PHILOSOPHY
AND THE EMOTIONS

PHILOSOPHY
AND THE EMOTIONS

A READER

edited by STEPHEN LEIGHTON

broadview press

National Library of Canada Cataloguing in Publication

Philosophy and the emotions: a reader / edited by Stephen Leighton.

Includes bibliographical references.
ISBN 1-55111-371-6

1. Emotions (Philosophy)   I. Leighton, Stephen R.

B105.E46P48 2003   128'.37   C2002-905700-0

Broadview Press Ltd. is an independent, international publishing house, incorporated in 1985. Broadview believes in shared ownership, both with its employees and with the general public; since the year 2000 Broadview shares have traded publicly on the Toronto Venture Exchange under the symbol BDP.

We welcome comments and suggestions regarding any aspect of our publications – please feel free to contact us at the addresses below or at broadview@broadviewpress.com.

North America
Post Office Box 1243, Peterborough, Ontario, Canada K9J 7H5
3576 California Road, Orchard Park, NY, USA 14127
Tel: (705) 743-8990; Fax: (705) 743-8353;
e-mail: customerservice@broadviewpress.com

UK, Ireland, and continental Europe
Thomas Lyster Ltd., Units 3 & 4a, Old Boundary Way,
Burscough Rd, Ormskirk, Lancashire L39 2YW
Tel: (1695) 575112; Fax: (1695) 570120
email: books@tlyster.co.uk

Australia and New Zealand
UNIREPS, University of New South Wales
Sydney, NSW, 2052
Tel: 61 2 9664 0999; Fax: 61 2 9664 5420
email: info.press@unsw.edu.au

www.broadviewpress.com

Broadview Press Ltd. gratefully acknowledges the financial support of the Government of Canada through the Book Publishing Industry Development Program for our publishing activities.

This book is printed on acid-free paper containing 30% post-consumer fibre.

Typesetting and assembly: True to Type Inc., Mississauga, Canada.
PRINTED IN CANADA

Certified Eco-Logo
30% Post.

Contents

ACKNOWLEDGMENTS

This work began as a result of a series of email conversations with Patricia Greenspan and from a sense that there was an important, ongoing intellectual development in theories of emotion that needed to be recorded. I would like to thank Pat and express my appreciation for permission to collect these works.

James, William, "What is an Emotion?," *Mind*, 1890. Reproduced by permission of Oxford University Press.

Errol Bedford, "Emotions and Statements About Them," *Proceedings of the Aristotelian Society*, Vol. LVII (1956-57). Reprinted by courtesy of the Editor of the Aristotelian Society: Copyright ©1956.

Robert Solomon, "A Subjective Theory of the Passions," from *The Passions: Emotions and the Meaning of Life*, by Robert Solomon, Hackett Publishing Company, Inc., 1993. (Originally appeared in his book *The Passions*, Doubleday and Company, 1976.) Reprinted with permission from Hackett Publishing Company, Inc.

Patricia Greenspan, "A Case of Mixed Feelings: Ambivalence and the Logic of Emotion," from *Explaining Emotions*, ed. Amelia Rorty, University of California Press, 1980. Copyright ©1980 The Regents of the University of California. Reprinted with permission.

Jenefer Robinson, "Emotion, Judgment, and Desire," *The Journal of Philosophy*, Vol. LXXX, No. 11 (November, 1983). Reprinted with permission from the author and *The Journal of Philosophy*.

Michael Stocker, "Psychic Feelings: Their Importance and Irreducibility," *Australasian Journal of Philosophy*, 1983. Reprinted with permission from the *Australasian Journal of Philosophy*.

William Lyons, "Physiological Changes and the Emotions," from *Emotion*, by William Lyons, Cambridge University Press, 1980. Copyright ©1980 by William Lyons. Reprinted with permission from the author.

Robert Solomon, "On Emotions as Judgments," *American Philosophical Quarterly*, 1988. Reprinted with permission from *American Philosophical Quarterly*.

Claire Armon-Jones, "The Thesis of Constructionism" from *The Social Construction of Emotions*, edited by Rom Harré, Blackwell Publishers, 1986. Reprinted with permission from Blackwell Publishers.

Ronald de Sousa, "The Rationality of Emotion," from *The Rationality of Emotion*, by Ronald de Sousa, MIT Press, 1987. Reprinted with permission from the MIT Press.

Jenefer Robinson, "Startle," *The Journal of Philosophy*, Vol. XCII, No. 2 (February,1995). Reprinted with permission from the author and *The Journal of Philosophy*.

P.E. Griffiths, "Modularity, and the Psychoevolutionary Theory of Emotion" *Biology and Philosophy*, Vol. 5 (1990). Reprinted with permission.

Stephen Leighton, "On Feeling Angry and Elated," *The Journal of Philosophy*, Vol. LXXXV, No. 5 (May, 1988). Reprinted with permission.

Martha C. Nussbaum, excerpted passage from *The Therapy of Desire*, by Martha C. Nussbaum, Princeton University Press, 1994. Copyright © 1994 by Princeton University Press. Reprinted by permission of Princeton University Press.

I should note the addition of one explanatory note, a master Reference list containing all sources mentioned in the papers, and the use of endnotes rather than footnotes, where possible. Finally, let me thank family, friends, colleagues, and the people at Broadview Press for standing by me in a project that has taken me much too long to complete.

INTRODUCTION

While philosophical speculation into the nature and value of emotions is at least as old as the Presocratics, William James's "What is an Emotion?" reinvigorated interest in the question. Coming to grips with James's proposals, particularly in light of subsequent concerns for the difficulties inherent in a so called private language, led philosophers away from analyses centred on feelings to ones centred on thoughts (judgments, beliefs, and so on). Such an analysis returns us to a vision of the emotions that traces its ancestry back to the Stoics.

This cognitive approach has proven to be enormously insightful and influential. Indeed, it has been so successful and productive a way of thinking that, in many ways, it has become the departure point for present-day philosophical thinking about the emotions.

The papers collected here record important stages in the contemporary emergence and development of the cognitive or judgmental analysis of the emotions. They centre on James's question and often respond explicitly to each other. Taken together, they provide a sense of what a cognitive view of the emotions maintains, what it denies, how it has arisen, the points of dispute among those impressed by this way of thinking, the diversity collected together under the moniker of a cognitive or judgmental analysis, and the tremendous explanatory power of the view. An appreciation of these papers is by no means the end of the matter, but rather an introduction to it: the debates continue and adapt.

One good way to get a grip on these matters is to begin with the first essay and read on, though it may be helpful to have a general sense of the arguments from the start. To avoid testing the reader's patience, I shall be brief. I give special attention to the emergence of the theory and thereafter merely point to some important issues and claims.

In "What is an Emotion?," James maintains that our normal understanding of emotions—in which a perception of something excites an emotion which is then expressed in the body—is mistaken. Rather, "*bodily changes follow directly the* PERCEPTION *of the exciting fact, and ... our feeling of the same changes as they occur* IS *the emotion.*"[1] The bodily component is, in the first instance, a visceral reaction, but James also includes more general bodily symptoms and further physical reactions. Contrary to our normal intuitions, then, fleeing in fear is not to be explained by feelings of fear, but, instead, the feelings of fear are themselves to be explained by the physiology involved in fleeing in fear.

James's proposals raise numerous questions, some empirical, some analytical. Is there one causal sequence central to emotion? What exactly are the relevant components and their order? How should distinctions between relevant physiological disturbance, bodily symptom, immediate reaction, or more considered behaviour be drawn and related to emotion and the feeling thereof? If emotion is the causal sequence described above, what becomes of the cause of the emotion (presuming emotion and its cause are distinct)? If emotion is some part of the sequence, what part, and why this part? What then becomes the logical status of the other parts of the causal sequence?

Howsoever these matters are resolved, further issues emerge when relating the theory to our everyday experience of the emotions. We have a wide range of emotions, and, while emotional confusion is common enough, we do have considerable facility to distinguish among them. Does the appeal to physiological realization (or feeling or both) enable us to distinguish as we do? It seems that resorting to recollection of physiological manifestation (and/or felt nature) is hardly sufficient. We seem to lack the psychological powers to keep straight the myriad of emotions we do keep straight—if we can only appeal to physiological-psychological upset. For example, how can one tell the difference between fear and excitement in these terms alone?

Trying to remedy these difficulties by speaking of the cause of the physiological- psychological upset also seems insufficient: upon seeing a bear some fear; others are excited. Thus, cause itself will not differentiate among our emotions. Even the triangulation of cause, physiological reaction, and felt component seems insufficient to explain our apparent ability to distinguish among these and other emotions—as the contrast between fear and excitement suggests. If so, James's view does not make sense of our experience of the emotions. The approach has been found wanting.

Erroll Bedford rejects thinking of emotions in terms of feelings. He puts his point dramatically when he writes: "To discuss the details of these theories would complicate, without affecting my argument, which is meant to show that an emotion is not any sort of experience or process."[2] Bedford offers many criticisms, including the point that we simply could not keep our diverse and varied emotions distinct if the account of emotions were centred on feelings. Interestingly, Bedford's argument is not just about the psychological power of particular humans to remember and recall: he deploys the private language argument with the aim of showing that the identities of feelings are incidental to and parasitic upon emotion itself. Thus, to attempt to define emotion by feeling is hopeless. If anything, feeling is to be defined in terms of emotion. As Ryle put it: "Pains do not arrive already hall-marked 'rheumatic,' nor do throbs arrive already hall-marked 'compassionate.'"[3] An approach to emotion centred on feelings is thought simply wrongheaded.

In part, Bedford attends to the language of emotion to gain insight. As well as seeing a role for behaviour or the disposition to behave, he notes that the language of emotion both describes and assesses. In emphasizing emotions as assessments, the analysis has turned in a cognitive direction and has done so in a way that attempts to provide a more plausible basis for distinguishing among the emotions we do distinguish among. That a situation is and is seen to be *dangerous* seems important to it being a matter of fear; that the same situation seems *pretty neat and stimulating* seems important to the matter being one of excitement; that someone *insults* you seems important to the matter being one of anger, and so on. For Bedford, the presence of emotion and particular emotions involves a subtle interplay between disposition to behave, behaviour, assessment, and social context.

Bedford's understanding of appraisal is not primarily individual but is set in terms of social practices and meanings. Thus, not only does he move towards a cognitive analysis, but he does so in a way that highlights the roles of social practices. Bedford thinks that typically an appraisal relevant to emotion implies an objective claim about the world, not just how the person experiencing the emotion thinks of it. Thus, whether a Mr. Davies was embarrassed or ashamed by the revelation that he was the model for Peter Pan is not simply a fact of his particular behaviour, or disposition to behave, or his appraisal, but has also to do with his social context. His situation, if anything, is embarrassing, not shameful. Thus, we see him to be embarrassed by the matter. Still, in making the objective claim the standard case, Bedford makes room for the possibility that Davies can rightly insist that he is ashamed, not embarrassed. The issue of whether first-person assessments or third-person assessments are vital to the determination of emotion arises here and elsewhere in the papers. What is not the case, according to Bedford, is that the feelings of Mr. Davies, if any, are determinant of what his emotion is.

Robert Solomon's articulation of a cognitive theory of emotion is, in many ways, its full flowering. Like Bedford, Solomon is unimpressed with any contribution feelings might make to the fact or identity of emotion. Like Bedford, he takes emotions to be a kind of appraisal. Indeed, in a later chapter in the book from which the present selection is taken, Solomon provides impressive maps that differentiate among a variety of emotions, doing so in terms of their cognitive content. Also like Bedford, Solomon wants to give the social nature of emotion its due. But Solomon is particularly struck by the subjectivity of the emotions, their surreality. Thus, rather than emphasizing any objective claims regarding emotions, he stresses the highly personal appraisal involved in the emotions. The judgmental-appraisal thesis to which both Bedford and Solomon adhere is held independently of their views on the objectivity or subjectivity of the emotions.

A focus on evaluations allows explanation of much else relevant to emotion. My desire to send flowers to Martha, my phoning her and listening intently to what she says, are usefully explained by my love for her—where that love is understood as certain kinds of judgments I make about what a wonderful person she is. Likewise, my wish to avoid Philip, my tendency to avoid, and my avoidance of him can be understood in terms of my fear of him—where my fear is understood as an evaluative judgment about how dangerous he is to me. Thus, by centring on our evaluations, the place of desires, behaviour, and dispositions to behave can be explained. Moreover, by centring on the relevant evaluations, one can readily differentiate among emotions, here love and fear.

What of the physiology of emotion? It does not seem to be accorded the logical connection to evaluation that, say, desire or behaviour has. To be sure, there are, or may well be, identifiable sorts of physiological changes that occur with emotions. These can be seen to be necessary and causally involved, but the understanding of emotion is obtained through its evaluations, not through its physiological ongoings. What of feelings? They, too, may be present but are thought to remain too amorphous to be definitive of the emotion. At best, they are a typical accompaniment. The judgments present determine the emotion.

The fact and nature of the intentionality of emotions, their object directedness, the status of emotion's "object" are all matters Solomon explores. So too is the issue of which kinds of judgments emotions are. Solomon writes:

> An emotion is a *judgment* (or a set of judgments), something we *do*. An emotion is a (set of) judgment(s) which constitute our world, our sur-reality, and its "intentional objects." An emotion is a basic judgment about our Selves and our place in our world ...[4]

This statement is further explicated when he writes: "Emotions are self-involved and relatively *intense* evaluative judgements ... [and] ... [t]he judgements and objects that constitute our emotions are those which are especially important to us, meaningful to us, concerning matters in which we have invested our Selves"; and "Emotions are *constitutional* judgements."[5] If Solomon has succeeded in delineating the type of judgment that constitute emotions, he will have differentiated emotion from dispassionate judgment and all other psychological phenomena. Are there judgments of the sort he describes? Are they emotions? Necessarily?

The critics have doubts. As suggested earlier, criticism, at least for the most part, has come from those who find something profoundly plausible in this move to cognition. Thus while it is allowed that a great deal about emotion can be explained in terms of a cognitive turn, that this is what emotion is doubted.

Patricia Greenspan repudiates the idea that judgments can fully account for emotions. The logical structure of emotions and the relevant judgments do not match, as she hopes to show by examining the logic of emotion and judgment. For example, she argues that a basically rational person might arrive in time at a summary judgment over a matter (all things considered ...). Even so, one's emotional reaction to the same matter need not blend or sum things up. We remain emotionally ambivalent, moved this way and that, despite a reconciliation in relevant judgments. That emotion can resist summing or blending while the judgment is summed suggests that emotion and judgment are not identical. So, too, it seems that a change in judgment need not beget change in the corresponding emotion. Here, too, judgment and emotion do not track each other. Greenspan deploys these and other considerations to argue that attempts to explain emotion by appealing to features of our judgments cannot capture the whole. At the very least, something important is missing. If so, emotion is not (wholly) constituted by the relevant judgments.

Jenefer Robinson is impressed by Greenspan's considerations, agreeing that attempts to identify emotions in terms of cognition are wanting. Like many critics of cognitivism, she suggests that the cognitions thought constitutive of particular emotions might be entertained in a dispassionate way. This is not to suggest the irrelevancy of cognition to emotion, just its insufficiency. Further, Robinson holds that the considerations Greenspan advances point to a role for desire as constitutive of the emotions, since emotions share certain formal features with desires (which dispassionate cognition alone does not share), including intensity, resistance to summing, tolerance of inconsistency, and resistance to change. Thus to plausibly account for emotion not only do we need cognition but also relevant desires.

Left there, one might suppose that desire is a further feature, one simply to be added on. Views of emotion of this sort can be and are defended. But Robinson's position is more complex: she holds that in order for cognition and desire to be emotion, relevant cognition must itself be coloured and caused by relevant desire. At the same time, she allows that in certain cases an occurrent emotional state might be identical with nothing but thought—so long as that thought has the right links to the agent's desire.

The criticisms so far, if correct, seem to allow for modified versions of the cognitive theory. Michael Stocker, while sympathetic to these criticisms, has greater reservations, reservations suggesting that a cognitive theory is not readily remedied. Too little has been said about feelings. His argument uses a conception of psychic feelings, which he thinks is needed in an adequate philosophical psychology generally and more particularly in accounts of various passions. Stocker holds that the affectivity of emotion cannot itself be reduced to or be wholly understood in terms of reason and desire. Indeed, reason and desire themselves are not fully understood without affectivity. If so, it is not possible to give an account of the emotions without appeal to affectivity—and that appeal cannot itself be explained by a further appeal to reason or desire. Thus, Stocker is far more sanguine than many recent philosophers have been about the relevance and non-dependent role of feeling to emotion.

William Lyons returns us to familiar territory. Like James, he thinks that physiological change has a role in the concept of emotion and takes it to be one part of a causal sequence that is emotion. He suggests that the relevant physiological changes are temporary and unusual ones of the autonomic nervous system. In addition, he holds that emotion is present when these changes are caused by (or at least taken to be caused by) a person's cognitive-appetitive evaluation of a situation. We have a causal sequence reminiscent of James, but now the cause of the physiological change is cognitive, evaluative, and appetitive structures. Lyons is not suggesting that *particular* physiological changes are parts of the concept of *particular* emotions, but rather that physiological change is part of the concept of emotion in general.

Lyons's analysis gives emphasis to ongoing or occurrent emotional states. Because his proposals include the cognitive-evaluative components discussed by Solomon, his proposals should be able to accommodate the insights found in Solomon's view. In addition, they can explain the connections between emotion, desire, disposition to behave, and behaviour. Strikingly, Lyons's proposals tie the account of emotion more closely to our bodily nature. On this view, Solomon and others have failed to adequately appreciate an important element in emotion.

While it is unlikely that Lyons's analysis is particularly illuminating of the place and role of what Stocker has called psychic feelings, it is noteworthy that it can make some sense of the felt nature of emotion, since it is at least reasonable to argue that the relevant physiological changes give rise to bodily feeling.

Solomon hardly feels defeated by these and other criticisms and has been vigilant in responding to them. In "On Emotions as Judgments," he attempts to show certain misunderstandings and/or inadequacies in the criticisms and to adapt his view to accommodate the insights of his critics, all the while remaining strongly cognitivist in his approach. His interest is not primarily to defend the view that emotions are just judgments, but to counter objections and to clarify the role judgment takes.

Solomon is particularly concerned to rebut the ubiquitous criticism that the relevant judgments can be made dispassionately (see Robinson). By drawing attention to the manner or mode of judging, to the importance of whole networks or systems of interconnected judgments, to a contrast between the occurrence of emotion and its standing condition, to judgments' essential ties to expression and particular connections with desires, Solomon hopes to dispel much of the power of that objection. Moreover, where the objection might still seem to have application, Solomon points out the very particular or exceptional nature of the case. Here it is striking that both Solomon and Stocker refer to cases where there is a disassociation of emotion from judgment; both see Aristotle's account of anger as something of a model. Yet, they reach very different conclusions: Stocker takes these matters to show the inadequacy of the cognitivist approach; Solomon takes them to show its power.

Whether or not cognition is sufficient for emotion, whether or not judgment is necessary in all cases, whether or not the exact kind of judgment has or can be specified, whether or not cognition is in part coloured by desire or feeling, whatever the place for physiological change, subjectivity, intentionality, surreality, and so on, none of the theorists considered so far question that cognitive-evaluative structures are significant to the structure of our emotions. A cognitivist approach to emotion remains illuminating and worth pursuing.

If so, then one issue only touched upon in the above is the extent to which emotions are or are not socially constructed. Theorists of a cognitivist bent are inclined to be sympathetic to concerns for social construction, something that can be seen in the writings of both Bedford and Solomon.

Claire Armon-Jones explores the idea of emotion as a social construction. Her view is that emotion is not (or is not simply) a natural phenomenon, but cognition based, constituted (in part or whole) by the manner in which it is conceptualized. Cultural belief profoundly shapes conceptualization and, thus, becomes central in the constitution (construction) of the emotions. The constructions themselves are seen to serve socio-cultural functions both in terms of what is appropriate and what is inappropriate. Moreover, because different cultures can and often do have different cultural beliefs, emotions can be and are differently constructed—differences in common emotions and their appropriateness ensue, different emotions entirely are constructed. The possibility of experiencing emotions such as courageous patriotism, amae, ennui, guilt, or shame, and the nature, significance, and appropriateness of each depend on the web of belief as constructed within societies.

Armon-Jones identifies different versions of the constructionist view, preferring those that make some room for natural responses to situations. As well, she situates constructionist views in terms of traditional and contemporary theories of emotion, cognitive aspects of emotion, intentional objects, and so on, giving particular emphasis to how the felt nature of emotion is to be accounted for. Once more, the relatively independent role for feeling—implicit in James and suggested by Stocker—is repudiated.

If it is agreed that emotions are or are in part constructed within society, one needs an account of how this formation can occur. Ronald de Sousa's analysis of emotions and deployment of paradigm scenarios has proven to be a leading way to account for the genesis and nature of emotion. Explanation by appeal to paradigm scenarios attempts to do justice to what is involved in emotion, how the elements come to have the role they have, and how emotion is constructed in the particular way it is. Facts about humans' biological, chemical, and neurological nature can be brought together with features of human psychology, culturally specific beliefs, matters of personal and idiopathic belief, and development in one overarching narrative. Different peoples and different persons can and do construct differently. Here it is worth noting that the construction is in terms of both causal and logical factors, therein allowing for the rationality (and irrationality) and arationality regarding our emotions. It is also worth noting that the construction is not restricted to society as a whole, but allows for, say, sub- cultural construction, construction by gender, by family, by personal situation, and so on. Thus, de Sousa's framework is well set to account for differences in our emotional lives at many different levels.

The emphasis, so far, has been on relatively complex and sophisticated emotions such as shame, guilt, love, and even courageous patriotism. Focusing on such examples makes the centrality of cognition and social construction within an account of the emotions plausible. In "Startle," Robinson calls attention to much more basic emotional or quasi-emotional phenomena by reporting on work on the startle reaction and considering its philosophical implications. Within a startle reaction, there seems no room for the cognitions featured in Bedford's and Solomon's accounts. Rather, the reaction seems to be a bodily response to a particular kind of stimulus, one which makes certain features of the environment salient and does so in terms of an organism's overall existence or well-being—or so Robinson argues.

Whether the startle reaction should be seen as an emotion or a proto-emotion, it seems related to and continuous with emotion. Moreover, Robinson argues that complex emotions, such as indignation, embody the structure of the startle reaction, though they do so with evaluations also being salient. Thus, she uses the structure of the startle reaction to provide a framework for understanding the emotions generally, one which, in effect, understands emotions in terms of the biological functioning and well-being of organisms and appreciates various ways this is achieved. Seeing matters this way, she argues, better enables one to explain a variety of features of our emotional life that seem poorly explained in the cognitivist framework. Here, then, the ubiquity of the cognitivist framework is seriously challenged.

Paul Griffiths's psycho-evolutionary approach also challenges the ubiquity of a cognitive- evaluative framework. He finds the claims of cognitivism and its variations inadequate. Griffiths wants to work within the distinctions and understandings relevant to a scientific psychology. He reports on what appear to be cross-cultural patterns of emotive expression, understood in terms of certain affect programs. The programs themselves are complex, responding to certain stimuli and having certain behavioural outputs. The place for innateness and the role for learning are to be seen in terms of these programs and fitted within evolutionary theorizing.

Affect programs are distinct from, considerably independent of, and can conflict with the system of beliefs and desires. By making these programs paradigmatic emotional events, Griffiths's approach is considerably different from cognitivism. Moreover, because the programs cut across cultures, he identifies some basic emotional phenomena that are not subject to social construction (contrary to the theories of at least some social constructionists).

More complex emotions such as guilt and romantic love are also explained. These cases do involve cognitive, cultural, and other factors, some doing so in terms of one or more affect programs (certain cases of fear), while others do not seem similarly related (hope, envy, and jealousy). By proceeding in this way, and because of doubts about the success of our intuitive classifications of the emotions, the classifications of Griffiths's psycho-evolutionary approach are to replace our normal ways of categorizing emotions. If successful, its advantages are not simply a neater, clearer system, but also a framework that more readily makes sense of irrational emotions, cases where the normal cognitions are absent, the disruptive nature of emotion, and so on.

Stephen Leighton returns our attention to feelings and their appropriateness to particular emotions. Dissatisfied with wholly cognitivist analyses of emotion and Rylean-inspired views that the identity of the feelings of particular emotions is simply determined by the relevant cognitive complex associated with the emotion, a number of alternatives are developed, contrasted, and compared in order to make sense of the apparent fact that there is something that grief feels like, which is different from what anger or elation feel like, and where there is a kind of suitability of feeling to particular emotion types. By distinguishing how we come to *identify* particular feelings as being relevant to particular emotions from how we *define or delimit* particular feelings as being relevant to particular emotions, and by taking diverse feelings to have diverse values, Leighton hopes to make better sense of the aptness of particular feelings to particular emotions and to do so in a way that does not leave the suitability of feeling in emotion simply contingent upon principles of association, conjunction, and so on. If so, a place for feelings in emotions, where the feelings have an independence from other constituents, becomes much more plausible.

The book ends by returning to its cognitivist beginning. Martha C. Nussbaum advocates a fundamentally cognitivist analysis, albeit one different from that of Solomon. In this excerpt from *The Therapy of Desire*, she uses the device of a student, Nikidion, to give voice to the Stoic philosopher Chrysippus's account of emotion, doing so in a way that renders it plausible (often in light of the many criticisms to which cognitivism has been subject). Nussbaum presents the basis and genesis of the view; appreciates the roles emotions and particular emotions have; and notes their interconnections and basic structures, as well as the role for evaluative cognition, the requirement that emotion concerns matters of high worth regarding some uncontrolled external item. Moreover, in order to appreciate the complexities involved, she tests the prospects for cognition as necessary to emotion, constituent of emotions, sufficient for emotion, and identical with emotion.

In view of previous proposals, one particularly interesting feature about Nussbaum's cognitivism is the extent to which it tries to include under the conception of cognition (necessary to, sufficient for, and identical with emotion) features often proposed to be central to emotion but themselves taken to be different from cognition. Her "inclusive" strategy contrasts the strategy of Bedford and Solomon. What Solomon and Bedford might argue not to be part of emotion, Nussbaum will allow to be part, but a part explained by a special sort of judgment rather than in contrast to it.

Notes

1   William James, "What is an Emotion?" *Mind*, 1890: 189-90.
2   Erroll Bedford, "Emotions and Statements About Them," *Proceedings of the Aristotelian Society* (1956) 110, note 1.
3   *Gilbert Ryle, The Concept of Mind* (London: Hutchinson, 1949) 105.
4   Robert Solomon, *The Passions* (New York: Anchor Books, 1977) 185.
5   Solomon 187, 194.

❧ BACKGROUND ❧

What is an Emotion?

William James

The physiologists who, during the past few years, have been so industriously exploring the functions of the brain, have limited their attempts at explanation to its cognitive and volitional performances. Dividing the brain into sensorial and motor centres, they have found their division to be exactly paralleled by the analysis made by empirical psychology, of the perceptive and volitional parts of the mind into their simplest elements. But the *aesthetic* sphere of the mind, its longings, its pleasures and pains, and its emotions, have been so ignored in all these researches that one is tempted to suppose that if either Dr. Ferrier or Dr. Munk were asked for a theory in brain-terms of the latter mental facts, they might both reply, either that they had as yet bestowed no thought upon the subject, or that they had found it so difficult to make distinct hypotheses, that the matter lay for them among the problems of the future, only to be taken up after the simpler ones of the present should have been definitively solved.

And yet it is even now certain that of two things concerning the emotions, one must be true. Either separate and special centres, affected to them alone, are their brain-seat, or else they correspond to processes occurring in the motor and sensory centres, already assigned, or in others like them, not yet mapped out. If the former be the case we must deny the current view, and hold the cortex to be something more than the surface of "projection" for every sensitive spot and every muscle in the body. If the latter be the case, we must ask whether the emotional "process" in the sensory or motor centre be an altogether peculiar one, or whether it resembles the ordinary perceptive processes of which those centres are already recognised to be the seat. The purpose of the following pages is to show that the last alternative comes nearest to the truth, and that the emotional brain-processes not only resemble the ordinary sensorial brain-processes, but in very truth *are* nothing but such processes variously combined. The main result of this will be to simplify our notions of the possible complications of brain-physiology, and to make us see that we have already a brain-scheme in our hands whose applications are much wider than its authors dreamed. But although this seems to be the chief result of the arguments I am to urge, I should say that they were not originally framed for the sake of any such result. They grew out of fragmentary introspective observations, and it was only when these had already combined into a theory that the thought of the simplification the theory might bring to cerebral physiology occurred to me, and made it seem more important than before.

I should say first of all that the only emotions I propose expressly to consider here are those that have a distinct bodily expression. That there are feelings of pleasure and displeasure, of interest and excitement, bound up with mental operations, but having no obvious bodily expression for their consequence, would, I suppose, be held true by most readers. Certain arrangements of sounds, of lines, of colours, are agreeable, and others the reverse, without the degree of the feeling being sufficient to quicken the pulse or breathing, or to prompt to movements of either the body or the face. Certain sequences of ideas charm us as much as others tire us. It is a real intellectual delight to get a problem solved, and a real intellectual torment to have to leave it unfinished. The first set of examples, the sounds, lines, and colours, are either bodily sensations, or the images of such. The second set seem to depend on processes in the ideational centres exclusively. Taken together, they appear to prove that there are pleasures and pains inherent in certain forms of nerve-action as such, wherever that action occur. The case of these feelings we will at present leave entirely aside, and confine our attention to the more complicated cases in which a wave of bodily disturbance of some kind accompanies the perception of the interesting sights or sounds, or the passage of the exciting train of ideas. Surprise, curiosity, rapture, fear, anger, lust, greed, and the like, become then the names of the mental states with which the person is possessed. The bodily disturbances are said to be the "manifestation" of these several emotions, their "expression" or "natural language"; and these emotions themselves, being so strongly characterised both from within and without, may be called the *standard* emotions.

Our natural way of thinking about these standard emotions is that the mental perception of some fact excites the mental affection called the emotion, and that this latter state of mind gives rise to the bodily expression. My thesis on the contrary is that *the bodily changes follow directly the PERCEPTION of the exciting fact, and that our feeling of the same changes as they occur IS the emotion.* Common sense says, we lose our fortune, are sorry and weep; we meet a bear, are frightened and run; we are insulted by a rival, are angry and strike. The hypothesis here to be defended says that this order of sequence is incorrect, that the one mental state is not immediately induced by the other, that the bodily manifestations must first be interposed between, and that the more rational statement is that we feel sorry because we cry, angry because we strike, afraid because we tremble, and not that we cry, strike, or tremble, because we are sorry, angry, or fearful, as the case may be. Without the bodily states following on the perception, the latter would be purely cognitive in form, pale, colourless, destitute of emotional warmth. We might then see the bear, and judge it best to run, receive the insult and deem it right to strike, but we could not actually *feel* afraid or angry.

Stated in this crude way, the hypothesis is pretty sure to meet with immediate disbelief. And yet neither many nor far-fetched considerations are required to mitigate its paradoxical character, and possibly to produce conviction of its truth.

To begin with, readers of this Journal do not need to be reminded that the nervous system of every living thing is but a bundle of predispositions to react in particular ways upon the contact of particular features of the environment. As surely as the hermit-crab's abdomen presupposes the existence of empty whelk-shells somewhere to be found, so surely do the hound's olfactories imply the existence, on the one hand, of deer's or foxes' feet, and on the other, the tendency to follow up their tracks. The neural machinery is but a hyphen between determinate arrangements of matter outside the body and determinate impulse to inhibition or discharge within its organs. When the hen sees a white oval object on the ground, she cannot leave it; she must keep upon it and return to it, until at last its transformation into a little mass of moving chirping down elicits from her machinery an entirely new set of performances. The love of man for woman, or of the human mother for her babe, our wrath at snakes and our fear of precipices, may all be described similarly, as instances of the way in which peculiarly conformed pieces of the world's furniture will fatally call forth most particular mental and bodily reactions, in advance of, and often in direct opposition to, the verdict of our deliberate reason concerning them. The labours of Darwin and his successors are only just beginning to reveal the universal parasitism of each special creature upon other special things, and the way in which each creature brings the signature of its special relations stamped on its nervous system with it upon the scene.

Every living creature is in fact a sort of lock, whose wards and springs presuppose special forms of key,—which keys however are not born attached to the locks, but are sure to be found in the world near by as life goes on. And the locks are indifferent to any but their own keys. The egg fails to fascinate the hound, the bird does not fear the precipice, the snake waxes not wroth at his kind, the deer cares nothing for the woman or the human babe. Those who wish for a full development of this point of view, should read Schneider's *Der thierische Wille*,—no other book shows how accurately anticipatory are the actions of animals, of the specific features of the environment in which they are to live.

Now among these nervous anticipations are of course to be reckoned the emotions, so far as these may be called forth directly by the perception of certain facts. In advance of all experience of elephants no child can but be frightened if he suddenly find one trumpeting and charging upon him. No woman can see a handsome little naked baby without delight, no man in the wilderness see a human form in the distance without excitement and curiosity. I said I should consider these emotions only so far as they have bodily movements of some sort for their accompaniments. But my first point is to show that their bodily accompaniments are much more far-reaching and complicated than we ordinarily suppose.

In the earlier books on Expression, written mostly from the artistic point of view, the signs of emotion visible from without were the only ones taken account of. Sir Charles Bell's celebrated *Anatomy of Expression* noticed the respiratory changes; and Bain's and Darwin's treatises went more thoroughly still into the study of the visceral factors involved,—changes in the functioning of glands and muscles, and in that of the circulatory apparatus. But not even a Darwin has exhaustively enumerated *all* the bodily affections characteristic of any one of the standard emotions. More and more, as physiology advances, we begin to discern how almost infinitely numerous and subtle they must be. The researches of Mosso with the plethysmograph have shown that not only the heart, but the entire circulatory system, forms a sort of sounding-board, which every change of our consciousness, however slight, may make reverberate. Hardly a sensation comes to us without sending waves of alternate constriction and dilation down the arteries of our arms. The blood-vessels of the abdomen act reciprocally with those of the more outward parts. The bladder and bowels, the glands of the mouth, throat, and skin, and the liver, are known to be affected gravely in certain severe emotions, and are unquestionably affected transiently when the emotions are of a lighter sort. That the heart-beats and the rhythm of breathing play a leading part in all emotions whatsoever, is a matter too notorious for proof. And what is really equally prominent, but less likely to be admitted until special attention is drawn to the fact, is the continuous co-operation of the voluntary muscles in our emotional states. Even when no change of outward attitude is produced, their inward tension alters to suit each varying mood, and is felt as a difference of tone or of strain. In depression the flexors tend to prevail; in elation or belligerent excitement the extensors take the lead. And the various permutations and combinations of which these organic activities are susceptible, make it abstractly possible that no shade of emotion, however slight, should be without a bodily reverberation as unique, when taken in its totality, as is the mental mood itself.

The immense number of parts modified in each emotion is what makes it so difficult for us to reproduce in cold blood the total and integral expression of any one of them. We may catch the trick with the voluntary muscles, but fail with the skin, glands, heart, and other viscera. Just as an artificially imitated sneeze lacks something of the reality, so the attempt to imitate an emotion in the absence of its normal instigating cause is apt to be rather "hollow."

The next thing to be noticed is this, that every one of the bodily changes, whatsoever it be, is *felt*, acutely or obscurely, the moment it occurs. If the reader has never paid attention to this matter, he will be both interested and astonished to learn how many different local bodily feelings he can detect in himself as characteristic of his various emotional moods. It would be perhaps too much to expect him to arrest the tide of any strong gust of passion for the sake of any such curious analysis as this; but he can observe more tranquil states, and that may be assumed here to be true of the greater which is shown to be true of the less. Our whole cubic capacity is sensibly alive; and each morsel of it contributes its pulsations of feeling, dim or sharp, pleasant, painful, or dubious, to that sense of personality that every one of us unfailingly carries with him. It is surprising what little items give accent to these complexes of sensibility. When worried by any slight trouble, one may find that the focus of one's bodily consciousness is the contraction, often quite inconsiderable, of the eyes and brows. When momentarily embarrassed, it is something in the pharynx that compels either a swallow, a clearing of the throat, or a slight cough; and so on for as many more instances as might be named. Our concern here being with the general view rather than with the details, I will not linger to discuss these but, assuming the point admitted that every change that occurs must be felt, I will pass on.[1]

I now proceed to urge the vital point of my whole theory, which is this. If we fancy some strong emotion, and then try to abstract from our consciousness of it all the feeling of its characteristic bodily symptoms, we find we have nothing left behind, no "mind-stuff" out of which the emotion can be constituted, and that a cold and neutral state of intellectual perception is all that remains. It is true, that although most people, when asked, say that their introspection verifies this statement, some persist in saying theirs does not. Many cannot be made to understand the question. When you beg them to imagine away every feeling of laughter and of tendency to laugh from their consciousness of the ludicrousness of an object, and then to tell you what the feeling of its ludicrousness would be like, whether it be anything more than the perception that the object belongs to the class "funny," they persist in replying that the thing proposed is a physical impossibility, and that they always *must* laugh, if they see a funny object. Of course the task proposed is not the practical one of seeing a ludicrous object and annihilating one's tendency to laugh. It is the purely speculative one of subtracting certain elements of feeling from an emotional state supposed to exist in its fullness, and saying what the residual elements are. I cannot help thinking that all who rightly apprehend this problem will agree with the proposition above laid down. What kind of an emotion of fear would be left, if the feelings neither of quickened heart-beats nor of shallow breathing, neither of trembling lips nor of weakened limbs, neither of goose-flesh nor of visceral stirrings, were present, it is quite impossible to think. Can one fancy the state of rage and picture no ebullition of it in the chest, no flushing of the face, no dilatation of the nostrils, no clenching of the teeth, no impulse to vigorous action, but in their stead limp muscles, calm breathing, and a placid face? The present writer, for one, certainly cannot. The rage is as completely evaporated as the sensation of its so-called manifestations, and the only thing that can possibly be supposed to take its place is some cold-blooded and dispassionate judicial sentence, confined entirely to the intellectual realm, to the effect that a certain person or persons merit chastisement for their sins. In like manner of grief: what would it be without its tears, its sobs, its suffocation of the heart, its pang in the breast-bone? A feelingless cognition that certain circumstances are deplorable, and nothing more. Every passion in turn tells the same story. A purely disembodied human emotion is a nonentity. I do not say that it is a contradiction in the nature of things, or that pure spirits are necessarily condemned to cold intellectual lives; but I say that for *us*, emotion dissociated from all bodily feelings is inconceivable. The more closely I scrutinise my states, the more persuaded I become, that whatever moods, affections, and passions I have, are in very truth constituted by, and made up of, those bodily changes we ordinarily call their expression or consequence; and the more it seems to me that if I were to become corporeally anaesthetic, I should be excluded from the life of the affections, harsh and tender alike, and drag out an existence of merely cognitive or intellectual form. Such an existence, although it seems to have been the ideal of ancient sages, is too apathetic to be keenly sought after by those born after the revival of the worship of sensibility, a few generations ago.

But if the emotion is nothing but the feeling of the reflex bodily effects of what we call its "object," effects due to the connate adaptation of the nervous system to that object, we seem immediately faced by this objection: most of the objects of civilised men's emotions are things to which it would be preposterous to suppose their nervous systems connately adapted. Most occasions of shame and many insults are purely conventional, and vary with the social environment. The same is true of many matters of dread and of desire, and of many occasions of melancholy and regret. In these cases, at least, it would seem that the ideas of shame, desire, regret, etc., must first have been attached by education and association to these conventional objects before the bodily changes could possibly be awakened. And if in *these* cases the bodily changes follow the ideas, instead of giving rise to them, why not then in all cases?

To discuss thoroughly this objection would carry us deep into the study of purely intellectual Aesthetics. A few words must here suffice. We will say nothing of the argument's failure to distinguish between the idea of an emotion and the emotion itself. We will only recall the well-known evolutionary principle that when a certain power has once been fixed in an animal by virtue of its utility in presence of certain features of the environment, it may turn out to be useful in the presence of other features of the environment that had originally nothing to do with either producing or preserving it. A nervous tendency to discharge being once there, all sorts of unforeseen things may pull the trigger and let loose the effects. That among these things should be conventionalities of man's contriving is a matter of no psychological consequence whatever. The most important part of my environment is my fellow-man. The consciousness of his attitude towards me is the perception that normally unlocks most of my shames and indignations and fears. The extraordinary sensitiveness of this consciousness is shown by the bodily modifications wrought in us by the awareness that our fellow-man is noticing us *at all*. No one can walk across the platform at a public meeting with just the same muscular innervation he uses to walk across his room at home. No one can give a message to such a meeting without organic excitement. "Stage-fright" is only the extreme degree of that wholly irrational personal self-consciousness which every one gets in some measure, as soon as he feels the eyes of a number of strangers fixed upon him, even though he be inwardly convinced that their feelings towards him is of no practical account.[2] This being so, it is not surprising that the additional persuasion that my fellow-man's attitude means either well or ill for me, should awaken stronger emotions still. In primitive societies "Well" may mean handing me a piece of beef, and "Ill" may mean aiming a blow at my skull. In our "cultured age," "Ill" may mean cutting me in the street, and "Well," giving me an honorary degree. What the action itself may be is quite insignificant, so long as I can perceive in it intent or *animus*. *That* is the emotion-arousing perception; and may give rise to as strong bodily convulsions in me, a civilised man experiencing the treatment of an artificial society, as in any savage prisoner of war, learning whether his captors are about to eat him or to make him a member of their tribe.

But now, this objection disposed of, there arises a more general doubt. Is there any evidence, it may be asked, for the assumption that particular perceptions *do* produce widespread bodily effects by a sort of immediate physical influence, antecedent to the arousal of an emotion or emotional idea?

The only possible reply is, that there is most assuredly such evidence. In listening to poetry, drama, or heroic narrative, we are often surprised at the cutaneous shiver which like a sudden wave flows over us, and at the heart-swelling and the lachrymal effusion that unexpectedly catch us at intervals. In listening to music, the same is even more strikingly true. If we abruptly see a dark moving form in the woods, our heart stops beating, and we catch our breath instantly and before any articulate idea of danger can arise. If our friend goes near to the edge of a precipice, we get the well-known feeling of "all-overishness," and we shrink back, although we positively *know* him to be safe, and have no distinct imagination of his fall. The writer well remembers his astonishment, when a boy of seven or eight, at fainting when he saw a horse bled. The blood was in a bucket, with a stick in it, and, if memory does not deceive him, he stirred it round and saw it drip from the stick with no feeling save that of childish curiosity. Suddenly the world grew black before his eyes, his ears began to buzz, and he knew no more. He had never heard of the sight of blood producing faintness or sickness, and he had so little repugnance to it, and so little apprehension of any other sort of danger from it, that even at that tender age, as he well remembers, he could not help wondering how the mere physical presence of a pailful of crimson fluid could occasion in him such formidable bodily effects.

Imagine two steel knife-blades with their keen edges crossing each other at right angles, and moving to and fro. Our whole nervous organisation is "on-edge" at the thought; and yet what emotion can be there except the unpleasant nervous feeling itself, or the dread that more of it may come? The entire fund and capital of the emotion here is the senseless bodily effect the blades immediately arouse. This case is typical of a class: where an ideal emotion seems to precede the bodily symptoms, it is often nothing but a representation of the symptoms themselves. One who has already fainted at the sight of blood may witness the preparations for a surgical operation with uncontrollable heart-sinking anxiety. He anticipates certain feelings, and the anticipation precipitates their arrival. I am told of a case of morbid terror, of which the subject confessed that what possessed her seemed, more than anything, to be the fear of fear itself. In the various forms of what Professor Bain calls "tender emotion," although the appropriate object must usually be directly contemplated before the emotion can be aroused, yet sometimes thinking of the symptoms of the emotion itself may have the same effect. In sentimental natures, the thought of "yearning" will produce real "yearning." And, not to speak of coarser examples, a mother's imagination of the caresses she bestows on her child may arouse a spasm of parental longing.

In such cases as these, we see plainly how the emotion both begins and ends with what we call its effects or manifestations. It has no mental *status* except as either the presented feeling, or the idea, of the manifestations; which latter thus constitute its entire material, its sum and substance, and its stock-in-trade. And these cases ought to make us see how in all cases the feeling of the manifestations may play a much deeper part in the constitution of the emotion than we are wont to suppose.

If our theory be true, a necessary corollary of it ought to be that any voluntary arousal of the so-called manifestations of a special emotion ought to give us the emotion itself. Of course in the majority of emotions, this test is inapplicable; for many of the manifestations are in organs over which we have no volitional control. Still, within the limits in which it can be verified, experience fully corroborates this test. Everyone knows how panic is increased by flight, and how the giving way to symptoms of grief or anger increases those passions themselves. Each fit of sobbing makes the sorrow more acute, and calls forth another fit stronger still, until at last repose only ensues with lassitude and with the apparent exhaustion of the machinery. In rage, it is notorious how we "work ourselves up" to a climax by repeated outbreaks of expression. Refuse to express a passion, and it dies. Count ten before venting your anger, and its occasion seems ridiculous. Whistling to keep up courage is no mere figure of speech. On the other hand, sit all day in a moping posture, sigh, and reply to everything with a dismal voice, and your melancholy lingers. There is no more valuable precept in moral education than this, as all who have experience know: if we wish to conquer undesirable emotional tendencies in ourselves, we must assiduously, and in the first instance cold-bloodedly, go through the *outward motions* of those contrary dispositions we prefer to cultivate. The reward of persistency will infallibly come, in the fading out of the sullenness or depression, and the advent of real cheerfulness and kindliness in their stead. Smooth the brow, brighten the eye, contract the dorsal rather than the ventral aspect of the frame, and speak in a major key, pass the genial compliment, and your heart must be frigid indeed if it do not gradually thaw!

The only exceptions to this are apparent, not real. The great emotional expressiveness and mobility of certain persons often lead us to say "They would feel more if they talked less." And in another class of persons, the explosive energy with which passion manifests itself on critical occasions, seems correlated with the way in which they bottle it up during the intervals. But these are only eccentric types of character, and within each type the law of the last paragraph prevails. The sentimentalist is so constructed that "gushing" is his or her normal mode of expression. Putting a stopper on the "gush" will only to limited extent cause more "real" activities to take its place; in the main it will simply produce listlessness. On the other hand the ponderous and bilious "slumbering volcano," let him repress the expression of his passions as he will, will find them expire if they get no vent at all; whilst if the rare occasions multiply which he deems worthy of their outbreak, he will find them grow in intensity as life proceeds.

I feel persuaded there is no real exception to the law. The formidable effects of suppressed tears might be mentioned, and the calming results of speaking out your mind when angry and having done with it. But these are also but specious wanderings from the rule. Every perception must lead to *some* nervous result. If this be the normal emotional expression, it soon expends itself, and in the natural course of things a calm succeeds. But if the normal issue be blocked from any cause, the currents may under certain circumstances invade other tracts, and there work different worse effects. Thus vengeful brooding may replace a burst of indignation; a dry heat may consume the frame of one who fain would weep, or he may, as Dante says, turn to stone within; and then tears or a storming-fit may bring a grateful relief. When we teach children to repress their emotions, it is not that they may *feel* more, quite the reverse. It is that they may *think* more; for to a certain extent whatever nerve-currents are diverted from the regions below, must swell the activity of the thought-tracts of the brain.[3]

The last great argument in favour of the priority of the bodily symptoms to the felt emotion, is the ease with which we formulate by its means pathological cases and normal cases under a common scheme. In every asylum we find examples of absolutely unmotivated fear, anger, melancholy, or conceit; and others of an equally unmotivated apathy which persists in spite of the best outward reasons why it should give way. In the former cases we must suppose the nervous machinery to be so "labile" in some one emotional direction, that almost every stimulus, however inappropriate, will cause it to upset in that way, and as a consequence to engender the particular complex of feelings of which the psychic body of the emotion consists. Thus, to take one special instance, if inability to draw deep breath, fluttering of the heart, and that peculiar epigastric change felt as "precordial anxiety," with an irresistible tendency to take a somewhat crouching attitude and to sit still, and with perhaps other visceral processes not now known, all spontaneously occur together in a certain person; his feelings of their combination *is* the emotion of dread, and he is the victim of what is known as morbid fear. A friend who has had occasional attacks of this most distressing of all maladies, tells me that in his case the whole drama seems to centre about the region of the heart and respiratory apparatus, that his main effort during the attacks is to get control of his inspirations and to slow his heart, and that the moment he attains to breathing deeply and to holding himself erect, the dread, *ipso facto*, seems to depart.[4]

The account given to Brachet by one of his own patients of her opposite condition, that of emotional insensibility, has been often quoted, and deserves to be quoted again:—

> "I still continue (she says) to suffer constantly; I have not a moment of comfort, and no human sensations. Surrounded by all that can render life happy and agreeable, still to me the faculty of enjoyment and of feeling is wanting—both have become physical impossibilities. In everything, even in the most tender caresses of my children, I find only bitterness. I cover them with kisses, but there is something between their lips and mine; and this horrid something is between me and all the enjoyments of life. My existence is incomplete. The functions and acts of ordinary life, it is true, still remain to me; but in every one of them there is something wanting—to wit, the feeling which is proper to them, and the pleasure which follows them.... *Each of my senses, each part of my proper self, is as it were separated from me and can no longer afford me any feeling; this impossibility seems to depend upon a void which I feel in the front of my head, and to be due to the diminution of the sensibility over the whole surface of my body, for it seems to me that I never actually reach the objects which I touch.... I feel well enough the changes of temperature on my skin, but I no longer experience the internal feeling of the air when I breath....* All this would

be a small matter enough, but for its frightful result, which is that of the impossibility of any other kind of feeling and of any sort of enjoyment, although I experience a need and desire of them that render my life an incomprehensible torture. Every function, every action of my life remains, but deprived of the feeling that belongs to it, of the enjoyment that should follow it. My feet are cold, I warm them, but gain no pleasure from the warmth. I recognise the taste of all I eat, without getting any pleasure from it.... My children are growing handsome and healthy, everyone tells me so, I see it myself, but the delight, the inward comfort I ought to feel, I fail to get. Music has lost all charm for me, I used to love it dearly. My daughter plays very well, but for me it is mere noise. That lively interest which a year ago made me hear a delicious concert in the smallest air their fingers played,—that thrill, that general vibration which made me shed such tender tears,—all that exists no more."[5]

Other victims describe themselves as closed in walls of ice or covered with an india-rubber integument, through which no impression penetrates to the sealed-up sensibility.

If our hypothesis be true, it makes us realise more deeply than ever how much our mental life is knit up with our corporeal frame, in the strictest sense of the term. Rapture, love, ambition, indignation, and pride, considered as feelings, are fruits of the same soil with the grossest bodily sensations of pleasure and of pain. But it was said at the outset that this would be affirmed only of what we then agreed to call the "standard" emotions; and that those inward sensibilities that appeared devoid at first sight of bodily results should be left out of our account. We had better, before closing, say a word or two about these latter feelings.

They are, the reader will remember, the moral, intellectual, and aesthetic feelings. Concords of sounds, of colours, of lines, logical consistencies, teleological fitnesses, affect us with a pleasure that seems ingrained in the very form of the representation itself, and to borrow nothing from any reverberation surging up from the parts below the brain. The Herbartian psychologists have tried to distinguish feelings due to the *form* in which ideas may be arranged. A geometrical demonstration may be as "pretty," and an act of justice as "neat" as a drawing or a tune, although the prettiness and the neatness seem here to be a pure matter of sensation, and there to have nothing to do with sensation. We have then, or some of us seem to have, genuinely *cerebral* forms of pleasure and displeasure, apparently not agreeing in their mode of production with the so-called "standard" emotions we have been analysing. And it is certain that readers whom our reasons have hitherto failed to convince, will now start up at this admission, and consider that by it we give up our whole case. Since musical perceptions, since logical ideas, can immediately arouse a form of emotional feeling, they will say, is it not more natural to suppose that in the case of the so-called "standard" emotions, prompted by the presence of objects or the experience of events, the emotional feeling is equally immediate, and the bodily expression something that comes later and is added on?

But a sober scrutiny of the cases of pure cerebral emotion gives little force to this assimilation. Unless in them there actually be coupled with the intellectual feeling a bodily reverberation of some kind, unless we actually laugh at the neatness of the mechanical device, thrill at the justice of the act, or tingle at the perfection of the musical form, our mental condition is more allied to a judgment of *right* than to anything else. And such a judgment is rather to be classed among awarenesses of truth: it is a *cognitive* act. But as a matter of fact the intellectual feeling hardly ever does exist thus unaccompanied. The bodily sounding-board is at work, as careful introspection will show, far more than we usually suppose. Still, where long familiarity with a certain class of effects has blunted emotional sensibility thereto as much as it has sharpened the taste and judgment, we do get the intellectual emotion, if such it can be called, pure and undefiled. And the dryness of it, the paleness, the absence of all glow, as it may exist in a thoroughly expert critic's mind, not only shows us what an altogether different thing it is from the "standard" emotions we considered first, but makes us suspect that almost the entire difference lies in the fact that the bodily sounding-board, vibrating in the one case, is in the other mute. "Not so very bad" is, in a person of consummate taste, apt to be the highest limit of approving expression. "*Rien ne me choque*" is said to have been Chopin's superlative of praise of new music. A sentimental layman would feel, and ought to feel, horrified, on being admitted into such a critic's mind, to see how cold, how thin, how void of human significance, are the motives for favour or disfavour that there prevail. The capacity to make a nice spot on the wall will outweigh a picture's whole content; a foolish trick of words will preserve a poem; an utterly meaningless fitness of sequence in one musical composition set at naught any amount of "expressiveness" in another.

I remember seeing an English couple sit for more than an hour on a piercing February day in the Academy at Venice before the celebrated "Assumption" by Titian; and when I, after being chased from room to room by the cold, concluded to get into the sunshine as fast as possible and let the pictures go, but before leaving drew reverently near to them to learn with what superior forms of susceptibility they might be endowed, all I overheard was the woman's voice murmuring: "What a *deprecatory* expression her face wears! What self-*abnegation*! How *unworthy* she feels of the honour she is receiving!" Their honest hearts had been kept warm all the time by a glow of spurious sentiment that would have fairly made old Titian sick. Mr. Ruskin somewhere makes the (for him) terrible admission that religious people as a rule care little for pictures, and that when they do care for them they generally prefer the worst ones to the best. Yes! in every art, in every science, there is the keen perception of certain relations being *right* or not, and there is the emotional flush and thrill consequent thereupon. And these are two things, not one. In the former of them it is that experts and masters are at home. The latter accompaniments are bodily commotions that they may hardly feel, but that may be experienced in their fullness by *Crétins* and Philistines in whom the critical judgment is at its lowest ebb. The "marvels" of Science, about which so much edifying popular literature is written, are apt to be "caviare" to the men in the laboratories. Cognition and emotion are parted even in this last retreat,—who shall say that their antagonism may not just be one phase of the world-old struggle known as that between the spirit and the flesh?—a struggle in which it seems pretty certain that neither party will definitively drive the other off the field.

To return now to our starting-point, the physiology of the brain. If we suppose its cortex to contain centres for the perception of changes in each special sense-organ, in each portion of the skin, in each muscle, each joint, and each viscus, and to contain absolutely nothing else, we still have a scheme perfectly capable of representing the process of the emotions. An object falls on a sense-organ and is apperceived by the appropriate cortical centre; or else the latter, excited in some other way, gives rise to an idea of the same object. Quick as a flash, the reflex currents pass down through their preordained channels, alter the condition of muscle, skin, and viscus; and these alterations, appperceived like the original object, in as many specific portions of the cortex, combine with it in consciousness and transform it from an object-simply-apprehended into an object-emotionally-felt. No new principles have to be invoked, nothing is postulated beyond the ordinary reflex circuit, and the topical centres admitted in one shape or another by all to exist.

It must be confessed that a crucial test of the truth of the hypothesis is quite as hard to obtain as its decisive refutation. A case of complete internal and external corporeal anaesthesia, without motor alteration or alteration of intelligence except emotional apathy, would afford, if not a crucial test, at least a strong presumption, in favour of the truth of the view we have set forth; whilst the persistence of strong emotional feeling in such a case would completely overthrow our case. Hysterical anaesthesias seem never to be complete enough to cover the ground. Complete anaesthesias from organic disease, on the other hand, are excessively rare. In the famous case of Remigius Leims, no mention is made by the reporters of his emotional condition, a circumstance which by itself affords no presumption that it was normal, since as a rule nothing ever *is* noticed without a pre-existing question in the mind. Dr. Georg Winter has recently described a case somewhat similar,[6] and in reply to a question, kindly writes to me as follows: "The case has been for a year and a half entirely removed from my observation. But so far as I am able to state, the man was characterised by a certain mental inertia and indolence. He was tranquil, and had on the whole the temperament of a phlegmatic. He was not irritable, not quarrelsome, went quietly about his farm-work, and left the care of his business and housekeeping to other people. In short, he gave one the impression of a placid countryman, who has no interests beyond his work." Dr. Winter adds that in studying the case he paid no particular attention to the man's psychic condition, as this seemed *"nebensächlich"* to his main purpose. I should add that the form of my question to Dr. Winter could give him no clue as to the kind of answer I expected.

Of course, this case proves nothing, but it is to be hoped that asylum-physicians and nervous specialists may begin methodically to study the relation between anaesthesia and emotional apathy. If the hypothesis here suggested is ever to be definitively confirmed or disproved it seems as if it must be by them, for they alone have the data in their hands.

POST SCRIPT

By an unpardonable forgetfulness at the time of dispatching my MS. to the Editor, I ignored the existence of the extraordinary case of total anaesthesia published by Professor Strumpell in *Ziemssen's Deutsches Archiv für klinische Medicin* xxii, 321, of which I had nevertheless read reports at the time of its publication. [*Cf.* first report of the case in MIND X, 263, translated from *Pflüger's Archiv.* Ed.] I believe that it constitutes the only remaining case of the sort in medical literature, so that with it our survey is complete. On referring to the original, which is important in many connections, I found that the patient, a shoemaker's apprentice of 15, entirely anaesthetic, inside and out, with the exception of one eye and one ear, had shown *shame* on the occasion of soiling his bed, and *grief*, when a formerly favourite dish was set before him, at the thought that he could no longer taste its flavour. As Dr. Strümpell seemed however to have paid no special attention to his psychic states, so far as these are matter for our theory, I wrote him in a few words what the essence of the theory was, and asked him to say whether he felt sure the grief and shame mentioned were real feelings in the boy's mind, or only the reflex manifestations provoked by certain perceptions, manifestations that an outside observer might note, but to which the boy himself might be insensible.

Dr. Strümpell has sent me a very obliging reply, of which I translate the most important passage.

I must indeed confess that I naturally failed to institute with my *Anaesthetiker* observations as special as the sense of your theory would require. Nevertheless I think I can decidedly make the statement, that he was by no means completely lacking in emotional affections. In addition to the feelings of *grief* and *shame* mentioned in my paper, I recall distinctly that he showed *e.g., anger,* and frequently quarrelled with the hospital attendants. He also manifested *fear* lest I should punish him. In short, I do not think that my case speaks exactly in favour of your theory. On the other hand, I will not affirm that it positively refutes your theory. For my case was certainly one of a very centrally conditioned anaesthesia (perception-anaesthesia, like that of hysterics) and therefore the conduction of outward impressions may in him have been undisturbed.

I confess that I do not see the relevancy of the last consideration, and this makes me suspect that my own letter was too briefly or obscurely expressed to put my correspondent fully in possession of my own thought. For his reply still makes no explicit reference to anything but the outward manifestations of emotion in the boy. Is it not at least conceivable that, just as a stranger, brought into the boy's presence for the first time, and seeing him eat and drink and satisfy other natural necessities, would suppose him to have the feelings of hunger, thirst, etc., until informed by the boy himself that he did all these things with no feelings at all but that of sight and sound—is it not, I say, at least possible, that Dr. Strumpell, addressing no direct introspective questions to his patient, and the patient not being of a class from which one could expect voluntary revelations of that sort, should have similarly omitted to discriminate between a feeling and its habitual motor accompaniment, and erroneously taken the latter as proof that the former was there? Such a mistake is of course possible, and I must therefore repeat Dr. Strümpell's own words, that his case does not yet refute my theory. Should a similar case recur, it ought to be interrogated as to the inward emotional state that co-existed with the outward expressions of shame, anger, etc. And if it then turned out that the patient recognised explicitly the same mood of feeling known under those names in his formal normal state, my theory would of course fall. It is, however, to me incredible that the patient should have an *identical* feeling, for the dropping out of the organic sounding-board would necessarily diminish its volume in some way. The teacher of Dr. Strümpell's patient found a mental deficiency in him during his anaesthesia, that may possibly have been due to the consequences resulting to his general intellectual vivacity from the subtraction of so important a mass of feelings, even though they were not the whole of his emotional life. Whoever wishes to extract from the next case of total anaesthesia the maximum of knowledge about the emotions, will have to interrogate the patient with some such notion as that of my article in his mind. We can define the pure psychic emotions far better by starting from such an hypothesis and modifying it in the way of restriction and subtraction, than by having no definite hypothesis at all. Thus will the publication of my article have been justified, even though the theory it advocates, rigorously taken, be erroneous. The best thing I can say for it is, that in writing it, I have almost persuaded *myself* it may be true.

Notes

1   Of course the physiological question arises, *how* are the changes felt?—*after* they are produced, by the sensory nerves of the organs bringing back to the brain a report of the modifications that have occurred? or *before* they are produced, by our being conscious of the outgoing nerve-currents starting on their way downward towards the parts they are to excite? I believe all the evidence we have to be in favour of the former alternative. The question is too minute for discussion here, but I have said something about it in a paper entitled "The Feeling of Effort," in the *Anniversary Memoirs of the Boston Natural History Society,* 1880 (translated in *La Critique of Philosphique* for that year, and summarised in MIND XX, 582). See also G.E. Müller's *Grundlegung der Psychophysik,* 110.

2   Let it be noted in passing that this personal self-consciousness seems an altogether bodily affair, largely a consciousness of our attitude, and that, like other emotions, it reacts on its physical condition, and leads to modifications of the attitude,—to a certain rigidity in most men, but in children to a regular twisting and squirming fit, and in women to various gracefully shy poses.

3   This is the opposite of what happens in injuries to the brain, whether from outward violence, inward rupture or tumor, or mere starvation from disease. The cortical permeability seems reduced, so that excitement, instead of propagating itself laterally through the ideational channels as, before, tends to take the downward track into the organs of the body. The consequence is that we have tears, laughter, and temper-fits, on the most insignificant provocation, accompanying a proportional feebleness in logical thought and the power of volitional attention and decision.

4   It must be confessed that there are cases of morbid fear in which objectively the heart is not much perturbed. These however fail to prove anything against our theory, for it is of course possible that the cortical centres normally percipient of dread as a complex of cardiac and other organic sensations due to real bodily change, should become *primarily* excited in brain-disease, and give rise to an hallucination of the changes being there,—an hallucination of dread, consequently, coexistent with a comparatively calm pulse, etc. I say it is possible, for I am ignorant of observations which might test the fact. Trance, ecstasy, etc., offer analogous examples,—not to speak of ordinary dreaming. Under all these conditions one may have the liveliest subjective feelings, either of eye or ear, or of the more visceral and emotional sort, as a result of pure nerve-central activity, with complete peripheral repose. Whether the subjective strength of the feeling be due in these cases to the actual energy of the central disturbance, or merely to the narrowing of the field of consciousness, need not

concern us. In the asylum cases of melancholy, there is usually a narrowing of the field.

5 Quoted by Semal: *De la Sensibilité générale dans les Affections mélancoliques*, Paris, 1876, pp.130-35.

6 "Ein fall von allgemeiner Anaesthesie," *Inaugural Dissertation*. Heidelberg, Winter, 1882.

Toward a Cognitive Conception of Emotion

EMOTIONS AND STATEMENTS ABOUT THEM

Errol Bedford

The concept of emotion gives rise to a number of philosophical problems. The most important of these, I think, concern the function of statements about emotions and the criteria for their validity. A solution to these problems is offered by what I shall call the traditional theory of the emotions, and I should like to begin by discussing some aspects of this. According to this view[1] an emotion is a feeling, or at least an experience of a special type which involves a feeling. Logically, this amounts to regarding emotion words as the names of feelings. It is assumed that to each word there corresponds a qualitatively distinct experience which may, although it need not, find 'expression' in outward behaviour. If it does, this behaviour entitles us to infer the existence of the inner feeling, and therefore to assert, with some degree of probability, statements of the form 'He is angry.' Looked at in this way, emotions naturally come to be thought of as inner forces that move us, in combination with, or in opposition to other forces, to act as we do. Briefly, anger is a specific feeling which leads the angry man to show the signs of anger (*e.g.*, striking someone) unless he is willing to, and able to, suppress them. It follows, I take it, that to explain behaviour by saying that a man acted as he did because he was angry, is to give a causal explanation, although, admittedly, a causal explanation of a special sort.

This is the accepted view of the older psychological textbooks. Stout distinguishes, indeed, between 'emotional dispositions' (*e.g.* liking and disliking, hate and love) and 'emotions,' but he affirms that the emotion itself in which an emotional disposition is actualised is 'always an acute state of consciousness' that, besides sensations and conative tendencies, 'also involves specific kinds of feeling which cannot be explained away as resultants or complications of more simple elements.'[2] Even James thinks that an emotion is a feeling, although he identifies the feeling with somatic sensations. In the famous passage in his *Principles of Psychology* he tells us that his theory is 'that the bodily changes follow directly the perception of the exciting fact, and that our feeling of the same changes as they occur IS the emotion.'[3]

I am going to argue that this involves a fundamental mistake: the logical mistake of treating emotion words as names, which leads in turn to a misconception of their function. There might, all the same, be more to be said for this view if it were less inadequate at the psychological level, if it did not presuppose a richness and clarity in the 'inner life' of feeling that it does not possess. What evidence is there for the existence of a multitude of feelings corresponding to the extensive and subtle linguistic differentiation of our vocabulary for discussing emotions? This assumption gains no support from experience. Indignation and annoyance are two different emotions; but, to judge from my own case, the feelings that accompany indignation appear to differ little, if at all, from those that accompany annoyance. I certainly find no feeling, or class of feelings, that marks off indignation from annoyance, and enables me to distinguish them from one another. The distinction is of a different *sort* from this. (Perhaps I do not remember very clearly—but then is not this part of the difficulty, that the words 'indignation' and 'annoyance' do *not* call up recollections of two distinct feelings?) I might add that at the present time this is psychological orthodoxy. The author of the chapter on 'Feeling and Emotion' in a standard textbook (Boring, Langfeld and Weld's *Foundations of Psychology*, 1948) remarks that 'there is little evidence that a peculiar, unique type of consciousness accompanies and identifies the different emotions.' (p. 100)

In any case, does the truth of such a statement as 'He is afraid' logically require the existence of a specific feeling? I imagine that it would nowadays be generally conceded that emotion words are commonly used without any implication that the person they refer to is having a particular experience at any given time. But it may be said, granting this, that such expressions as 'is afraid,' 'is angry,' nevertheless gain their whole meaning from an indirect reference that they make to experiences, and can only be defined in terms of feelings. A man can feel angry as well as be angry; the expression 'is angry' may not name an experience, but 'feels angry' surely does, and all that can be meant by saying that someone is angry is that he is liable to, and sometimes does, feel angry. I do not think, however, that this argument can prove what it sets out to prove, *i.e.* that anger necessarily involves a specific feeling. In the first place, 'feels angry' is often able to serve instead of 'is angry.' We can say, 'I felt angry about it for days afterwards.' A more important point is that one cannot understand what it is to feel angry without first understanding what it is to be angry. If we can assume the meaning of 'is angry,' or teach it (ostensively or by a descriptive account), we can go on to explain 'feels angry' by saying that it is to feel as people often feel who are angry. But how could we explain the expression 'feels angry' without presupposing that the person we are explaining it to understands 'is angry'? The only possible method open to us would seem to be this: to make him angry, *e.g.* by insulting him, and then to say to him, 'Well, feeling angry is feeling as you feel now.' The difficulty is that, if the view I am criticising is correct, we cannot ensure in this way that we have taught him the meaning of the expression. We have to be certain that he has experienced a specific feeling. Yet it is logically possible that the insult (or other stimulus, and it is a crucial point that there is no *specific* stimulus) has failed in its object—it may have produced no feeling, or the wrong feeling, or so confused a mixture of feelings that he cannot discriminate the essential from the inessential (the matter is, if anything, even more difficult from his point of view). We cannot exclude this by arguing 'He is angry, therefore he feels angry,' for how are we to know that he is angry? *Ex hypothesi* his behaviour is no proof of this. And having as yet no guarantee that he has grasped what the question means, we obviously cannot ask him whether he feels angry. Nor can we discover that he has understood the meaning of the expression by observing that he uses it in the same way as we do, for, *ex hypothesi* again, this will not prove that he means the same by it. The conclusion to be drawn, if I am right, is that being angry is logically prior to feeling angry, and therefore that being angry does not entail feeling angry, and *a fortiori* does not entail having any other feeling.

Now it may seem that this does not accord with the confidence we have in our beliefs about our own and other people's emotions respectively. But is this really so? We do not first ascertain that a man feels angry, and then conclude that he is angry. On the contrary, we realise that he is angry, and assume (perhaps wrongly) that he feels angry. Behavioural evidence for a statement about emotions is evidence in its own right, so to speak, and not because it entitles us to infer to private experiences. For if we have good grounds for the assertion that a person is jealous, we do not withdraw this assertion on learning that he does not feel jealous, although we may accept this as true. It is, after all, notorious that we can be mistaken about our own emotions, and that in this matter a man is not the final court of appeal in his own case; those who are jealous are often the last, instead of the first, to recognise that they are. This is scarcely consistent with the view that the criterion for identifying an emotion is the recognition of the special qualities of an experience; it is intelligible if the criteria are different from, and more complex than this. I am going to discuss these criteria shortly. For the moment, I only want to suggest that the traditional answer to the question 'How do we identify our own emotions?' namely, 'By introspection,' cannot be correct. It seems to me that there is every reason to believe that we learn about our own emotions essentially in the same way as other people learn about them. Admittedly, it is sometimes the case that we know our own emotions better than anyone else does, but there is no need to explain this as being due to the introspection of feelings. One reason for this is that it is hardly possible for a man to be completely ignorant, as others may be, of the context of his own behaviour. Again, thoughts may cross his mind that he does not make public. But the fact that he prefers to keep them to himself is incidental; and if they were known they would only be corroborative evidence, not indispensable evidence of a radically different sort from that which is available to other people. It is only in some respects, then, that each of us is in a better position to understand himself than anyone else is. Against this must be set the possibility of self-deception and a reluctance to admit that we are, for instance, vain or envious.

I must now meet what is, I think, the most serious objection that is likely to be made to this—the alleged impossibility of distinguishing, from an external observer's point of view, between real anger, say, and the pretence of it. It is sometimes claimed that although someone might behave as if he were angry, and give every appearance that he would persist in this behaviour, there would still be a sense in which he might be shamming. What then is the difference between being angry and merely pretending to be? It may be held that it can only lie in the fact that the man who is pretending is not in the appropriate state of inner feeling. Now this objection plainly rests on the attempt to assimilate being angry to other cases of 'being so and so' in which the only decisive evidence for whether someone is pretending or not is what he feels. One line of reply to it, therefore, would be to deny that there are any such cases. But it is doubtful whether this could be sustained. Pain is a specific sensation (or class of similar sensations) and it seems clear that being in pain does entail having that sensation, since 'I am in pain but I don't feel anything' is self-contradictory. If so, it is possible for someone consistently to pretend to be in pain, and yet to be deceiving us. We might, of course, be unwilling to believe anyone who after showing all the signs of pain confessed that he felt no pain; but the point is, that *if* what he says is true, it entails the falsity of 'He was in pain.' Can we say that being angry is similar to being in pain in this respect? Let us contrast the cases of a man who is angry and another, behaving in a similar way, who is only pretending to be. Now it may well be true that the former feels angry, whereas the latter does not, but in any case it is not this that constitutes the difference between the fact that the one is angry and the fact that the other is only pretending to be. The objection rests on a misconception of what pretence is. There is necessarily involved in pretence, or shamming, the notion of a limit which must not be overstepped; pretence is always insulated, as it were, from reality. Admittedly, this limit may be vague, but it must exist. It is a not unimportant point that it is usually *obvious* when someone is pretending. If a man who is behaving as if he were angry goes so far as to smash the furniture or commit an assault, he has passed the limit; he is not *pretending*, and it is useless for him to protest afterwards that he did not feel angry. Far from his statement being *proof* that he was not angry, it would be discounted even if it were accepted as true. 'He was angry, but he did not feel angry' is not self-contradictory, although it is no doubt normally false. If in a particular case it is difficult—as it may be—to settle the question, 'Pretended of real?,' that can only be because the relevant public evidence is inadequate to settle it. What we want is more evidence of the same kind, not a special piece of evidence of a different kind. Our difficulty in resolving the question 'Is he really in pain?' on the other hand, arises from the fact that the only decisive evidence is evidence that he alone is in a position to give. (I think that even in the case of pretending to be in pain there is a limit, only it is exceptional in depending on a subjective condition. It is decisively passed if a person truly says 'I feel pain.' There may, of course, be inductive evidence for accepting or rejecting his statement.)

This is confirmed by the difference between the two questions 'Do I really feel pain?' and 'Do I really feel angry?' Since there is little room for doubt about the answer, the former is not a query that anyone is very likely to put to himself; it may even be said that it is a meaningless question. But I am inclined to think that it could be asked as a classificatory question, as roughly equivalent to 'Is this pain or rather discomfort?' It is to be answered, if at all, by comparing the present feeling with other feelings definitely counted as pains, and considering whether it is sufficiently similar to be classed with them. One cannot resolve it by answering the question 'Am I really in pain?' since the answer to that question must depend on the answer given to the first. By contrast, 'Do I really feel angry?' is one of a class of similar questions that are common in everyday life. This question does not concern the comparison of feelings; in answering it one is trying to decide whether one is angry or not, and the answer 'Yes' can be mistaken in a way that a similar answer to the question 'Do I really feel pain?' cannot be.

II

Having, I hope, cleared the ground a little by putting some preliminary arguments against the traditional theory, I now want to consider whether an adequate alternative to it is provided by a dispositional theory of emotions, and to discuss the criteria for the use of emotion words. Can the concept of an emotion be fully elucidated without using non-behavioural, indeed non-psychological, concepts? I will try to justify the negative answer that I think should be given to this question.

To begin with, statements about emotions cannot be said to describe behaviour; they interpret it.[4] The situation seems to be that emotional behaviour, so to speak, is far from being homogeneous. The behavioural evidence for 'He was angry' varies with the person and the occasion; in different cases it is not the same, and possibly it may not even be partially the same. Conversely, the same, or similar, behaviour, can be differently, and correctly, interpreted in different circumstances, for example as anger, indignation, annoyance, exasperation or resentment. Accordingly, categorical descriptive statements, *e.g.* (1) 'He raised his voice and began to thump the table,' and hypothetical descriptive statements, *e.g.* (2) 'If I had gone on teasing him he would have thrown something at me,' are evidence for such statements as (3) 'He was very angry,' but they are not part of what these statements mean. Clearly, on hearing (3), it would be proper to ask for details, and such details could be given in (1) and (2). (1) and (2) would therefore give additional information to that already given in (3). To put the matter another way, (1), (2) and (3) are independent of one another in respect of truth and falsity. (1) may be true when (3) is false (a man can thump the table and raise his voice—to emphasise a point—without being angry), and (3) may be true although (1) is false (for not all angry men thump tables). The same holds of the relationships of (2) and (3). The truth of (2) is perfectly compatible with joining in the fun; anger, on the other hand, is consistent with not being prepared to throw things. I think that this would still hold with other statements substituted for (1) and (2). It does not seem to be possible, therefore, to analyse (3) into a set, however, complex, of categorical and hypothetical statements that describe individual behaviour. (3) does not sum up, but goes beyond, the behavioural evidence for it, and it would always be logically possible to accept the evidence and deny the conclusion. Although when we say (3) we are in a sense talking about the behaviour on which its truth rests, anger is not merely a disposition, and cannot be reduced to a pattern of behaviour, actual or potential.[5] All that can be said about the logical relationships between (3) and such statements as (1) and (2) is that it is a necessary, but not a sufficient, condition for the truth of (3) that some statements such as (1) and (2) should be true, without it being possible to specify which.

This last assertion may be challenged in at least two ways. It might be said, first, that the phrase 'necessary, but not a sufficient, condition' ought to be changed to 'neither a necessary nor a sufficient condition.' But since the only ground on which this could be maintained appears to be the traditional view, I shall not discuss it any further. I will only add that I do not believe that we either do, or should, take any notice of anyone's protestations that, for instance, he loves his wife, if his conduct offers no evidence whatever that he does. At the other extreme, those who want to be thoroughly behaviouristic about the emotions will argue that the phrase 'necessary but not sufficient' should be amended to 'both necessary and sufficient.' What I am suggesting is that people who share the same information and the same expectations about another person's behaviour may possibly place different emotional interpretations on that behaviour, if their knowledge is confined to descriptive statements about it. It may be urged that this difference of opinion can be eliminated as further evidence of the same type comes to light, and that it can only be eliminated in this way. The assumption underlying this—that the criteria for assertions about emotions are purely behavioural—is not, however, borne out by an examination of the way in which we actually use emotion words. These words, when used without qualification, carry implications, not merely about behaviour, but also about its social context. Consider the distinction between two emotions that have a close similarity, shame and embarrassment. The behaviour of an embarrassed man is often not noticeably different from that of one who is ashamed; but there is an important difference between the respective situations they are in. In a newspaper article last year, Mr. Peter Davies, the publisher, was said to be 'to his mild embarrassment' the original of Peter Pan. The embarrassment is understandable, and the epithet appropriate, whether its application is correct or not. Yet we can say at once that if the writer of the article had alleged that Mr. Davies was 'to his shame' the original of Peter Pan, this would have been incorrect; it is scarcely conceivable that it could be true. The reason for this is obvious, and it is logical, not psychological, since it has nothing to do with Mr. Davies' behaviour, still less with his feelings. It is simply that the fact that Barrie modelled Peter Pan on him is not his *fault*—it was not due to an act of his, and there is nothing reprehensible about it anyway. In general, it is only true to say of someone 'He is ashamed of so and so' if what is referred to is something that he can be criticised for (the criticism is commonly, though not perhaps necessarily, moral). It is, in other words, a necessary condition for the truth of the statement that he should be at fault. The word 'embarrassed' is not connected in the same way with blame and responsibility; the claim that it makes is the vaguer and weaker one that the situation is awkward or inconvenient and so on. 'He was embarrassed' may impute a fault to someone else, but not to the person of whom it is said. (I do not mean that we may not also impute a fault to someone of whom we say this. Sometimes one puts oneself into an embarrassing situation, sometimes one finds oneself in it. I mean that we do not impute it *in* saying 'He was embarrassed,' in the way we do if we say 'He was ashamed.') It may be pointed out that we can, after all, be ashamed of the faults of others. But I do not believe that this is true unless we accept the fault as our own; when, for instance, our children, or even our friends, commit anti-social acts in houses that we introduce them to. It is most unusual to be ashamed of the deeds of total strangers, although it is possible provided that responsibility is accepted through identification with the stranger in virtue of a common characteristic—'I was ashamed to see an Englishman lying dead drunk on the pavement.' A Frenchman would be unlikely to say this, although rising to a still higher level of generality he might change 'Englishman' to 'European.' (It is beside the point that such acceptance of responsibility may be irrational.) The connexion between shame and responsibility is not, of course, ignored in the traditional theory of emotions. It appears as the doctrine that every emotion must have an appropriate object; that it is impossible (psychologically) to experience the feeling specific to shame unless you recognise that you are open to criticism. But there are no limits to what men may feel; we can only set limits to what they can say. This is merely the misrepresentation of a logical point as a piece of implausible *a priori* psychology.

The point of the example is to show that although knowledge of facts that is quite independent of knowledge of behaviour cannot by itself establish a given interpretation of that behaviour, it can be sufficient definitely to exclude it. I suggest, then, that it is possible to rebut the contention that *e.g.*

A is jealous of B's relationship with C, by showing that the claim made about the situation in which A is, by such an assertion, *viz.* that he is in a certain marital, professional or other relationship (depending on the context) with B, is not satisfied. Certainly the contention that A is jealous is as a rule rebutted by evidence about his behaviour which is inconsistent with its truth. The reason why the claim that A is in a certain relationship with B is usually unquestioned, is that it is rarely false; the assertion that A is jealous is not usually made unless it is already known that the claim is satisfied, although it is frequently made on inadequate behavioural evidence. In general, then, this criterion is relevant to the *assertion* of statements, rather than the justification or rebuttal of statements that have *already* been asserted—it leads us to pick one word rather than another. For example, the decision whether to say that the driver of a car which has broken down for lack of water is indignant, or merely annoyed or angry, depends on whether the radiator is empty through (let us say) the carelessness of a garage mechanic who undertook to fill it for him, or through his own carelessness ('annoyed with himself' but not 'indignant with myself'). Indignation, but not annoyance, seems to imply unfairness, particularly unfair accusation, or breach of an agreement. Thus, if the garage mechanic is later taxed with his carelessness, it could not be said that he was indignant, unless he was in a position to reply 'But you said you would do it yourself, sir' or something similar.

Statements about emotions may also involve another, and somewhat different, type of commitment, which has an even closer bearing on the elucidation of their function. It can be illustrated in the contrast between hope and expectation, and I think this throws some light on the question why one is, and the other is not, usually counted as an emotion. The most apparent difference between them is that hoping for and expecting an event express different degrees of confidence that the event will happen. To expect something is to believe that it is more likely than not to happen. In the case of hope it is only necessary that it should not be an impossibility. This is, however, not the only, nor the most crucial, difference. Phrases which express a low degree of confidence, *e.g.* 'I think it may...,' 'Perhaps it will ...' cannot be substituted without loss for 'I hope that....' The expression 'I hope that ...' implies, in addition to a very vague estimate of probability, an *assessment* of whatever is referred to in the clause that follows. I think it is clear that one cannot hope for something, although one can expect something, without judging it favourably in some respect, or from some point of view. Compare (1) 'I don't favour a higher purchase tax but I expect it will be raised,' with (2) 'I don't favour a higher purchase tax but I hope it will be raised.' (1) creates no surprise; (2) demands further explanation. Does he think it bad for the country, but profitable to him personally because he has a large stock of goods on which he has already paid tax? Does he regard it as unsound fiscal policy in general, but advisable temporarily in an inflationary economy? Failing an answer to questions such as these (2) is surely a puzzling remark, and (3) 'I don't favour a higher purchase tax in any respect, but I hope it will be raised' seems to me to be self-contradictory. (Since—to mention one reason—one can only favour events under human control, and hope is not restricted in this way, 'I favour ...' does not precisely represent the implication of 'I hope that...,' but it will do for the purpose of the present example. I need hardly say that it is not my intention in this paper to give an exhaustive—or, indeed, a more than roughly accurate—account of the particular concepts that I use as examples.) It is a psychological truism that men do not, with some exceptions, hope that their opponents will win; it is a truth of logic that they can-not hope that their opponents will win without approving of this in *some* respect. Thus 'I hope that ...' is commonly used to declare, or to commit one-self to, an allegiance, and although disagreement *about* hopes is disagreement about the interpretation of facts, disagreement *in* hopes is not—it is one of the forms that disagreement about value may take (*e.g.* 'I hope the Socialists will get in.' 'Well, I don't. I think it would be a disaster for the country.') This is a further reason why it would be absurd to say that questions of the form 'Do I feel regret for...?' 'Do I really hope that...?' could be settled by intro-spection. 'Do I really hope that the Tories will get in?' is plainly a question a wavering Tory supporter might put to himself. This may amount to asking himself whether, granted that he thinks a Tory government better than a Labour one, he is concerned enough about the election result, or whether he is not too indifferent to say, if he is honest, that he *hopes* for a Tory victory. If so, he will not answer it by searching his feelings, for they have nothing to do with the matter, but by reflecting, for example, that when the party's policy was attacked, he did not bother to defend it, or by remembering that after all he has agreed to do some canvassing. But it is just as likely, if not more likely, that the answer to the question will be a *decision* about his allegiance, reached by reconsidering the merits of the two parties. (Contrast 'Do I really feel pain?' discussed above.)

To generalise from this example: emotion words form part of the vocabu-lary of appraisal and criticism, and a number of them belong to the more spe-cific language of moral criticism. Normally, the verbs in their first-person use imply the speaker's assessment of something, and in their third-person use they carry an implication about an assessment by the person they refer to.[6] It is perhaps worth mentioning that there are certain cases in which a third-per-son statement gives the speaker's verdict on that person; a factor which cer-tainly complicates discussions of character. Such terms as 'vain,' 'envious' and 'resentful' are terms of censure.[7] There is an overlap between the lists of emo-tions, and the lists of virtues and vices that are given by philosophers. The overlap is not complete; some virtues (*e.g.* veracity) are not connected with emotions, and some emotions (*e.g.* regret) cannot be treated as elements of character and are not merits or defects.

So far I have discussed the conditions which appear to govern the truth and falsity of statements about emotions. While emotion concepts do not form an altogether homogeneous group, I believe that this is correct as a broad outline. But there is one respect in which it needs to be supplemented. This concerns the sense in which emotions (as opposed to statements about emotions) can be justified or unjustified, reasonable or unreasonable. It is fairly obvious, to begin with, that the behavioural criteria for the use of emotion words are not connected with the application of these predicates. The way in which a man behaves will determine whether he is or is not angry. But *if* he is angry, the behavioural evidence for this is not in itself relevant to the question whether his anger is justified or unjustified. On the other hand, if the claim that an emotion word makes about a situation is not satisfied, this is often indicated by saying that the emotion is unjustified or unreasonable. The attribution of the emotion, that is to say, is not withdrawn, but qualified. An example will make this clearer. Suppose that B does something that is to A's advantage although A thinks that it is to his disadvantage (*e.g.* B, a solicitor administering A's affairs, sells some shares that A believes [wrongly] will appreciate). Now it would be misleading to say simply, except to a fully informed audience, 'A resents what B did'— this surely carries the incorrect implication that B has injured A. To guard against this it is necessary to add 'but his resentment is quite unjustified,' or some equivalent expression. A's belief that B has done something that affects him adversely is, however, a necessary condition if the word 'resentment' is to be used at all. The distinction between what the situation is, and what it is believed to be, is normally unimportant, and for this reason emotion words make an objective claim unless special precautions are taken to exclude or cancel it (*e.g.* 'He was afraid but no one else was' [there was no real danger], 'Your surprise is quite unjustified' [it was only to be expected]).

But this is not the whole story and the question whether an emotion is justified or not does not always turn on an issue of fact. There is a second group of emotions (not, I think, necessarily exclusive of the first) in respect of which the qualifications 'unjustified,' 'unreasonable' refer to a different implication, and have quite a different force. Contempt, disgust, and pride are typical of this group. If I were to say that a music critic's contempt for Bartok was unjustified, I should not be asserting a fact; I should be challenging his assessment of Bartok. It is impossible to give any simple paraphrase of this remark, but it could be taken, in part, as more or less equivalent to saying that Bartok is a better composer than the critic allows. While the critic's assessment of Bartok determines, among other considerations, whether I shall assert or deny that he is contemptuous of Bartok, it does not determine whether I shall say that his contempt is justified or not; *that* depends on my opinion about his assessment.

How far can these distinctions be accounted for by theories in which emotion concepts are treated as psychological concepts? I am inclined to think that if an emotion were a feeling no sense could be made of them at all. It may be said that an emotion is unjustified when a feeling is inappropriate or unfitting to a situation. But I find this unintelligible. Feelings do not have a character that makes this relationship possible. In any case, the interpretation suggested is not what is meant by saying that *e.g.* a critic's contempt is unjustified. In general, I do not think it can be maintained that logical predicates apply either to feelings or to sensations. What reasons could be given for or against a feeling, or for or against its 'inappropriateness' to a situation? If someone were to say 'I felt a pang this afternoon,' it would be meaningless to ask whether it was a reasonable or unreasonable pang. The matter is different if he says 'pang of regret,' but the phrase 'of regret' does not *name* the feeling, as I have already argued, and the pang of regret is justified, if it is, not as a feeling, but because his regret is justified. Nor do these predicates apply to bodily sensations, such as feeling giddy or having a pain in one's leg. This, I think, explains the fact that while we often say 'You ought (or ought not) to be (or feel) ashamed (etc.),' we cannot say this of feelings;[8] a point that has created difficulties for moral philosophers who adhere to the traditional theory about emotions. Sir David Ross, for instance, recognises that 'ought' does not apply to feelings, and he assumes that from this it follows that it has no application to emotions, except in an 'improper use.' According to him 'we cannot seriously say' *e.g.* 'You ought to feel ashamed.'[9] He is, therefore constrained to interpret this remark as meaning that a certain feeling is 'right or fitting' in the circumstances, which, as I shall argue shortly, misconstrues its point. If, however, we do not presuppose that the primary function of 'I feel ashamed' is to report a feeling, there is no objection to allowing—what is surely the case— that 'You ought to feel ashamed' employs 'ought' in a perfectly 'proper' sense, indeed in the same sense as in 'You ought to apologise.'

A dispositional theory of emotions may be thought to be on stronger ground, since it can be argued that behaviour may be unreasonable or unjustified. To use a previous example again, to say that someone has an unjustified contempt for Bartok is to say, I take it, on this view, that certain categorical and hypothetical statements are true of him, and that these statements describe behaviour that is unjustified. In other words, the assertion that contempt for Bartok is unjustified means that a certain pattern of preferential behaviour is unjustified. But what is this pattern of behaviour? Presumably it will consist in doing (or being prepared to do) things of this sort: switching off when Bartok's music is announced on the Third Programme, wasting free tickets to a concert of his music, never buying records of Bartok, going for a walk when a neighbour plays his music on the violin, and so on; in short, choosing against this composer whenever a choice presents itself. Now let us suppose that contempt for Bartok is unjustified, as it undoubtedly is. Even so, this behaviour may be perfectly reasonable or justified, and therefore cannot

constitute an unjustified contempt for Bartok. It is open to a different interpretation, that the person who behaves in this way is simply uninterested in
this composer's music, or in modern music generally. Consistently to choose
against something is not necessarily to condemn it, or to be contemptuous of
it, because this choice is susceptible of rational explanation in other ways.

III

I must now amplify what I have said in passing about the functions performed
by statements that refer to emotions. It is generally assumed that these functions are to report feelings, or to report, predict, or explain behaviour. Now
although some statements containing emotion words are used in these ways,
and particularly as explanations, the force of the qualifications 'unjustified'
and 'unreasonable' in itself suggests that this is much less common than
might be thought, and my contention is that it would be a mistake to imagine that the primary function of these statements is to communicate psychological facts. Their principal functions are judicial, not informative, and when
they are informative, it is often not merely psychological information that
they give. Consider the following remarks, as they might be used in suitable
contexts in everyday life:

(1) 'They are very jealous of one another.'
(2) 'I envy Schnabel's technique.'
(3) 'I feel ashamed about it now.'
(4) 'I never feel the slightest pang of regret for what I did.'
(5) 'I am quite disgusted with the literary men' (Keats).
(6) 'Well, I hope you are ashamed of yourself.'
(7) 'His pride in the Company's record is unjustified.'
(8) 'He is very disappointed in you.'

I think these are all typical examples, and they have been chosen at ran-
dom, except that I have taken care to ensure that in each case it is clear that
the operative word is the emotion word, *i.e.*, I have avoided such instances as
'He is very disappointed by your failure to get there in time.' Of these examples, the first is different from the rest, its point, I assume, being to inform
the hearer that a certain relationship exists between the persons referred to,
e.g. in a suitable context, that they are rivals in their profession. The other
remarks have what I have termed, for want of a better word, a judicial function. (2) praises Schnabel; it resembles, say, 'Schnabel has a brilliant technique,' although it is more tentative and personal, and implies more than
this—it would only be said by another pianist. (3) is an admission of responsibility, or perhaps a plea in mitigation, and (4) is the justification of a choice.
(5) and (6) imply highly unfavourable assessments. In (5) Keats condemns

literary men, and he goes on (Letter of 8 October, 1817) to give part of his reasons for feeling disgusted by an anecdote about Leigh Hunt. The force of (6) seems to lie in its mixture of blame with imputation of responsibility—there are two general lines of reply to it, either (a) 'No, I think I was quite right' or (b) 'No, it wasn't my fault.' (7) is either a way of saying that the person referred to is taking more credit than he deserves, or of saying that the Company's record is not as good as he believes. The normal conversational point of (8), I think, would be to convey blame.

In general then, the affinities of (1) to (8) are not with descriptive statements about what people feel and do, but with a different type of statement altogether. (4), for instance, is very close to 'My choice was quite correct (sound, justified)' and (8) to 'You have not done as well as he expected.' These are not put forward as exact paraphrases; I only wish to suggest that they do not miss the point in the way that any psychological interpretation does. We do not counter such statements as (1) to (8), if we disagree, by challenging an alleged fact. If this is accepted, it can only be consistent with a psychological analysis of emotion concepts if either (a) a naturalistic theory of value is presupposed, or (b) these usages are treated as non-literal.

(a) It may be said that a judgement of value is a report or expression of an individual's feelings, and that it would not be surprising, therefore, if emotion words (reporting or expressing feelings) had a function somewhat similar to that of value words. I can only make one or two remarks about this here. Earlier on I discussed a moral emotion, shame, and tried to show that the concept of shame is logically dependent on the moral notion of wrong action. I believe, then, that there are specifically moral emotions in this sense only: that the use of some emotion words ('remorse,' 'shame,' *etc.*) presupposes moral concepts. There are no specifically moral (or for that matter, aesthetic) experiences, and consequently no judgement of value can be a report, or an expression, of an experience. In the case of example (3), no statement that merely reported a feeling could be equivalent to it, since such a statement would not be an admission of responsibility. To accept responsibility for a past action (in the ordinary sense in which it is the opposite of taking credit for something), one has to admit that one did the action and to concede that it was wrong. But there is no experience which, taken in itself, is inconsistent with refusing to admit the one or concede the other. Even if there were a specific experience which always accompanied the admission of responsibility, this would be something logically accidental.

(b) It could be argued that although such words as 'regret' and 'pride' name emotions in their primary sense, they are used in a different sense in the examples. This will no doubt be turned by some into the objection that a consideration of such usages can throw no light on the nature of the emotions. What does this amount to? There exist uses of emotion words that are unquestionably figurative or metaphorical, *e.g.*, 'angry masses of cloud,' 'the raging waves of the sea foaming out their own shame.' Statements (1) to (8) are precisely the literal uses that would be contrasted with these, and no one is likely to maintain, therefore, that they are figurative in the strict sense. It may more plausibly be argued that they are extended or derivative senses of emotion words. But what, then, are the sense from which they are extended or derived? No use of *e.g.* 'envy,' 'ashamed,' or 'pang of regret' appears to exist which is more basic, primary, or literal than that of the examples. There is perhaps a temptation to suppose, because we associate emotion with violent feelings and behaviour, that the word 'disgusted' is somehow being used more literally when it is used by or of a man who is actually feeling nausea, than it is by Keats in the sentence I have quoted. But all that this proves, it seems to me, is that the experiences of those who are disgusted are different on different occasions. No doubt, to be disgusted with the literary men is not the same as being disgusted with the state of the kitchen sink, the one criticism is moral, and the other is not; but there is a very close and intelligible connexion between them which should not be obscured by treating one sense as more primary than the other.

IV

What kind of an explanation of behaviour are we giving when we account for it in terms of emotions? I should like, in conclusion, to sketch the general lines on which I think this question ought to be answered. As this is no more than a corollary of the preceding discussion I can put it very briefly.

The traditional theory gives the answer that emotion words explain behaviour by specifying its cause, *i.e.* a certain feeling or inner experience. But surely, when we ask what caused someone to do something, we usually neither expect nor receive an answer in terms of feelings. The answer takes the form of a reference to some external circumstance, if that is relevant, or to some thought, memory, observation, *etc.*, that accounts for the action. If we refer to feelings at all, this appears to be a type of explanation that we fall back on as a last resort, because it is unilluminating and only one step removed from saying that the action is unaccountable. What seems to me to be wrong, then, on this score, with the traditional view is that it does not do justice to the explanatory power of emotion words. For the fact is that to know the feeling that may have preceded an action is not to understand it, or to understand it only very imperfectly. One can remember an action that one did many years ago, an action that one no longer understands, and the question 'Why did I do it?' can remain in the face of the clearest recollection of what it felt like to do it. If emotion words merely named some inner experience that preceded or accompanied behaviour, to explain behaviour by using them would not give the insight that it does.

A quite different answer to this question is proposed by Professor Ryle in *The Concept of Mind.* Referring to what he calls 'inclinations' or 'motives,' professor Ryle writes, 'The imputation of a motive for a particular action is not a causal inference to an unwitnessed event but the subsumption of an episode proposition under a law-like proposition' (90). Again, 'To explain an action as done from a certain motive is not to correlate it with an occult cause, but to subsume it under a propensity or behaviour-trend' (110). And as I understand him, explanation in terms of mood-words is of a generally similar character. Mood and motive explanations, despite their differences, have this in common, that they are explanations by reference to types of disposition (97). Now although I have been simply following Professor Ryle in what he here denies, I find the positive side of this less adequate. It does not seem to me that emotion words explain merely in the relatively superficial way that dispositional words explain, if 'the glass broke because it was brittle' is to be taken as a model, however rough, of this kind of explanation. To refer to a man's laziness or fondness for gardening is to account for what he does on a particular occasion by removing the need for a *special* explanation of it; by showing that his conduct is not in any way surprising or unusual, but part of the regular pattern of things that he does or is likely to do. To assimilate emotion words closely to dispositional words is to give an incomplete account of their explanatory function; they explain behaviour more fully than could be done by saying, in effect, that it was only to be expected. ('To say that he did something from that motive is to say that this action, done in its particular circumstances, was just the sort of thing that that was an inclination to do. It is to say 'he *would* do that'' *Ibid.* 92-3.) I would suggest that emotion words go beyond this sort of explanation in two ways. First, by setting the action to be explained, not merely in the context of the rest of an individual's behaviour, but in a social context. 'He was rude to you because he was jealous' resembles 'I helped him because he was a friend' in accounting for his behaviour by the reference it makes to his relationship with other people. Secondly, emotion words explain by giving the reason for an action, in the sense of giving a justification for it. 'He refused an interview because of his contempt for journalists' explains the refusal by connecting it with an assessment made by the person whose behaviour is referred to. In this respect it has some analogy with, for instance, 'He reads Gibbon because he thinks highly of his style.' Emotion concepts, I have argued, are not purely psychological: they presuppose concepts of social relationships and institutions, and concepts belonging to systems of judgement, moral, aesthetic, and legal. In using emotion words we are able, therefore, to relate behaviour to the complex background in which it is enacted, and so to make human actions intelligible.

Notes

1   The details vary. For example, it is very commonly held that every emotion must have an object, and therefore that it is an experience involving a 'cognitive' ele-

ment, not a pure state of feeling. 'We must hold,' writes McTaggart, 'that the cogitation of that to which the emotion is directed, and the emotion towards it, are the same mental state, which has both the quality of being a cogitation of it, and the quality of being an emotion directed towards it' (*The Nature of Existence*, Vol. 2, 146). (I think it is important to ask what 'directed towards' could mean here.) Russell claims that emotions also involve bodily movements. In *The Analysis of Mind* he says that 'An emotion—rage, for example—[is] a certain kind of process.... The ingredients of an emotion are only sensations and images and bodily movements succeeding each other according to a certain pattern' (284). To discuss the details of these theories would complicate, without affecting, my argument, which is meant to show that an emotion is not any sort of experience or process.

2   *Manual of Psychology*, 5th Edn., p. 375 and p. 371.

3   Vol. 2, 449. James prints the passage in italics.

4   This is not to say that we do not also use the word 'description' in such a way that (3) (immediately below) might form part of a description of some incident. When I say that (3) does not describe I am making what could be looked on as a technical distinction between description and interpretation, which is meant to indicate a difference of order between (3) and (1) or (2). Higher order statements explain and interpret what lower order statements describe.

5   Let me give an analogy. 'Jones is responsible for this muddle' is a statement about the behaviour its truth is dependent on, although it is not shorthand for a set of statements describing that behaviour.

6   But the words 'right,' 'unreasonable,' *etc.*, when used to qualify third person statements sometimes serve as endorsements of, or refusals to endorse, this assessment on the speaker's part. I discuss this point below.

7   A point noted in respect of envy by Aristotle at *E.N.* 1107*a*.

8   In the same, *i.e.*, moral, sense. A doctor might maintain that his patient ought not to feel any pain, when the physical condition is not as a rule painful or when he has given a dose of morphine that would alleviate the pain of most patients. 'Ought not to' here means (roughly) 'would not normally.' He might equally be prepared to give a reason why a patient feels giddy, *i.e.*, a causal explanation. This is not a reason *for* feeling giddy, which is an impossibility.

9   *Foundations of Ethics*, 45 and 55.

A Subjective Theory of the Passions

Robert C. Solomon

Like Leporello, learned literary men keep a list, but the point is what they lack;
while Don Juan seduces girls and enjoys himself—Leporello notes down the time,
the place and a description of the girl. —Kierkegaard, *Journals*

Like Leporello, psychologists.... But the point is what they lack. A description
of someone else's emotion is one thing; understanding one's own is something else. And our problem is to understand, *for me (us)*, subjectively, what it
is to *have* an emotion.

1. INTENTIONALITY

All consciousness is consciousness of something. —Edmund Husserl

Emotions are not feelings, yet feelings are typically if not almost always associated with our emotions. And yet neither are emotions *merely* their objective
manifestations in neurology or behavior, although we may agree that such
manifestations might always be found. But this hardly constitutes a "theory of
the emotions." The most prominent feature of our emotions has yet to be
introduced—that which distinguishes them from mere feelings and that
which firmly ties them to behavior and our world.

Emotions are *about* something. One is never simply angry; he/she is angry
at someone *for* something. Even an "angry young man" is angry about something (namely, everything). It is impossible to fall in love without falling in
love *with someone*, whether or not he or she is largely a fabrication of the
romantic imagination, whether or not he or she represents a "stand-in" for
someone else, a mother, a dead brother, or an old and not-forgotten lover.
One is not simply afraid, but afraid of something, even if the object of fear is
something unknown. There are emotions which seem virtually always about
something specific, for example, sadness; there are emotions that are typically general, for example, despair, resentment, and guilt. In these emotions, a
particular incident seems to act as a catalyst, crystallizing out the ornate pre-
cipitate that soon becomes supersaturated consciousness.

There are passions which need not even begin with a particular incident or object, which need not be *about* anything in particular; these are *moods*. The difference between an emotion and a mood is the difference in what they are *about*. Emotions are about particulars, or particulars generalized; moods are about nothing in particular, or sometimes they are about our world as a whole. Euphoria, melancholy, and depression are not about anything in particular (though some particular incident might well set them off); they are about the whole of our world, or indiscriminately about anything that comes our way, casting happy glows or somber shadows on every object and incident of our experience. It is with particular reference to moods that Heidegger suggests the notion of "being tuned" to the world. I again insist that this distinction between emotions and moods is not a sharp distinction, and that the relationship between emotions and moods is one of mutual support and even identity. Every emotion, no matter how specific, structures our world and has definitive influences on the whole of our experience. And every mood, no matter how apparently metaphysical, can usually be found to have a number of nodal points, around which the rest of the structure is shaped.

Following recent phenomenological tradition, this feature of emotions can be called their *intentionality*; that is, all emotions are *about* something. That which the emotion is about is called its *intentional object*, or simply its object. As a matter of logic, every emotion has its particular object. Furthermore, it is this particular object which constitutes the emotion. To understand an emotion, therefore, it is necessary to understand its "object." This raises difficulties, however, which are among the most stubborn problems of contemporary philosophy.

The following two sections may seem formidable to the non-professional reader. They are necessary to my thesis, however, although I have simplified them as much as possible (so much so, I am afraid, that my colleagues will find mammoth gaps at several turns; these can be substantiated in appropriate journals). I ask the reader to bear with me in what follows. The thrust of my argument should become evident soon enough.

The peculiarity of the intentional object becomes evident when cases are considered in which this object does not exist (if, that is, the "object" is a person or a thing), or in which the object is not true (if the "object" is a proposition or claim of some kind), or is not the case or has not occurred (if the "object" is a "fact" or incident or state of affairs). I may be afraid of communists under the bed, although there are no such communists; I may be angry with John for stealing my car when in fact he did not. For most transitive verbs, "P verbs Q" may be analyzed as a relationship between P and Q (e.g., "John kicks Fred"). Since there are no Communists, however, my fear cannot be analyzed as a relationship between me and the Communists, and the object of my fear cannot be "the Communists." Since John has not in fact stolen my car, my anger cannot be a relationship between me and the fact that John has stolen my car. There is no such fact. But, then, what am I angry about? Surely not my *belief* that John has stolen my car. (Why should I be angry at my belief and blame it on John?) I am angry *that John stole my car.*

Because the object of an emotion need not exist in order for it to be such an object, it has been often suggested that this "object" is a peculiar sort of "nonexistent" (or "subsistent" or "irreal") object. At the turn of this century, logicians populated fantastic universes with such nonexistent and even self-contradictory "objects" in order to account for those cases of emotions (and beliefs, assertions, dreams, and illusions) in which the intentional objects were not "real." But now consider the case in which I am rightfully afraid or justifiably angry, such that there really is a cell of Marxist-Leninist guerrillas hiding under my bed or John really has stolen my car. Are the intentional objects of these emotions the Communists and the facts themselves, or are they intentional objects of some mysterious sort (as in the former cases) which stand "in front of" or "beside" the real objects? Either way, the result gives rise to intolerable confusions and paradoxes. If one argues that the intentional object is an object, person, incident, or fact in the real world, then it appears that a great many emotions are not intentional after all. On the other hand, if it is argued that the intentional object is a special kind of object, not a real object (a real person or incident or fact), then the account of cases in which there are bona fide objects is absurdly complicated. On the one hand, we want to say that all emotions and their objects are "in the world," not simply "in our minds." On the other hand, we must take account of the fact that many if not all emotions have objects which are not wholly real, which are in part imagined, in part distorted, and which are peculiar to the emotion in question.

In the past seventy years, logicians have often followed the German genius Gottlob Frege in distinguishing certain linguistic contexts which he called "indirect" and which are now usually called "opaque." An opaque context, for example, "John believes that ..." or "Fred is angry at ..." is distinguished by the fact that only certain descriptions can be used to complete the sentence without changing its meaning and its truth. For example, it might be true that "John believes that Stendhal wrote *The Red and the Black.*" As a matter of fact, Stendhal was the pen name of Henri Beyle. Yet although it is true that "Beyle wrote *The Red and the Black,*" it is not true that "John believes that Beyle wrote *The Red and the Black,*" since John does not know this identity. Similarly, it is true that John loves Mary. It is also true that Mary was a prostitute in St. Louis for five years before meeting John, a fact she has never told him. Consequently, it would not be true to describe Mary *qua* John's lover as an "ex-prostitute," even though the woman he loves is in fact an ex-prostitute. The significance of calling these contexts "opaque" is that the descriptions of the "objects" of belief or emotion must be geared to the mode of conceiving of them by the person who has them, not upon the "facts." A man may be afraid of his own shadow; but we can be sure that the object of his fear is not his own shadow, but rather something else which he sees *through* his shadow. The notion of "opacity" is an attempt to get around the problem of mysterious and unreal "intentional objects" in favor of an analysis of the linguistic apparatus we use to describe certain "acts" or "attitudes." Given the confusion and absurdities that have been generated by the notion of intentionality, we can easily understand the motivation of this move. However, it is clear that what I am afraid of or angry *about* is not simply a certain kind of sentence. It is an object (or person, incident, state of affairs), which may or may not "really" exist or be the case. What are we to say of such objects? How are we to account for the "opacity" of their descriptions?

Underlying the various dilemmas the notion of "intentionality" has produced, there is an insidious dualism which I have already rejected. In general, it is the "mental-physical" dualism so celebrated by Descartes. With particular respect to the emotions, this dualistic analysis, which has been actively promoted by philosophers on both sides of the English Channel, distinguishes two "components" of an emotion: (1) having the emotion, a feeling, an act or "attitude," and (2) the object of the emotion: a thing or person or incident or state of affairs or "fact" (see, for example, D.F. Pears).[1] The first is mental or subjective, and the second is "in the world" and objective. But as soon as this distinction is introduced, the status of such "objects" becomes impossibly problematic. How can an object be "in the world" but not exist? Or if one says that such objects need not exist, then how can they be "in the world"? What of those cases in which the object of the emotion is indisputably real, "in the world"? And how, then, is the emotion *logically* connected to its object?

It is this set of paradoxes that lay behind my theory of "subjectivity" in Part I. Emotions are subjective; their objects are not simply objects of the world, not "facts," not part of an anonymous and scientifically ascertainable Reality. The objects of the emotions are objects of *our* world, the world as we experience it. (In the case of moods, the object is our world as a whole.) Once again, this is not to defend an absurd "two-worlds" view, a "private" world within which we enact our emotional dramas and a public world of "the facts." There are rather two standpoints, one detached and one personally involved. All objects of our emotions are in surreality: Reality is irrelevant except on reflection. It is always open to question whether or to what extent those objects are also in *the* world and publicly verifiable. There are cases, for example, in the extremes of paranoia, panic, or romantic raptures, in which the object of emotion may have no status in Reality at all; it may be "just a matter of self-delusion." On the other hand, there are many cases in which the object of the emotion has an indisputable position in Reality: when I am angry at what in fact is the case, when I hate someone who is very much flesh-and-blood. But the objects of emotions are rarely Real or unreal;[2] they virtually always have *some* basis in Reality (the most extreme paranoid does not *make up* the objects of his fear), and no object of an emotion is simply what it is "in Reality." The objects of an emotion are objects of great personal importance to us; Reality knows nothing of "personal importance." I am indignant about the Strangelove tactics employed by my Government in instigating a revolution in Chile; in Reality, that is "just the way things are." For me (and hopefully, for all of us), those tactics are a matter of great concern. But that concern, unlike "the facts," is not part of the Reality in question, except *for us.* Thus, the object of an emotion, in this sense, is *never* simply an object (person, incident, fact) in *the* world, in Reality. It's an object—an object of considerable importance—in *our* world, in our surreality. The objects of emotions are the objects of the world experienced through our concerns and values. Even where the object has no status in Reality, it is based upon the world as we experience it, interpreted, and hypostatised, projected into the world by our concerns and values. No matter how much a lover is the fabrication of our own fantasies, the basis of the fabrication and the evidence for his or her existence must be the "facts" or the "real" world. This is true not only in those familiar cases in which we glamourize and glorify our lovers with attributes they possess only to a very limited extent (Lauding intelligence as "genius," reasonable looks as "beauty," adequate sex as "voluptuousness"), but even in extreme fantasies, the wandering knight in the medieval morality play who falls in love with a few golden locks or possibly a shoe or two strewn strategically around a cave or a castle. There must be at least a lock or a shoe, or at any rate a reputation or rumor.

The intentional object of an emotion is not a peculiar kind of object that is common to both those emotions which also have a "real" object as well as to those which do not.[3] An intentional object is nothing other than an object, as subjectively experienced, whatever its status or basis in the "real" world. Even in cases of delusion and fantasy, the intentional object is experienced as "in the world," this is, in *our* world. Its status as an intentional object (of emotion) need have nothing to do with its status in Reality; but neither, then, does it make sense to speak of intentional objects as either real or not real, *qua intentional objects.* The conception of such objects is applicable only within the subjective point of view. As soon as one attempts to extend it to the sphere of objectivity, the result will be instant paradox and confusion.

Returning again to the discussion of subjectivity, it is clear what is so seriously wrong with the analysis of emotions into "components": An emotion is not distinct or separable from its object; the object as an object of this emotion has no existence apart from the emotion. The object of my being angry with John for stealing my car is not the alleged fact that John stole my car (for he may not have), nor is it simply John. The object is irreducibly *that-John-stole-my-car.* But even this is an incomplete description. Having long wanted to get rid of my car, I may also be *relieved* that John stole my car. Of course, the fact which stands at the base of my anger is identical to the fact which stands at the base of my relief. But my anger and my relief are not separate feelings or acts or attitudes which are directed toward one and the same object. The object of my anger is an offense; the object of my relief is a boon. Thus the object of my anger is not the same as the object of my relief. The distinction between the emotion and its object begins to collapse. The emotion is determined by its object just as it is the emotion that constitutes its object (which is not to say, except in extreme cases, that it creates its own "facts"). There are not two components, my anger and the object of my anger. Borrowing a clumsy but effective device from the translators of more difficult German philosophical concatenations, we might say that every emotion has the unitary form of "my-emoting-about...," "my-being-angry-about...," "my-loving...." I will not attempt to maintain this typesetter's nightmare in the text, but it must be kept in mind when attempting to understand the intentionality of the emotions; there are no ultimately intelligible distinctions between the emotion and its object. The emotion is distinguished by its object; there is nothing to it besides its object. But neither is there any such object at all without the emotion.

This technical point can support and be supported by an immensely practical consideration. A change in beliefs typically inspires a change in emotions. How can this be? If an emotion were a feeling, the explanation would be a still tentative hypothesis about psychosomatic disorders—like losing one's headache five minutes after one's mother-in-law has left the house. Most feelings are absolutely indifferent to what we believe. But my being angry at John for stealing my car changes radically upon being told that my car has not left the garage all evening. Believing this, my anger vanishes in an instant, not as a matter of cause-and-effect, but rather as a matter of logic. I *can't* be angry at John for something I believe he did not do. Similarly, my evaluation of a situation has everything to do with my emotions of embarrassment and pride, not merely as cause but as their structure. I cannot be embarrassed if I do not believe my situation to be awkward; I cannot be proud if I do not believe myself to have accomplished something or to have been bestowed with some honor. The relationship between beliefs and opinions on the one hand and emotions on the other is not a matter of causation or coincidence but a matter of logic. The emotion is logically indistinguishable from its object: Once its object has been rejected there can be no more emotion. A headache hangs on with a momentum of its own for minutes or perhaps hours after its instigating cause has ceased, but my anger vanishes immediately upon the refutation of the "fact" I was angry about.

Now we can understand, too, why it is so important to insist not only that an emotion is not identical to a feeling but that a feeling is not even a component of emotion. Of course, emotions may typically involve feelings; they may even always involve feelings. But feelings are neither necessary nor sufficient to differentiate emotions. An emotion is never simply a feeling, even a feeling plus anything. One can be angry without ever feeling angry—for days or weeks or years. Moreover, it makes no sense to say that someone feels angry unless he *is* angry. On the traditional view of emotions as feelings, of course, this claim would seem strange indeed; how could one not feel whatever one feels in anger without being angry? But one could have those same feelings after drinking three cups of coffee or swallowing some amphetamine; what one feels is not anger or angry but simply flushed, excited, irritable, etc. when I do have those feelings when I am angry, the feelings are at most an accompaniment to the anger, like the excitable fans following an athletic team. I am angry at John for stealing; now I find out he did not steal. My anger vanishes instantly, but the feeling—that is, the pulsing and flushing—remains for a moment. Even though those feelings were induced by my anger and are now the same feelings I had when I was angry a moment ago, they are no longer feelings of anger. They are just feelings. One cannot feel angry without being angry.

To say that emotions are *intentional* is to say that they *essentially* have logical connections with the objects of our world. This is why I found it necessary to spend so much time introducing our notion of subjectivity in Part I. Emotions are not "mental" states or events or acts, if by that one means that they are "in our minds" rather than in our world. An emotion is not something locked "inside," even in those cases in which it is brutally suppressed and kept from expression. An emotion is a structure linking ourselves and the objects of our world which provides the structures of our world. We have yet to understand the nature of these structures and their immense importance to us. In breaking down the old Cartesian picture of the emotions, however, as feelings and sensations in our minds that have at most contingent (if not downright mysterious) connections to our world and its objects, a major step has been made in laying the groundwork for a new subjective theory.

2. EMOTIONS, OBJECTS, AND CAUSES

She's so in love with me she doesn't know anything.
That's why she's in love with me.   —Marx (G.), *A Day at the Races*

The intentionality and nature of an emotion have nothing to do with its *causes*. This point was made briefly before when I insisted that my anger, even if caused by a drug I had taken, is still anger, and nothing else. What I am angry about is not the drug or my having taken the drug. (In fact, I may have forgotten, or may never have known, that I had taken any such drug.) Similarly, I may be particularly prone to romantic fantasies and "falling in love" because of protracted sexual deprivation; but even if the cause of my consequent love is sexual deprivation, the object of my love is not my sexual deprivation or someone to cure my sexual deprivation. Whether or not my love survives the cure of its cause, the cause is no part of the love itself.

This technical distinction between the causes and the objects of emotions is absolutely vital considering the all-too-frequent dismissal of emotions on the basis of the knowledge of their causes. For example, under the dramatic influence of lysergic acid, one's view of the world may become one of universal affection and enthusiasm, one's relationships with others "clarified" in such a way that intimacy becomes possible where it had not been before. Drug-induced expression of long-suppressed anger, envy, and hatred may display the emotional structure of our everyday world as a purple dye might render visible the otherwise invisible membranes of a tiny piece of tissue. The cause of this clarity, and perhaps even the cause of the emotions themselves, is the drug. Yet the emotions are nothing other than what they are. They are no less "real" (surreal) because their chemical causes are in this case known with certainty. (Our everyday emotional life is similarly chemically dependent; that does not make our everyday emotions any less "real" [surreal] either.) The distinction between "real" (surreal) and "false" emotions has nothing to do with their causes. An emotion is distinguished by its object, not by its causes, and the "surreality" of an emotion depends only upon its role in our subjective lives, however it may have originally been instigated.

There are several very different categories of causes of emotions. The easiest to distinguish from the emotion and its objects are those physiological and chemical causes already discussed. A convincing case can be made for any number of causal laws concerning the effect of certain neurological changes and emotions, despite the fact that a subject need never know anything about them. (In fact, very few people know even the most elementary of these laws, and no one, as yet, knows very many of them.) Slightly more complicated are such factors as inherited temperaments, which may similarly lie beyond any conceivable knowledge of the subject and can no doubt be traced to some complex series of genetically regulated physiochemical process. The same might be hypothesized about human instincts, if there are any (aggression? territorial imperatives? motherly love?), but it is preferable to suppose—at least as a matter of practical principle if not as a theoretical necessity—that what in any case is called an "instinct" is in fact a motive, a *psychological* factor, whatever its physiological substrate.

The distinction between *cause* and *object* of emotion becomes difficult with the introduction of *psychological* causes. Learned emotional reactions, for example (which probably includes all of them), might be causally explained in terms of emotional traits and habits (for example, having "a bad temper," being "a Romantic at heart," having "a streak of jealousy" or "a morose personality"); or in terms of past experiences or training (for example, "He was brought up cruelly and without love," or "His first girl friend crushed him when she left," or "He saw his parents having intercourse when he was three and ever since ..." or "Well, he was brought up by *those* people"). The complication arises because, in every case, the cause of the emotion might be argued to be necessarily *experienced*. In some cases, this raises no special problems: For example, whether or not one recognizes himself as "bad-tempered" or as "an incurable Romantic," such causal factors do no more than describe a *pattern* of emotional reactions into which any particular emotional reaction finds a suitable place. But consider the kind of case which is so crucial to Freud's early clinical experiences: An ongoing set of emotions is causally attributed to a childhood trauma in which, for example, a young boy was sexually assaulted by his aunt. (Complicating the case, of course, may be the idea that the trauma has been repressed, but, for my purposes here, let's suppose that the subject ["patient"] has already accepted this causal hypothesis after some time in therapy, and he now attempts to understand its effects upon him.) What is the object of an emotion with such an experience as its cause? A first guess would be: the sexual assault. Notice, however, that the fact of the assault is not sufficient to play this causal role: Unlike the causal theories linking physiology and emotion, this hypothesis requires the connection of the *fact experienced* and the emotion. But even this is not nearly sufficient.

Early in his career, Freud commented that if the "memories" of his patients were true, the perverseness of the private life of the outwardly staid bourgeois Viennese was no less than shocking, to put it mildly. He soon came to the conclusion, however, that most of the traumas he investigated were based upon fantasies, not facts; fabrications, and not memories. Accordingly, so far as the cause of the emotion is concerned, the facts need have nothing to do with the case; it is simply the experience that is at stake. Insofar as the emotions are subjective phenomena, the distinction between Reality and surreality cannot be drawn; what is essential is only that the incident occurred in one's surreality. (This raises grave problems for those psychologists who would make any attempt to identify the "stimulus" of behavior in an objectively designated set of circumstances [so many days without food, such and such an incident before the subject's eyes]. Even a rat has a surreality, and so never merely responds to a "stimulus."[4])

Even this is not sufficient; if the cause of the emotion is the experience, is it not identical with the object of that experience? It is not. First of all, the object of an emotion is not an experience, but the object of experience; it is not the experience toward which I feel anger or guilt or shame or fear, but toward my aunt and what she (supposedly) did to me. Moreover, the experience that is the cause of the emotion is past experience, but the object of our emotion must be in our present experience, even if the object itself refers to a past experience.[5] (Of course, the object of the present experience will very probably be, as Freud so richly illustrated, considerably edited and embellished due to subsequent experiences and associations.) The cause is the original experience in the sense that, as in Freud's theoretical papers, a certain kind of experience is linked in a causal lawlike generalization to certain kinds of subsequent emotions and fixations in adults. The cause is past, and it does not matter whether I am now aware of it; the object, on the other hand, must be the object of my *present* experience (even if it is a past event). The cause and the object are thus different, even if they should refer to "the same fact."

Even more complicated still are those causes of an emotion which are both present and related to the object of the emotion. For example, one says that he became angry because he saw a certain item in the newspaper; it was the spying of the item that caused him to be angry, but what he was angry about was presumably what the newspaper item was *about,* or something of which it reminded him. Or one falls in love because the other just happens to say something precisely right at the right time; but one does not fall in love with the comment, which only acts as a catalyst for an emotion directed toward the whole person. Similarly, sex might easily act as such a cause for falling in love, but we must not confuse the cause for the emotion, which is always directed at the person and never at the sexual activity (no matter how central to the relationship).

The distinction between object and cause is most confused because of the kind of case in which the object seems to *be* the cause. For example, I might be made (that is, caused to be) angry by John's stealing my car. In this case, we are tempted to say that the cause of my anger and its object are the same— John's stealing my car. But what if it is the case that John did not steal my car? The object would still be *his stealing my car*; the cause would not be his stealing my car but only my believing that he did. And so the two are not the same, not only in those cases in which what I am angry about is not the case but also in those cases in which what I am angry about is the case. The object of an emotion is *never* identical to its cause. The object is always *subjective,* a part of the world as one sees it, whether or not it is in fact the case or not. The cause is always *objective,* it must be the case if it is to be the cause. (It makes no sense to say that A caused B if A never occurred.) Moreover, the cause must not be a cause *for me,* but, in line with the objective or scientific method in general, it must be demonstrable for *anyone* that it is the cause. A cause plays a role in a lawlike generalization which can be proven only through comparison and extrapolation with other more or less similar cases. The cause of my anger can be shown to be my having taken amphetamines because there is a lawlike generalization which has been well confirmed in a great many cases to the effect that amphetamines make a person irritable and therefore tend to make him angry at the least disturbance or apparent offense. The object of my anger, on the other hand, requires no such lawlike generalization or confirmation. As far as the object of my anger is concerned, I can consider it one of a kind. This is not to say that the objects of my anger may not fall into a neat and discernible, even familiar, pattern. Nor is it to deny that I may be unaware of the objects of my anger. It is only to say that the objects of anger (and all emotions) are strictly subjective, dependent only upon the person who "has" them. The causes of an emotion, however, have nothing to do with subjectivity and individual experience. The cause of my anger can be John's stealing my car only insofar as there is some demonstrable evidence that the knowledge of such thefts typically bring about such reactions. If, for instance, John has often taken my car without my permission (but with my knowledge) but I have never before gotten angry, then clearly it is not simply his having stolen my car that has caused me to be angry this time. Nevertheless, I may indeed be angry that he has stolen my car.

Psychology and physiology are typically concerned with the objective (that is, scientific) aspects of the emotions. Accordingly, they are primarily interested in their causes—in lawlike generalizations between certain stimulations or circumstances and typical emotional reactions. But if what characterizes an emotion is its object—as distinguished from its cause—we can appreciate how far short of a comprehensive understanding of the emotions any psychological or physiological theory must fall. To balance this account (and it need not condemn the "objective" approach by any means) my analysis will remain wholly within the subjective standpoint. I will make no attempts to theorize about the particular causes of emotions (what Freud would call their "aetiology"). *To me,* my passion is my way of seeing and structuring my world, whatever might be going on in the synapses of my brain, whatever long-forgotten childhood traumas may have set up this or that "complex" of reactions, and whatever chemicals might be peddling their unseen influence in my experiences. Of course, a change in such causes will manifest itself as a dramatic change in our emotional lives as well. What makes the causes of our emotions so insidious—whether they are "complexes" set up by our peers and parents in childhood or chemicals wittingly or unwittingly ingested—is precisely the fact that they have no place in our experience at all.

The causal instruments which may cause such changes in experience are not the sphere of the philosopher but rather the neurologist, the developmental psychologist, and the pharmacologist. One might say that their interest, not ours, is the "technology of the experience," the discovery of techniques and instruments to alter our consciousness "from the outside." As a philosopher, however, I am only interested in what R.D. Laing has called the "politics of experience," changing oneself from within. The strategies of politics are ideology and persuasion, changing the object of passion rather than the cause. And however we might change other people by any number of causal techniques, it is only self-overcoming that interests me here. If we adapt Lévi-Strauss's well-known declaration about society for philosophical purposes: "Our own society is the only one which we can transform and not destroy, since the changes which we should introduce would come from within" (*Tristes Tropiques*). To change someone else, whether for "better" or for "worse," is, in a sense, to "destroy" him. But to change oneself is to *grow.*

3. EMOTIONS AS JUDGMENTS

It is judgment that makes it possible, in fact indispensable, to think teleology as well as mechanical necessity in nature.   —Kant, *Critique of Judgment*

What is an emotion? An emotion is a *judgment* (or a set of judgments),[6] something we *do*. An emotion is a (set of) judgment(s) which constitute our world, our surreality, and its "intentional objects." An emotion is a basic judgment about our Selves and our place in our world, the projection of the values and ideals, structures and mythologies, according to which we live and through which we experience our lives.

This is why our emotions are so dependent upon our opinions and beliefs. A change in my beliefs (for example, the refutation of my belief that John stole my car) entails (not causes) a change in my emotion (my being angry that John stole my car). I cannot be angry if I do not believe that someone has wronged or offended me. Accordingly, we might say that anger involves a *moral* judgment as well, an appeal to moral standards and not merely personal evaluations.[7] My anger *is* that set of judgments. Similarly, my embarrassment *is* my judgment to the effect that I am in an exceedingly awkward situation. My shame *is* my judgment to the effect that I am responsible for an untoward situation or incident. My sadness, my sorrow, and my grief *are* judgments of various severity to the effect that I have suffered a loss. An emotion is an evaluative (or a "normative") judgment, a judgment about my situation and about myself and/or about all other people.

Needless to say, this is not the usual portrait of the emotions. The emotions are usually thought to be *consequent* to judgments, perhaps a slightly delayed reaction to their import, but not the judgments themselves. Or, even more usually, the notion of judgment is omitted altogether, and the emotion is said to follow—again as a "reaction" to—some incident before us. (Thus, James's theory, as well as the theories of McDougall and most motivational theorists, holds that the emotion is the feeling that follows a perception of some disturbance in the "external world," and most behaviorists, insofar as they recognize the category of emotions at all, hold that the emotion is nothing but a preparatory or avoidance reaction to a disturbing "stimulus.") But an incident or a perception of an incident alone is never sufficient for emotion, which always involves a *personal evaluation* of the *significance* of that incident.[8] How else could we account for the fact that different persons have very different "emotional reactions" to the same incidents? Of course, it can be correlated with and attributed to differences in background and "conditioning," but that explains only the genesis of the differences, not their nature. Those differences can be easily accounted for once we have given up the influential model of the emotions as passive "reactions." They are not reactions but interpretations. They are not responses to what happens but evaluations of what happens. And they are not responses to those evaluative judgments but rather they *are* those judgments. Of course, we might still say that an emotion is a "reaction," namely, a conscious judgmental reaction to what happens before us and involving us. But there is nothing passive about that reaction (except, of course, that it presupposes something happening, which may or may not be the person's own doing, to which he reacts). There is no *given* in the emotions, except of course the "facts" of the case. But they are no more than an author's research notes, from which he has yet to choose his leading heroes and villains, themes and plots, digressions and climaxes.

Not all evaluative judgments are emotions. Legislating a dispute between two of my friends, I disinterestedly judge in favor of one against the other. At the supermarket, I casually judge one cantaloupe better than the other. Walking out of a Bogart double feature, I calmly argue the superiority of *Casablanca* over *To Have and Have Not*. Of course I could become "emotional" about any one of these issues, if I owe a heavy allegiance to one friend rather than the other, if I am a finicky and no doubt neurotic connoisseur of cantaloupe, if I feel a strong romantic preference for Ingrid Bergman rather than Lauren Bacall; in short, depending on what we have called my personal "investments." But it is clear that most such judgments are not "emotional" and are not emotions. The key to the difference is the adverbs, "disinterestedly," "casually," and "calmly." Emotions are self-involved and relatively *intense* evaluative judgments. They are always, whether implicitly or explicitly, judgments involving oneself as well as whatever else—disputes, cantaloupes, movies, other people or situations. The judgments and objects that constitute our emotions are those which are especially important to us, meaningful to us, concerning matters in which we have invested our Selves. Not surprisingly, most of our emotions involve other people, not only as their objects but also intersubjectively, in our concerns for our relationships, trust and intimacy, suspicion and betrayal, what others think of us as well as, insofar as we identify with them, what we think of them.

There are no a priori limits on the scope and objects of the emotions. One might have invested himself in anything and thus be emotionally committed to just about anything—pets and gardens, collections of model ships or medieval coins—with a passion that is more usually reserved for lovers and children. But what distinguishes the emotions is not *what* they value but *that* they value, that they endow our lives with meaning. A man whose life is meaningless is a man who is not emotionally committed, or whose commitments are not at all what they seem. *There* is the content of Camus's sense of "the Absurd"—not a sense of "confrontation" but a sense of emptiness, not the ruthless conclusion of Reason but the hollow logic of a reasoning that has no passionate base to which to anchor itself.

Emotions are self-involved not only in the sense that they are important to us; they are also *about* us, about our Selves, whether explicitly or not. Every emotion, as a uniquely subjective judgment, involves a judgment of both one's Self and his surreality. It is through our emotions that we constitute ourselves. In many emotions, this self-involvement is explicit and obvious, as in pride and shame, self-love and guilt. Many emotions, particularly those which tie us closest to other people, are what I shall call "bipolar" neither solely about oneself nor solely about another person and not a conjunction of the two but rather about the *relationship*, as in love and hate, anger and jealousy. Many emotions, however, leave the judgment of Self implicit or in the shadows, in admiration and worship, indignation and envy, for example. Anger, which always involves a judgment that one's Self has been offended or violated, may nonetheless focus its fervor strictly outward toward the other person. Resentment, although clearly self-involved and based upon a personal stance of defensiveness, protects its Self with a projected armor of objectivity, focusing all of its attention on its alleged oppressors. But in every case, explicitly or not, the Self is an essential pole of emotional judgment, the standpoint from which our judgments of our world and of other people begin.

The ultimate object of our emotional judgments is always our own sense of personal dignity and self-esteem. Whatever its particular object and strategy, whether it is committed to collecting butterflies or to ruling Asia, an emotion is ultimately concerned with personal status, self-respect, and one's place in his or her world. Insofar as an emotion is "about" another person, as in love or hate, anger or pity, it is the constitution of an intersubjective identity, a relationship of one sort or another, perhaps competition or comparison, within which one attempts to elevate his self-esteem. Sometimes, as in love and mutual respect or admiration, the strategy is to work together and jointly increase self-esteem, through mutual identification (in hate as well as in love) and through "self-expansion" (including another as part of one's Self). In anger, however, the strategy may be rather to boost oneself up with the leverage of accusation, casting oneself in the role of martyr or "defender of the right." In pity, one might boost his self-esteem through contrast with another person, much like himself, whose fortunes are considerably less fortunate. Even those emotions which ostensibly are not about our Selves at all, envy and resentment, faith and worship, are judgments whose ultimate object is our own self-esteem. This is not to say, however, that they always succeed in attaining this object. It will be my task in Part III to show just how, despite the common goals of our emotions, some emotions are eminently more successful than others.

Emotions are not only judgments about our present situations. Emotions are also judgments about our past, editing and organizing the countless incidents and acts of our previous years into coherent and meaningful heritages, depending upon our judgment of the present circumstances. (In love, for example, one tends to view his or her entire life as "preparing for this." But in anger at the same person, history shifts quite quickly to a history of offences and betrayals.) Most importantly, emotions include intentions for the future, *to act*, to change the world and change our Selves, to revenge ourselves in anger, to punish ourselves in guilt, to redeem ourselves in shame, to restore our dignity in embarrassment, to help another person in pity, to caress and care for another in love, to destroy—but at a safe distance—an oppressor in resentment. In the next chapter, I will call this future-oriented aspect the "ideology" of the emotions. It, too, is an intrinsic part of our emotional judgments, even those that ostensibly focus themselves exclusively on the past, for example, remorse, sadness, and grief.

It is important to stress continually the difference between the emotion itself as a judgment and our reflective judgments about our emotions (judgments about our judgments). My being angry is my making a judgment; my recognition that I am angry is a reflective judgment about my anger (as is my judgment that my anger is justified, that, on reflection, the other person deserves [or doesn't deserve] my wrath, etc.). The self-involvement of anger, however, is not limited to the judgment of the anger alone; it may be shared by my reflective judgments which may also be aimed at the maximization of self-esteem. Reflective judgments are often straightforwardly objective; "I see myself as if I were someone else." And they always appear to be so. But there is a tangle of logical and pragmatic relationships between my judgments (my emotions) and my reflective judgments about my judgments such that it is impossible to separate them entirely. If I judge *that* I am angry, that judgment lends vital support to my being angry. (We often make ourselves angry precisely by reflecting on the idea that we are or ought to be angry.) Similarly, the denial that I am angry (when I am) surely affects the anger. It may not rid us of it, of course, or even diminish it. (In fact, traditional theory, particularly Freud's theory, would tell us that such anger denied is always intensified by the denial.) But the denial of a judgment of anger, like a lie regarding one's beliefs (see Chapter 13), has inevitable complications in the formation of other judgments and conceptions of our Selves. In the various versions of the Myth of the Passions, anger was thought to be an atomic force or feeling that remained pretty much the same whether reflectively recognized ("conscious") or not. But in this theory, the anger has a position in a network of emotional judgments which includes the reflective judgments about our emotions. Accordingly, anger acknowledged and anger denied are not the same anger at all; they are constitutive of very different emotional surrealities.

If emotions are judgments, why should it seem as if they "happen" to us? Why do we not remember making them?—as we might remember choosing between two automobiles at the car lot? How can we do something without knowing it? Not all judgments are reflective or deliberate; and not all judgments are articulated as such. Our prototype of a "judgment" is that explicitly rational, publicly expressed, deliberated decision that one finds in a courtroom or an assessor's office. But not all emotions are explicit; we make thousands of judgments every day— reaching for the light switch, glancing at the clock, turning off the fire under the scalding cappuccino—perceptual judgments, aesthetic judgments, even moral judgments, that are never articulated, deliberated, or "thought about." Emotions are such judgments, undeliberated, unarticulated, and unreflective (except on rare occasions; "Should I be angry or not?" "Should I allow myself to continue to love her or not?"). Emotions can become deliberate without lessening their intensity (though this flies in the face of one of the most established doctrines of the traditional "reason vs. the passions" dispute). They can of course become articulate (whenever we verbally express them, for example) and we are all familiar with the fact that our emotions often become more intense *as* we express them. (This, too, must be explained, since Freudian theory and most psychological theories since seem to think that emotions are "ventilated" through expression and are intensified through suppression.) And emotions *can* become reflective, aware of themselves, their purposes, and their objects. It is clear that not all emotions can stand the scrutiny of reflection, and most of us have experienced the wilting of unreasonable anger in the light of reflection. But, again, the fact that some emotions are so affected does not imply that all are.

It is because our judgments have already been made when we normally come to reflect on them that we are able to view them as "not ours" at all. By focusing on the feelings and flushings that typically accompany our emotional upheavals in times of crisis, it may well seem as if the emotion—mistakenly identified with the feeling that accompanies it—is involuntary and an unrequested result of the secretions of the autonomic nervous system. But this strategic confusion of cause and effect is only a vehicle of irresponsibility, a way of absolving oneself from blame for those fits of sensitivity and foolishness that constitute the most important moments of our lives.[9] It is the emotion that causes the feeling, our judgment that spurs the adrenal glands into actions, not the secretions that cause the emotion. The Myth of the Passions has so thoroughly indoctrinated us with its notion of passivity that we are no longer capable of seeing what we ourselves are doing. Once the Myth is exploded, however, it is obvious that we make ourselves angry, make ourselves depressed, make ourselves fall in love. We are like infants who for months watch our legs bobble before us, and then one day we discover that we ourselves are doing the bobbling. Once discovered, it is not a lesson unlearned. Once we have accepted responsibility for our emotions we will not ever allow them to slip away from us again.[10]

4. A NOTE ON MORALITY AND AESTHETICS

"Stealing money is wrong" expresses no proposition that can be either true or false. It is as if I had written "Stealing money!!"—where the shape and thickness of the

exclamation marks show that a special sort of moral disapproval is the feeling which is being expressed.   —A.J. Ayer, *Language, Truth and Logic*

It is only the expression of sentiment that gives the arts their meaning.
     —Leo Tolstoy, "What Is Art?"

The idea that an emotion is an evaluative judgment wreaks havoc with several long-cherished theories of morality and aesthetics. On the one hand, there is a long tradition of moralists who have argued that morality is a matter of reason, of principle, of duty, in which the passions must be allowed to play either no part whatever or, at best, a secondary and supportive role (in guilt and remorse, for example). Kant, for example, wholly excluded the passions from his conception of "moral worth," and he once called them "pathological" where duty is concerned.[11] On the other hand, there is an equally long tradition according to which all values, including moral values, are matters of emotion, of "sentiment" rather than reason and judgment. Hume's often-quoted phrase "Reason is, and ought to be, the slave of the passions" is the hallmark of one such theory and is still accepted by a great many British and American philosophers as the cornerstone of any adequate moral philosophy. But if in fact every "sentiment" is already a matter of judgment by its very nature, then the alleged distinction which lies at the base of this long-standing dispute between rationalists and "cognitivists" on the one hand and teleologists and "emotivists" on the other has no comprehensible interpretation. An ethics of principle differs from an ethics of sentiment only in the fact that the judgments of the latter remain unreflective and unchallenged whereas those of the former are tediously rationalized and canonized. The one is an ethics of prejudice, whereas the other is typically an ethics of dogma.

A similar set of considerations applies to the long-standing dispute over various "expression" theories of art—all of which embody the popular idea that art and its objects appeal directly to our emotions as expressions, in some (usually mysterious) sense, of the artist's emotions. Hydraulic models are often invoked in this context (as if a poem or a painting were the "outpouring" of its creator's "bursting" sensitivities), and the theory is in virtually every case a *causal* one, the ideas that the *affect* of the viewer (or reader, listener, etc.) is *induced* by the work, which is in turn the *effect* of the artist's own sensibilities. Thus, it is suggested that the most appropriate viewing (reading, hearing) is also the most naïve, the least mediated or interfered with by critical judgment (thus, the general disdain of critics, who are thought to be unduly judgmental and ruinously critical in a realm that is supposed to give free and unhampered flow to the passions alone). But if it is true that art appeals to and expresses our emotions (and this surely is at least part of the aesthetic story), then aesthetic appreciation is already riddled with judgments, including judgments about the medium, about the subject matter, about the artist, and about the art *as* art. Accordingly, the traditional versions of the "expression" theory—and the objections to it—require some serious reconstruction.[12]

5. EMOTIONAL CONSTITUTION: "THE WAY THE WORLD IS"

There are no facts, only interpretations.   —Nietzsche, *The Will to Power*

There is no way the world is. —Nelson Goodman, "The Way the World Is"

Emotions are *constitutional* judgments. They do not just *find* interpretations and evaluations of our world, identifying objects of fear and loathing, for spite and loving, intimately binding us to this person but repulsively separating us from that one, giving us a sense of superiority concerning him, a sense of inferiority regarding her. They constitute them. They do not merely *apply* standards of interpretation and evaluation to our experience but in an important sense *supply* them. This is not to say that, through our emotions, we create *de novo* the ideals and values of our world. None of us is that original. Nor is it to say that our emotions constitute "the facts" of the world. Objectively, we need not hesitate in admitting the independence of Reality from our passionate tamperings within it. But the Way the world is for us is never simply the way the world is. We do not live in Reality but in surreality, a world that is populated with objects of value and objects of fear, gains and losses, honors and injustices, intimacies and inequalities. It is our passions—and our emotions in particular—that *set up* this world, *constitute* the framework within which our knowledge of the facts has some meaning, some "relevance" to us. This is why I insist that the emotions are constitutive judgments; they do not find but "set up" our surreality. They do not apply but supply the framework of values which give our experience some meaning.

Consider the difference between a magistrate's declaration, "The defendant is guilty," and the similar statement by a court reporter telephoning his editor after the hearing. There is a sense in which they have both "said the same thing," namely that the defendant is guilty. But there is a vital difference. The magistrate, by virtue of his position, *makes* the defendant guilty by declaring that he is. The reporter only reports that he is. Regarding our own emotions, we are always in the position of the magistrate (although in uncritical reflection we may act as reporter as well). Our emotions are self-confirming judgments about our world and about our Selves. We might say that the emotions are preverbal analogues of what J.L. Austin called "performatives"— judgments that *do* something rather than simply describe or evaluate a state of affairs.[13] In anger, we judge that a friend's casual comment is offensive; but anger is not merely a report or a "reaction" to an offense; it *declares* that the comment is offensive precisely in the same way that the magistrate declares that the defendant is guilty. One does not become angry because the comment *is* offensive: the comment is offensive by virtue of its being an object for anger. A megalomaniacal artist may become angry at the compliment that his use of color is as good as that of Pierre Bonnard (he thinks it is *better* than Bonnard). The comment is itself not offensive, but it is so constituted in the artist's anger. The emotions, like magistrates, do not find but rather are responsible for the objects of their judgment.

Of course, a single judgment can be overruled. The magistrate's verdict can be reversed by an appellate court; an emotion may seem unwarranted or absurd in the court of reflection. But it is important to stress that neither can be shown to be "incorrect" or "wrong," for such terms apply only to descriptive judgments, which claim to "correspond to the facts," not to constitutive judgments, which do not "correspond" to anything. Consider a simple Austinian example: "I christen this ship the S.S. *Albanie*"; the name might well be ridiculous, or politically inappropriate, or not what was intended. But the christening cannot be wrong about the name of the vessel, for the vessel has no name before it is christened. (Austin calls these "infelicities," as opposed to "mistakes.") The magistrate's declaration may be ill considered, unjustified, irresponsible, or absurd. It may even be "unconstitutional," in which case it may be shown to be beyond the bounds of his jurisdiction. Such constraints, however, only point to the constitutional limitations of the individual magistrate: They do not deny his magisterial or constitutional powers. It is through the legal system and by virtue of his position *within* it that he is empowered to declare guilt and innocence. But then we might say it is the legal *system*, acting through its representative, that constitutes the defendant as guilty through its choice of laws and interpretations.[14] The same can be said for the emotions: One's anger may be unjustified (the allegedly offensive comment may have been an obvious compliment—that is, obvious to everyone else); it may be unwarranted (the comment may have been misunderstood or heard inaccurately). It may be overly harsh (the intensity of the anger may be out of proportion to the seriousness of the offense) or it may simply be absurd (since the person did not say anything at all). On reflection, the anger may indeed be recognized to be unreasonable, inappropriate, unfair, or foolish. But for the anger itself, its object is no less offensive (and the anger no less "real") than anger that is fully reasonable, appropriate, and fair. As a constitutive judgment, anger is never simply "incorrect" or "wrong." Its object is as it is constituted.

A single emotion may be but a near-repetition of any number of others (a "pet peeve," for example, or Don Juan serial romanticism), rigidly following its predecessors and a set of standards that have become virtually stagnant and dogmatically unquestionable ("instinctive"). A single emotion, viewed in isolation from the rest, may appear to be following rather than constituting the guidelines and structures of our surreality and our personality. But together, our emotions form an organic system of projected rules and standards within which any particular emotion takes its place, borrowing from but also contributing to that system in much the same way that a magistrate both borrows from the law and contributes to a common-law and "constitutional" legal system. Every emotion is a judgment that presupposes the entire body of previous emotional judgments to supply its context and its history as well as "paradigm cases" for it to consider if not follow. But every emotion is also an individual bit of legislation, whether striking out on its own and shifting the weight of precedent, attempting to establish itself as a new paradigm case, or merely reinforcing the biases of our already established emotional constitution. No two cases and no two emotions are precisely the same, even if they should differ only in the fact that one has come before the other. (Our emotions, unlike the law, make a great deal of this particular and objectively trivial difference: Some repetitions are celebrated as rituals—for example, making love with the same lover or making sacrifices to an object of worship. Others are damned as tedious and offensive: For example, one word of advice can be gladly accepted as an indication of well-meaning concern, whereas the second or third "word" of identical advice becomes offensive, intrusive nagging or lack of respect in one's intelligence.)

We do not create but are taught the forms of interpretation and standards of evaluation which we employ in our emotional judgments, by our parents and our peers, by instruction and by example. Our problem, in this society at least, is that there are virtually always alternative sets of such forms and standards, providing competing laws and loyalties at war with each other. Our parents typically disagree with our peers, and what we learn through instruction is often at odds with what we learn from examples. We are taught both selfishness and selflessness, aggression and meekness, ambition and resignation, competition and compromise, the need to belong and the ideal of autonomy. We are proven superior in one world and inferior in another, all of which is confused by the persuasive ideology which teaches us that all of us are "equal" in some ill-defined sense. We are taught to stand up and fight by the same culture that teaches us to "turn the other cheek," and we are taught the power of possessions by many of the same people who advise us of the evils of greed and covetousness. And the upshot is that we must always choose among alternatives. Our emotions are always legislative decisions. Our pettiest anger and our most casual romances are existential commitments to a system of constitution, a decision about the way our world will be.

Even where there is but a single set of criteria (for example, in those small timeless societies that anthropologists paternalistically call "primitive") every application of a rule is in fact legislation regarding the existing system. Philosophers and jurists have long been concerned with the fact that, no matter how precise the law, there is never a unique and indisputable application to any particular incident.[15] Regarding the emotions, this becomes important every time we must decide whether two cases are "the same," and every such decision establishes or reinforces a certain precedent for future decisions. For instance, it may be clear that verbal insults are appropriate objects for anger and indignation, but it remains an open question which comments in which contexts are to be interpreted as insults. Adolescents, for example, have a practice of filling their jibing with comments of the form "your mother ..." and "you couldn't even ..." which in any other social circle would appear to have all the earmarks of brutal offensiveness. Yet, in that context, an angry response is considered inappropriate and even despicable. We often find people like our megalomaniacal artist becoming offended and angry at compliments, and it is not unknown for persons to become grateful for the most cruel mockeries. And all of this is to say that there are no fixed standards of interpretation or evaluation for any emotion, and so *every* emotion must be viewed as constitutional, as an existential decision concerning the way one is to view his world.

The constitutional character of the emotions is a partial account—and a partial vindication—of the often alleged "dogmatism" and "blindness" of the emotions. When we are emotional—it is always objected—we do not have an "open mind"; we have already determined what we shall see and what we shall not. This is true. But the role of the emotions in our lives is not the same as that of those "objective" judgments in which we seek and compare, observe and experiment, test and confirm. An emotion is not a hypothesis, following certain rules of inquiry and aspiring to truth and accuracy. An emotion is an evaluative framework, which sets up, not follows, a set of rules and guidelines for itself. A child's fear of dogs, for example, is never a hypothesis or mere belief—subject to confirmation or refutation—about dogs. The fear is a predetermined framework within which dogs are *presumed* to be dangerous. Of course, such fears may well be "irrational," based upon some latent symbolic role of dogs whose manifest content is clearly unjustifiable. But such "phobias," as Freud described them, are no different in their structure than the legitimate fear of a child who has actually been attacked and bitten by several dogs before. The origin of the fear is different, and the warrant of the fear—as seen in reflection and therapy—differs accordingly. But every emotion, whatever its origins and whatever its warrant, is a before-the-fact constitutive judgment, a predisposition to react in certain ways. Compared with "open-minded" and disinterested curiosity, such predetermination will indeed seem dogmatic. But we do not *live* with open minds and curiosity, accepting whatever comes our way. We survive on our predeterminations and expectations, on our resolute decision to treat cruelty as wrong, not as a fact of life, to be grateful for kindnesses rather than take them for granted, to esteem the respect of other people, and to take every opportunity to act according to our predetermined ideals. The "dogmatism" of the emotions ought rather to be viewed as something of a virtue, one always to be coupled with objective open-mindedness perhaps, but one whose closed-mindedness, or *resoluteness* (to use Heidegger's more flattering term), is a presupposition of any meaningful or moral view of the world. Where the constitution of meaning and the establishment of standards is concerned, "open-mindedness" is no more than another name for wishy-washy indecision.

Consider what it means to "fall in love": To begin with, it is not a matter of "falling" at all, but of choice, a matter of constitution. But what does this mean? Our language of love is typically passive, from its poetic metaphors to its quasi-religious aetiology ("We were made for each other"). It is surely true that love often begins with an apparently spontaneous "attraction" or "chemistry," that we sometimes have the sense of someone as exactly the "right" person, as if the categories of companionship have been set up for us in advance. In fact, they *have* been "set up in advance"—not for us but *by* us. Our love is not a conclusion, a well-confirmed judgment of praise based upon intensive research into the virtues and vices, talents and failures, of this particular person, as if we were personnel officers interviewing for an open post. Love is a set of constitutive judgments to the effect that we *will* see in this person every possible virtue, ignore or overlook every possible vice, celebrating faults as well as charms in the context of his or her total personality.

We constitute, not find, the charms and virtues of the person whom we *choose* to love. In desperation and loneliness, we loosen our ideals to fit a broader class of people. At the extremes of desperation, we might reduce our criteria to the minimal requirement that the other person need only love us (or seem to love us) in return, no matter *who* he or she is. But even this open commitment, indiscriminate as it is, is a commitment, and a basis for the shared experiences and mutually reinforcing opinions that soon provide "something to love" in anyone. Then there are those cases in which we "fall in love at first sight," often with someone who bears little or no resemblance to the prototypes one has envisioned and adopted in the past. But even here, it is not a matter of "finding" a set of virtues which "cause" one to "fall," but rather is a matter of discovering (or rediscovering) a set of attributes that have long been circumscribed by emotional legislation that has been developing for a lifetime, perhaps unheeded or ignored because of the more superficial and misleading demands of peer group pressures, self-imposed false images, or a certain (also self-imposed) blindness to one's own needs and circumstances.

Stendhal's famed notion of "crystallization" is part of the same phenomenon, a consequent commitment rather than mere "discovery." It might be said that the lover "creates," not finds the virtues he continually discovers. "The facts," perhaps, are there to be found. But it is not "the facts" one discovers but newly imposed interpretations. There is no blemish that cannot be viewed as a beauty mark, no moral failing that cannot be viewed as a "wicked" charm of some peculiar but enticing variety. Similarly, André Gide's parasitic concept of "decrystallization" is not a matter of a lover's losing virtues or our discovering new vices and flaws but rather a matter of reconstituting our attitudes toward the other with diminished resolve and commitment, an attempt to break down the sense of shared identity and re-establish ourselves as *separate* individuals. And, at the extreme, there is the pathetic man or woman who guards his or her individuality so vigorously that he or she finds everyone flawed and "unworthy" of his or her intimacy. Of course, he or she always finds convincing reasons for rejecting this or that person (and aren't there always such reasons?).

The parameters of love are a set of ideals and standards which one legislates for oneself. They may be so narrow that they include one and only one person, or so stringent that they in fact (but not, of course, in intention) include no one. They may be so broad as to include any of an indefinitely large class of people, or they may be so indiscriminate and promiscuous as to include virtually anyone. But in any case, love is not so much "attraction" as it is resolution, a commitment to trust and share, to mutually praise and encourage, to mutually identify and esteem.

What we have just said about love is true of all emotions; every emotion establishes a framework within which we commit ourselves—or refuse to commit ourselves—to our world and to other people. Every emotion lays down a set of standards, to which the world, other people, and most importantly, our Selves are expected to comply. Of course, there are emotions and emotional systems that resemble the self-indulgent and less than honest rules of a rainy-day children's game, reinvented from moment to moment and momentarily absolute—until the slightest change of fortune dictates a self-serving change. At a party, we find ourselves outraged at the "obnoxiousness" of one character, disdainful of the timidity of another. On reflection, we come to see that each of these emotions was but a self-indulgent attempt to defend ourselves against a growing sense of insecurity and self-imposed isolation. Accordingly, we determined in advance to find some sufficient fault with each of the people whom we viewed as our antagonists, thus constituting the party as a whole as an alien and repulsive landscape within which we were glad to feel excluded and delighted to leave. Without reflection and occasionally "catching ourselves," such constitutional abuses might be continued indefinitely, choosing criteria inconsistently and arbitrarily for the defensive convenience of the moment. "Incapacity to love" is typically the result of such adjustable criteria, not simply a matter of "not finding the right person" but a matter of rigorously excluding every candidate for affection with some made-for-the-occasion criticism. ("He's too short" but "He's too tall"; "she's too intellectual" but "she's not smart enough.")

It is such inconsistency and arbitrariness that give the emotions a bad name. But, rendered reflective and maintained consistently, it is this same predetermined and "before the fact" resoluteness that stands at the foundation of all love and respect, all ideals and values, all relationships and senses of community. The way we are, and the way our world is, is the collective and systematic resultant of all of our various judgments—from person to person and from time to time—our judgments of value and our judgments of status, our judgments of power and our judgments of responsibility, our judgments of trust and judgments of intimacy. If we may adapt another line from Shelley, we might say that the emotions are "the unacknowledged legislators of [our] world."

6. THE MYTHOLOGY OF THE PASSIONS

... we are no less guilty of anthropomorphizing than the most unregenerate savages. Of this same fallacy we are guilty every time we think of anything whatsoever with the least warmth—we are endowing it with human attributes.
—B. Berenson, *Italian Painters of the Renaissance*

The systematic unity of the judgments of the emotions corresponds to a systematic unity of the objects of the emotions. What we have been calling the "object" of an emotion is in fact only its focus, circumscribing an incident or singling out a person or an action for particular consideration. The status of an object as an object of fear or reverence, love or anger, hatred or envy, depends upon its role and its relations in surreality as a whole. Thus, the object as well as the emotion that constitutes it belongs to an extensive system of such objects. At its extreme, for example, in moods or in a very prominent emotion (a romance or rage that virtually defines a person's life), the systematic connections of an emotional object may extend to the whole of our surreality. In rare cases, an emotion may be sufficiently "out of character" or a situation may be sufficiently unusual such that its connections to other objects is minimal. But most often, the object of any single emotion belongs to an extensive drama which permeates a certain realm of our experience. To underscore the dramatic nature of these systematic connections— as well as to underscore their often fantastic imagery and dependence upon the imagination—I want to call these extended objects of our emotions "*mythologies*."

Our emotions subjectively reorder our world, casting minor characters from the rambling plot of Reality as epic heroes and protagonists in its own intensive theatrics. We ourselves, our friends and enemies, become the focus of our world, which itself becomes a stage for the personal Thespianism of everyday life. For the emotions, the Realities of power and politics provide only the skeleton of plot, the bare bones of characterization that are listed in the cast of *dramatis personae*, introducing but not determining the surreality that is constructed around them. The emotions create their own hierarchies of status and importance, their own sense of power, often in the face of objective impotence. The emotions have their own surreal politics, sometimes in spite of the fact that their struggles for status and power are purely subjective and often without any result more manifest than the smug expression of "psychological" satisfaction.

By "mythology," I do not mean, according to the usual cynical self-righteous definition, *somebody else's* foolish and primitive theory, a fantastic but erroneous account of a phenomenon that we can explain "correctly."[16] Nor is a mythology merely "idle play or coarse speculation" (Lévi-Strauss). Neither is it true that the purpose of mythology is to make the world "intelligible." According to this familiar account, a myth is an alternative to (or a species of) scientific explanation, and scientific explanation (or our more "advanced" form of scientific explanation) is naturally preferable. The purpose of mythology is rather to make the world *meaningful* (which must, of course, include or presuppose an account which makes it intelligible, but these are not the same). The Greeks distinguished sharply between *logos* and *mythos*; the first was concerned with truth, the second with imagination and meaningfulness.

> To the Hellenic mind *logos* and *mythos*, "reasoning" and "myth," are two antithetic modes of thought. The former includes everything that can be stated in rational terms, all that attains to objective truth, and appears the same to all minds. The latter includes all that cannot be subject to verification, but contains its truth in itself or, and this amounts to the same thing, in powers of persuasion arising out of its own beauty.
> —P. Grimal, *Larousse World Mythology*

Unlike our Christian conceptions of faith (which, needless to say, are not "mythologies" at all, but rather the "gospel truth"),[17] the Greek mythologies were never accepted as the "truth" at all, but only as allegories of the imagination that portrayed the world in fanciful and dramatic garb.[18]

If a mythology is not literally "true," neither is it "false," for it is not an attempt at explanation (whatever its objective underpinning) but interpretation. It is not merely a story but neither is it a quasi-scientific or objective account of our world.[19] A mythology is a subjective interpretation of our world, one which may require an objective basis, but which may also allow itself the luxury of a lifetime of allegories and fantasies in its constitution of its world. No mythology may controvert "the facts," but no mythology is limited to "the facts." The mythology of emotion interprets those facts in a dramatic setting, invoking its most powerful and familiar images to do so. It does not surprise us, having been raised in a society dominated by sexual and Christian mythology, that our emotional expressions are typically cast in sexual and Christian terms—for example, "Screw you" and "Damn you" or "Go to hell" and "Bugger yourself." Good love affairs are "made in heaven," and lovers are often credited with possession of a spark of the Divine. In a society that has more concern for and spends more time with animals and agriculture, the expressions and the mythologies behind them are more likely to contain a zoological and botanical vocabulary, tracing human events to biological ancestors and casting all forces in animal forms. There are remnants of this in our expressions (for example, "you dirty rat" and "you pig") and our frequent treatment of friends, lovers, and enemies in terms most appropriate to pet cats and dogs (occasionally to caged birds and fish, "chicks," insects and worms). It is only to be expected that our highly urbanized lives would be more impoverished in these comparisons than the farming societies of ancient Egypt and Babylon. (Once again, the anthropomorphism that is often used to characterize a more "primitive" society is only a matter of a difference in experience and allegories; is our mythical condemnation of an antagonist to hell any less primitive than the Egyptian recognition of the divine indifference of a spoiled cat?)

The basic categories (or what Jung called archetypes) are status and power, and it matters little whether these categories are expressed in biological or theological or even "scientific" terminology.[20] Nor does it matter, for the purposes of the emotion or the mythology, whether its terms are to be taken literally or not. Of course, one does not believe for a second, when James Cagney accuses his antagonist of being a "dirty rat," that he has made a zoological discovery. But this categorization structures the role of the antagonist in Cagney's world and prescribes the treatment he is to receive. Only a few of us literally believe that we are giving directions when we angrily tell someone to "go to hell," but the phrase is an apt indication of our attitude. We would very much like the offensive Other to spend some time in the flames, though it would not be merely our decision (and therefore not our responsibility) for sending him there. Or again, when one finds him or herself uttering a religious appeal in the throes of extreme pain or sexual pleasure, it is of no importance whether the theology invoked is literally believed or not; it is sufficient that it is such an appeal, an attitude of awesome helplessness and giving oneself over.

The categories of mythology and emotion are often hidden by the rich imaginative tapestries of the fables and fantasies expressing them. But the essence of every mythology and every emotion is a set of the most powerful values in our lives, our sense of power and impotence, our sense of uniqueness and identity, our sense of belonging and exclusion, our sense of status and interpersonal roles. In metaphorical terms, these concerns easily translate into images of activity and passivity, genetic identity through myths of genesis and reincarnation, allegories of up and down, heaven and hell, in and out (whether sexual or digestive [eating and excreting], a structure from which Lévi-Strauss gets considerable mileage, and which Freud used similarly in his notion of "identification"). The basic ingredients in myth, as Lévi-

Strauss has pointed out, are typically concerned with kinship and status, including the apparently autonomous but demonstrably common rituals and experiences of eating and sexuality, terror and horror, power and impotence, identity (eating or being eaten) and exclusion (being exiled) and the rites of sacrifice and magic, murder and worship. We *live* these categories, whether literally embellished in allegory or not, and it is only the blindness of a restrictedly "scientific" fetishism that refuses to see the indisputable surrealities that underlie the admittedly fantastic and unreal stories of mythology. Far from pure fantasy, and far from the exclusive distinction between *logos* and *mythos* of the Greeks, every mythology has its demonstrable logic. Thus, every emotion has its logic as well, and, in another chapter, in which we shall discuss in detail this "logic of the emotions," we might well call that structural analysis "mythologic" as well, the logic of mytho-logy, though without thus confusing the logic of mythologies with the logic of objective thinking. The two are, in some features, very different indeed.

The mythology of emotion is the construction of surreality in dramatic form. It always, therefore, includes anthropomorphism, whether the casting of animals, plants, and idols with human attributes or the elevation of human forms to godlike status. (There is little difference between the elevation of the human to the divine, and the secularization of the divine in human terms.) The scope of such anthropomorphism varies, of course; some peoples, with a preference for teleological explanation, will allow themselves to use it anywhere. For others, notably ourselves, who insist that objective explanations must be as causal as possible, saving teleological accounts as a desperate explanatory measure,[21] the scope of anthropomorphism must be extremely restricted indeed, limited only to other people (since the treatment of them, at least, certain behaviorists and radical reductionists aside, may be "anthropomorphic" without the threat of protest). This is part of the reason (though the explanatory arrow might well turn the other way) that our emotions are primarily intersubjective, taking other people as their objects. When we do allow ourselves to get angry at the weather or fall in love with plants or automobiles, such emotions are necessarily accompanied by a peculiar anthropomorphization that may well strike us, in our more objective moments, as childish, foolish, or amusing. But it is the nature of emotion that it constitutes our world in mythological and meaningful terms, and that means *human* terms. And it is here that our emotions and mythologies so often run counter to our science; our science stresses the impersonal, the inhuman, the mechanical, forces of nature, whereas our emotions and our mythologies stress the personal, the human, the purposes and wills of our animated world. In a society with a conception of science which lies closer to mythology, it is only to be expected that men will have a rapport with nature that we typically lack. In our society, we allow ourselves the luxuries of teleological explanation only in the realm of interpersonal relations (and perhaps with a pet or two). Accordingly, our world of meaning is limited to the social world, while the natural world, the world of nature, is ever more closed off to us the better we understand it. And perhaps, when one day the physiologists have given us an adequate causal account of human behavior ...

The danger is always the confusion of our mythology with science; the Greeks were always careful to keep these apart. But with the recent relativization of science and rediscovery of the importance of mythology, the line between them is increasingly blurred, elevating once clearly mythological disciplines to the status of candidates as scientific theories, and inversely, relegating the claims of established science to the role of alternative mythologies. It is easy to see how this has happened; as scientists became increasingly aware of the *constructive* nature of the "theoretical" or "hypothetical" entities they invoked in their explanations, the emphasis moved from the *truth* of their accounts to their coherence and adequacy, their "elegance" and their explanatory richness. But with this shift, once discarded theoretical constructions reappeared with new claims for recognition, and confirmed scientific theories found themselves humbly unable to demand exclusive recognition. By mixing the verificationist demands of science with the dramatic demands of mythology, the lines between the two have all but disappeared. For example, science will tell us authoritatively that the movement of the stars and planets depends solely on the laws of gravity and so on. But what a lifeless view! And what, then, should the stars and the heavens *mean* to us? An occasional topic of "wonder"? Suppose instead that we supposed, on the basis of precisely the same facts plus a few other questionable correlations, that the movements of the heavens were not distant clockwork but rather direct influences on our own lives, dispositions, fortunes, and abilities? How much more "meaningful" the stars would become in that case. Objectively, the defense of these additional correlations and postulated "influences" may be exceedingly difficult. But subjectively it is not the objective defensibility that is at stake; it is meaningfulness. And, short of an actual breach in the objective correlations (and they are intentionally imprecise to preclude any such breach), the objective view cannot refute the subjective view, and the subjective view has an appeal that the objective view cannot have. It is exciting; it is dramatic; it portrays our lives as pawns in the distant arms of cosmic forces. The fact that it *may* be false, or at least without specifiable content, is of little subjective interest.

The line between subjectivity and objectivity, mythology and "the facts," may be difficult to discern in emotion, but the distinction can in most cases be clarified.[22] Of course, there will always be legions of the soft-headed who will believe in any subjective substitutions for objective and well-confirmed scientific theories just because they are more exciting (if only because they are very new or very old). Just as often there will always be those "hard-headed realists" who will not accept any belief which is not based on the cold-blooded confirmations of science. But there is enough room and need in our lives for mythology that we do not have to usurp the established claims of science. For example, the woman I love is scientifically but a few dollars' worth of chemicals, or a textbook illustration of cardiac type A, or an exemplary sociological specimen of the female *Bourgeois americanus*, subspecies *Rebellious bohemius*. To me, however, she is an answer to a prayer (whatever my religion), an incarnation of ideals and hopes. Her skin is hardly an epidermis populated by freckles, warts, hairs, sebaceous glands, and scar tissues; my love makes that view impossible (even were I an overzealous medical student or dermatologist), and I cannot help but describe her complexion (with varying degrees of clumsiness) in poetic metaphors. You may accuse me of being "unscientific," if you like, but I will hardly take that as a term of abuse. Similarly, I glorify if not exaggerate her intelligence and her beauty, her talents and her sensuosity, not by way of falsification—I do not deny a single "fact" about her—but by way of celebration, as a religious community might celebrate and even worship the attributes of its spiritual leader, whatever they might be. You might complain that no emotion is "objective," but an emotion, like a Greek allegory, is not intended to be objective or merely "true." Its purpose is to lend our surreality and our lives some significance. Love need not be blind; and an objective recognition of "the facts" about our lovers and ourselves is not the least bit incompatible with our love.

As in our general discussion of subjectivity (Chapters 2 and 3) we must again warn that there is no easy criterion, from the first-person or subjective viewpoint, to distinguish Reality from subjective falsification. In the world of the paranoid schizophrenic, the world of hallucinatory wish fulfillment, the world of fictional literature and film, and in the world of unbridled emotion, the mythologies of the emotions may well give themselves to imaginative abandon, express themselves in the degenerate forms of histrionics and adventurism, or quash all fine distinctions in Manichean divisions of good and evil which have little correlation with the subtleties of our knowledge of Reality. But mythology and Reality are no more at war than subjectivity and objectivity in general; the one supports the other. Reality provides mythology with its problems and parameters, its factual ingredients and its chronological sequence. Mythology interprets and selects, edits and personifies, aggrandizes and dramatizes, our Reality and gives it meaning. In Reality, we are all recruits standing in line at preparing to be classified by an impersonal doctor according to our warts and bare qualifications. It is only with mythology that we come to see ourselves and other people as fellow strugglers in a common quest. There is no Reality so degrading that a man cannot mythologize himself as a martyr, someone else as an oppressor from whom he shall liberate himself or against whom he shall avenge himself. There is no loss that cannot be used as a cause for mourning, a celebration of the transience of happiness, no error that cannot become a Christian morality play of guilt and redemption, and no person whom we cannot love, with whom we could not share a piece of our world, no matter how small. It is by mythologizing the world (in which boredom is an essential but hopefully not dominant aspect) of our everyday lives, that we create the sense of drama. It is something less than a creative enterprise as such, but its imaginative and constitutive character leaves open room for creativity that few people ever attempt to use, except in the wholly unreflective desperation of an untoward passion that requires the misuse of the imagination to rationalize its already unintelligible scenario into some coherent mythology. Our emotions are our personal projections onto our own world. The fact that our emotional surrealities are so tediously similar and often degrading and our projections so uniformly defensive speaks to the fact that we have, because of the reflective myths (in the derogatory sense) in which our emotions have been couched, taken poor advantage of our most powerful and most personal instruments for making our lives meaningful—our emotions.

Notes

1   In S. Hampshire, ed., *The Philosophy of Mind* (New York: Harper & Row, 1966).

2   A distinction some German philosophers attempt to squeeze between with a concept of *irreal.*

3   See, e.g., A. Kenny, *Action, Emotion and Will* (New York: Humanities Press, 1963). Cf. Robert Gordon, "The Aboutness of Emotions," *American Philosophical Quarterly*, 1974.

4   See Charles Taylor, *The Explanation of Behavior* (London: Routledge & Kegan Paul, 1964), for a telling formulation of these objections.

5   Lévi-Strauss, for example, argues that all "recollected experience" must be treated as "contemporaneous experience" (*Le Temps Retrouve*, p. 62).

6   It is a matter of indifference whether one says that an emotion is a judgment or a set of judgments. If one circumscribes a single judgment by a simple declarative sentence ("*a* is *b*"), then every emotion is a complex of judgments. But this criterion is surely arbitrary; how many judgments is "Fred is a repulsive and lecherous bore?" One? Two? Or three? All emotions are constituted by complex judgments with a number of dimensions, but the question of individuation may be ignored.

7   It is not always clear that anger involves such standards. Sometimes it surely does. John Rawls, in *A Theory of Justice* (Cambridge, Mass.: Harvard University Press, 1971), Sec. 73, suggests that it does not, contrasting anger with indignation. See my chapter 11.

8   See Jean-Paul Sartre, *The Emotions: A sketch of a Theory*, trans. B. Frechtman (New York: Philosophical Library, 1948), Introduction and Chap. 1.

9   One of the few places in which we must side with traditional Christianity against the rapacious thrusts of Nietzsche is on the matter of the voluntariness of the

emotions. Nietzsche objects to the biblical teaching that a man is responsible not only for what he does but for what he "feels" as well. Nietzsche argues that this thesis is unintelligible; but here, for once, we must violently disagree with him and defend an insight of Christian psychology that has too long been lost under the metaphysics of its theology. But see, too, Nietzsche's discussion of "the four errors," in which such strategic confusion of cause and effect plays a central role (*Gay Science*).

10   Perhaps we should make the distinction between getting into emotional states (making an initial judgment) and simply being in one (that is, getting angry vs. being angry). But nothing turns on this distinction. Being in an emotional state as well as getting into one, like God's maintenance of the universe as well as his creation of it, requires continuous and devoted activity. We are responsible, in other words, for being in an emotional state just as much as we are for getting into one.

11   A milder version of this position is currently maintained by Rawls, op. cit., esp. Sec. 3.

12   Kant's notion of "feeling," which he used like our "emotion" and contrasted with mere sensation in his third critique, might be used as a historical prototype for such reconstruction. His notion allowed him to squeeze in between his usual dichotomy of "subjective-objective" to include a form of "intersubjective" validity that is clearly appropriate in these contexts. (We might lament the fact that he did not consider similar applications in the realm of moral judgements.)

13   J.L. Austin, *How to Do Things with Words* (Oxford: Clarendon Press, 1962).

14   The fact that the court "finds" the defendant guilty is a verbal symptom of absolutist pretensions. The court makes, not finds, guilt. One is reminded of De Sade's perverse legal relativism, "a man is hanged in Istanbul for an act for which he would be handsomely rewarded in London." The notion of guilt (or innocence) makes no sense outside a constitutional system of laws. (Thus, the tired but clever quip that one could eliminate crime altogether by simply eliminating the criminal statutes that constitute certain acts as crimes.)

15   This problem of application greatly exercised Kant, for example (*Metaphysics of Morals*).

16   Our use of "myth" in our discussion of the Myth of the Passions and the Myth of Innocence, for example, had this particular significance.

17   Cf. Ernest Renan, who in 1855 distinguished the "Semites" from the other peoples of the ancient world because they "never had a mythology," rather a "clear and simple conception of God." Thus, we so often find that "myth" is a category reserved for other people's mythologies. Because, for example, Egyptian allegories are so filled with animal spirits and Greek stories so filled with anthropomorphic gods, these become characteristic of myth, but the tales of miracles and divine vengeance which populate the New and Old Testaments are not thought of as "myths" at all, despite the fact that they are usually as fantastic as anything that one could find in either Egyptian or Hellenic fables.

18   For example, see P. Grimal, *Larousse World Mythology* (Paris: Larousse, 1968). I am grateful to my brother, Jon D. Solomon, for some exciting discussions on this topic.

19   The now popular thesis that science itself is but contemporary mythology has admirable reason behind it—the insistence that we do not use our science with a superior air to ridicule and dismiss vital mythologies which are more primitive (i.e., less scientific) and magic-oriented (i.e., concerned more with teleological explanations and questionable causal principles than the mechanical canons of Newtonian physics). But the thesis thus stated yields only confusion, since the very virtue of a myth, unlike science, is that it does not endeavor to be unbiased and anonymous, to account for the world in unreligious terms. Contemporary science is not itself a myth, although one can persuasively argue that it has usurped just that position in our lives which myths once held, leaving nothing (except for the passing enthusiasm of "scientific curiosity") in its place. (See, for example, Nietzsche on myth in *Gay Science*, in which, seventy years ago, he warned of the despair and cults of power that would soon replace the collapse of the very human if also all-too-human and brutal myths that had always structured and given significance to men's lives.)

20   Cross-mythological identities in structure, of course, have been the central concern of Claude Lévi-Strauss and the anthropological movement that has loosely been identified with him appropriately called *structuralism*. Although we are not concerned here with the range of myths in various societies or with the defense of the "fundamental properties" of the human mind that Lévi-Strauss claims the structures of myth display, no employment of any theory of myth today can proceed without taking account of the vital claims of this movement. On the one hand, "structuralism" can be easily enough criticized as a new quasi-empirical version of the age-old Cartesian French fetish for universal rational structures. But the field in which Lévi-Strauss has forced this once introspective and restrictively European and bourgeois probe is dramatically new, for it no longer forces "primitive" people into the netherworld of nonrationality but recognizes them (in the style of Rousseau) as "reduced models" of the rational structures in all of us. I shall not be defending any such universal claim here, but the claim I am making, that myths are rational structures, whatever their literary or allegorical embellishments, is one which is deeply rooted in structuralist claims. See, importantly, *Tristes Tropiques, Pensée Sauvage,* and *Mythologique,* Vol. I.

21   For example, Immanuel Kant, in his *Critique of Judgment,* trans. Meredith (Oxford: Oxford University Press, 1952).

22   This, again, is Sartre's dilemma in *Being and Nothingness,* Pt. I, Chap. 2, Sec. iii.

❧ OBJECTIONS AND MODIFICATIONS ❧

A Case of Mixed Feelings:
Ambivalence and the Logic of Emotion

Patricia S. Greenspan

Traditional philosophical treatments of the emotions have usually emphasized questions of their *rationality*, and some philosophers have raised the related question whether they should be identified with *judgments*, or elements of cognition.[1] In contemporary literature, these questions are brought together by Robert C. Solomon, most recently in an article called "The Logic of Emotion," which argues that emotions have a logic of sorts which connects them quite firmly to judgments, and that they therefore are in many ways open to rational control.[2] Other current authors, though they may agree that emotions generally correspond to judgments, would apparently prefer not to *identify* the two; and some stress ways in which emotions are typically irrational.[3] But there is one important fact about the emotions—indeed, a kind of logical fact— which none of them brings to bear on this dispute, although they may often be ready enough to grant it.[4] This is *the possibility of ambivalence*: contrary emotions with the same object in a basically rational person. Briefly: ambivalence seems to be possible in persons not so irrational as to hold genuinely contrary judgments.

I suppose that most people think of ambivalence in connection with some rather complex, and debatable, claims of psychoanalytic theory, like the claim that a child unconsciously hates a parent it consciously loves, where the parent is its rival in the Oedipal triangle. Indeed, if psychoanalytic theory is even roughly correct, the phenomenon of ambivalence is widespread and subtle enough to require an extended treatment. I shall not give it one here, however—our understanding of even the simplest emotions is just too fuzzy, at this point. Instead, I shall keep my argument close to common sense and focus on one very revealing yet relatively simple and uncontroversial example of ambivalence, an example roughly familiar to us as a case of "mixed feelings." I think I can extract this case from suggestions found in Spinoza, one philosopher who does make much of the possibility of ambivalence (besides anticipating Freud with some of his general views about knowledge and freedom).[5] In what follows, after constructing and defending my example (Section I), I shall show how it bears on the question whether emotions should be identified with judgments (II-III) and then draw out some implications for the tangled question of the rationality of the emotions (IV). (As my argument proceeds, I shall try to *untangle* the rationality question somewhat by making a few rough distinctions.)

By putting "logic" in scare quotes much of the time, I mean to cancel out any suggestion that the logic of emotion is really analogous to that of judgment. In fact, I shall be arguing *against* that view, by stressing the logical differences between emotion and judgment, expanding on some of them (and raising further questions about them) in a long set of endnotes. At the same time, though, I think it may be useful to examine an artificial "logic" of emotion (a task I merely begin in this paper), just to see where the analogy must break down. For there *are* some significant parallels between emotion and judgment, which I shall point out, here and there, as my argument proceeds. Hence, even if the two should not be identified, I think we may be able to learn something interesting by exploring their interrelations. I shall explore them here, however— except in a few of my (optional) endnotes—just insofar as they bear on my case of mixed feelings.

I shall argue, then, that insofar as emotions have a "logic," it is one that tends to set them apart from judgments, though it also calls for a noncognitive assessment of their rationality. In my last section, on the second point, I shall present some initial thoughts on a subject that I do not think philosophers have dealt with sufficiently: the special motivational force of emotions, the pressure they exert on us to express them somehow in behavior. In a way, my argument will end with some questions about the nature of this special motivational force. We do not yet understand it fully; but I think we do know enough about it to question the familiar ideal of "philosophic detachment" from the emotions. Because of their motivational force, I shall argue, the emotions may often be useful to us—may play an essential role, for instance, in social communication—as long as we can control their behavioral consequences. In effect, then, my argument will bear out some of Solomon's more restrained comments on rational control of the emotions, while rejecting his central argument for them, which involves identifying emotions with judgments. But before I get to my critical points, I need to argue, using Spinoza, that ambivalence is indeed possible, and possible, moreover, without some sort of abnormal breakdown in reasoning.

I

In his treatment of the emotions in Part III of the *Ethics*, Spinoza allows for ambivalence—he calls it *fluctuatio*, or vacillation (p. 142)—as a result of a kind of transfer of emotions which he calls *imitatio*, imitation (p. 148). In his particular system, it seems to rest primarily on the resemblance of various possible objects of emotion. He introduces the subject of ambivalence in Proposition XVII:

> If we conceive that a thing, which is wont to affect us painfully, has any point of resemblance with another which is wont to affect us with an equally strong emotion of pleasure, we shall hate the first-named thing, and at the same time we shall love it. [p. 142]

Spinoza's claim here relies on his view that love and hate amount to the "primary" emotions pleasure and pain (*laetitia* and *tristitia*, often translated— more accurately, I think—as "joy" and "sorrow"), attributed to some object as cause (p. 140; see p. 138). I shall not attempt a scholarly account of Spinoza's overall system of the emotions; but this point should help us construct, in a moment, an example much more plausible than those Spinoza himself actually gives. In the quote above, the object of emotion is seen as causing both pain and pleasure—pain in its own right, and pleasure because of its resemblance to something else that causes pleasure in its own right. Spinoza does not tell us here what sorts of resembling "things" he has in mind; but his later remarks indicate that they would standardly be persons (or persons seen as experiencing pain or pleasure), including ourselves.

Proposition XXVII, his central proposition on imitation, runs as follows:

> By the very fact that we conceive a thing, which is like ourselves, and which we have not regarded with any emotion, to be affected by any emotion, we are ourselves affected by a like emotion. [p.148]

The proof of XXVII adds:

> If, however, we hate the said thing like ourselves, we shall, to that extent, be affected by a contrary, and not similar, emotion. [p. 148]

Thus, on Spinoza's view, a kind of sympathy based on resemblance leads us to "imitate" others' emotions, or at least the emotions of others we do not hate. Taken by itself, XXVII may not seem to bear on the possibility of ambivalence, since it is apparently limited to objects toward which we have no contrary emotion, like hatred. But in light of Spinoza's further comments, it does suggest at least one way in which ambivalence might result from imitation.[6] If something like ourselves (another person, with whom we identify) causes us pain *by* gaining pleasure for itself— by getting something we would like to have ourselves, for instance—then according to Spinoza, it ought to cause us *both* pain and pleasure, and hence be an object of *both* hatred and love. Insofar as we imitate it, it causes us pleasure by virtue of the very same fact that simultaneously causes us pain: its fulfillment of our own competing desire. Thus, it is unaffected by XVII's exclusion of objects of prior hatred, and points toward situations of *rivalry* as one potentially rich source of cases of ambivalence.

Spinoza himself focuses on various other sorts of cases of ambivalence, as arising from the propositions I have quoted; and he does not make explicit any link of situations of rivalry.[7] But I think that the general connection he sets up between ambivalence and imitation would be most effectively illustrated by a case of rivalry. Cases of rivalry are emphasized, of course, in the discussions of ambivalence in psychoanalytic theory; but they should be especially interesting to us because, assuming that one does sometimes identify with others and share in their emotions, ambivalence towards a rival seems perfectly *rational*, even if by definition it involves a kind of inconsistency. Consider sibling rivalry, for instance: it seems quite *appropriate* to have "mixed feelings" toward a person one both to some extend identifies and competes with. I shall take up the question of "perfect" rationality in my last section; but for the moment, I think we may grant that ambivalence is at least compatible with what I shall call "basic" rationality. It is certainly not unreasonable, that is, even if it falls short of some higher rational ideal, like Spinoza's ideal of complete freedom from external emotional influence; for it need not involve any abnormal breakdown in reasoning.[8]

As they stand, however, Spinoza's comments do not seem to yield an intuitively compelling example of ambivalence, even once we turn to a case of rivalry. He seems to imply, for instance, that any rival would be sufficiently like ourselves to give rise to a sympathetic emotion; and this may certainly be doubted. We might even question his assumption, moreover, that emotions as strong as love and hatred (or for that matter, any conflicting emotions) are directed toward the rival himself, insofar as he causes both pleasure and pain. I think it would be better to concentrate on Spinoza's fundamental emotions of pleasure and pain (joy and sorrow, or positive and negative feeling; perhaps the most natural terms in common speech would be "happiness" and "unhappiness"), taken as directed toward some *facts involving* a rival. We should also restrict our attention to cases where we have some special reason (other than simple resemblance to ourselves) for identifying with a particular rival. For even if Spinoza is wrong about the extent of our identification with others, there clearly are some people (our close friends and relatives, for instance) whose happiness we sometimes participate in, because of love, perhaps, as he suggests in Proposition XXI (p. 145). Using this insight, then, but ignoring the details of Spinoza's system, I think we can construct a case of ambivalence which *is* intuitively compelling.

Instead of treating pleasure and pain as episodes of feeling, let us take the more modern view (not all that foreign to Spinoza himself), and consider those emotions as propositional pro and con attitudes—"being pleased" or (less naturally) "pained" (in common speech, being happy or unhappy) that something is the case; that a rival has won for himself the prize one was competing with him for.[9] Our initial question then becomes: could two statements ascribing contrary emotions with the same (propositional) object:

I am happy that he won (feel good about his winning).
I am unhappy that he won (feel bad about his winning).

both be true of me? I think they could, in a case where I am the rival of a close friend whose feelings I tend to share. Suppose that a friend and I are in competition for some honorific position; we both want to become chairman of the same department, for instance (to take a somewhat implausible example). What emotions might I feel, not toward my rival himself, but toward the fact that he turns out to win, when I hear it over the telephone, say? I think we might plausibly hold, in some conceivable cases, that I have mixed feelings. I feel both pleased (at least to some extent) and pained—happy "for" him (as we say)—since I know that he deserves the honor and has been hoping for it, but unhappy on my own account, since my own desire has been frustrated.

Perhaps in many such cases my unhappiness would vastly outweigh my happiness; and of course there may be cases where I would not really be happy for my rival, even if I said I was; where I would not really identify with him strongly enough for my negative feelings at losing out to be accompanied by any positive emotion, however weak. On the other hand, in many cases my ambivalence might extend beyond emotions directed toward my rival's victory to those directed toward my rival himself. But these possibilities do not affect my point here. I just want to make the rather weak claim that the two statements above might *sometimes* both be true of me to *some* extent—whatever else may be true as well—on the assumption that I am reacting reasonably. This claim results from what I take to be Spinoza's main insight on the subject of ambivalence—his view that we often "imitate" others' emotions, as applied to my case of friendly rivalry—and I think it provides us with a fairly ordinary and unproblematical example of ambivalence, one defensible without appeal to irrational forces like "the Unconscious," as in psychoanalytic theory.

Some further insights of Spinoza's should help us defend the example against various possible objections: attempts to deny that it represents a genuine case of ambivalence. For instance, someone might maintain that I could not really have contrary feelings toward my rival's victory at one and the same time; instead, I would waver between them, feeling happy at some times, unhappy at others. Spinoza would grant, I think, that this describes any pleasure and pain I actually experience—my emotions taken as episodes of feeling—since he uses the word *vacillation* for cases of ambivalence. Yet he clearly states that in such cases one has contrary emotions "at the same time" (p. 142). The point of his remarks should be evident: we may be said to have or exhibit a particular emotion (and indeed, I might add, to exhibit it consciously) over a span of time which includes, but is not limited to, the times (supposing there are some) when we are actually experiencing it. Thus, if I waver, over time, between happy and unhappy feelings about my rival's victory (I momentarily feel bad when I first hear the news on the phone, say; but then I immediately consider my friend's good fortune and momentarily feel good), we would reasonably conclude that I have "mixed feelings" throughout the overall time span involved, and not that I am continually changing my mind.[10]

But are my feelings really contrary emotions with precisely the same object? Someone might maintain that what I really feel bad about is not my rival's victory but my own loss. In the case as envisioned, however, my rival's victory entails my loss; so it would be natural enough for me to feel bad about both, even if I might sometimes manage to keep them rigidly distinct. Again, I am not claiming that ambivalence in such situations is inevitable, but only that it *can* occur in a basically rational person—a person whose reasoning comes up to the normal standards, even if it falls short of some ideal of perfect rationality. Someone might maintain, though, that the "contrary" emotions we attribute to that person do not really conflict in themselves, but simply happen to give rise to conflicting tendencies—to act, for example, or to feel. However, I think that, by grounding various pairs of emotions in the fundamental distinction between pleasure and pain, or positive and negative feeling, Spinoza in effect (whatever his intentions) stresses the genuinely contrary basis of many emotions. Emotions, or those amounting to pro and con attitudes, seem to involve taking "positions," of sorts, on their objects, and thus may be said to be capable of logical conflict.

Philosophers may try to dismiss their logical conflict by fiddling with the object of contrary emotions, building into it the reasons for a positive or negative reaction, so that contrary emotions may be taken as directed toward *different* objects. This is a legitimate move for certain purposes; but I think we should not let it keep us, here, from retaining our common sense description of cases of ambivalence. By varying my case of mixed feelings a bit, I think I can show that the reasons for an emotion certainly *need* not be taken as defining its object. Suppose that in fact I do not realize, at first, that my rivals' victory frustrates any of my own desires; I have always fancied that I had no political ambitions, say, so I am initially quite surprised to find that I feel bad about the news I hear on the phone. Only after a moment of reflection am I able to discover the reasons for my emotion. Yet surely I might know what its object is—what I am unhappy *about*—before I discover its reasons; and it seems wrong just to insist that its object (in every sense of "object") must *change* as I come to understand my reaction to it. Nor need my increase in understanding in any way resolve the conflict between my positive and my negative feelings. (In fact, since both of them might seem appropriate to me upon reflection—I might accept my political ambitions once I become aware of them—I need not even try to resolve the conflict.) Intuitively, then, I think we can take my happiness and my unhappiness as contrary attitudes toward the same object, which conflict with each other quite apart from any tendencies they "happen" to give rise to. I shall try to explain how they could both be appropriate (and what it might mean to call them "contrary") in my third section; but first I want to go on to show how a basically rational person would handle contrary judgments. I shall argue that emotions differ from judgments in that they resist qualification and summing, moves we can normally make to resolve a conflict among judgments. On some interpretations, Spinoza himself seems to identify emotions, or those based on pleasure and pain, with certain sorts of judgments.[11] My ensuing argument will question this general view—though I shall now avoid any reference to Spinoza and consider the issue in its own right.

II

Should emotions be identified with judgments? I can think of two main sorts of judgments to which they might be said to correspond: *evaluations* of the situations in which they arise; and their *grounds,* or the descriptions of those situations on which such evaluations would be based.[12] In the case where I have mixed feelings about my rival's victory, the grounds of both my positive and my negative feelings might seem to be the same: the judgment that my rival has won. So initially, at least, the first alternative looks more plausible. I shall return to the second alternative in my next section; but for the moment, let us consider some extremely simple evaluations as candidates for my contrary emotions in the case that concerns us:

His winning is good.
His winning is bad.

These, of course, are naturally interpreted as genuine (logical) contraries, judgments that conflict in themselves—apart from any tendencies they might or might not give rise to—since they cannot both be true at the same time. But would a basically rational person who does interpret them as contraries be likely to *hold* both of them at the same time? I shall argue that, even if his contrary emotions persist, he would sooner or later manage to resole any such conflict among judgments, thus casting doubt on the identification of emotions with judgments.

Let us return, then, to the case where I waver in reaction to the news of my rival's victory, when I first hear it over the phone. Do I then believe both of the contrary judgments given above? Could two statements ascribing them to me as pro and con attitudes toward the same (propositional) object:

I think it is good that he won (judge his winning good).
I think it is bad that he won (judge his winning bad).

both be true at the same time?[13] Certainly they *need* not be true to support my mixed feelings; I might already have made up my mind (as I pondered my chances beforehand) that my rival's victory would be on the whole good, or on the whole bad, and yet feel both happy and unhappy about it when the news arrives. On the other hand, I might initially waver between the two contrary judgments, just as I waver between positive and negative feelings in reaction to them. In that case, however, I think we would reasonably conclude that I would not immediately make up my mind—that I *withheld* full assent for a moment or two, instead of according it to both judgments at once. Either of these possibilities cuts against the identification of emotions with judgments, or judgments of the sort now under consideration. But even if we ignore them, and grant that I might start out confused enough to accept two contrary judgments, my confusion would have to end rather quickly—or at any rate, more quickly than my ambivalence must—if I am to count as a basically rational person.

How would we normally handle such a conflict between judgments? First, I think, we would *qualify* both judgments, by building into them a description of the reasons for them. The resulting judgments, for instance:

His winning is good in that it satisfies a desire of someone I identify with.
His winning is bad in that it frustrates a desire of my own.

would no longer be genuine contraries, though they still might give rise to contrary emotions. I might continue to waver between happy and unhappy feelings about my rival's victory—though probably at longer intervals (experiencing *no* particular feelings much of the time)—once sufficient time has passed for me to resolve any conflict among judgments. Further, my contrary emotions need not "blend" into a single intermediate emotion, even after enough time has passed for me to *sum* their corresponding judgments: add them together, as a second step in their reconciliation, to form a single "all things considered" judgment, either:

His winning is on the whole good.

or:

His winning is on the whole bad.

Even if my feelings of unhappiness (say) are clearly much stronger than my feelings of happiness at my rival's victory, I still may continue to experience both, instead of opting entirely for those that are "overriding."

There may be some cases, of course, in which I am unable to make up my mind—to decide which of two contrary judgments is overriding, or even how they might be qualified. But then, supposing that I *am* convinced that they are genuine contraries, and hence that they could not be simultaneously true, I would treat the two judgments as merely *prima facie*, instead of giving my full assent to both—assuming, once again, that I am a basically rational person. Belief in both judgments, even if not impossible, would seem to be unreasonable—to involve some sort of abnormal breakdown in reasoning— in a way that ambivalence does not. Even if it falls short of perfect rationality (the question I shall consider in my last section), ambivalence is at any rate *less* irrational than full assent to judgments one knows to be contrary. We cannot simply decide to treat emotions, like judgments, as merely *prima facie*, so "all-out" emotions may only correspond to *prima facie* judgments, since they resist the sort of qualification and summing that lets us reconcile contrary evaluations.

There are often limits, first of all, to the distinctions we can capture in feeling. A distinction, for instance, between unqualified happiness at my rival's victory and (say) happiness-for-him—an attitude that would not conflict with the unhappiness I feel on my own account—will not help us here; for reasons cannot just be "built into" emotions, in the way that they can be built into judgments. That is, even if I do feel happy for my rival, or happy about his winning *in that* it satisfies a desire of someone I identify with, I would normally still feel happy about his winning—*simpliciter*—so that my emotion cannot be said to be truly qualified. Hence emotions should not be identified with qualified evaluative judgments. (I say "should not," rather than "could not," here and elsewhere, because any such attempt at reduction *could* manage to swallow some counterintuitive consequences, in the interests of simplicity, say. I just mean to argue that this attempt does have counterintuitive consequences, in relation to cases of "basically" rational ambivalence.) Consider how qualification would *change* my initial contrary judgments, for instance: insofar as they both involve taking positions on some object, qualification weakens them, and thereby keeps them from conflicting with each other. But as I illustrated above, in dealing with questions about the object of my contrary emotions, my emotions may very well remain stable as I alter my conception of the reasons for them. It is perfectly conceivable that my unhappiness at my rival's victory should be completely unaffected—in object, quality, strength, and what have you—by the process of discovering the reasons for it and qualifying its corresponding judgment. If so, moreover, it certainly might still conflict with the happiness I feel because I identify with my rival as well as competing with him.

In general, then, it seems that a change in judgment, like the change it undergoes in being qualified, need not give rise to any change in the corresponding emotion; so intuitively, at least, emotions and judgments seem to be individuated somewhat differently.[14] Further, emotions need not change (except insofar as they naturally fade over time) at the second stage in our reconciliation of contrary judgments, as our qualified evaluations are combined to form a single "all things considered" judgment. Nor does there seem to be anything unreasonable about our failure to change them. For one thing, an emotion seems to be appropriate relative to a particular set of grounds, and not necessarily a unified evaluation of one's total body of "evidence." It is enough that it be justified by *some* (adequate) reasons, even if the overall *weight* of one's reasons favors a contrary emotion instead. Thus, emotions may persist, even when they are accompanied by stronger opposing feelings, in a basically rational person. In my next section, after considering another possible way of identifying emotions with judgments, I shall expand on this brief observation concerning the "logic" of the emotions. I shall conclude that it would be better to stick to our offhand (and much looser) characterization of emotions as *attitudes*—attitudes that generally correspond to judgments, but which seem to exhibit a logic of their own.

III

Instead of identifying emotions with evaluative judgments, someone might argue that they ought to be identified with judgments giving the grounds for a particular evaluation, what we would normally think of as the reasons for exhibiting the emotion in question, the facts that seem to make it appropriate. In the case where I have mixed feelings about my rival's victory, the reasons for my happiness and my unhappiness might seem to be identical with their common propositional object:

> He won.

However, the discussion of qualified evaluations in my last section suggests a way of filling out this judgment to distinguish between my two emotions, at least where I am aware of the reasons for them. We can build the reasons into the judgment, and thus replace it with two:

> He won, thereby satisfying a desire of someone I identify with.
> He won, thereby frustrating a desire of my own.

Still, like the qualified evaluations in my last section, these judgments are not logical contraries— both, in fact, are true—though of course they would be likely to give rise to contrary feelings. They also fail to capture the positive or negative "point" of the emotions—or at any rate, of the emotions I mean to be considering—since belief in judgments like the two just above need not involve any pro or con attitudes. Of course we could manage to interpret such belief as involving *different* attitudes toward a common object. For instance, in holding the second judgment, I might be made out as applying a complex predicate to my rival—as judging that-he-won-thereby-frustrating-a-desire-of-my-own—but this would not itself amount to a con attitude. Rather, it would seem to give the reason for one, for my negative reaction to the news I hear on the phone, and if we want to preserve the force of this claim, we need to preserve some distinction between my emotional and judgmental attitudes.

We can preserve the distinction by returning to the evaluative judgments I discussed in my last section, by considering emotions as analogous to them, but not identical. Thus we can speak of emotions as sometimes conflicting with judgments, in those all-too-familiar cases of "head/heart" conflict, and as conflicting in a logical sense with one another. Since judgments like the two just above do not conflict logically, it seems that any explanation of the possibility of ambivalence must refer beyond them. How is it that my happiness and my unhappiness at my rival's victory can somehow conflict in themselves, apart from any associated behavioral conflicts? So far, I have simply taken for granted our intuitive view that these emotions *are* in some sense logical contraries; but now I want to suggest a way of interpreting it. I suspect that the notion of contrariety must be understood somewhat differently for emotions than for judgments (relative, as I have suggested, to a particular limited set of grounds), so that emotions can be identified with judgments only at the cost of obscuring a logical distinction.

What I have in mind is this: contrary judgments are defined as judgments that cannot both be true; but my case of friendly rivalry makes it clear that we could not accept an analogous definition of contrary emotions. Like judgments, emotions may or may not "fit the facts," and above I have spoken of those that do as "appropriate." But appropriateness is not quite analogous to truth. For one thing, it depends on the adequacy of certain reasons for an emotion, the facts that make it suited to its object (assumed to exist), as in the two statements given just above.[15] For judgments, on the other hand, questions of truth and justification are often distinct. I shall let myself blur over the distinction, though, in the argument that follows, since I take it that contrary judgments cannot both be fully justified, any more than they can both be true. If we grant, then, that appropriateness is the value for emotions which comes closest to truth for judgments, we might expect contrary emotions to be emotions that cannot both be appropriate. But we have seen above that, in at least one case, contrary emotions might both be appropriate for different reasons. Where I am in competition with a close friend, happiness at his winning might be adequately justified by my identification with him, and unhappiness by my concern for my own interests, even though each of these reasons would seem to count as reason *against* exhibiting the contrary emotion. Ambivalence is possible, then, in a basically rational person. But how can we explain its possibility?

For emotions, I would suggest, support by some (adequate) reasons is enough for appropriateness; so contrary emotions might both be appropriate and, hence, I take it, "basically" rational, even if emotions are not under rational control to the extent that judgments are. (I assume that, except in extreme cases, they are under *some* control: we can usually avoid exhibiting emotions we take to be *in*appropriate.) But even if they are both appropriate, could contrary emotions be appropriate for exactly the same reasons? I think not—in which case contrary emotions might be defined instead as emotions it would be inappropriate to exhibit *for the same reasons*. The reason for an emotion is necessarily a reason *against* its contrary, in short; and thus two contrary emotions may be said to be contrary in a logical sense—to conflict "in themselves," as I have put it above. But however contrariety is defined for emotions, we seem to treat them differently from judgments when we evaluate them against their background of reasons pro and con. The judgments of a person whose reasoning comes up to the normal standards are justified in relation to the total background; but his emotions, even when they are appropriate, may sometimes rest on particular limited portions of the background, if my treatment of the case of friendly rivalry is correct.

Thus, instead of identifying emotions with judgments, I think we should take both of them as attitudes of different sorts, and try to distinguish between them initially by describing differences in their logic—in how we "reason" with them, insofar as our reasoning comes up to the normal standards. I have sketched one such difference here, but I am sure there are many others (and a deeper explanation of the one I have sketched). Perhaps by describing them we can best explain the concept of an emotion (answer the philosopher's general question, "What is an emotion?") since the attempt to force emotions into some presumably clearer category (whether cognitive or noncognitive, mental or physical, physiological or behavioral) seems to have failed consistently.[16] The claim that emotions are attitudes is uninformative enough to be widely acceptable as a starting point; so perhaps we can make some progress toward understanding the emotions if we limit ourselves to asking what sorts of attitudes they are, how their logic differs, for instance, from that of judgments.

I have suggested that we treat emotions differently when we evaluate them against their background of reasons. Briefly: an emotion is appropriate as long as there are adequate reasons *for* it, whatever the reasons against it. My suggestion is meant to help explain how ambivalence is possible in what I have loosely termed a "basically" rational person. But does it also indicate that cases of ambivalence—and indeed, the emotions generally—involve a kind of *ir*rationality, in contrast to judgments, even though they do come up to the standards we think of as normal? Presumably, the normal standards are designed to fit beings who are subject to emotions—and subject to whatever irrationality emotions bring with them—so there may be a sense in which emotions are intrinsically irrational. Though we have *some* rational control over them, our control is limited; they are based on reactions to particular facts, as they come into consciousness, rather than consideration of all the relevant reasons. (Here, I think, is where a deeper explanation of basically rational ambivalence would lie.) However, I think we should be wary of applying to emotions the cognitive criteria for rationality in judgments, as we can see by trying to illustrate this argument with my case of friendly rivalry. Certainly—someone might maintain—it would be *more* rational for me to reconcile my conflicting emotions as time passes. A perfectly rational person would come to take a detached view, and suppress any emotions that were not supported by the overall weight of his reasons. This argument may sound plausible; but I think that a closer look at my example will make us reject it. Emotions do involve irrationality in any number of ways, but even a case of conflicting emotions might be defended as perfectly rational in light of the special relationship between emotions and behavior.

IV

My preceding argument was structured as an answer to the question whether emotions should be identified with judgments; and its upshot was a rough account of how contrary emotions might both be appropriate—what notions of contrariety and appropriateness would make sense of that possibility. Starting with an intuitive treatment of my case of friendly rivalry, I tried to explain the possibility in terms of the way emotions are justified by reasons in a basically rational person. A stronger claim, about some higher rational ideal, was not needed to distinguish emotions from judgments, since holding two judgments one knows to be contrary would seem to be downright unreasonable, besides falling short of "perfect" rationality. Now, though, I want to consider whether the stronger claim can be made as well. The conclusions of my preceding argument should not be affected by this one; but this one should let us see just *how* rational my case of mixed feelings really is, assuming that its rationality is not determined by cognitive criteria. I shall argue that it would sometimes be a mistake to treat emotions like judgments, and reconcile them in cases of conflict, even if one could. On a standard of rationality that evaluates emotions according to their behavioral consequences—which takes into account, for instance, the social value of identification with others— ambivalence might sometimes be *more* rational than forming an "all things considered" emotion that resolves the conflict.[17]

I shall illustrate this point in a moment; but let me begin by explaining two qualifications. First of all, even if it is wrong to treat emotions like judgments generally, there may still be enough similarity between the two to allow for their comparison on cognitive criteria, in relations to a total body of evidence. I have admitted as much above, in effect, by characterizing them both as attitudes directed toward an object, with appropriateness taken as the value of emotions which comes closest to truth for judgments. For example, I have assumed that my happiness at my rival's victory is appropriate as long as he has indeed won and I have adequate reason for sharing his happiness at winning; under these conditions, my emotion can be thought of as fitting the facts, like a true judgment. But "adequate reason" for an emotion need not be sufficient to ground a corresponding judgment—it might not count as "evidence" at all. It is clear enough, for example, that my identification with a friend would not give me adequate (cognitive) reason for adopting his beliefs. I shall not deny, then, that the emotions in my case of mixed feelings are in some sense less rational than judgments; but I shall defend them as perfectly rational relative to the *non*cognitive functions of emotion, with emotions considered particularly as *motivating* attitudes, attitudes with special motivational force.

Second, though my defense of this view must rest on some sort of reference to behavior, I shall continue to ignore the conflicts in behavior that conflicting emotions may or may not give rise to. I shall assume that, though emotions may sometimes motivate (exert a kind of pressure toward) irrational behavior, they need not always disrupt deliberation, even if they conflict. Except in extreme cases, we seem to have some control over how we act on them—*more* control than we have over whether we exhibit them or not. For instance, if I waver between positive and negative reactions to my rival's victory, I might be led in extreme cases—where my emotions are especially strong, say—to alternate between friendliness and hostility in his presence. My behavior toward him might very well be inconsistent and self-defeating, and hence irrational. But this is not a necessary consequence of my conflicting feelings; I would ordinarily be able to control their effects on my behavior without actually resolving my emotional conflict. My question is: supposing that I am under pressure to act on my conflicting emotions in *some* way or other (if only to control their effects), *must* my behavior be any less rational than it would be if I resolved the conflict? Let us approach this question by considering a case where I do resolve the conflict, in the way that we commonly reconcile contrary judgments. I think we shall see that I might lose something important in the process.

Suppose, then, that I do manage to sum my conflicting emotions. We have been assuming that my unhappiness is stronger than my happiness, so perhaps the most likely result would be a somewhat tempered negative reaction to my rival's victory.[18] But then I would no longer participate in his emotion, and share his point of view, though sympathy would have had some effect on what I do feel. From the standpoint of self-interest, then, his feelings might be overridden; and from an impersonal standpoint, on the other hand, they might simply counterbalance my own. A neutral reaction to my rival's victory would also fail to express my identification with his interests—I simply would not care who happened to win—though this solution might well be recommended by some philosophers. The philosopher's ideal of "perfect" rationality is often an ideal of *detachment* from particular points of view. But with emotions taken as motivating attitudes, whose behavioral effects are ordinarily open to control, I think it is clear that conflict between emotional extremes may sometimes serve a purpose that would not be served by moderation. Commitment to different points of view, in short, can motivate behavior unlikely to arise from emotional detachment.

In my case of mixed feelings, for example, how might I exercise rational control over my behavior, in light of my emotional conflict? I think I could best handle the conflict by focusing on my happy feelings in my rival's presence. Assuming that I want to preserve our friendship, I should offer him sincere congratulations, take part enthusiastically in any victory celebrations, avoid dwelling on my own disappointment, and so on. Of course, I could conceivably manage to do all this even if I did not really take an interest in his happiness; but then I would merely be going through the motions, probably unconvincingly: we can often *perceive* the difference between detached and emotional behavior. Genuine emotional identification with others, then, motivates spontaneous sympathetic behavior, behavior that expresses our concern for others' interests for their own sake. I think it should be obvious that such behavior facilitates social relations, and thus promotes an important human end, in a way that detached behavior, or behavior arising from tempered self-interest, would not be likely to. Indeed, even if my conflicting emotions blended to form a positive reaction to my rival's victory, my happiness for him would presumably be weaker than it would be if I failed to resolve the conflict. By allowing the conflict, but controlling its behavioral effects, I can express my strong commitment to someone else's interests without losing sight of my own.[19]

Some philosophers would argue, of course, that judgments, particularly evaluative judgments, also have motivational force. But without taking a position on that issue, I think we can see that the emotions we are discussing motivate behavior in at least one *special* way. Being pleased about something amounts to a pleasurable state, which an agent would naturally act to promote in himself. Positive feeling can itself be positively reinforcing; that is, happiness motivates behavior partly by *rewarding* it, so it is in some ways a more reliable motive than the judgment that something is good, particularly when the judgment is weakened by qualifications.[20] It provides an agent with a further reason for action because it actually increases the desirability (for him) of one of the options he chooses among. Emotions are typically more variable than judgments; but assuming that happiness at others' good fortune is indicative of a long-range tendency, behavior expressing it would tend to be reassuring to others. It would encourage them to think that they could depend on the agent to consider their interests in the future. For even if judgments have *some* motivational force, emotions usually seem to have more; and it usually seems to be easier to change one's mind, and drop a judgment, than it is to alter a pattern of emotional reaction. Thus, emotional identification with others, as opposed to merely including them in one's detached calculations, can lend a special kind of support to social communication. Providing that the agent has control over the behavior it motivates, its behavioral consequences may make it perfectly rational—ideally suited to promoting human ends—even where it involves emotional conflict.

This is just one fairly simple and obvious example of how the emotions can be useful to us, in view of their motivational force. They are "adaptive," let us say for short; for with proper control, they can help us adapt to our social (and material) environment. Since social adaptation serves some chief ends of morality, moreover, we can begin to appreciate the obvious *moral* significance of the emotions, even supposing that emotions and moral *judgments* are quite distinct. Indeed, the emotions very likely have moral significance beyond what I need to argue for here in defense of their rationality. Without any reference to the informational role I am assigning to them, we might want to say that they function morally just in so far as they actually let us perceive the world from other people's different points of view, by "mirroring" them in our own, as it were, instead of merely viewing them all from some neutral standpoint. Does moral motivation depend, in fact, on our commitment to "points of view," as opposed to detachment? Would I support my friend's chairmanship with equal enthusiasm, for instance, if all I could do were to observe his happy feelings from a distance? A kind of Humean moral stress on the emotions, but without any version of the "emotivist" account of morality, may seem to emerge from questions like these about their special motivational force. But we need not try to settle such questions here. The argument from social communication suffices to establish *one rational* purpose for the emotions, whatever their further rational or moral purposes. Even in promoting our selfish ends in society, that is, we seem to rely on emotional behavior for the information it provides about the future.

Someone might maintain, though, that a perfectly rational *person* would not *need* the emotions to reassure others about his future behavior. He could be relied on to act in strict accordance with detached calculations of the good, since (unlike a "basically" rational person) he would never be subject to weakness of will. But I think that this argument holds only for someone assumed to be living among others who are also unusually rational, so that they can be depended on to take his qualified judgments as strongly motivating. Even so, of course, they might take emotional behavior as a particularly useful sign of someone's tendency to act in their interests, since emotions are typically harder to fake than judgments. As I have suggested, emotions exert a kind of pressure on us to act, at least partly, by affecting the very options we choose among. But at any rate, though judgments may have motivational force as well, I would insist that any *realistic* ideal of perfect rationality must take account of the stronger link, as people are in fact constituted, between emotions and behavior. Instead of detachment, it should stress control over the behavioral consequences of emotion; for with such control, emotions play an important role in motivating rational behavior.[21] On any remotely realistic ideal, then, suppressing an emotion may sometimes be *less* rational than controlling its behavioral consequences.

Since this point seems to apply even to a case of conflicting emotions, like my case of friendly rivalry, I think we may conclude that the "logic" of emotion permits ambivalence. In general, there seem to be two phases of our reasoning with an emotion: to it from its object and from it to behavior. We are far from understanding the logic of the two phases, in particular, the special motivational force of emotions needs further explanation, and I have suggested that we need to understand it if we are to make any progress toward explaining the general concept of an emotion. For the moment, however, I think we may conclude that, where both phases are under proper rational control, even conflicting emotions may be perfectly rational in at least one important sense, given the fact that the agent and the others he interacts with are not perfectly rational. Exhibiting the emotions may be the best way of promoting the agent's ends—that is, the emotions may be "adaptive" as well as appropriate—even if (as philosophers often argue) emotions are in some sense intrinsically *irrational* and impose some *limitations* on rational control. Indeed, the fact that emotions resist control may be part of the reason why they are useful to us, and hence in our sense rational—part of what gives them their motivational force, and thus lets them serve (in my particular example) as a way of binding ourselves to one another.

Someone might maintain, of course, that we would really all be better off with no emotions whatever, and no need for emotions to bind ourselves to each other. Just above, I have dismissed such cognitive ideals of "perfect" rationality as unrealistic; but in fact I think that the problem goes deeper than that. Some unrealistic ideals (utopian visions of society, for example) seem to provide us with a reasonable standard for action, since the attempt to live up to them presumably is likely to have good consequences, even though it can never quite succeed. But on the whole, I strongly suspect that approaching an ideal of complete detachment, in a world where we depend on the emotions for their special motivational force, would be likely to have rather *bad* consequences. Detachment is surely sometimes in order, in those extreme cases (for instance) where our emotions would otherwise be too strong to allow for control of their behavioral consequences. But where an emotion is both appropriate and adaptive, it may be clearly wrong to urge "philosophic detachment" from it.

Notes

I am indebted to my colleague Arthur Flemming for his extremely helpful comments on the earlier versions of this paper, including one I presented at a University of Chicago philosophy colloquium in November 1977.

1   This view is attributed to the Stoics, for instance. For a detailed historical survey of accounts of the emotions, see H.J.Gardiner et al, *Feeling and Emotion: A History of Theories* (Westport, Conn.: Greenwood, 1970).

2   See Robert C. Solomon, "The Logic of Emotion," *Nous*, XI, 1 (March 1977), 41-49; also, *The Passions* (Garden City, N.Y.: Anchor, 1976). Solomon does not seem to use "logic" in any very precise (or familiar) sense; but I shall not be much concerned here with the fine points of his argument, which I find both illuminating and obscure. A similar view emerges, though, in Donald Davidson, "Hume's Cognitive Theory of Pride," *Journal of Philosophy*, LXXIII, 19 (November 4, 1976), 744-757, see, e.g. p. 751.

3   For an examination of some irrational features of the emotions, see Amélie Rorty, "Explaining Emotions," *Journal of Philosophy*, LXXV, 3 (March 1978), 139-161, also published in this volume. Also, see Frithjof Bergmann, Review of *The Passions* by Robert C. Solomon, *Journal of Philosophy*, LXXV, 4 (April 1978), 200-208, for a refutation of Solomon from another point of view, which I heard at the meetings of the American Philosophical Association, Western Division, in April 1977. On some points, my argument will overlap with these, as well as some others (especially Solomon's; and also, of course, the classic treatments of the subject in Descartes and Hume). The differences are also important, however, and numerous and complicated, so for simplicity's sake I shall present my argument without much reference to other authors.

4   See, e.g., Solomon, *The Passions*, pp. 166, 283, 406. But see also Bernard Williams, "Ethical Consistency," in *Problems of the Self* (Cambridge: University Press, 1973), for a related treatment of the problem of conflicting desires.

5   I shall give page-references to the *Ethics*, using the translations by R.H.M. Elwes; see Benedict de Spinoza, *On the Improvement of the Understanding: The Ethics; Correspondence* (New York: Dover, 1955). For a classical *rejection* of the possibility of ambivalence, see David Hume, *A Treatise of Human Nature* (Oxford: Clarendon, 1964), p. 278. (But cf. René Descartes, "The Passions of the Soul," in *The Philosophical Works of Descartes*, ed E.S. Haldane and G.R.T. Ross (Cambridge: University Press, 1970), p. 408. Descartes' example–and his account of ambivalence in terms of different reasons—comes close to common sense; but Spinoza's general treatment of the subject contains an important insight, as we shall see.)

6   I shall adopt Spinoza's terminology; but I do not mean to suggest, of course, that the transference of emotions he picks out as "imitation" is meant to rest on any sort of conscious mimicry of others' reactions. I think it must involve *direct* transference, though, in some sense actually coming to *share* another person's happiness, e.g., instead of merely being made happy oneself by reflection on the fact that he is. With this restriction, however, I shall ignore distinctions that other authors might insist upon, and use interchangeably a range of expressions that in ordinary language do seem to fit the rough phenomenon Spinoza seems to have in mind. Thus, I shall speak of "identifying" with others, "participating" in their emotions, acquiring "sympathetic" emotions, and so forth, without taking myself

to depart in any significant way from Spinoza's general notion of imitation, though I *will* soon abandon his account of it in terms of resemblance.

7   Spinoza uses ambivalence in his account of jealousy (or our mixed feelings toward a person whose affections we have a rival *for*); cf. Prop. XXXV with its accompanying Note (pp. 153-154). But it does not seem to come into his account of envy (or our feelings toward the rival himself); cf. Prop. XXIV with its accompanying Note (pp 146-147). For Spinoza's further examples of ambivalence, see Prop. XXXI (p. 151), Corollary I to Prop. XL (p. 157), the Corollary to Prop. XLI (p. 158), and Prop. XLVII with its accompanying Note (pp. 160-161).

8   Spinoza's ideal applies only to those emotions he picks out as "passive"—cf., e.g., Prop. LVIII (p. 171) and the Note to Prop. LIX (pp.171-173)—but these seem to cover all the emotions we recognize as such in common life. For some further comments on Spinoza's ideal of freedom (particularly in relation to knowledge), see, e.g., the Note to Prop. LXVI in Part IV (p. 232) and the Note to Prop. IV in Part V (pp. 248-249).

9   I am not assuming that *all* emotions are plausibly made out as "propositional pro and con attitudes," but just that these are. Instead, I shall later characterize emotions in general simply as attitudes, of a sort that we can compare with at least some judgments.

First of all, many emotions, e.g., love and hatred, clearly have persons, rather than propositions, as their objects (and it should become obvious, later on, that the same is also true of many judgments, as I am parsing them; see n. 13). It may still be true that emotions are all in some sense *based on* propositional attitudes; perhaps love and hatred, e.g., could be reconstructed out of hypotheticals about what a rational person *would* feel about various possible facts involving the persons they are directed toward. Some such proposal would let us set up a kind of "logic of appropriateness" for the emotions (cf. n. 14); and it may provide us with a way of making some modern sense of the seventeenth-century attempt to build all emotions out of "primaries."

Second, I am not even sure (though I think it not unlikely) that all emotions can be interpreted as pro and con attitudes, as having some positive or negative "point," as I put it below. Spinoza, e.g., accepts desire as a third primary, besides pleasure and pain; see, e.g., the Note to prop. XI (p. 138) and his summary of his views under "Definitions of the Emotions" (pp. 173-174). But it is questionable whether desire really amounts to an emotion; and in any case, perhaps it *could* be made out as a pro attitude, with aversion as the corresponding con attitude. However, I shall leave such questions open here. Many emotions can be taken as pro and con attitudes, surely; and my argument below will make use of this view.

10   This suggests at least one rough point of analogy between emotions and judgments, but with important limitations. Judgments, too, may be held over time spans including, but not limited to, the times when they are actually *asserted* (whether in speech or just mentally.) So perhaps assertion, as a cognitive episode, plays a role for judgments, which is something like the role I have assigned to

emotional *experience*, or episodes of feeling. Taken as attitudes, as I take them here, emotions and judgments both may be said to be based on (at least the possibility of) certain mental occurrences; but clearly we can hold a judgment, or exhibit an emotion, without at the same time—or ever—expressing it in conscious thought or feeling.

On the other hand, I shall expand below on some of the crucial differences between judgment and emotion. For instance, not every expression of a judgment in thought—not every "mental utterance" of it—need actually count as an assertion. There are various possible degrees of assent to a judgment: one can merely "entertain" it, to examine its implications, say; or one can assent to it tentatively, pending further evidence, taking the judgment as merely *prima facie.* Perhaps we can sometimes "toy" with an emotion, try it out, as it were, to see how it fits the situation, and perhaps emotions can sometimes be exhibited without full conviction. But in any case, it is clear that we only have limited control over our ability to take such intermediate emotional positions, and, in general, to "change our mind" about an emotion, so the decision to withhold full assent from a judgment often may have no effect at all on the emotion we take to correspond to it.

Moreover, there seems to be an important analogy (again with important limitations) between contrariety in judgments and emotions. Its details will emerge as my main argument proceeds; but in general, I think we must take contrary emotions, like contrary judgments, as expressing conflicting "points" or "positions," and not just as amounting to conflicting properties or states. It is clearly possible for someone to exhibit two contrary emotions, just as he might hold both of two contrary judgments. But—someone might object—is it possible to *experience* conflicting emotions at one and the same time? I am not sure how this question should be answered; but in any case, I do not think it really threatens the limited analogy I wish to set up between emotions and judgments.

Is it possible actually to *assert* two contrary *judgments* at one and the same time? I have my doubts, but perhaps this point is undercut somewhat by the intermediate degrees of assent to a judgment which I sketched just above. Is it possible, instead, to give some sort of simultaneous mental utterance to two *prima facie* judgments? I still have my doubts, in fact, because of some general questions, also applicable to emotions, about the restrictions on occurrent thought. Perhaps it *is* impossible to experience simultaneous conflicting feelings (though we do speak of "mingled" pleasure and pain, say). But this point (supposing it holds) would not seem to apply particularly to *contrary* feelings. I think it may be impossible to experience any two very *different* feelings, whether or not they are contraries, at one and the same time. Can we actually be said to experience hope and hatred simultaneously, for example? My doubts are even stronger about occurrent feelings which are directed (and often appropriately directed) toward the same object, e.g. love and anger.

In general: how many mental occurrences can take place in the same mind at exactly the same time? Doubtless certain combinations are possible; but those that are ruled out would clearly include many that could not be plausibly taken as contraries, at least in the sense of "contrary" that seems to be relevant here. Later on in my main argument (after bringing in some of the points I anticipate here), I shall try to pin down the relevant sense of "contrary," for emotions, by analogy with judgments. For the moment, though, I think we may conclude that the relevant sense is *not* explained by reference to possible real-world combinations of emotion or judgment.

11   I owe this point (and much of my treatment of Spinoza) to Arthur Flemming. Spinoza takes pleasure and pain as "confused ideas" (see, e.g., his "General Definition of the Emotions," pp. 185-186); and on some interpretations his "ideas" come out as judgments. His characterization of the judgments that amount to emotions seems to depend very heavily, though, on the peculiarities of his overall system; so I shall limit my attention to some simple modern candidates below.

12   Solomon seems to suggest both alternatives in different places. For the first view, with judgments taken as evaluations, see, e.g., T*he Passions*, pp. 149, 187; but he also at least allows for the possibility of the second view, with judgments taken as giving the grounds for evaluations, e.g., in "The Logic of Emotion," p. 47. I shall eventually conclude that the first view *is* more plausible, even though the second may give better support to the claim that emotions and judgments always *correspond* (see n. 14).

13   As my parenthetical insertions are meant to indicate, I am not parsing these statements as they are standardly parsed by authors who make out judgments as propositional attitudes. The attitude in question is standardly taken as simply *belief* (not a pro or con attitude), directed toward *contrary* propositional objects which give the content of the two evaluative judgments, as follow:

I think (it is good that he won).
I think (it is bad that he won).

But on this interpretation, my contrary judgments would not seem to be analogous to the contrary emotions ascribed to me above, with contrary *attitudes* taken as directed toward a *common* propositional object. Instead, to exhibit the analogy, I suggest that we take the attitude involved in judgment as some sort of attitude of predication (in this case, "judging good" or "judging bad") applied to an object (in this case, a propositional object) which amounts to the subject of predication. Thus, I would parse the two statements above as follows:

I think it is good (that he won).
I think it is bad (that he won).

These statements clearly ascribe to me contrary pro and con attitudes directed toward a common propositional object. (For a similar interpretation of *none*valuative judgments, however, we would need to make some changes. They can be taken as attitudes of predication toward a common object; but the attitudes need not be contrary pro and con attitudes, and the object need not be propositional.)

14   Some further "logical" differences between emotions and judgments emerge from an interesting variant of my example, which I had intended to use in a side-argument designed to strengthen the case against emotions as qualified evaluations. In fact, this example may turn out to be in some ways more revealing than the one I focus on; but it is not a case of basic rationality (or even, necessarily, of ambivalence), so it might just constitute a distraction from the main argument presented in my text. Consequently, I shall restrict it to notes, outlining it here, and exploring some of its implications for the attempt to identify emotions with evaluative judgments; and then, in n. 15, showing how it forces us to distinguish appropriateness from truth.

My variant case rests on the possibility of conflicts between emotions and evaluative judgments themselves, of having an emotion one does not consider appropriate. Where emotions, like evaluative judgments, involve taking positions pro and con on some object, it seems that our emotional and judgmental "positions" can sometimes conflict. I might actually believe, for instance, that my rival's victory is good without qualification, though simply out of competitiveness I feel bad about it. What if I feel extremely guilty about my competitiveness—so guilty, in fact, that I consider my emotional reaction completely inappropriate? (I think my guilt-feelings *are* appropriate, say.) For I do not really want the chairmanship at all. My negative feelings at not attaining it stem from a lifelong aversion to losing *anything* that I recognize as completely irrational. It seems at least possible, in this variant case, that I do not hold even the qualified judgment: "His winning is bad in that it frustrates a desire of my own." (I think it could only be *good* to frustrate *that* desire, suppose.)

Indeed, this variant case suggests that the argument for identifying emotions with evaluative judgments may be trading on an important confusion. In general, it seems that an emotion will be *appropriate* just as long as some evaluative judgment is *true*. Perhaps this means that the belief that one's emotion is appropriate corresponds to an evaluative judgment; but it does not mean that the emotion itself corresponds to that judgment. Thus I have spoken of emotions and judgments just as corresponding "generally" above, though perhaps a stronger claim can be made for cases of basic rationality, where the agent does take his emotional reactions to be appropriate. This, in fact, may be what really stands behind philosophers' several attempts to identify emotions with judgments—what gives that view its initial appearance of plausibility—for we might say that, insofar as they are *reasonable*, emotions have a kind of cognitive "content" which evaluative judgments express. Where an agent's emotions are "basically rational," that is, they involve an implicit commitment to some claim (perhaps unspecified) that would support them as appropriate. (We might think of this implied claim as spelling out the *rational* content of an emotion.) This is a suggestion worth looking into, I think, in exploring the logical interrelations between emotion and judgment. But it rests on the (at least partly) normative emotion of "rationality"; so I see no way to get from it to a descriptive thesis identifying emotions with evaluative judgments.

More needs to be said, of course, about the various logical terms I am applying to emotions, here and elsewhere: "appropriate," "rational," "reasonable," and the like. I shall say a bit more about them below, but by no means enough.

15   Reflection on my variant guilt case above (see n. 14) has led me to a stronger argument for distinguishing appropriateness from truth. Holding a judgment involves some kind of commitment to its truth, even apart from the requirements of rationality. To hold it *is* just to think that it is true; and to assert it is to say so. But the guilt case seemed to indicate that we can have or exhibit (or even experience) an emotion without any commitment to its appropriateness. (Perhaps, in fact, it is this disanalogy between emotions and judgments which explains those I outlined, e.g., in n. 10 above; it certainly drives a wedge between assertion of a judgment and emotional experience.) Here it seems that appropriateness comes closer to justification than truth (as I suggest just below); for at least in cases of irrationality, we can hold a judgment without thinking it justified. We can cling to it obstinately, as it were, in the face of strong counterevidence; or just blindly, without even evaluating its evidence at all. (Consider, e.g., some people's belief in God.)

On the other hand, we might not want to equate appropriateness with justification, either. Like truth in judgments, appropriateness does not seem to depend on everything we might want to count as a reason for an emotion, but only on reasons that somehow serve to link it to a real-world object. First of all, there may be extrinsic reasons for an emotion, reasons why it is useful in attaining our ends. (I shall touch on some of these—particularly social reasons—in my last section, under the heading of "adaptiveness.") For instance, in a threatening situation in which others are depending on my calmness, I may have reason to avoid exhibiting fear, to keep myself from having the feeling at all, that is (in accordance with my use of "exhibit" throughout this paper), even though the feeling would be perfectly appropriate. For the situation I face may be so extremely threatening that my fear would be too strong to hide from others, if I felt it. So in this case, we might want to say that an appropriate emotion would not be justified, at least on the grounds that seem to apply to emotions.

But second, if I may complicate this discussion further, there seem to be some important differences between the grounds on which emotions and judgments would be deemed justified. A reason that would justify a judgment, presumably, is reason for thinking the judgment true, not just some noncognitive reason for holding it, e.g., in order to please others or to make oneself feel secure. Suppose, then, that I model my reaction to some situation on my observations of another person, not because I identify with him but just because he is generally sensitive and rational in such matters, a reliable guide to emotional appropriateness. In this case, he is wrong, however; so my reaction might seem to be justified but not appropriate. I have adequate reason for thinking it appropriate, say; but I do not have adequate reason for the emotion. (In fact, my way of arriving at it would in most cases seem ridiculous, though it is analogous to a common and legitimate path to judgments.) I can only conclude that appropriateness falls somewhere in between justification and truth, and that the relations between these notions (for emotions as well as judgments) are confusing. But I can think of no notion that comes closer to truth than appropriateness; so I shall continue to suppose here that it is the basic rational value of the emotions. If there is a better notion, my argument can simply be rephrased in terms of it.

16 For a concise account of several such attempts, ending in a Wittgensteinian "paradigm case" view (and thus, in effect, in a rejection of the general question), see William P. Alston, "Emotion and Feeling," in *The Encyclopedia of Philosophy*. Vol. I, ed. Paul Edwards (New York: Macmillan, 1967). It remains a crucial issue, of course—which the "paradigm case" view does not shed much light on—just how emotion is related to phenomena in those other categories (in what sense emotional attitudes, e.g., are "based on reactions to particular facts, as they come into consciousness"—my brief suggestion below). But I think, by now, it is clear enough that we cannot easily make out emotions as identical to any of those phenomena; and if, as attitudes, they must involve various dispositions to exhibit those phenomena, it also seems clear enough, by now, that it is difficult to make them out as simply identical to those dispositions. (It is also clear that the dispositions must be extremely complex, for both emotions and judgments.)

17 My argument for this final point need not be taken, like that in my central sections, as an argument for distinguishing emotions from judgments. Judgments can also be evaluated on noncognitive criteria at times; and in this case, someone might argue that I would be better off stopping at the first stage of their reconciliation, and resisting the urge to decide between the qualified evaluations above. However, where grounds for forming a single judgment are available to me, I think it must always seem odd, at least, to refuse to take them into account. We seem to recognize some rational "push" toward moving on to the second stage of reconciliation for judgments. Though we may sometimes resist it, and refuse to sum them, I think this requires a stronger justification than the one I go on to sketch for emotions. I would suggest, then, that cognitive criteria are somehow more essential to the proper evaluation of judgments; but my further remarks can be made out as independent of this view.

18 There are various different senses in which we may speak of the "strength" of an emotion (e.g., felt intensity vs. force as a motive); and in any case, there may be other factors (e.g., the importance assigned to it as a reason) which determine whether a particular emotion is "overriding." To avoid some difficult issues, then, I shall not limit my argument to any single imagined outcome of the attempt to sum emotional contraries.

19 Losing sight of my own interests—completely repressing my *un*happiness—might in fact be worse than ignoring someone else's feelings. Arthur Flemming has

pointed out the dangers of *servility*, for some agents, in this connection. But even supposing that I have no tendencies toward servility, I may have reason to retain my emotional point of view. Without some counterbalancing reaction, some private disappointment, e.g., identification with a rival might often have damaging consequences, like bottled-up hostility. Even a healthy self, in short, needs occasional reinforcement.

20   This need not hold for every positive feeling, for every emotion "based on" positive feeling (cf. n. 9), in the sense that it involves taking a pro attitude toward some object. Thus, e.g., love need not always be positively reinforcing; in some circumstances, hatred may actually feel better and be preferred. Indeed, perhaps there are even some circumstances in which the "primary" positive feelings I am discussing here would actually be annoying, on the whole (where we really— perversely—were *hoping* to be disappointed about something, say). But I think they must always be to some extent pleasurable, even if the pleasure can sometimes be outweighed by accompanying "pains," and even if it is wrong (as I think) to *equate* positive and negative feeling ("being pleased" and "being pained") with simple pleasure and pain. (In fact, since it is emotional *attitudes* I mean to be discussing here, it would be wrong to equate them with *any* features of experience.)

In general, I mean to suggest, just above, that part of the special motivational force of an emotion has to do with extralogical facts about the nature of positive and negative feeling, granting the "logical" fact with which my main argument began: that like evaluative judgment, it involves some sort of pro or con attitude toward an object. Judgmental pro attitudes may also be to some extent positively reinforcing; and it is hard to say precisely why emotion is generally more so, or more so, at least than evaluative judgment alone (which is all I really need to grant here). But this point does seem intuitively clear.

21   This claim should hardly be surprising to a post-Freudian era (e.g., in view of the likely effects of repression, which I bring up only briefly in n. 19). For that matter, something not unlike it seems to lie behind Descartes's various comments, and especially his general approach to examples in "Part Third."

Note that control over the behavioral consequences of emotion may also give us some indirect control over their expression in experience. I may be able to restrict myself to happy feelings in my rival's presence, e.g., simply by getting involved in his victory celebrations and refusing to think about the grounds for my own disappointment. We need a more detailed treatment of the relation of attitudes to experience and behavior, to flesh out my many hints in this last section. (I hope to flesh them out somewhat in a forthcoming book, *Emotions and Reasons*. For some initial comments on the question of motivational force, but without much reference to the emotions, see "Behavior Control and Freedom of Action," *Philosophical Review*, LXXXVII, 2 (April 1978), 225-240, esp. 230-233. A fuller discussion of these topics would have to deal with the possibility of identifying emotions with desires; but I have focused here on the attempt to identify them with judgments. Since this paper was completed, I have benefited from comments by Jerome Neu whose recent book on the emotions charts an opposing view; see *Emotion, Thought, and Therapy* (Berkeley, Los Angeles, London: University of California Press, 1977), esp. pp. 148-49. For some later remarks on the subject, emphasizing the distinction between judgments proper and the general category of "thought" which Neu equates with belief (see esp. pp 36-37), see "Emotions and Evaluation" (unpublished, presented at the December 1979 meeting of the American Philosophical Association, Easter Division).

EMOTION, JUDGMENT, AND DESIRE[1]

Jenefer Robinson

In this paper I discuss some of the relationships among emotion, judgment, and desire. First I examine the theses that an emotion can be identified with a judgment, and mention four ways of distinguishing the kind of judgment it might be. However, none of these ways succeeds in drawing a sharp distinction between judgments central to emotions and "dispassionate" judgments. Next I point out that emotions share certain formal properties with desires, which mark them off from dispassionate judgments. I then argue that the judgmental element in our emotions should be thought of as a way of thinking about something which is governed by our desires and which is "colored" by our desires in the sense that it shares some of the formal properties of desires previously mentioned. I claim that these two features distinguish the judgmental or cognitive element in emotion from dispassionate judgments. Furthermore, in the light of this analysis we can see why the four ways of characterizing "emotional" judgments, distinguished earlier, should have been found plausible. I conclude that although an occurrent emotional state cannot be *defined* as a conception of something determined by desires, a particular occurrent emotional state may be identical with the occurrence of nothing but a thought, provided it has the right historical links with the agent's desires.

I

There are good reasons for supposing that some sort of appraisal or evaluative judgment is a necessary condition on emotion. Whether I am in love or angry or afraid or anxious or joyful, it seems as if an essential component in the situation is that I appraise[2] it in a certain way: I appraise you as having certain virtues (love); or I appraise myself as having been wronged (anger) or in danger (fear); or I appraise a situation as menacing and uncertain (anxiety) or wonderful (joy). Notice that I have not specified that the appraisal be of the object of the emotion, since there are some emotions that do not seem to have a particular object, such as nameless anxiety or pointless joy. Even in these cases, however, there seems to be an appraisal which is essential to the emotion in question: I appraise the world in general as menacing or uncertain or as full of wonderful things.[3]

Many of the most influential theories of what an emotion is can be shown to be inadequate because they neglect the centrality of judgment or appraisal to emotion. Thus an emotion cannot be merely a feeling in Ryle's sense of bodily sensation,[4] such as a qualm, a throb, a chill, or a sinking feeling, partly because a qualm is not an emotional qualm unless its immediate cause[5] is an appraisal of the situation at hand: a qualm of remorse is (partly) caused by my realizing that I have done something wrong, whereas a qualm of seasickness is caused only by the boat's rolling motion. Again, an emotion cannot be merely a piece of behavior, since, as Errol Bedford has pointed out, the behavior associated with two different emotions, such as shame and embarrassment, may be identical;[6] we can distinguish these emotions only by examining the different judgments that (partly) cause the behavior in question. My cringing may be due to my judgment that I have behaved in a way that is morally wrong (shame) or merely socially unacceptable (embarrassment). Finally, an emotion cannot be identified with a set of physiological changes, since it is only those which originate in an evaluative judgment that count as "emotional": my heart may begin to pound and my face to flush because I judge you have wronged me (and so I am angry) or merely because I have run up the stairs too fast.[7]

It seems plausible, then, that a judgment or appraisal is a necessary condition for an emotion. However, any theory that *identifies* emotion and judgment is open to serious objections. Robert C. Solomon, for example, in his book *The Passions*, claims that an emotion *is* "an evaluative (or a "normative") judgment, a judgment about my situation and about myself and/or about all other people,"[8] but none of his examples bears out this view. Thus my embarrassment cannot be identical with "my judgment to the effect that I am in an exceedingly awkward situation" nor can my sadness be identical with my judgment "that I have suffered a loss" (187) nor can my anger at John for stealing my car be identical with "my judgment that John has wronged me."[9] These examples all fail for the same reason: it is possible to make the judgment without feeling the corresponding emotion. Moreover, it seems likely that any examples one might think up would fall prey to the same objection.

Sometimes Solomon seems to be defending the rather different thesis that an emotion is a special *kind* of judgment. Thus he says that emotions are "self-involved and relatively *intense* evaluative judgments…. The judgments and objects that constitute our emotions are those which are especially important to us, meaningful to us, concerning matters in which we have invested our Selves."[10] Elsewhere he claims that emotions are "urgent" judgments: "emotional responses are emergency behavior."[11]

The suggestion that there are two kinds of judgment, dispassionate judgments and those which are central to emotions, is a valuable one, but unfortunately none of the features Solomon mentions succeeds in distinguishing the two. An "emotional" judgment cannot be a judgment that is particularly *intense,* for the simple reason that judgments are not the sorts of things that admit degrees of intensity. Nor can the judgments central to emotions be identified as those which are especially "meaningful" to us; just because a judgment concerns something of crucial importance to us, it does not follow that I cannot be dispassionate about it. Thus in a clear-sighted moment I may make the dispassionate judgment that my adored husband is a drunkard and a liar. Finally, it is not true that the judgments central to emotion are necessarily urgent or emergency judgments. My contemptuous judgment that Ruth is shirking her duty, my compassionate judgment that Philip is much to be pitied, and my fearful judgment that the dollar is dangerously declining may be made after long and careful scrutiny of the grounds for the emotion. Moreover, there are other more obviously urgent judgments which are not emotional. The judgment "I had better go now" may be made urgently and perhaps rests on grounds that have not been at all carefully scrutinized; yet it may be a purely prudential or practical judgment, and not central to any emotion.

II

A more general argument designed to show that *no* emotion can be identified with a judgment has been advanced by Patricia Greenspan. She points out that our emotions have certain formal properties that are not shared by the corresponding evaluative judgments. First of all, in cases where our emotions are ambivalent, the corresponding judgments may not be. Suppose I judge that my dear friend Sally's winning the prize (for which I also applied) is both good and bad. I may resolve the conflict in judgment by qualifying it: her winning is good for some reasons and bad for others. My emotions, however, may continue to fluctuate between sadness and happiness: they resist qualification. Secondly, I may "sum up" my judgment, concluding that *on the whole* it is good that Sally won (on the whole it is bad), but again my emotions resist summing in this way: even if I judge that on the whole Sally's winning is good, my emotions may continue to fluctuate between sadness and happiness. Greenspan concludes that the "logic" of our emotions differs in important ways from the logic of our judgments, for it is not *irrational* for my emotions to resist qualification and summing: "emotions may persist even when they are accompanied by stronger opposing feelings, in a basically rational person."[12]

Interestingly, the formal features of emotions which Greenspan points out link them not with dispassionate judgments but with desire. I want to argue that there are at least four ways in which the "logic" of emotion resembles the "logic" of desire,[13] all of which help to distinguish the emotions from dispassionate judgments.

I have already remarked that judgments cannot be more or less intense.

One important feature of both emotions and desires is that they do allow degrees of intensity. Moreover, this is no accident, since the intensity of an emotion is based upon the intensity of the underlying desire. Thus if I am intensely afraid of bees, I have an intense desire to avoid them; if I am intensely in love with Joe, then I have an intense desire to be with him, to care for him or whatever.

Secondly, one of the features of emotions which Greenspan focuses on, namely resistance to summing, is also a feature of desires. Again, this is no accident, since my failure to sum up my conflicting emotions is due to my failure to sum up the corresponding desires. When Sally wins the prize, I am happy because I desire that she achieve her desires and I am sad because I desire that I achieve my desires. My emotions fluctuate between happiness and sadness because I fail to sum up the two desires that gave rise to them. Making the judgment that *on the whole* Sally's winning the prize is good (or bad) does nothing to resolve the conflict in my desires which produces the conflict in my emotions.

Resistance to summing is closely linked to two other features of emotions which they share with desires: tolerance of inconsistency and resistance to change. As the Greenspan example shows, inconsistent emotions may coexist in a rational person: the reason for this is that the related desires may also coexist in a rational person. It is perfectly rational for me to maintain both my desire that I do well and fulfill my desires and my desire that my friends do well and fulfill their desires. Perhaps it will be said that I ought to rank my desires and thereby resolve the conflict. However, even if I do succeed in ranking my desires, it does not follow that in order to be rational I should drop the second-ranked desire altogether: I may still have both desires and still have the corresponding emotions without sacrificing my rationality. Similar examples are not hard to find: I may both love and hate John, feel pity and envy for Philip, despise and admire Ruth, and these conflicting emotions may be perfectly rational, just as the conflicting desires that underlie them may be perfectly rational. By contrast, it is not possible simultaneously to judge dispassionately that John is on the whole both lovable and hateful, that Ruth is on the whole both admirable and despicable, or that it is on the whole both good and bad that Sally wins the prize, without laying oneself open to a charge of irrationality. Of course the evidence may change so that I may rationally change my judgment, or the evidence may be inconclusive so that I shift back and forth in my judgment or—more likely—suspend judgment altogether. But if the evidence stays the same and points in one direction, then the rational person will accept the evidence and the conclusion it dictates.

A third important feature of emotions which links them to desires is their resistance to change. The Greenspan example shows how two inconsistent emotions and their corresponding desires can persist unchanged in a "basically rational" person. I desire both my own good and that of Sally, and I cannot simply "drop" one of these desires; hence I cannot simply "drop" the corresponding emotion. But there is nothing irrational in this behavior if, as Greenspan argues, there are adequate (although necessarily different) reasons for the two emotions (see 234-38). And in this case there certainly are, since the two emotions are based in two equally rational desires.

It is, however, a further common feature of both emotions and desires that they persist even when they are in fact irrational. I may, for example, have an irrational desire to play Russian roulette, a desire which remains no matter how many good reasons I find for not satisfying it. Similarly, I may know that Ruth is an altogether admirable person, yet persist in despising her. For example, my desire to feel superior to someone with Ruth's qualities of character may persist despite my realization that it is irrational for me to feel superior to someone of such courage and virtue.

In this section I have mentioned four formal features of emotions which link them to desires rather than to dispassionate judgments. In the next section I shall expand upon the nature of this close connection between desire and emotion.

III

In the first section of this paper I briefly examined the theory that an emotion is a special kind of judgment, but failed to find any satisfactory way of characterizing that judgment. In section II I pointed out that emotions have formal properties in common with desires. I now want to suggest that the cognitive or judgmental element in an emotion is of a special kind, in that (1) it is not a dispassionate judgment that, say, an object A has a property P, but rather a conception or way of thinking of A as P, and (2) this way of thinking is both governed (caused) by our desires (values, interests, goals, and so on) and also "colored" by our desires in the sense that it shares some of the formal features of desires. I will first illustrate these two theses with respect to love and then try to draw some more general conclusions.

If I am asked to make a dispassionate judgment about Joe, I may declare that he is ugly, morally despicable, and a boring companion. Nevertheless, I am in love with Joe. I find him lovable, although dispassionately I judge him not to be lovable at all. I think of him as lovable, and my behavior is governed by the fact that I so think of him. I may love Joe because he is friendless, lonely, and has so many failings, believing, in my unliberated way, that I have a mission to regenerate and rejuvenate him and that caring for him is indeed the highest mission there is for any truly womanly woman. In short, I think of Joe as lovable because I have certain relevant desires with respect to him, to be with him, to care for him, to make him happy, etc. The judgmental element of my love (Joe is lovable because he is friendless, alone, unattractive, despicable, etc.) is not the *ground* of my love; it is rather the *consequence* of my pre-existing desires. I have a desire to regenerate and rejuvenate Joe, and hence I evaluate as lovable a man whom perhaps nobody else so evaluates: my desires directly determine my conception of my beloved. For the same reason they also determine whom I pick out as a lover in the first place: looking for a lonely, worthless man to cherish, I naturally warm to Joe.

I am aware that in saying that my desires *determine* how I think I am not speaking very precisely. What I mean to suggest, however, is that my desires are an important causally determining factor in how I conceive of things emotionally and may in extreme cases be the sole cause of how I think. Usually, of course, the way I think of something is determined in large part by the way it actually is, but our emotional conceptions are also determined by the way we want it to be and by the way we want things in general to be (i.e. our goals, interests, and values). In an extreme and obviously irrational case I may love a man in virtue of properties which I desire him to have (his "hidden virtues") but none of which he actually possesses. More normally, there is a mismatch to a greater or lesser degree between how we want something to be and how it actually is, and hence potentially a corresponding mismatch between an emotional conception of it and how it actually is. However, I do not mean to imply that we are always blinded by our emotions: even when the way things are is not consistent with the way I want things to be, I can always try to be dispassionate, i.e., to discount the effect of my desires, rather than allow my desires to determine how I conceive of things. And very often the way things are is consistent with the way I want things to be, and then my emotions appear to be rational. However, even if the way I conceive of a situation emotionally corresponds to the way things actually are, the history of my conception is different if it is emotional: it is my desires which play the most important causal role in determining how I think of the situation, and not the way the situation actually is.

Emotional conceptions are not merely determined by desires; they are also colored by desires in that they share some of the formal features of desires which I discussed earlier. Two emotional conceptions of something resist summing: if I both pity and envy Philip, then I have two inconsistent conceptions of him which I may not sum. I may think of him alternately as one who is suffering greatly (in a way I do not desire for myself) and as one who has an opportunity to exhibit Christian courage (which I do desire for myself). Secondly, as this example also shows, it is possible to entertain inconsistent conceptions of the same person or situation without being irrational: my two conceptions of Philip are both based on inconsistent but equally rational desires of mine. Moreover, as in the case of emotion and desire, one (or both) of two conceptions I hold about something may indeed be irrational. Perhaps some will say that my envy of Philip, who is dying a slow, painful, and lonely death is irrational. Thirdly, our emotional conceptions of things are resistant to change, just as the desires that determine them are resistant to change. I may continue to find Joe lovable for many years despite the ever-increasing evidence of his worthlessness. The fourth mark of desire and emotion which I distinguished is that both are susceptible to degrees of intensity, and this is not a property of conceptions any more than of judgments; only the desires that determine our conceptions can be more or less intense.

I have argued that the cognitive element in emotion is an emotional conception, i.e., a conception of something which is determined by and colored by our desires (goals, values, and interests). If I am right, then a number of puzzles about the emotions can be solved in a novel way.

1. Emotional reactions are not generalizable. Because my conception of Joe is governed by my desires with respect to Joe, it does not follow that I will have the same conception of anybody who has Joe's properties.[14] I love Joe because he is friendless and alone and has many failings, but I do not love everybody who has these properties: my desires to cherish and so forth are satisfied by my cherishing Joe. Moreover, far from loving everyone with a certain set of properties, I rather find lovable in my beloved properties I would find intolerable in anyone else. Thus, although John's belching disgusts me, I am amused by Joe's.[15]

2. My view explains why it is that "the same judgment" can be made either emotionally or impartially. I can judge impartially that John has wronged me. If, however, I am angry at John, then I think of him as wronging me and my so thinking of him is determined and colored by my desires. My thoughts have a different history and different formal properties from my impartial judgment.

3. More generally, if my account is right, we can see why the cognitive element in emotion might be thought to have some of the properties I discussed in section I of this paper. Since our emotional conception of something is determined by our desires, it may well be based on insufficient grounds, or, even if the grounds are sufficient, they may not have been well scrutinized. Again, it is not surprising that our emotional conceptions concern matters of great importance to us, since they are, as I have said, the product of our desires. None of these features of emotional conceptions marks them off from dispassionate judgments, but it is now easy to see why they might have been thought to.

The main objection to my view might be that I have got things back to front: it is not desires that determine judgments or conceptions, but judgments or conceptions that determine desires. For example, it would seem that when I am afraid of the approaching grizzly bear, I make a (dispassionate) judgment that it is dangerous, and I have a desire to escape from the danger, which is a *consequence* of that judgment. If I am right, however, even in this commonplace example, the reverse is true. If I am afraid of the bear, this entails that I have an intense desire to stay alive and unharmed and to avoid threatening situations, and it is these desires and goals that determine the way I think of the bear: I conceive of it as a threat to these deeply held desires. By contrast, if I am excited and exultant when I see the bear, then I may have the desires to court danger and test my courage which are more intense than my desire to stay alive and unharmed, and it is these desires and goals which determine how I think of the bear, as an opportunity for me to exercise my wits and courage. In both cases, I conceive of the bear as dangerous, but it is only if I have an intense desire to avoid danger that I am afraid: the conception does not cause the desire, but vice versa.

We can see this even more clearly in an irrational case of fear. Suppose, for example, that I am afraid of ladybugs. The standard view would be that I judge ladybugs to be dangerous and as a result of this (dispassionate?) judgment I want to avoid ladybugs. But this cannot be right, since as a matter of fact I do not judge ladybugs to be dangerous. Rather, no matter how hard I try, I cannot help *thinking* of ladybugs as dangerous (and hence acting as if they were) even though I judge them (dispassionately) to be harmless. If I am afraid of ladybugs then I have certain desires vis-à-vis ladybugs, and the way I think of them is determined by these desires.

IV

So far I have argued that the cognitive element in an emotion is a conception of something determined and colored by desires. The question now arises whether we can *identify* an emotion with this cognitive element; i.e., can we define having an emotion as having a conception of something that is both determined and colored by our desires?

To answer this question we need to make a distinction between a "standing" and an "occurrent" emotion.[16] It has often been pointed out that one can be in an emotional condition without actually doing or feeling anything right now: I may be in love with Joe, angry with Ruth, and contemptuous of Susan, but right now I am filling in my income tax return, and none of these "standing" emotional conditions is "occurrent." By contrast if I am turning purple and yelling at Ruth, we say I am in an occurrent state of anger.[17] Now, it seems clear that having a certain conception of something, which is determined by our desires in the way I have suggested, is a necessary condition for having an emotion either in a standing or occurrent sense. But is it sufficient for either?

My answer is that normally it is not sufficient for either, but that it may be in certain cases. If, for example, I am in a standing condition of love for Joe, then normally I do not merely think of him in a certain way and have certain desires with respect to him: I normally behave in a certain way too, and typically I also experience certain feelings, and undergo certain physiological responses. But suppose I am in a standing condition of *nostalgia* for Paris. This may mean simply that I have a certain conception of Paris, which is the product of my desires vis-à-vis Paris; I wish I could return to the Paris of yesteryear and be young again; I wish things now were as rosy as they then seemed, etc. etc. I may never *do* anything out of nostalgia or even have a tendency to do anything. I never undergo any physiological changes or their accompanying bodily sensations. I simply have a tendency to think certain thoughts.

What then counts as an occurrent state of my nostalgia? William Lyons, who places great weight on the distinction between occurrent and standing emotion, seems to suggest that the relevant occurrence is always an abnormal physiological change of some kind (see note 6), but in my example, I never undergo such changes. Surely the truth is that the relevant occurrence may be of several different kinds: when I am in an occurrent state of nostalgia, all I do is think certain thoughts about Paris, thoughts which have their origin in my desires, interests, values, and goals. Similarly, if I am in an occurrent state of contempt, I may exhibit contemptuous behavior, feel certain feelings or, less likely, experience certain physiological changes, but I may simply think "What a contemptible fellow!" What makes this a *contemptuous* thought is its history, the fact that it originated in the particular desires, interests, etc. that I have.

My conclusion, then, is that having a conception colored and determined by desire may be both necessary and sufficient for the presence of a standing emotion and is always at least necessary. Furthermore, in certain very "bare" cases of occurrent emotion, the occurrence in question may be nothing more than the having of a thought that expresses this conception, always provided that the thought has the right history.

Notes

1 To be presented in an APA Symposium of the same title, December 29 1983. Robert C. Solomon will comment; his comments are not available at this time.

2 The word 'appraisal' is used by Magda Arnold in, for example, "Human Emotion and Action," in T. Mischel, ed., *Human Action: Conceptual and Empirical Issues* (New York: Academic Press, 1969), and by R.S. Peters in, for example, "Emotions and the Category of Passivity," *Proceedings of the Aristotelian Society*, suppl. Vol. LXII (1961/2).

3 There is a large literature on emotions and objects. See in particular, William Alston, "Emotion and Feeling," *Encyclopedia of Philosophy*, vol. 2, Paul Edwards, ed. (New York: Collier-Macmillan, 1969); Anthony Kenny, *Action, Emotion and Will* (London: Routledge & Kegan Paul, 1963); and J.C. Gosling, "Emotion and Object," *Philosophical Review*, LXXIV, 4 (October 1965): 486-503.

4 In his discussion of feelings, Gilbert Ryle allows that there may be a "tinge of metaphor" in our talk of feelings where there is none in our talk of sensations; see *The Concept of Mind* (London: Hutchinson, 1949): 82.

5   The remoter causes may include a person's interests, values, etc.

6   "Emotions," reprinted in D. Gustafson, ed., *Essays in Philosophical Psychology* (London: Macmillan, 1967): 86. Bedford's conclusions from the example are not quite the same as mine.

7   William Lyons argues at length that an ("occurrent") emotion should be identified with an abnormal physiological state caused by the subject's evaluation of his or her situation; see *Emotion* (New York: Cambridge, 1980); parenthetical page references to Lyons are to this book.

8   New York: Doubleday, 1976. 187.

9   Solomon, "Emotions and Choice," reprinted in Amelie Rorty, ed. *Explaining Emotions* (Berkeley: University of California Press, 1980), 258.

10 *The Passions*, 188.

11 "Emotions and Choice," 264.

12 "A Case of Mixed Feelings: Ambivalence and the Logic of Emotion," in Rorty, ed. *op. cit.*, p. 234. I have paraphrased her example, changing some minor and irrelevant features. Parenthetical page references to Greenspan are to this article.

13 Throughout the paper I examine connections between emotion and desire, a word I use to stand for both wishes and wants, both forward-looking and backward-looking desires. Later I shall talk about values, goals, and interests in the same breath as desires. It seems to me that these three concepts are closely related to the concept of desire and may be analyzable in terms of it.

14 Compare Ronald de Sousa's remarks on the "nonfungibility" of love, "Self-Deceptive Emotions," reprinted in Rorty, 292-94.

15 William Lyons disagrees. He argues that if, say, John loves Frieda "because he believes that she is shy, and that shy people are generally speaking more kind and affectionate than extroverts," then it follows that John will love anyone insofar as she (he?) is shy. Lyons argues by analogy: "Surely my finding Ferguson intensely irritating because he belches constantly will be evidence that I will quite likely be irritated with anyone who belches constantly" (73-4). Lyons' account ignores the fact that at the heart of love are not evaluations based on properties of the beloved, but desires directed toward a beloved individual: it is our desires which dictate what properties we find lovable and not vice versa.

16 For this distinction, see Lyons 53-57.

17 A great many things sometimes go by the name of "standing" emotions, not just love, anger, contempt, and so on but character traits (anxious, irascible, kindly), moral qualities (courageous, indolent, vain), qualities of mind (sentimental, ironic) etc. Ryle even includes an interest in symbolic logic as an example of an emotion. It is not clear that all these involve having a conception of something determined by desires, but some of them, such as character traits, certainly do.

PSYCHIC FEELINGS:
THEIR IMPORTANCE AND IRREDUCIBILITY

Michael Stocker

SECTION 1: THE IMPORTANCE AND THE NATURE OF PSYCHIC FEELINGS

Much of contemporary philosophical psychology is inadequate, and pathologically so. It omits, denies, or radically misunderstands affectivity or feeling. Thus, it comes at least close to depicting people as dissociated, detached, depersonalised, hollow, or perhaps even as schizophrenic or psychopathic.

In this paper, I shall begin to remedy this inadequate depiction by beginning a discussion of psychic feelings—one area of affectivity. In particular, I focus on the psychic feelings of care, concern, and interest. I emphasise 'begin.' For the topics involved—even only those concerning these psychic feelings—are vast and complicated ones, involving many of the areas and problems of philosophical and moral psychology.

Concentrating on care, concern, and interest, I here begin a better understanding of the psyche. My plan is as follows: I shall take it as given that we cannot understand the human psyche without imputing desire and reason, including belief, to it. But in addition, I shall argue, we must impute affectivity to it. For, first, a depiction of our psyche without affectivity either is incomplete or is a depiction of a radically deficient, perhaps even a pathological person. Second, desire and reason, themselves, cannot be understood without imputing affectivity either to them or to the psyche. Third, affectivity cannot be understood in terms of reason and desire.[1]

If these claims about affectivity are not denied by contemporary philosophers, neither are they endorsed. What is notable, rather, is the absence of discussion of affectivity, much less of the relations between it and reason and desire. This is true of near enough all contemporary philosophical psychologies, not only belief-desire or functionalist ones, which alone might seem the target of this paper.[2]

The importance of affectivity can easily be presented. So consider this passage by R. Angell, which so nicely depicts what happens to at least many people:

Even those of us who have not been spoiled by ... the fulfilment of the wild expectations of our early youth are aware of a humdrum, twilight quality to all our doings in middle life, however successful they may prove to be. There is a loss of light and ease and early joy, and we look to other exemplars—mentors and philosophers ... —to sustain us in that loss.[3]

It is obvious that the psychic feelings of light and ease and early joy, as well as those of a humdrum, twilight quality are important. So too, it is obvious that we are concerned that those we love and care for be interested in what they do, and that they care for those they live and work with. We are also concerned that they hold and act upon their values with care, concern, and interest.

Indeed, psychic feelings are necessary, though by no means sufficient, for a good life. Without them, one's life, including one's life of action, is certain to be marred by such maladies of the spirit as meaninglessness, emptiness, dissociation, ennui, accidie, spiritual weakness, and tiredness.[4] In short, a life deficient in such feelings is a deficient life. (To be sure, it would at least often be better that evil people, insofar as they remain evil, lack these feelings and, thus, not be interested in, full of care and concern for, their evil activities.) Further, it is obvious that the feelings characteristic of melancholy and depression are to be avoided. However, the total lack of feeling, totally flat affect, as found in such psychotic states as extreme depersonalisation, is also— probably even more—to be avoided.

Thus, I take it to be obvious both that we have what I call psychic feelings and also that they are essential for at least various forms of a good or even a tolerable life, and for various sorts of bad lives.[5] Any theory of the psyche which denies, omits, or misunderstands such feelings will, therefore, be inadequate both descriptively and evaluatively. Thus, to take only one point of particular current interest: if theories of artificial intelligence do not allow for psychic feelings, their models of the mind will fit, indifferently, a radically deficient, even pathological, mind, and a healthy mind. (Whether, given their goals, this is a criticism of such theories is not in question here.)

Even granting that psychic feelings are important, it may be wondered why I call them psychic, not, say, bodily; and why I call them feelings, not, say, emotions, moods, or attitudes. The entire paper is occupied with these questions. Sketching their answers should, thus, help to introduce my principal concerns.

As a start to explaining why these are called psychic, not bodily, let us recall what Descartes says about emotions or passions, which contain what I call psychic feelings: '... we feel as though they were in the soul itself.'[6] This is to contrast those feelings with bodily ones, which, as he says, 'we relate to our body, or some of its parts ... which we perceive as though they were in our members.' Related to this distinction are the distinctions between what the feelings are about and what we must understand in order to understand the content and the genesis of the feelings or of the activity giving rise to them.

The connections between psychic and bodily feelings need to be explored; but in another work. (Similarly, the connections between psychic feelings and the body—e.g., whether they require a body—need to be explored; but in another work.) Some feelings do seem both bodily and psychic: e.g., some of those involved in sexual desire, in the exultation of climbing a difficult cliff, and in certain forms of disorientation and tension. On the other hand, it does not seem that being interested in a philosophy problem, say, need involve any bodily feelings. (Cf. n. 10.)

Notwithstanding the complex relations between psychic and bodily feelings, we can and should here concentrate solely on psychic feelings or psychic aspects of feelings. First, their nature qua psychic needs elucidation. Second, it is heuristically important to focus on psychic, non-bodily feelings or aspects. (Henceforth, I will not distinguish between psychic feeling and psychic aspects of feelings.) For many philosophers simply identify feelings with wholly bodily feelings. So, for example, one influential line runs that since bodily feelings are conceptually irrelevant to emotions, feelings as such are conceptually irrelevant to them.[7] As suggested above, the premise may well be false. As we will see below, the conclusion is, in fact, false.

The second question was why call these feelings, rather than emotions, moods, or attitudes. (Henceforth, by 'feeling' I will mean 'psychic feeling,' unless otherwise made clear.) This question cannot be answered adequately now. First, it involves the details of the paper far more intimately than even the previous question. Second, it requires an adequate understanding of the distinctions among emotions, moods, and attitudes. (This paper is intended also as a contribution to advancing that understanding.) The best I can now say in reply to that second question is that psychic feelings must themselves be understood if we are to understand emotions, moods, and attitudes. Whether, after this, we will see that, in some sense or other, psychic feelings are, or may be likened to, emotions, moods or attitudes need not delay us now.[8]

Why I say that psychic feelings must be understood to understand emotions, moods, and attitudes can be brought out by noting a point made by Aristotle and Wm. James. In *Rhetoric* II, 2, Aristotle characterises anger in terms not only of the rational and the conative, but also the affective: pain. To be angry, I must be pained by the thought of being wronged, and I must intend to retaliate.[9] James, of course, not only requires bodily feelings for strong emotions, such as rage, he holds that the emotions actually are the bodily feelings. Nonetheless, I will borrow his words about feelings and—where he says that without bodily feelings—I will say that without psychic feelings, such as care, concern or interest, there is no rage, but only, for example,

> some cold-blooded and dispassionate judicial sentence confined entirely to the intellectual realm, to the effect that a certain person or persons deserve chastisement for their sins.[10]

In these ways, then, psychic feelings are essential for anger and rage. Further, the intensity of psychic feelings is at least one of the important differentiae between anger and rage; and it is one of the important determinants of the waxing or waning of the one into the other. So too, for other emotions, moods, and attitudes: without psychic feelings, there would be, e.g., only cold-blooded thought or desire; and there would not be the differences between other emotions, moods, and attitudes, which differ in intensity, such as fear and terror; nor would there be at least some of the waxings and wanings of emotions, moods, and attitudes.[11]

Investigating these matters would involve a study of the 'laws' of the affinities and vicissitudes of feelings: e.g., of how at least some feelings have a life of their own, seeking out certain objects to colour, while shunning other objects. But these issues, though necessary for a complete understanding of feelings, are beyond our present concern.

So far, it has been shown that feelings are important. It must now be shown that feelings cannot be understood in terms of desire and reason, and also that without feelings, desire and reason themselves cannot be understood. To do this, I shall first consider some simple non-eliminative would-be reductions of feeling to desire and reason. Eliminative reductions are not explicitly discussed here. However, they are shown to be mistaken first, by the importance and thus the reality of the feelings considered here, and second, by the arguments against non-eliminative reductions. Those reductions are, in sec. 2, a reduction of feeling to desire, and in sec. 3, to reason. These reductions fail either by omitting feeling or by circularly invoking it. In short, they are either feelingless or circularly feeling-laden. In sec. 4, I argue that the failures of these simple attempts are in no important way due to their simplicity, but are rather due to their failing to acknowledge the irreducibility of feelings.

That these claims about understanding and irreducibility do not depend on any special, problematic notions of understanding or reducibility will, I trust, become clear. I intend this paper to be as neutral as possible on issues concerning these notions. Similarly, I intend this paper to be as neutral as possible on such issues of philosophical psychology as materialism and functionalism. All I intend this paper to do in regard to these various issues is to help make clear some phenomena that any credible theory must account for.

Having set out what I intend to show and what I do not intend to show, it is important to set out my methodology. I present cases of what I take to be clear and important examples of feelings or feeling-laden states and then argue that both the presence and the nature of these feelings are omitted or only circularly included by the reductions considered. As will become clear—and as may already be clear from my discussion of Angell, Aristotle, and James—it is difficult, if not impossible, to give a proof, i.e. a conclusive proof, that feelings are important or that they are omitted. All that can be done, I think, is what I here try to do: offer examples, with discussion, which show these points.

In what follows, I shall use the following provisional typology of psychic feelings. First, there are those which seem objectless and at least primarily characterise the psyche: e.g. being excited, full of mental or psychological energy, having high spirits or *thumos* (as in *Republic*, 439 ff). Second, there are those which take an object, and are thus about the 'world': e.g. being excited by or interested in something. Third, there are those which are about, and even seem to be in, the world: e.g. seeing that something is interesting. There are important and difficult connections among these sorts of feelings. So for example, it seems that I can see that something is interesting with or without being interested in it and with or without being full of interest or excitement. A full account of these relations must wait for another work. Here, my concern is to show that feelings are important and irreducible, and I use and discuss this provisional typology only to further this end.

SECTION 2: IRREDUCIBILITY TO DESIRE

Desire is clearly and intimately connected with feeling. For example, to care for someone involves a desire to be with or benefit that person. But the question for us is not about connections. It is, rather, about the reducibility of feeling to desire.

Let us start with feelings about cognitive matters—feelings of, or connected with, attention, perception, and the like. Interest in something, finding it interesting and attractive, may well seem to be a form of desire. As a first approximation, to be interested in what one is seeing would be to desire to continue to see it. To care for philosophy, say, would be to want to engage in it and engage in it well, perhaps to advance it or simply to understand it. To be excited by philosophy would be to have strong and insistent desires of the sort just mentioned.[12]

Objectless forms of feeling might also seem understandable in terms of desire. High spiritedness and excitement would perhaps be understood in terms of the quantity and quality of desires; so too, would their contraries, such as boredom, low spiritedness, and the like.

The move towards understanding feelings in terms of desire is made even more attractive once the role of desire in various emotions is seen: Fear involves the desire to flee; anger, the desire to retaliate; love, the desire to possess or benefit. And it might seem reasonable to hold that at least part of the feeling associated with any of these emotions simply is the relevant desire(s). Pleasures and pains are also reasonably thought to be among the feeling components of emotions. Following well-known moves, they might be thought to be characterisable in terms of what we desire to get or to avoid. Such characterisations of pleasure and pain are discussed at the end of this section, after a general discussion of desire and feeling.

These suggested reductions are only first approximations. But they may well be attractive. Indeed, once it is also seen how important desire is in other accounts of the mental and of human life and action—in, e.g., desire plus belief psychologies—this reductive move might seem not only attractive, but near enough to being irresistible.

But, as I shall now argue, we cannot understand such feelings in terms of desire—unless desire is taken as itself possessing an irreducible element of feeling.[13] To show this, I will sketch a general and, I think, current view of desire. I shall argue that precisely because it does not hold that feeling is an irreducible element of desire, we cannot understand feeling in terms of such desire. As I shall note below, that view of desire may also be inadequate as an understanding of desire itself—again, precisely because it does not hold that feeling is an irreducible part of desire.

I shall call this the explanatory-theoretical account of desire. For it understands desire as what, perhaps along with belief, explains or gives direction to, or energy for, action. It is the notion of desire which comes out as, or can be understood as given by, preferences and preference functions. This, then, is desire from the 'inside.' From the 'outside,' desires or desired objects are what the being or thing in question goes after, seeks, overcomes obstacles to get, protects, and so on. Among theorists who use such a notion of desire, we find H. Putnam in 'The Mental Life of Some Machines,'[14] D.M. Armstrong in *A Materialist Theory of the Mind*,[15] D. Davidson in 'Belief and the Basis of Meaning,'[16] B. Aune in *Reason and Action*,[17] and many others, especially those who subscribe to a belief-desire psychology.

To show the explanatory-theoretical account of desire inadequate, both for an understanding of feelings and also for an understanding of desire itself, I shall start by examining a special case of that account. I call this special case the biological-functional account, for it, or some of its main forms, can be most easily taken as trying to understand desire in terms of the biological function of desire. Such an understanding is offered by various contemporary theorists. But it will be useful—if only to show that not only we moderns make errors about desire—to consider Spinoza. He writes that the mind

> ... endeavours to persist in its own being, and that for an indefinite time ... This endeavour when referred solely to the mind is called *will*, when referred to the mind and body in conjunction it is called appetite.... Further ... desire is generally applied to men, in so far as they are conscious of their appetites, and may accordingly be thus defined: *Desire is appetite with consciousness thereof.*[18]

Why I call this a biological-functional account should be clear enough. Putting it briefly: of natural necessity, people desire their own self-preservation or perfection. Indeed, that seems to explain both what desire is and why we have it. Self-preservation and perfection, often taken as basic and ineluctable sources of motivation, are too well-known to need comment here. And the connections between feeling and these concerns for self seem obvious. What could be felt as more important, more moving or interesting for people than their own wellbeing or existence? What could be more vivid than what conduces, or what one believes to conduce, to one's own wellbeing or existence?

But these connections with feeling are given neither by the notion of desire as here characterised nor by the notion of feeling.[19] To see this, we should note two points. First, we can conceive of people who do not care for or about their own wellbeing or existence. Such people might well, therefore, not find life-improving or preserving things interesting or vivid. This claim, however, is not decisive. For even if it is right, all that is shown is that self-preservation and perfection need not interest a person, need not evoke, be the object of, desire. Perhaps for all that, interest in something simply is a desire for it.

However, this is mistaken. For—and this is the second point—a being can seek things including his own wellbeing, without feeling. It need not be interested in, moved by, care for or about, be concerned with the things it seeks. To avoid a suggestion of contradiction, my point would be better put this way: Simply seeking one's own wellbeing might be held to be, as such, a sort of care, concern, interest, or the like. Machines such as lathes which look after themselves— e.g. monitor and tend to their supply of oil—might in this sense be called self-tending machines. Perhaps, too, in this sense they could be said to be interested in, concerned about, or care for their own wellbeing. Nonetheless, of such machines at least, we can hold that they need not have feeling-laden concern, interest, and care. Their interests do not interest them, even though they serve their interests with great success and assiduity. So too, lower animals, e.g. protozoa, can be said to care for themselves in the sense that they seek food, avoid harm, and the like. But we need not ascribe feeling-laden interest, care, or concern to them.

These examples also show that feeling cannot be characterised in terms of feelingless action. Perhaps these machines and lower animals can be said to engage in self-caring action— seeking food, avoiding harm, and the like. From this it might well follow that their actions can be called caring, concerned or interested. So too, they may strive harder for one goal than another. From this it might well follow that they can be said to care more or be more concerned or interested in one goal or another. Nonetheless, we need not ascribe feeling-laden interest, care or concern to such acts. Nor, therefore, need we invoke feelings to develop an energetics of desire. Since, if this is correct, the attempt to characterise feeling in terms of action introduces no essentially new options or problems, I shall henceforth largely ignore the clearly important relations between feeling and action.

Consideration of these machines and lower animals shows that there are both feeling-laden and feelingless forms of care, concern and interest. Thus, feeling cannot be located simply by care, concern and interest, but only by feeling-laden instances of them. This, first, heightens the need for a general characterisation of feeling—a task beyond this paper. Second, it makes even clearer and more justified the methodology and the task of this paper. It shows how essential clear examples of feeling are and how essential it is to show that feeling is irreducible. It does both of these by showing, once again, that 'states' characterised in terms of feelingless desire can be feelingless or feeling-laden.[20]

It might be objected that the above examples work in my favour only because they are devoid of awareness (a form of reason). The thought here is that were a machine or lower animal aware of seeking and attaining its own preservation or enhancement, then the seeking and attaining would be feeling-laden: with awareness, there would be feeling-laden care, concern and interest. I think that, when restricted to machines and lower animals, simple inspection shows this claim to be mistaken.

More to the point, however, a similar claim about people is mistaken. It is conceptually possible for people knowingly to seek and attain their preservation or enhancement, even under those descriptions, where the seeking, the prospect, and the attainment of what is sought are all feelingless.[21] This is not merely conceptually possible. We can meet people who feel nothing about taking care of themselves. As is well known, it is characteristic of various sorts of neurotics and psychotics to complain that they feel nothing about such things.[22]

There is a familiar response to such claims: The people do have the feelings in question, but—e.g., because of blocking, denial, repression,...—they are not fully or even partially aware of having them. This response is often grounded in a psychological theory which would deny my suggestion that it is psychologically possible not to be interested in the life-enhancing things one is seeking or in the seeking of them. But this disagreement is unimportant. For the response agrees with my point that there is a conceptual gap between people seeking something, even what is life-enhancing, and their being interested in it or the seeking: The seeking is not the same as the interest even if they are necessarily connected—even if, for example, we could not seek such things without interest.

The point here is perfectly general. It might be that humans cannot, e.g., do a certain feelinglessly characterisable act unless we also have a certain feeling or feeling-laden property. But this would be absolutely no objection to my claim if, as in this case, the impossibility is due to the fact that in such situations we must have feelings: where, first, that connection is licensed by an essentially feeling-laden psychological theory; and second, the interpretive or explanatory feeling-laden features of the theory are not, in turn, reducible to feelingless ones. (Cf. n. 19 and sec. 4 where this issue also arises.)

Here we should pause to note that this objection allows for psychic feelings which people are not fully or even partially aware of having. Awareness of one's feelings can, I suggest, range from full reflective and attentive awareness, to a clear but non-attentive awareness, through dim or confused awareness, to total unawareness. This raises difficult general issues about feeling and also about awareness, e.g. its connections with attention and reflection. But to show that feelings are irreducible, these issues need not be settled, nor need it even be allowed that one can be less than fully aware of one's feelings. Therefore, I will make only a brief comment on how these issues bear on our question.

Allowing for feelings we are not aware of having helps make it clear that the distinction between pairs of feeling-laden and feelingless correlates—e.g., interested care and interestless care—is not the same as that between (occurrently) experiencing a feeling or emotion and only (perhaps dispositionally) having it. By the latter pair, I have in mind what is exemplified in the following: Even though I am still angry—'have anger'—about your taking the car, since I am now not thinking about it, I am now not feeling angry—'experiencing anger.' Both experiencing and having anger involve feeling.

Were that not so, there would be no difference between a person who merely has anger, though is not experiencing it, and a person who has, perhaps not occurrently but dispositionally, only the thoughts and desires that help constitute anger. There are important reasons for distinguishing between such people, not the least of which is to account for important occurrent conscious and unconscious differences between them. Consciously, the angry person may act differently, e.g. walk stiffly; and may have feeling-laden, though not angry, ways of seeing people, e.g. as distasteful. Unconsciously, the person may have highly charged, repressed, hostile intentions. Thus, neither form of feeling-laden anger is reducible to feelingless desire, i.e. to desire as that notion is given by biological-functional account. (So too, of course, for other emotions and their 'component' feelings.)

The general case of the explanatory-theoretical account of desire can now be dealt with summarily. Remember, in essence such an account understands desire simply as what explains, gives direction to, or energy for, action. Thus, insofar as the biological-functional account of desire is feelingless, so is the explanatory-theoretical one. For there is no essential difference between them in this regard. This is at least suggested by the fact that the two accounts of desire come together in various accounts of the teleological activities of lower animals, plants, and even non-living things. And, as I trust is clear, feeling need not be invoked to allow for such teleologically-characterised desire or goal-seeking.

If I am right, then on either the biological-functional account or the explanatory-theoretical account of desire, Angell's people of middle years could still have, and have in the same ways, the desires and goals they had when young. But on the contrary, it is clear that even if they still have the

desire or on the being with such a desire. Considerations which allow us to admit that there can be a feelingless desire should also allow us to hold that fulfilling such a desire need involve no feeling at all, much less hedonic feeling. Similarly, considerations which allow us to hold that a being can have a feelingless desire should also allow us to hold that the being could fulfil that desire without any feeling at all, much less hedonic feeling.

If this very brief sketch of an argument does point the way to the truth, then we see that accounts of the hedonic in terms of the conative must use a notion of feeling-laden desire. This would not be circular. For, pleasure, enjoyment, pain are not the whole of feeling. But it is inadequate. It founders on the heterogeneity of feeling. My argument for this would pursue the following lines: Desire cannot be laden with just any feeling, if those accounts are to succeed. For example, fascination (or the feelings it involves) and interest do not fit the bill. People can be interested in, even morbidly fascinated by, what they find repulsive, disgusting, horrible, evil,... precisely because of what makes it such. Consider the tale in the *Republic* (439) about Leonitus', or his eyes', desire to see the corpses. Or consider the attention-seizing quality of some physical deformities. Here we have feeling-laden desire to see something for its own sake. But there need not be any pleasure or enjoyment in the seeing or in what is seen. So too, one may, without enjoyment or pleasure, but with interest, want to do, and indeed do, for its own sake what one believes to be one's duty, e.g. care for the wounded.[28]

Without here continuing the argument, I suggest that similar considerations show that pleasure or enjoyment is the feeling with which desire must be laden, if satisfying such desire is to be sufficient for pleasure or enjoyment. Thus my conclusion that conative accounts of the hedonic either omit the relevant feeling or are circular. Thus also my conclusion that there are mutually irreducible feelings.[29]

SECTION 3: IRREDUCIBILITY TO REASON

Let us now turn to attempts to understand feelings in terms of reason. I shall examine two inter-related sorts of attempts. The first takes feelings to be understandable in terms of how we see or understand the world. The second takes feelings to be judgements, questions, imagined scenes, and the like. I will argue that attempted reductions of feelings to these forms of reason either omit feeling or are circular. I shall not discuss, but only raise, the question of whether there are or can be feelingless forms of reason. (I believe reason is understood as being feelingless, at least by many contemporary philosophers. But I shall not pursue this here.)

There are important connections between various forms or occurrences of feeling and reason. These connections show, first, that psychic feelings are not totally arational, the way, say, an ache in a muscle is. Second, they show that feeling is not simply a matter of, not reducible to, desire, whether feelingless or feeling-laden. These important theoretical points will not be pursued here. For our present question is whether feeling is reducible to reason.

To examine that issue, let us now turn to some cases of connections between feeling and reason. So for example, when one is interested in something, its presence or absence may be especially vivid. At a party, the hungry person's eye may be captured by the food, the collector's eye by the antique rugs, the lubricious person's eye by sexual possibilities; and to one possessed by universal enthusiasm—as children and mystics from time to time are— 'everything' is seen vividly, 'everything' captures the imagination. In short, then, attention and interest seem conceptually connected.[30] So too, when one is concerned to get someplace in a hurry, slow drivers by the dozens seem to vie with each other to block the way. And when in a bad mood, many ordinarily unnoticed things come to the fore with insistent force.

Further, as argued by Heidegger, Sartre, and others, various features we see in the world are 'created' by our interests. So a mountain is (seen as) an obstacle only for someone wanting to get beyond it. A piece of metal is a screwdriver because of its uses. And uses have importantly to do with interests.

Sartre's general account of emotions in his *Sketch for a Theory of the Emotions* and also in *Being and Nothingness* is couched in terms of the world's being seen in various determinate ways. This seems correct for at least many emotions, moods, and attitudes. So, for example, depression involves seeing the world as being 'not for you.' Jealousy involves interpreting incidents jealously.

We get an idea of what philosophers mean when they suggest—and why they suggest— that feelings and emotions are understandable in terms of more discursive or propositional forms of reason in various recent articles: e.g. E. Bedford's 'Emotions,' G. Pitcher's 'Emotion,' R. Solomon's 'Emotions and Choice,' and J. Neu's 'Jealous Thoughts.'[31] So Bedford is concerned to deny the importance, indeed the role, of feelings in emotions, arguing instead that emotions are to be considered a complex of belief, evaluation, and action. Pitcher argues similarly, explicitly denying that emotions require, or often even have, feelings—or sensations, as he calls physical or mental sensations or feelings. He writes,

> If P hopes that she will come today, he simply believes she might come and considers that her coming would be a good thing. He may also experience one or more sensations, but he need not; and even if he does it is doubtful that they will be part of his *hope*. (p. 338)

In 'Emotions and Choice,' Solomon concludes that 'emotions are judgements' (p. 257), holding e.g., 'My anger *is* my judgement that John has wronged me.' (p. 258) In 'Jealous Thoughts,' Neu writes that

... the lover of a patient of a psychoanalyst may always raise the questions: 'What is missing?,' 'What is the analyst providing that I cannot?,' 'Are there things that my lover can say to her analyst that she cannot say to me?,' and so on. (pp. 431-32)

Having set the stage, he immediately adds what is crucial for us:

To imagine the elimination of jealousy is to imagine the elimination of the possibility of these questions, for these questions *are* jealousy. To have these doubts and worries is to be jealous. (Jealousy is not a sensation or a headache, it is in its essence a set of thoughts and questions, doubts and fears.) (p. 432)

One must agree that making certain judgements, asking certain questions, and having certain thoughts are importantly connected with, perhaps are constituents of, certain feelings, emotions, and the like. However, the question for us is not one about connections or about some constituents. It is, rather, about the reducibility of feeling to these or other forms of reason. I do not think such reductions work—unless the forms of reason are, themselves, feeling-laden.

Three sorts of psychic feelings were mentioned at the outset: feelings of the person, e.g. being full of interest; feelings of the world, e.g. being interested in the world; and feelings in the world, e.g. seeing the world to be interesting. In what follows, I shall concentrate on the second and third sorts. But the arguments used to show that they are not reducible to feelingless reason also show this of the first sort of feeling. In ways shown below, the second and third sorts of feelings are naturally allied to different forms of reason. Put in terms of seeing, feelings of the world are naturally allied with ways of seeing the world, e.g. seeing it with interest. Feelings in the world are naturally allied with ways the world is seen to be, e.g. seeing it to be interesting. However, since I am concerned with both sorts of feelings, there is now no need to distinguish between them or between those forms of reason.

Let us start with the relations between interest and attention, e.g. the hungry person's attention to, vivid seeing of, the food. Certainly, if the person did not notice—or having noticed, did not pay attention to—the food, that might make us question the person's interest in food and thus the hunger. (Here we put aside complexities such as those involved in a person's deliberately averting attention from what is attractive—as a hungry dieter might do.) As I shall now argue, however, feeling is not reducible to feelingless reason.

I may pay attention to something, indeed it can fill up my whole field of attention. Nonetheless, I need not be interested in it and I need not find it to be interesting. Here I am thinking not only of what one may do when bored—e.g. pass or kill time by watching a wretched and uninteresting programme on television, perhaps only to keep one's mind off how boring everything is. I am thinking also of how a person may become through and through occupied with details in a way which merits calling both the involvement and the details mechanical or merely habitual. The details and what they are details of—a job, a personal relationship, or whatever—may well fill one's attention without one's being interested in or by them or what they are details of. Perhaps they were once interesting, which may have accounted for their then filling one's attention. But now only their attention-filling remains.

Shifts in ways of seeing also go the other way, of course. So, having fallen on the ice, the very same knowledge of (and wishes to avoid) the dangers of walking on ice are 'emotionally present' to me. They concern me to the point of my being afraid. Before the fall, I had, as is said, only an intellectual appreciation of the very same dangers (and a rather pro forma desire to avoid them). Then I only saw the dangers, now I also feel them.

For a related sort of case, which emphasises 'categories' of understanding rather than objects of attention, consider a person who has become used to and continues to use categories of understanding and perception, even after interest, care and concern have gone. So for example, jaded aesthetes, now uninterested in matters of taste, beauty, and so on, may still pay attention to the things they used to, and may still see, categorise, and understand the world in the ways they did when passionately interested and caught up in the aesthetic. So too, people whose jealousy has burned out may continue to put jealous constructions on innocent goings-on, may still make their lovers give accounts of time spent apart, and so on. But now they do this without care, concern or interest. One natural way to put this is that though they still see the same things, they are no longer touched by them, they are no longer open to them.

As just seen, the possibility of a gap between reason—e.g. ways of seeing—and feeling does not depend on the extensiveness of the ambit of the reason. Fear of walking on ice is very localised; jealousy is also localised, involving seeing only a small part of the world in a particular way. But aestheticism or seeing the world aesthetically can extend to, near enough, one's entire world. Nonetheless, here too, there is a conceptual gap between reason and feeling: one may continue to see aesthetically, but no longer care. So too, Sartre's explicitly world-encompassing ways of seeing the world instrumentally or magically admit of this gap between reason and feeling. Sartre characterises emotionality in terms of seeing the world magically as opposed to instrumentally. However, one can see the world magically or as magical, but have no emotions or feelings at all. The magical might be too commonplace or one might be too stolid to be moved by it. Correlatively, the world seen instrumentally or as being instrumental might be seen with, or seen as having, various sorts of emotions (and associated feelings) such as loneliness or awe.[32]

For these various reasons, then, I conclude that feeling cannot be understood in terms of the sorts of feelingless reason we have been considering.[33] Indeed, as seen, some of the forms of reason which are so essential, say, to emotions—e.g. seeing the world jealously, or more generally with interest— are feeling-laden, not feelingless.

Let us now return to the attempts to understand feelings in terms of the more discursive forms of reason—i.e. in terms of judgments, questions, and the like. Drawing on the above argument, we can easily see that there is a feelingless way to take these forms of reason, but that so taken they cannot be used to reduce feeling, or the feeling aspects of emotion, to reason. So a person may make the judgment 'I have been betrayed' or ask the question 'Have I been betrayed?' or have the vision of the betrayal clearly in mind, but for all that not be jealous. For each of these cognitive goings-on is compatible with not caring about—and also not being concerned with or interested by— being betrayed. The person might be, as is said, all played out. Similarly, P might make Pitcher's judgements, but because P does not care whether she comes, not hope she does, P might be, for example, a parent coolly contemplating the arrival of a child's friend. (It cannot be objected on Pitcher's behalf that evaluations, e.g. 'her coming would be a good thing,' are feeling-laden. For then, on his view, hope and presumably other emotions would be feeling-laden.) So too, one might make Solomon's judgment about John, but because one does not care about being wronged by him, not be angry at him.

To be sure, judgments, questions, scenes, can be taken as essentially involving feeling: The judgments can be made, the questions asked, the scenes imagined, out of care, concern or interest, e.g. out of jealousy, hope or anger. Only when feeling-laden do these judgments, questions, and scenes seem even close to being the jealousy, hope, or anger.[34] But for the reasons advanced in regard to feeling-laden desire, feelings cannot be reduced to feeling-laden reason—precisely because such reason is feeling-laden.

To conclude this section, let us note another parallel between it and the previous one. There it was suggested that there are feeling-laden desires— e.g. full-blooded ones. It was left open whether there are feelingless ones. Here it has been suggested that there are feeling-laden forms of reason. It has been left open whether there are feelingless ones. So for example, I have not discussed whether we can give a feelingless account of the assent needed for belief.

If all forms of reason, or even if only those of belief, are feeling-laden, this would bear on many issues, e.g. ethical cognitivism. But I do not here wish to discuss such issues.[35] To do this, we would need to go beyond the scope of this paper. We would need an account of the relevant notions of reason—e.g. of understanding, conceptual connections, knowledge—that figure in these disputes. As well, we would need an account of how the relevant forms of reason are feeling-laden.[36]

SECTION 4: IRREDUCIBILITY TO MORE COMPLEX ACCOUNTS

My arguments so far have been directed against extremely simple and briefly-sketched reductive accounts. A natural objection would be to ask about more complex ones. After all, it seems easy enough to discern people's feelings by noting a 'large enough slice' of their desires, beliefs, bodily and behavioural goings-on.

Since the more sophisticated accounts, such as those that would make use of large-scale descriptions, have yet to be propounded, it seems difficult to assess them. Thus, the following are meant only as some reasons why I think my arguments tell against complex reductive accounts too.

First, let us agree that we can discern what feelings people have by noting a large enough slice of their life, even if it is described feelinglessly. It is difficult to imagine a person with no feelings or feelings quite different from ours if that person has, or is said to have, the same interwoven myriads of beliefs, desires, and goings-on as we do. My explanation for this, however, in no way licenses a reduction. It is, rather, that we impute those feelings to those people so described because we understand the people by means of an irreducibly feeling-laden psychological theory, such as our naïve, everyday one. According to it, such people have such feelings. As indicated in sec. 2 (and n. 19), the use of such a theory tells entirely in my, not the reductionist's, favour.

Second, it does not seem that what is lacking from the simple feelingless accounts is complexity, so that the lack could be made good by yet other feelingless states or goings-on. This can be seen, I suggest, by considering the notion of interest in some object. At least certain forms of such interest are pre-eminently ways of desiring that object. Reason, behaviour, functional states, and bodily manifestations are relatively unimportant compared to desire, even though they, too, are clearly bound up in such interest. Thus, if my claim of irreducibility is mistaken in regard to such interest, a reduction in terms of feelingless desires should at least come close to working. But if I am right, that reduction not only fails, it fails miserably.

My argument might be faulted for using too simple an understanding of desire. It might be held that the relevant desires are, or involve, hierarchies of and about the desires as I presented them: e.g. to be interested in some object O, one must desire to have O; but further, one must also desire to have that desire, one must see one's desire for O in a certain light, and so on. We need not investigate the soundness of such claims. As was seen, a feelingless desire for O is not even close to being a correct understanding of being interested in O. And as can easily be seen, little, if any, progress is made by augmenting that feelingless desire with feelingless hierarchies of or about desire: e.g. with a feelingless desire that one have a desire for O, a feelingless way of seeing or appreciating that one have a desire for O, and so on.

What might well help is an understanding of what it is to have an interest in O put in terms of desiring with interest or pleasure that one desire O, or seeing with interest or pleasure that one desires O. But these higher-order elements are themselves feeling-laden. If we can recur to higher-order feeling-laden elements, there is no reason not to start at the ground level with feeling-laden elements: e.g. desiring O with interest or pleasure.

SECTION 5: CONCLUSION

The above arguments are clearly not sufficient to still all doubts about more complex reductive accounts. Perhaps it would be useful to sketch another sort of reason that might incline people to think that some such reductive account must be true. Suppose it is agreed that we cannot get an account of, say, care or interest in terms of desire and reason, as those latter notions are deployed in the accounts so far considered. How, it might be asked, could those or similar accounts be made successful by the incorporation of feeling? How would the addition of some inner pang, say, improve the account? In short, feelings are too much of an inner phenomenon and too poor conceptually to bolster up accounts of care, concern, interest, and so on.

A complete reply would require an account of the nature of psychic feelings and especially of how, like other psychic elements, they are connected with the inner and the outer. Here, it should be sufficient to note the following. Undoubtedly some psychic feelings are pang-like. A momentary tingle of psychic tension or excitement might be pang-like. It might also provide an example of an entirely inner goings-on. Whether it is pang-like or objectionably inner is perhaps interesting, but, for our concerns, beside the point. Indeed, the present objection is entirely misguided.

It must be remembered that the psychic feelings I have been concerned with—care, concern and interest—have been shown, first, to have conceptual complexity. Just consider, for example, their relations with objects. Second, as shown, those psychic feelings can and often should be thought of not as merely connected with, but rather as 'modes' of, action, desire and reason. So, one acts with interest, one desires with interest, one sees with interest. At least these psychic feelings, then, are not conceptually impoverished the way pangs are supposed to be; nor are they any more objectionably inner than are desire and reason or, for that matter, action.[37]

As acknowledged, I have not proved that feelings are irreducible to complexes of desire and reason. But I believe I have given good reason to think that they are irreducible. In arguing for this, I have been concerned to stress the intimate connections between feelings and other psychic elements, as well as bodily goings-on and behaviour. I have also suggested that feelings might well be thought of as modes of desire and reason, as well as forming complexes with them.

Much remains to be discussed. To mention only some topics that have arisen here: How are feelings bound up with a good or bad life? Which feelings play these roles? How are care, concern and interest interrelated? How many different sorts of feelings are there? How are they interrelated? How are they related to desire and reason, and to functional states, bodily goings-on and behaviour? How are bodily and psychic feelings related? Are there feelingless forms of desire, or of reason, or of action, or ...? That is, are those accounts of desire, reason, action,... which present them as being, or allow that they might be, feelingless inadequate accounts of those notions? Or are they adequate accounts of what are 'only humanly' inadequate forms of desire, reason, action...?

These and similar questions must be answered for a full understanding of psychic feelings. Nonetheless, we have, I believe, seen enough to conclude that we do have psychic feelings, that they are important, and that they are interconnected with, but irreducible to, desire and reason.[38]

Notes

1   This, as I understand it, is what Plato suggests in the later parts of the *Phaedrus* (253 ff), *Symposium* (205 ff), and *Republic* (580 ff), where reason is said to require for its perfection its own proper desire, pleasure, and feeling. This contrasts with the view that is, or may seem to be, suggested in the earlier parts of these dialogues: viz., reason, desire, and feeling stand to each other only in such external and political relations as being controlled by, rebelling against, or cooperating with the others. I leave it open in this paper how we are ultimately to understand talk of 'parts' of the psyche—e.g. whether these are really, or only analytically, separable. Thus, my view may differ, in this regard, from Plato's.

2   There are, of course, some notable exceptions such as M. Scheler, *Formalism in Ethics and Non-Formal Ethics of Values* (Evanston: Northwestern UP, 1973), especially pages 256-64 and 332-44; S. Strasser, *Phenomenology of Feeling* (Pittsburgh: Duquesne UP, 1977); Wm. Alston, 'Feelings,' *Philosophical Review*, 1969; G. Rey, 'Functionalism and the Emotions,' *Explaining Emotions*, ed. A.O. Rorty (Berkeley: U of California P, 1980), especially pp. 176-80 under 'the qualitative'; J. Haugeland, 'Understanding Natural Language,' *The Journal of Philosophy*, 1979, esp. sec. 5; and R. Lawrie, 'Passion,' *Philosophy and Phenomenological Research*, 1980. These, however, are exceptions to the way feeling is—i.e., is not—treated by philosophers. Feeling seems to enjoy the same lack of attention in cognitive psychology, that area of psychology now so important to, and closely allied with various philosophical currents. To quote R.B. Zajonic in 'Feeling and Thinking,' *American Psychologist*, 1980, 'Contemporary cognitive psychology simply ignores affect. The words *affect, attitude, emotion, feeling,* and *sentiment* do not appear in the indexes of any of the major works on cognition ...' (152, fn. 3). He proceeds to list these works and to mention several exceptions.

3 'The Sporting Scene—Distance,' *The New Yorker*, September 22, 1980, p. 127.

4 See my 'The Schizophrenia of Modern Ethical Theories,' *The Journal of Philosophy*, 1976, and 'Desiring the Bad—An Essay in Moral Psychology,' *The Journal of Philosophy*, 1979. The former argues that there is a moral need for our values to be held and acted upon with such feeling. The latter argues both that 'weakness of will,' e.g. doing what is believed bad, can be explained by, indeed is entirely natural given the absence of such feelings, and also that their presence is necessary for explaining 'strength of will,' e.g. doing what one believes good.

5 See e.g. E. Jacobson, *Depression* (New York: International UP, 1971); H. Kohut, *The Analysis of Self* (New York: International Universities Press, 1971); O. Kernberg, *Borderline Conditions and Pathological Narcissism* (New York: Jason Aronson, 1975); and E. Erikson, *Insight and Responsibility* (New York: W.W. Norton and Co., 1964), esp. ch. 4.

6 *The Passions of the Soul*, I, 25, translated by E.S. Haldane and G.R.T. Ross. The next quote is from I, 24. See also I, 27-29.

7 For one source of this line, see E. Bedford, 'Emotions,' *Proceedings of the Aristotelian Society*, 1956-57. See also the works cited in n. 31.

8 For a start on these distinctions, see Scheler, *op. cit.* The closest he comes to what I call psychic feelings is, I believe, his category of vital feelings, not his category of psychic feelings. But vital feelings need not be, in my sense, psychic. They can be, near enough, wholly bodily, e.g. feeling physically tired. (Vital feelings differ importantly from sensations, which are also bodily.) Further, some of the psychic feelings I here consider are not, in his sense, vital feelings.

9 Aristotle requires, not belief, but thought, i.e. *phantasia*. 'Thought,' which is W.R. Roberts' translation, seems accurate so long as it is slanted more to imaging than merely entertaining. Aristotle's claim, which seems correct, bears on various issues about emotions: e.g. whether and how we can have emotions about fictional characters. On *phantasia* see F. Brentano, *The Psychology of Aristotle* (Berkeley: U of California P, 1977), p. 69; K. Lycos, 'Aristotle and Plato on "Appearing,"' *Mind*, 73, 1964; and M. Nussbaum, *Aristotle's De Motu Animalium* (Princeton: Princeton UP, 1978, essay 5.

10 'What is an Emotion?,' reprinted in *The Emotions*, ed. K. Dunlap (New York: Hafner Pub. Co., 1967), p. 17. See also p. 103. (James' article, originally from *Mind*, 1884 is found on pp. 11-30 of the book; ch. 25 of *The Principles of Psychology* on pp. 93-135; C. Lange's 'The Emotions,' on the intervening pages.) Further—also unfortunately inconclusive—discussion of the role of bodily feelings in emotions is found in ancient, medieval, modern, and contemporary philosophy: e.g. Aristotle's *De Anima*, I, 1, and *Nicomachean Ethics*, III, 10; Aquinas, *Summa Theologica*, 1-2, Q. 22; J. Dewey, 'The Theory of Emotion,' *The Early Works* (1882-98), v. 4 (Carbondale, Ill: Southern Illinois UP, 1971), esp. pp. 152-88—originally from *Psychological Review*, I, 1894 and II, 1895; M. Perkins, 'Emotion and Feeling,' *Philosophical Review*, 1966; and Wm. Gean 'Emotion, Emotional Feeling, and Passive Bodily Change,' *Journal for the Theory of Social Behaviour*, 1979. See also N.J.H.

Dent's and J. Benson's 'Varieties of Desire,' *Proceedings of the Aristotelian Society*, Sup. Vol., 1976.

11   The psychoanalytic notions of cathexis and change are, thus, clearly related to my understanding of feeling. But I shall not pursue these relations here.

12   Some other cognitive feelings, such as vividness, seem recalcitrant to such an understanding in terms of desires. For something's being vivid or seen vividly has little, if anything, to do with desiring to see it or desiring it in a certain way—despite the fact that desiring something may be explanatorily connected with its presence or absence being vivid. But even if only some cognitive feelings are understandable in terms of desire, that would be significant. Perhaps the others could be understood in terms of reason.

13   I say 'such' as a reminder that, as suggested in n. 12, only some feelings seem even prima facie to lend themselves to a conative understanding. Henceforth in this section, as contrasted with the following one, I shall be concerned only with such feelings.

14   *Mind, Language, and Reality* (Cambridge: Cambridge UP, 1975), vol. 2, pp. 410-11.

15   New York: Routledge & Kegan Paul, 1968, p. 152.

16   *Synthése*, 1974, pp. 313-14.

17   Dordrecht: Reidel Publishing Company, 1977, pp. 57-58.

18   *Ethics*, III, ix, trans. by R.H.M. Elwes. The only feelings or feeling-laden states (*affecti*) Spinoza uses to define emotions are pleasure and pain—defined as transitions to greater or lesser perfection—and desire (III, xi). I would argue that all these definitions omit feelings. However, apart from n. 21 and the end of this section, I shall not do this here, since all I now require is that the quoted characterisation of desire can be taken as feelingless. I am concerned with the notion of feelingless desire, not its attribution. For similar reasons, I shall not argue that other, e.g. contemporary, philosophers are committed to such a notion of desire.

19   To be sure, these connections are given by our naïve, everyday—and clearly feeling-laden— psychological theory which holds that, apart from sickness and some other exceptional states, one's own wellbeing and what one believes to conduce to it are indeed vivid, interesting, and moving. But precisely because it is feeling-laden, this psychology cannot be invoked to supply the reductive links between desire and feeling.

20   Third, this shows how 'elastic' are the notions of care, concern and interest. 'Care' can be used to cover psychic feelings; full-blown emotional states, akin to some forms of love as in 'I really do care for you'; caring activities 'properly associated' with such an emotional state; and what may be routinised or institutionalised forms of activity which may well be completely feelingless, as is given by the notion of 'caring professions' or 'day care.' (So too for concern and interest.) In this paper there is neither the time nor the need to discuss the interrelations among these forms of care. My thanks are due to Jenny Teichman for discussing this with me.

21 Two points should be noted here. First, this way of putting the matter may naturally make us wonder whether hierarchical understandings of desire would get around the present problem. But as discussed in sec. 4, hierarchies of feelingless desire are as inadequate as are first-order feelingless desires. Second, the claim in the text can readily be modified to show that, contrary to Spinoza, a transition to a higher (lower) state of perfection need not involve, much less be, a pleasure (a pain). This is discussed at the end of the section.

22 Here I am thinking of, at an extreme, those suffering from various forms of schizophrenia and pathological narcissism—on which see the works cited in n. 5.

23 For reasons given at the outset, I would prefer not to use this second and weaker thesis. It brings us into a direct confrontation with behaviourism and functionalism, as such, not just their present versions. Indeed, it is similar to the 'missing qualia' objections to functionalism advanced by N. Block and others. (See his 'Troubles with Functionalism,' *Minnesota Studies in the Philosophy of Science*, vol. 9, ed. W. Savage (Minneapolis: U of Minnesota P, 1979).) The major differences center on the differences between qualia and psychic feelings—e.g. whether their *esse* involves *percipi*. My thanks are owed to John Campbell for discussing this and much else in the paper with me.

24 On this notion of desire, see K. Duncker on desire and striving in 'On Pleasure, Emotion, and Striving,' *Philosophy and Phenomenological Research*, 1940; and also B. O'Shaughnessy, *The Will* (Cambridge: Cambridge UP, 1980), under 'act-desire,' e.g., vol. 1, p. li. My thanks are owed to Graeme Marshall for discussing this notion of desire and much else in the paper with me.

25 For an important discussion of how these accounts bear on traditional disputes over hedonism, see Duncker, *op. cit.*

26 See 'Enjoyment,' *Philosophical Review*, 1980. His exact formulation is found on p. 518.

27 Similar arguments show that Rylean attempts to understand pleasure in terms of various adverbial notions—e.g., acting with interest—either omit the feeling or are circular. So too, these arguments show that even such pleasure as can be understood adverbially—e.g. in terms of acting with pleasure rather than as sensations or experiences of pleasure—must be recognised as involving an irreducible feeling.

28 Claims that if there is desire, there must be pleasure or enjoyment seem simply expressions of dogmatic psychological hedonism. So, of course, does the suggestion that whatever one finds or believes pleasurable or enjoyable must motivate one to seek or keep it. On these hedonistic claims, and for a discussion of the above example of caring for the wounded, see J.C.B. Gosling, *Pleasure and Desire* (London: Oxford UP, 1969), ch. 5, esp. pp. 70-71. See also Duncker, *op. cit.*

29 My thanks are owed to Kent Bach for discussing this with me.

30 See A.R. White, 'The Notion of Interest,' *Philosophical Quarterly*, 1964, p. 320.

Some philosophers seem even to identify interest and attention. See, for example, S. Alexander, 'Foundations and Sketch-Plan of a Conational Psychology,' *British Journal of Psychology*, 1911: Not only is feeling 'not independent of conation' (p. 242), but 'If the name "attention" be preferred to conation, I have no objection ...' (p. 243). In 'Consciousness and Intentionality in Heidegger's Thought,' *American Philosophical Quarterly*, 1975, F. Olafson writes that 'Noesis as attention has, as Husserl points out, an especially personal character since shifts of attention express the interests of the ego in a uniquely direct way.' (p. 92) Although the cited passages of *Ideas*—part 3, ch. 9 of the English edition; especially, I presume, sec. 92—are consistent with talk of 'the interests of the ego,' interests are not explicitly mentioned there. G. Taylor in 'Justifying the Emotions,' *Mind*, 1975 can, I think, be taken as suggesting that attention—her 'thought-concentration' of pp. 391 and 400—is interest, care or concern. But she can also be taken as suggesting that it is only a precondition for, or a sign of, them.

31   Pitcher's article appeared in *Mind*, 1965, Solomon's and Neu's in *Explaining Emotions*. Page numbers in parentheses are to these publications. Solomon's paper, in a shorter version, originally appeared in *The Review of Metaphysics*, 1973.

32   It might be objected that Sartre's account of affectivity is in terms not only of reason but also of ways of living a world which has, or upon which we have projected, affective meanings. (See e.g., *Sketch for a Theory of Emotions*, London: Methuen and Co., 1971, pp. 77-78.) But he often does attempt to characterise emotionality and affective meanings in feelingless ways. Further, obvious extensions of my argument show that for the notion of living a world to be adequate for affectivity, that notion must, itself, be feeling-laden. For as these arguments show, there are any number of feeling-laden and feelingless ways of living a world, whether or not it, itself, is feeling-laden or feelingless. (These arguments also show that, contra Sartre, affective meanings must also be in us, not simply in the world: e.g. we must be interested in a world seen to be interesting.) Sartre's inadequate treatment of affectivity is especially surprising given the roles played by emotions in (and the emotionality of) his writings: e.g. his use of anguish, boredom, and nausea. My thanks are owed to Max Deutscher for discussing this with me.

33   These arguments also impose a requirement on those conceptual and genetic accounts of feeling given in terms of earlier, perhaps archetypal or infantile, scenes and scenarios. (See e.g. Jacobson, *op. cit.*; Neu, *op. cit.*; and R. de Sousa, 'The Rationality of Emotions,' *Dialogue*, 1979 and *Explaining Emotions*.) For even if an adult's emotion of, say, jealousy in a certain situation S is explained by S's being like some earlier situation S*, we still need an account of what it is for either S or S* to be feeling-laden. We still need an account of what it is to be interesting or magnetising, as A.O. Rorty puts it in regard to this issue in 'Explaining Emotions,' *The Journal of Philosophy*, 1978 and *Explaining Emotions*. My thanks are owed to Jerome Neu for discussing this issue with me.

34 Neu, in discussion, said that by questions, doubts, and worries, he meant feeling-laden ones. In the appendix to 'Emotions and Choice,' added for *Explaining Emotions*, Solomon writes,

> One might make a judgment—even much of a set of judgments—in an impersonal and uninvolved way, without caring one way or the other. But an emotional (set of) judgment(s) is necessarily personal and involved. Compare 'What he said to me was offensive' (but I don't care what he thinks) and 'He offended me!' Only the latter is constitutive of anger. (... the latter is, in part, a judgment about my own self-esteem.) (p. 276)

If this says that emotions involve feeling-laden judgments, judgments made in feeling-laden ways, I agree completely. But this may be saying something else: perhaps, that by collocating enough feelingless judgments—the full set of judgments—emotion is guaranteed; or perhaps that there are certain feelingless judgments—e.g. 'He offended me'—that guarantee emotion. I disagree with both. The former is discussed in sec. 4; and in any case, the latter is the more probable interpretation, since 'He offended me' seems to be only one judgment, even if it involves many others. Here we must note that judgments, too, can be taken to be feelingless or feeling-laden. It may be read as saying that, as I noted, my self-esteem was attacked. But, obviously, I need not care about that. It may also be read as saying that I felt the attack, it struck home, my self-esteem was wounded. But, first, this would seem feeling-laden. It is a report, one might say, of how I feel. And second, even read in this second way, it is insufficient for anger. For I may not care about being so wounded, just as I may not care about suffering a physical hurt. So, for 'He offended me' to come even close to constituting anger, it must be feeling-laden, and perhaps multiply so.

35 Some of these issues are discussed in I. Scheffler, 'In Praise of the Cognitive Emotions,' *Teachers College Record*, 1977, and my 'Intellectual Emotion, Desire, and Action' in *Explaining Emotions*.

36 Without discussing the relevant notions, various philosophers have held that at least some feeling-laden forms of reason do admit of a cognitivist understanding. So for example, T. Nagel in *The Possibility of Altruism* holds that it is a conceptual truth that some beliefs or reasons must be able to motivate. R.M. Hare in 'What Makes Choices Rational?,' *The Review of Metaphysics*, 1979 and T. Sprigge in 'Metaphysics, Physicalism, and Animal Rights,' *Inquiry*, 1979 argue that having certain—presumably feeling-laden—wants follows as a matter of conceptual necessity from fully understanding another's state, e.g. of pain. J. McDowell in 'Are Moral Requirements Hypothetical Imperatives?,' *Proceedings of the Aristotelian Society*, sup. Vol. 52, 1978 writes that a conative 'colouring of the agent's view of the world' can be 'regarded as a cognitive state' (p. 24); see also his 'Virtue and Reason,' *The Monist*, 1979, esp. his objections to non-cognitivism is secs. 3, 6, and 7. M. Platts in 'Moral Reality and the End of Desire,' *Reference, Truth, and Reality*, ed.

Platts (London: Routledge and Kegan Paul, 1980), e.g. p. 81 suggests that seeing the world with wonder can be at once cognitively characterisable and feeling-laden. I am indebted to John Campbell for discussing these issues with me. See also his unpublished 'Can Actions be Motivated by Reason?' and his doctoral dissertation, *Kantian Conceptions of Moral Worth*, Princeton University, 1980.

37   For discussion of issues concerning the inner and outer natures of such feelings, see G. Matthews, 'Ritual and Religious Feelings,' *Explaining Emotions*, and, in an earlier version, 'Bodily Motions and Religious Feelings,' *Canadian Journal of Philosophy*, 1971.

38   I am greatly indebted to many people for their help with this paper. My greatest debts are owed to Kent Bach and Michael Bratman for the many discussions we had on these subjects. Along with those already acknowledged, I should also like to thank Annette Baier, Sylvain Bromberge, Chris Cordner, Michael Devitt, Bert Dryfus, Mark Johnson, Aryeh Kosman, Genevie Loyd, Kim Lycos, Gareth Matthews, Amelie Rorty, Robert Shope, Irving Thalberg, John Taurek, and an anonymous referee for this *Journal*. Versions of this paper were read to, and benefited from discussion by, various philosophy department seminars.

Physiological Changes and the Emotions

William Lyons

In this chapter I want to attempt to analyse a particularly neglected area in the philosophy of the emotions, the relations between physiological changes and emotions. I should remark that it is philosophers, not psychologists, who tend to neglect this aspect of the emotions. As I suggested in the introductory chapters, in philosophy the Cartesian view of the emotions has generally held the stage, and in recent years philosophers have concentrated almost exclusively on emotions as if they were purely internal mental events. Thus they have concentrated on puzzles to do with the cognitive and evaluative aspects of the emotions and their relation to the objects of emotions, often, as we have seen, in a way that did not adequately distinguish the evaluative strand from the purely cognitive. Excepting their denial that emotions are feelings, philosophers have had very little to say about the 'bodily motions' part of emotions, particularly in recent times, even though, somewhat ironically, it is this very aspect of emotions which distinguishes them from being just beliefs and desires of certain sorts.

So in this and the next chapter I will concentrate on these bodily aspects, the physiological changes and feelings. In detail, I will attempt in this chapter to clarify the physiological aspect by

(1) Trying to elucidate what exactly is to be understood by the term 'physiological change' in the context of an emotion;
(2) Showing that particular physiological changes are not part of the concept of any particular emotion and are only linked causally to the cognitive-evaluative-appetitive part of an occurrent emotional state;
(3) Showing, however, that the notion of a physiological change is part of the concept of an emotional state as such;
(4) And, finally, by drawing out some consequences of this analysis regarding the connection between physiological changes and feelings, and physiological changes and the observability of emotions.

THE TERM 'PHYSIOLOGICAL CHANGE' IN THE CONTEXT OF AN EMOTION

First a brief explanation of my use of the term 'physiological change' rather than the more usual phrases 'physiological disturbance' or ' bodily upset.'[1] I am chary of using terms such as 'disturbance' or 'upset' as they may lead one into the dual error of thinking that all physiological changes associated with emotion are of an alarming or disturbing nature and that all bodily changes associated with emotion are experienced by the subject of them. When, in discussing quotations from other philosophers, I do use such terms as 'physiological disturbance' and 'bodily upset,' I wish them to be neutral as regards such suggestions.

What exactly is meant by the phrase 'physiological changes'? I think that Goshen, in his article 'A systematic Classification of the Phenomenology of Emotions,' gives a useful catalogue of the sort of thing which this phrase refers to:

> The physiological phenomena which occur during the actual period of time in which the individual is experiencing an emotion (e.g. fear) include: increased pulse rate, increased respiratory rate, increased muscle tone, pupillary dilation and peripheral vascular changes such as flushing, sweating or pallor. The gastrointestinal tract might also exhibit increased levels of motility. The individual subjectively experiences certain sensations including muscular tension, tightness of the throat, dryness of the mouth and increased levels of alertness. The overall impression, psychologically, is that of an adrenergic response [Goshen, 1967, p. 488].

There are two points to notice here. In the first place, Goshen seems to mention only the unusual physiological changes which could be called disturbances or upsets. He should also have made mention of the physiological changes such as a *decreased* pulse rate and *decreased* respiratory rate, for there seems to be no good reason for believing that these do not also occur in emotional states, when, for example, a person is very happy and feeling unusually calm. Again, ennui, may involve a decreased pulse and respiratory rate, and muscular relaxation. It may prove to be the case that the majority of the changes linked with emotions show an increase of physiological activity rather than a decrease. Indeed, intuitively, this would seem to be the case. But since this is a purely empirical matter, and since there is no reliable evidence of this effect, it must be left open.[2]

Then, as a second point, Goshen seems to hint at but not carry through an important distinction when listing the physiological changes associated with emotion. The distinction is that between physiological changes which we are subjectively aware of and necessarily so, those which we are necessarily not aware of, and finally those of which we may or may not be aware depending on the circumstances. The subject must always be aware of tightness of the throat, dryness of the mouth, and perhaps, an increased level of alertness if these are feelings, for you cannot have unfelt feelings, that is feelings of which one is unaware. On the other hand it may be possible to define all these terms without reference to feelings. There seem to be no items in Goshen's list of which we are necessarily unaware. The only possible candidates for this category seem to be pupillary dilation and pallor; with the stipulation that there is no mirror about! But the very fact that such a stipulation must be introduced means that they are not really candidates for items of which we are necessarily (logically or empirically) unaware. So, the other items listed by Goshen appear to fall reasonably clearly into the third category, namely the physiological changes which we may or may not be aware of depending on the circumstances. We can feel increased pulse rate, increased respiratory rate, flushing, sweating, muscular tension, and probably, increased muscle tone and an increased level of motility in the gastrointestinal tract, and we can observe our pupillary dilation and pallor in a mirror; but it is also the case that all these changes can occur without our being aware of them, for example when asleep, unconscious, or drugged, or simply when our attention is wholly occupied by what is going on around us, or (in the case of pupillary dilation and pallor) we have no mirror about.

It is important to note that, in this chapter, I am only concerned with the physiological changes of which the subject may or may not be aware depending on the circumstances. I am only interested in the category of bodily changes which *can* exist without the subject of the changes being aware of them. The other category of bodily changes, from which some items on Goshen's list are drawn, includes bodily sensations, and the discussion of these I will defer to the next chapter. However, towards the end of this chapter, I will briefly discuss whether there is any connection between physiological changes and the bodily feelings which occur more or less simultaneously.

A final preliminary remark. It is important to stress that the word 'unusual' is to be understood whenever the phrase 'physiological change' is mentioned in connection with the emotions. Some physiological changes are always going on in our body but the ones which are linked with emotions are both noticeable and unusual. We do not link emotions with such things as a pulse rate, a respiratory rate and a skin colour but with an *increased* pulse rate or a *decreased* respiratory rate or an *unusual* colouring such as occurs with blushing.

However in that sense of 'unusual' the physiological changes resulting from feeling very cold or tired or from just having finished a 100 metre sprint are also unusual. How then do the physiological changes associated with emotion differ from these? They differ in two ways. In the first place they differ in terms of their causal ancestry. The physiological changes associated with feeling cold, such as shivering and going blue, result from a person's being too long in a very cold temperature and physiologists can trace the causal connections. The physiological changes associated with being emotional are those which result from a person's evaluation of his situation and neurophysiologists and experimental psychologists are beginning to trace out the causal links. A person can be very cold and embarrassed at the same time yet it is possible to separate off at least some of the physiological changes associated with feeling cold from those associated with being afraid by tracing the causal connections involved in each state. Even those untutored in physiology can work out that when a naked man who is a member of the Icebergs' Club and has just emerged from his midwinter dip in the icy river blushes, and his blushing coincides with the appearance of his boss's wife on the river bank, the blushing should not be put down to the cold but to embarrassment.

Secondly the physiological changes associated with emotions differ in kind from those associated with feeling cold, tired or over-exercised at least to the extent that they form a recognisable set which differs from the sets associated with these other physiological conditions, though there may be overlap between the sets. Physiologically there is a definite limit to the physiological changes which evaluative attitudes can give rise to and so these physiological changes form a recognisable set. No emotion, for example, can make us go blue or freeze our joints in the way that low temperatures can, and no amount of exposure to low temperatures can make us blush. As we have seen, neurophysiologists and experimental psychologists tell us that by and large the physiological changes associated with emotion are those which can be triggered off by activity in the limbic system of the brain, which in turn causes activity in the hypothalamus, and so by and large are those changes associated with discharges or other divergences from the normal equilibrium state of the autonomic (sympathetic and parasympathetic) nervous systems.

PARTICULAR PHYSIOLOGICAL CHANGES AND THE COGNITIVE-EVALUATIVE-APPETITIVE PART OF AN OCCURRENT EMOTIONAL STATE

It is not an uncommon view among psychologists and philosophers that there is a characteristic core-pattern of physiological changes unique to each particular emotion and that, unless there were such a core-pattern, we would never recognise emotions in others.[3] A more radical view along these lines (which was held, as we have seen, by J.B. Watson) would be to say that the word 'fear' or the word 'love' is the label of a distinctive core-pattern of physiological changes such that in recognising a particular physiological pattern in another we are recognising the particular emotion he or she is undergoing.

As these views concern an empirical matter, it is important to refer to the experimental evidence concerning them. Schachter and Singer, in their article 'Cognitive, Social, and Physiological Determinants of Emotional State,' give a short survey of the experimental evidence both in favour of and against the above views and conclude that, while the matter is empirically still 'an open question'[4] (Schachter and Singer, 1962, pp. 379-80) 'the numerous studies on physiological differentiators of emotional states have, viewed en masse, yielded quite inconclusive results. Most, though not all, of these studies have indicated no differences among the various emotional states' (Schachter and Singer, 1962, p. 397).[5] Goshen takes a more definite standpoint about the conclusion to be drawn from the experiments. He writes that 'When the different types of emotion (e.g. fear *versus* anger) are examined minutely in respect of physiological changes only, there does not appear to be any significant difference, so that physiological distinctions between differing emotions are only quantitative, and not qualitative' (Goshen, 1967, pp. 488-9).

While the experimental evidence so far available seems to give little or no comfort to the view that there is a pattern of physiological changes peculiar to each emotion, Goshen's conclusion does seem rather sweeping. For, while there is a reasonable presumption in favour of there being a core-pattern of physiological changes common to many emotions (occurrent emotional states), and while there is no solid evidence that there is any pattern of changes peculiar to each emotion, there are physiological changes which seem to be found more often in one group of emotions than in others. Perhaps this is what Goshen means by there being 'quantitative differences' only among the various emotions, though this phrase does not really capture the point I am making. To take an example, weeping (the activation of the tear ducts) seems to occur more often with occurrent states of grief, fear and elation than with, say, the occurrent states of disgust, hate or envy.

In a brief comment in his article 'Emotion and Feeling,' Alston gives us a more philosophical reason for not equating bodily upsets (as he calls physiological changes) with emotion. He argues that if emotions were considered to be bodily upsets then we would seem to be landed with the unacceptable conclusion that love, fear, jealousy and other emotions are just the same sort of thing as stomach upsets and startled reactions.[6] We could no longer give reasons for saying that queasiness is not an emotion or that love is not just a bodily upset. One could continue along Alston's line of thought by saying that if we made such an equation then there would be no point in having a term 'emotion' because there would be no difference between this term and the term 'bodily upset.' But this type of argument cannot be conclusive about such an empirical matter for it just may be the case that through ignorance we have in our language two terms, 'emotion' and 'bodily upset,' for one and the same thing.

The matter seems to have dried up more or less at that point. In recent years, whenever a philosopher has considered the relation between physiological changes and emotions, a rare enough event, he seems to have assumed that the evidence from experiments is that there is no relation at all between physiological changes and emotion. I want to make out a case that, while there is no conceptual link between the notion of any particular physiological change or any pattern of physiological changes and the concept of any particular emotion, there is a causal connection between the cognitive-evaluative-appetitive part of an emotional state and the concomitant physiological changes.

Schachter and Singer point out in their article that subjects excited by an injection of adrenaline (epinephrine), given in such a way that the patients did not realise that they were being injected with a drug, did not report having emotions till they were put in a context of euphoria or anger (Schachter and Singer, 1962, pp. 395-6). In other words, though undergoing strong physiological changes, notably an increased pulse rate and respiratory rate which gives a sensation of having palpitations, they did not consider themselves to be in an emotional state till they were provided with suitable 'cognitions.' That is, they did not consider themselves to be in an emotional state until they were placed in a situation in which they were more or less led into making the evaluation or appraisal peculiar to some emotion. Schachter and Singer point out that in 1924, Marañon had also found that he could not produce a genuine emotional reaction by injecting adrenaline into subjects till he provided them with 'appropriate cognition.'[7]

Considering these experiments, one is led into postulating that a person labels his own sensations of physiological changes with the name of a particular emotion, if and only if he connects their occurrence with a specific type of evaluation (or appraisal) of the situation, which in turn is associated with the concept of a particular emotion. A person will speak of his sensations of physiological changes, even though, unknown to him, they are chemically induced, as somehow connected with the emotional state of, say, love, if he believes that these physiological changes are somehow connected with the appraisal of the situation as one in which he believes he loves someone.

What the experiments which I have so far referred to do not tell us is whether the subjects *only* connect their physiological changes with their evaluation (or appraisal) of the situation if they *believe* that the evaluation somehow caused the physiological changes. This will be so irrespective of whether this belief in fact be true or not. However, some other experiments conducted by Schachter and Singer suggest that the subject of the physiological changes must believe that the evaluation of the situation, which is peculiar to some emotion, generated his physiological changes if that subject is to report having undergone some emotion (i.e. emotional state). When Schachter and Singer told certain of their subjects that the injection which they had just been given was of adrenaline, and also told them about the physiological changes and bodily sensations which would be produced by the adrenaline, then these subjects proved 'relatively immune' to attempts to manipulate them into thinking that they were undergoing an emotional reaction. That is, they proved 'relatively immune' to attempts to manipulate them into thinking that their physiological changes were part of an occurrent emotional state

(Schachter and Singer, 1962, pp. 395-6). It seems that they were immune because they knew that their evaluation of the context was not the cause of their physiological changes and bodily sensations. For the only difference between this set of experiments and the former ones was that, in this set, the subjects were told the exact *cause* of their physiological changes and the accompanying bodily sensations or feelings, namely the adrenaline.

These experiments seem to point to a conclusion that is parallel to Ryle's contention in Chapter IV of *The Concept of Mind*, that it is by applying a causal hypothesis that I identify feelings as being of a certain emotion (Ryle, 1949, p. 105). Though Ryle would not agree with this gloss, Schachter and Singer's experiments suggest that I say the feelings are of, say, love if I believe that the feelings are caused by my belief that I am now in love with someone. It seems that in like manner a person labels his physiological changes as emotional ones if he believes that they are caused by the evaluation (or appraisal) of the situation in a way that is peculiar to some emotion.

Bruce will link his own blushing with the emotion love only if he believes that his blushing is a result of his now seeing Moria with whom he believes he is very much in love. Someone else seeing Bruce blushing may identify the blushing as being from embarrassment because this person believes rightly or wrongly that yesterday Bruce accused Moira of being dishonest and vowed never to see her again so that, in consequence, he is embarrassed at being caught in the same room with her. What is clear is that, irrespective of the correctness of either identification, the identification is always attempted by means of a causal hypothesis of a certain sort. That is, by trying to work out what situation, or rather what view (evaluation or appraisal) of the situation, is causing the particular physiological changes in question.

THE NOTION OF A PHYSIOLOGICAL CHANGE
AND THE CONCEPT OF AN EMOTIONAL STATE

Another aspect of Schachter and Singer's experiments suggests that there is a conceptual link between the notion or concept of a physiological change as such and the concept of an emotional state as such. They pointed out that a number of subjects, inhibited by drugs from having any *noticeable* physiological changes, were placed in paradigm emotional contexts yet, having apprehended and evaluated (or appraised) the situation adequately, they did not report that they were undergoing an emotion (Schachter and Singer, 1962, p. 382). This experiment suggests that a belief that some unusual physiological changes are taking place is necessary if a person is to have grounds for claiming that he is in an emotional state; without this belief one cannot attribute an emotional state to someone (oneself or another).[8]

Of course, it may be the case that a person is undergoing physiological changes as a result of an evaluation peculiar to some emotion and yet doesn't know it, because he is somehow distracted or inhibited from knowing this. In such a case he would be undergoing an emotional state but not have grounds for asserting this. And this fact, that he could not assert that he was in an emotional state in such a case, would be further grounds for the claim that to believe one is in an emotional state, one must first believe that one is undergoing physiological changes caused by an evaluation (or appraisal) peculiar to some emotion. And, in turn, this would be further grounds for holding that there is a conceptual link between the notion of an emotional state and the notion of a physiological change.

If this is so, then Kenny may be far too sweeping when he writes in *Action, Emotion and Will* that 'There is a conceptual connection also between a feeling and its object, whereas the physiological process studied by psychologists lack intensionality. Bodily changes may be the vehicle of an emotion, but they are not themselves emotion' (Kenny, 1963, p. 38). I suggest that Kenny, in his proper anxiety to make it clear that 'the somatic phenomena characteristic of particular emotions occurred also in connection with quite different emotions' (Kenny, 1963, p. 39) that is, that there is no pattern of physiological changes peculiar to each emotion, may have put his position too strongly. He seems in the quoted passage to be saying, or to leave himself open to be interpreted as saying, that bodily changes are not part of the concept of emotion itself, that is, of emotion in its primary occurrent sense of emotional state. Whereas what he should be saying is that no particular physiological or bodily changes are part of the concept of any particular emotion.

Leaving aside the experiments which seem to show that physiological changes are an essential part of the concept of emotion in its sense of occurrent emotional state, there is another good reason (though not compelling argument) for holding this. In our ordinary locutions, we associate the notion of 'an emotional state' with unusual bodily activity such as extreme agitation or unusual bodily states such as an unusual colouring of the face. If I inform you that I have lost your book, your reaction may be to work yourself up so that you go red in the face, speak far faster and more loudly than normal, tremble and appear taut around the face. If so, it would not be out of place to say 'There's no need to get emotional about it. I'll buy you another copy.'

To sum up, then, in this section I have argued in various ways that it seems inconceivable to be in an emotional state and not to have undergone unusual bodily changes of some sort. To be *in* love (that is, to love emotionally, in a very strong sense), for example, but never to be in any unusually agitated or excited physiological state, or never to be in any unusually calm or serene physiological state seems inconceivable. This is true only of the phrase '*in love*,' as contrasted with the word 'love.' For the early stages of love, the 'in love' stage, are deemed to differ from the later stages precisely by being a period of strong occurrent emotional states, particularly as regard the bodily reaction and, if any, behaviour aspect.

So it is essential to a claim to be in love that a physiological change, which is in one sense a divergence from the normal physiological metabolism and which is discoverable at least by a careful observer, has taken place at some time in the presence of the person or as a result of one's attitudes towards and appraisal of that person. Just as it is absurd to make a dispositional claim to be in love but never to have had any feelings for the person concerned, so it is conceptually absurd to make a dispositional claim to be in love but never to have been in an extraordinary physiological condition. For such a claim is parasitic on the claim to be or at some time to have been in an emotional state, and this point is ultimately a point about the dispositional-occurrent distinction and about the concept of an emotional state, not about the concept of love as such.

I do not want to give the impression that the above arguments only apply to the 'in love' state or stage, for I would argue that the arguments should apply to any stage of any emotion. It is just that the point is easier to grasp when put in the context of the stronger, clearly emotional stage of love.

There is further, though weak, supporting evidence for the view I am urging in the fact that one of the ways in which we assess the intensity of an emotion is from the intensity of the various physiological factors associated with the occurrence of that emotion (that is, of that emotional state). If Jim and Sam are angry with one another so that Jim is red in the face, shaking and shouting, while Sam is pursing his lips, narrowing his eyes and speaking in an even but steely voice, an onlooker has some reasons for saying that Jim is more angry than Sam. Obviously, they cannot be compelling reasons, for it may be merely that Sam is dissembling or else better able to control himself.

Again, we so associate emotional states with unusual physiological changes, and we so associate marked physiological changes with paralysis of good judgement, that 'under emotional stress' is allowed as a plea of mitigation in the law courts of some countries. The murder which is committed as a crime of passion is not considered as criminal as the *sang-froid* murder because we associate emotions with hot blood and with physiological changes which often amount to a disturbance and clouding of sober good reason, cool calculation and balanced decision. I do not want to deny, of course, that part of the explanation of 'crime of passion' as a plea will also be tied up with the fact that, with certain emotions, such as jealousy, it may be very difficult to refrain from activity. Certain emotions have a very strong appetitive aspect, and so tend to issue in action, and the stronger the emotion the more ungovernable is the urge to act.

SOME CONSEQUENCES

Since we have seen that both feelings (bodily feelings as different from, say, feelings of elation which have more the character of a fully developed emotion) and physiological changes are associated with emotional states, it is time to ask whether the feelings associated with, say, love are the sensations caused by the physiological changes associated with the emotion.[9] As a question of cause and effect, like all such empirical matters, it can only be decided finally by experiment. However, since it is argued that the paradigm bodily feelings such as twinges, throbs and tickles, have at least proximate physiological causes, this is good reason for thinking the physiological changes which are associated with an emotion on some particular occasion will be the ones that cause the bodily feelings which are associated with that emotion on the same occasion. In simpler terms, since we associate, say, a throb, with some proximate physiological cause such as the heart beat and consequent pulse rate, then, if we associate the bodily feeling, throbbing, with love on some particular occasion, and the physiological change, increased pulse rate, with love on the same occasion, it is most likely that the throb is caused by this physiological change, the increased pulse rate, rather than by any other. This will be so because it is this physiological change which is most noticeable, and perhaps the only one noticeable, or indeed discoverable, and so has the best credentials for being associated with the unusual feeling, the throbbing.

This link between some physiological changes and feelings generates a new distinction for us between the physiological changes associated with emotion: between those which are introspectible and those which are not. For only those physiological changes which we can introspect will count as feelings, though by this I do not wish to imply that such physiological changes are only discoverable by introspection. A physiological change, such as an increased heartbeat and blood flow, may be felt and so introspected— for attending to the feeling will be attention to the felt physiological change—but it may also be discovered by feeling one's pulse and listening to one's heart beat. Feeling one's pulse is not introspection in the sense explained, though feeling one's pulse race is, because it amounts to an inner private awareness. It should also be clear that not all physiological changes associated with emotion can be paired off with a corresponding feeling. Only the introspectible ones will. We can discover that our pupils are dilated—by looking into a mirror—but not feel them dilating or feel that they are dilated.

But if it is the case that the bodily feelings associated with emotions are causally linked with at least some of the bodily changes associated with emotions (with particular emotional states), then this will be further good reason for asserting that it is unlikely that there are any *particular* physiological changes which are to be linked conceptually with any *particular* emotion. For, as there seem to be no particular bodily feelings (feelings in the sense of Ryle's throbs, twinges, and tickles) which can be linked conceptually to particular emotions,[10] and since there is an alleged causal link between a particular bodily feeling and a particular physiological change, so there will be no particular physiological changes, at least of the introspectible kind, which can be linked conceptually to particular emotions.

It is worth noting however that, all the same, we do consider physiological changes to be an important indicator that *some* emotion (no particular emotion perhaps, but some group of emotions) is present. If we can form a causal hypothesis of sufficient strength to enable us to say that such and such a physiological change in such and such a person is the result of that person's present view of the situation, that is, if we can identify the physiological change in question as being of such and such an emotion, then we can look upon the physiological change as a reflex indicator of the presence of that emotion. It can also serve as a check on the genuineness of that emotion (for we cannot manipulate or engineer our physiological changes in normal circumstances). Being reflex, such an indicator will be more trustworthy than a non-reflex one such as a verbal one and may well be evidence for or against the truth of such verbal avowals. If we know that Bruce has been 'keen on' Moira for some time and if we now see Bruce blush when she enters the room, we will quite likely believe that this is a sign that Bruce is still in love with her, in preference to believing Bruce's later nonchalant avowal that he no longer cares for her at all and had indeed forgotten all about her.

It is because the physiological changes caused by the emotions show on a person's face and body, and because these are the only observable item that is tied conceptually to the notion of an emotional state that, contrary to the views of some philosophers,[11] we can be said to observe another's emotions.[12] Though, as we have seen, particular physiological changes are not to be conceptually identified with particular emotions, physiological changes should be considered as part of occurrent emotions in general.

So far it may seem that I am saying that, if one can see anything which is causally linked to the core part of emotions (of occurrent emotional states), namely to the cognitive-evaluative-appetitive part, then one is seeing the emotion. But this would not be true, for in some cases it would be like saying that if one sees the vapour trail of a jet-plane then one is seeing the jet- plane. My case is different. I am saying that if one sees the body-work of such and such a jet- plane then one is seeing that jet-plane. I have argued that the core part of an occurrent emotional state is only causally linked to any particular feelings or particular physiological changes, which form the other part of such an emotional state. I have also argued that this position is not incompatible with holding that there is a conceptual link between the claim that there is an occurrence of a particular emotional state, and the claim that some sort of physiological changes, generally associated with a discharge of the sympathetic or parasympathetic nervous system, must therefore be present. This will not be true of any claim about behaviour or feelings, for one can be in an emotional state and not engaging in any behaviour, or be in an emotional state and not be aware of it. This claim about the conceptual link between emotional states and physiological changes entitles us to say that, when we see particular physiological changes which have been causally linked to a particular emotion, then we are seeing an occurrence of that particular emotion. That is, when we see particular physiological changes which have been causally linked to the evaluative component peculiar to some emotion, then we are seeing part of the occurrent emotional state of that particular emotion. Our reasons for identifying the occurrence as of that particular emotion, however, will be considerations other than the presence of the physiological changes, namely the evaluative component or some clues to it.

If it is true that behaviour is not linked conceptually to the notion or concept of an emotional state, then I cannot say that to observe emotional behaviour is to observe the emotion; it only amounts to observing the manifestation of an emotion. Observing behaviour causally linked to a particular emotional occurrence, but whose concept is not linked conceptually to the notion of that particular emotion or to the notion of an emotional state as such, is then logically on a par with observing the vapour trail causally linked to a particular jet-plane. And in such a case one is entitled only to say 'I see that he is in the grip of such and such an emotion' and not 'I see such and such emotion,' just as when one sees only a vapour trail one is entitled to say 'I see that a jet-pane has flown across the sky' and not 'I see a jet plane.' But I shall devote a later chapter to investigating the exact connection between emotions and behaviour.[13]

Notes

1   See for example, Alston (1967a, pp. 481-2).

2   There seems in fact to be reasonably well tested evidence about relaxing emotions. The activation of the parasympathetic nervous system seems to be the core of the physiological changes part of some emotional states. See G. Dumas (1948b), esp. pp. 116-18; and Izard (1972, Ch.I).

3   For example, Arnold (1960, Vol. I, and p. 179).

4   See also Schachter (1970).

5   This was also the result of the later attempts to distinguish at least some emotions, in particular fear and anger, by reference to the excretion of adrenaline and noradrenaline. See Marianne Frankenhaeuser (1975, esp. pp. 218-22).

6   Alston (1967a, p. 485): regarding this argument, I would like to suggest that one sense of 'startled reaction' (reacting with alarm at something apprehended and evaluated) is more akin to an emotion that to a stomach upset.

7   From 'Contribution à l'étude de l'action emotive de l'adrénaline,' *Revue Française d'Endocrinologie*, No. 2, 1924, pp. 301-25. See also Munn (1961, p. 325).

8   For further psychological work on this point, see Goldstein, Fink and Mettee (1972).

9   For psychological work on this point see Brady (1970, esp. p. 70).

10 For a fully argued version of this claim, the reader should consult Ryle (1949, Ch IV, pp. 83ff.), and Kenny (1963, Ch III, pp. 52ff).

11 For example, Aune (1963, p. 198).

12 Perkins (1965) puts forward literary examples which show that we speak of seeing emotions but not why we do so.

13 For further reading concerning experimental data about the physiological aspects of emotions, the reader is referred to p. 15, nn. 6 and 7.

ON EMOTIONS AS JUDGMENTS

Robert C. Solomon

Philosophers have often contrasted "reason and the passions," typically championing the former against the latter. Descartes and his compatriote Malebranche, for example, treated emotions as "animal spirits," distinctively inferior parts of the psyche. Leibniz thought of emotions as "confused perceptions" and Kant rather famously dismissed what he called "pathological love" (i.e. love as an emotion) from the love more properly commanded by the Scriptures and practical reason.

More than occasionally, one finds one of the enlightenment philosophers defending the passions against the excessive claims of rationality. David Hume, most notably, insisted that "reason is and ought to be the slave of the passions." Nevertheless, he agreed with a long line of philosophers in setting them off against one another and separating emotion from rationality. It is worth noting that such philosophers as Hume not uncommonly employ an emotionally emaciated concept of reason in their analyses, together with a cognitively rich if somewhat convoluted concept of emotion. Indeed, it is this inequitable divorce between emotion and reason that motivates the rather odd problems shared by but separating Hume and Kant—how passionless reason can move us and how non-rational passions can be moral and justifiable. What does not get questioned is the critical distinction between reason and passion, judgment and emotion. So too, into this century, William James famously defended a quite visceral conception of emotions as felt physiological disturbances, quite distinct from cognition. Today, philosopher Robert Kraut and psychologist Robert Zajonc maintain this traditional separation of emotions and cognition.

And yet, there is another tradition in philosophical analysis, not nearly so well known nor so widely accepted. Over 2500 years ago, Aristotle provided (in his *Rhetoric*, but not consistently elsewhere) a detailed analysis of anger in which judgments play a crucial role. Anger, he argued, was the perception of an offense (real or merely perceived), a kind of recognition coupled with a desire for action (namely, revenge). Moreover, the perception and the desire were not effects of emotion but its constituents. It would be *irrational* for a man *not* to get angry in certain circumstances, Aristotle insists. (The fellow would even be a "dolt," he adds.) Reason here is not distinct from passion but a part and parcel of it, just as passion is part of—and not an intrusion into—the rational life.

Seneca the Stoic argued a more elaborate general thesis about the nature of emotions, following his forerunner Chryssipis. On the Stoic analysis, too, emotions are judgments, ways of perceiving and understanding the world. Unlike Aristotle, however, Seneca saw these emotional judgments as essentially irrational—misinformed or in any case mistaken attitudes, distorted by desire, which philosophical reason, properly applied, would correct. Nevertheless, the distinction between passion and reason, emotion and judgment, now becomes an internal matter within the realm of judgments. Many years later, the Dutch philosopher Spinoza argued a similarly stoic thesis; for him, too, emotions are essentially "thoughts" moved by desire, though they are not necessarily unreasonable. Against James in this century, John Dewey defended a largely cognitive theory of emotion.

In the past twenty years or so, there has been a virtual triumph of the cognitivist theory, in the number of its defenders if not by virtue of any final arguments or agreement. In both philosophy and psychology the idea that an emotion necessarily requires cognitive ingredients, if it does not wholly consist of cognitions, has attracted many, many advocates. There is by no means agreement about the precise nature of these cognitions, whether they are peculiar to emotions or no different as such from other cognitions, whether they consist of beliefs, or thoughts, or judgments, whether they alone constitute an emotion or whether other factors, in particular "feelings," are also required. But the idea that emotions are cognitions is at least an idea that has gained the upper hand in the debate, an idea that has to be refuted rather than fight for recognition. Indeed, one philosophical reviewer has referred to the cognitive theory as the "new view" of emotions, in contrast to the older view of James and his many historical predecessors.

Emotions are constituted by judgments, as I have argued elsewhere (*The Passions;* New York: Doubleday, 1976). But against this strong cognitivist thesis and any others like it, there is a now-standard objection, though it is rarely spelled out in sufficient detail. Here is one typically blunt statement of the standard objection (there are many others) by Jerome Shaffer, from his recent essay, "An Assessment of Emotion":

> Perhaps it is this superfluity of the physiological/sensational component that has led some philosophers to identify emotion with judgments, appraisals, and evaluations. But the identification will not work. One can hold precisely those beliefs and desires in a dispassionate and unemotional way. So getting emotionally worked up must involve more than just beliefs and desires (Myers and Irani, eds., *Emotion: Philosophical Studies* [New York: Haven, 1983] p. 206).

In short, if "having an emotion *E*" is analyzed in terms of "making judgments *A, B, C*" (whether these are construed as constitutive of the emotion, as causally necessary preconditions of the emotion or as logical presuppositions of the description), then a counter-example to the pure cognitive thesis would be an example of a person's making judgments *A, B, C* without having emotion *E*. For instance, I have argued that anger is, basically, a judgment that one has been offended. Sally, who has a keen ear for the nuances of supposedly polite discourse, judges that she has been offended. Sally can make that judgment, for instance, because she studied conversational implicature at Berkeley, and knows that the perlocutionary force of utterance *U*, stated in language *L* and in context *C*, is that of an offense. But she does not, as we say, "take it personally." In fact, she is both amused (because she had not heard that utterance employed to make that insult before) and grateful (because it is just the example she needs for the paper on perlocutionary force that she is writing.

One way to deal with this objection is to weaken and modify the cognitivist thesis, to admit, in effect, that emotions are not constituted just by judgments but essentially involve some other ingredient(s)—feelings, physiological reactions, strong desires or frustration of desires or "affective tone" of some sort or other. I do not reject this option; my aim has been to relocate emotions in our geography of the mind, to redeem them from the "lower" realms of involuntary, unintelligent response to their proper status among such learned cognitive skills as judgment, belief and perception. Whether or not emotions are "just" judgments, or judgments plus desires or feelings, is not my primary concern. But I think that it is worth pursuing the strong cognitivist thesis as far as it will go, in order to show just how much of our emotional life is essentially cognitive and that judgments provide at least the complete skeleton if not the body of our emotions. My objective in this paper, accordingly, is to counter the standard objection ("one can hold precisely those beliefs and desires in a dispassionate and unemotional way"). In doing so, I will also try to clarify the concept of "judgment" that plays such a central role in the cognitivist thesis.

In particular, I want to argue that the analysis of emotions as judgments must not be understood as the simple-minded claim that each emotion is the assertion of a single judgment or belief (with or without an accompanying desire). Such an analysis can be easily shown to be inadequate (Stephen Leighton, *American Philosophical Quarterly*, Vol. 22, April, 1985). The judgments that constitute emotions must be understood as (1) particular kinds of acts of judgment, not just the affirmation of certain propositions, (2) systems of judgments, not single judgments, (3) essentially and not contingently tied to their expression, (4) "dispassionate" only in peculiarly pathological or philosophical circumstances, (5) tied to desires in a non-causal way, and (6) sustaining rather than simply initiating, structural rather than disruptive. I will not attempt to establish a sharp distinction between emotional and 'dispassionate' judgments, however, for—contrary to the view that I am attacking, in which emotions represent sudden intrusions into life—I believe that virtually all of our experience is to some degree 'affective' and even our most dispassionate judgments (which are not to be confused with opinions or pronouncements that are mere matters of indifference) can be adequately understood only within some larger emotional context.

I. JUDGMENTS AS MENTAL ACTS, NOT PROPOSITIONAL CONTENTS

The standard objection almost always seems to focus on the propositional *content* of the judgment: Sally judges *that* Jones has offended her. But the content of a judgment is not the whole of judgment. There is also the act of judging, and very different acts may be "directed toward" one and the same proposition. It has become routine in discussions of intentional states to make a distinction between asserting or doubting and *what* it is that is asserted or doubted, for example, or between the act of perceiving and what it is that is perceived. So too we can distinguish between Sally's making the judgments that constitute her getting angry and the proposition in the unemotional context of a Gricean investigation, but this is not the same making of the judgment that would be involved in her getting angry. She does not, as we say, "take it personally." She is rather amused and grateful, entertained by as she entertains the proposition in question. But though she judges that there has been an offense, she does not get angry. That is, she is not offended. The fact that she can assert that an offense (against her) has been committed without being offended does not show that she can make the judgments claimed to be essentially involved in the emotion of anger and not be angry. It only shows, what we already knew, that it is possible to assert or otherwise entertain propositions that are normally emotional without emotion.

It is worth noting that the distinction between propositional content and the entire act (and various 'levels' of acts) of judgment, so long employed so skillfully in discussing the utterance which constitutes the offense, tends to be wholly ignored in the standard objection. To counter that Sally can judge that she has been offended without being angry is no objection to the cognitivist analysis of anger as (in part) judging that one has been offended. Moreover, the judgment that she has been offended is no simple matter. There is the offender, Jones, and his remark. There is what he says, but there is also how he meant it. He asserted a certain proposition, presumably, but then he also intended for it to be taken a certain way, as an offense, or, perhaps, as a compliment. He might have said something offensive without meaning it as an offense, or he might have said something inoffensive with the intention of offending. So too we can distinguish between what Sally understands about Jones and his remark and "how she takes it." Recognizing Jones's intention is not the whole story, for she might know that Jones is trying to be offensive and not be offended (indeed, perhaps just because she knows how hard he is trying to be offensive). Or she may know that he is not trying to be offensive but is offended anyway. In her judgment, as in Jones's remark, we can distinguish between the proposition asserted and the holistic mental act(s) involved in the making of that judgment—what the offense means to her. It is one thing that she understands the meaning of the utterance, that is, the sentence in its context. She understands that the sentence was intended as offensive to her. But it is something more—considerably more—for her to also *be offended.* In Gricean circumstances she dispassionately judges that someone has said something (intentionally) offensive to her. When she gets angry, on the other hand, she gets offended. The propositions may be the same but the judgments are importantly different.

This is not to say, of course, that the propositional content of a judgment has nothing to do with a judgment's being a component of an emotion. The proposition that Jones offended Sally is not merely an incidental ingredient in Sally's anger, but neither is it entirely clear that such propositions are explicit in every judgment constitutive of an emotion. For example, the explicit propositional content of an angry microbiologist's judgments might be concerned wholly with microbiology and methodology; "your criticism of the experiment is invalid." Such judgments alone could not constitute an emotion, but combined with other judgments (e.g. that this is a matter of urgent personal gravity) they certainly could be components of emotion, and it is the way in which such judgments are made—indicated by the tautness of the voice, the clenched fist on the lectern—that make them part of emotion. But I say 'indicated,' for such non-cognitive features of judgment making are expressions of, not identical to, the emotional act judgment. It is the making of the judgment itself, not the accompanying bodily expression or the content of the judgment, that is accusatory, malevolent, vindictive. The propositional content of a judgment is germane and often essential to the emotion it (in part) constitutes, of course, but at some point our attention must be shifted from the propositional content to the whole act of judgment. Although the judgment that one has been offended is essential to anger it should not be thought that what distinguishes passionate from dispassionate judgment is just the assertion of that particular proposition.

The key claim in the standard objection is that one can make "the same judgment" without having the appropriate emotion. But, given what we have said above, it is not the case that judgments expressing the same proposition are thereby *the same* in the required sense. Sally sometimes judges dispassionately that she has been offended and at other times she is deeply hurt. Sometimes she simply judges that Jones has offended her; sometimes she makes that judgment and is therein offended and angry. In both cases, the judgment can be summarized, "Jones offended me (Sally)" but these are not "the same judgment," whether or not they involve the same proposition. Having an emotion is not just affirming the truth of a certain proposition. To object that the making of certain judgments is possible without having the respective emotion is to confuse the narrowly epistemic act of affirming the propositional content of a judgment with the many other ways in which judgments can be "made" which are essential to having an emotion.

II. JUDGMENTS AS SYSTEMIC

It is convenient and often sufficient to characterize an emotion in terms of a single judgment—particularly when distinguishing two emotions (shame and embarrassment, jealousy and envy). One might say, for example, that shame involves acceptance of responsibility whereas embarrassment does not, or that jealousy embodies some claim to a right that envy clearly lacks. But it would be a serious mistake to think that the analysis of an emotion therefore consists—as in the quaint offerings of some of the great philosophers—of a one line description. An emotion is a *system* of judgments. Anger is not just a judgment of offense but a network of interlocking judgments concerning one's status and relationship with the offending party, the gravity and the mitigating circumstances of the offense and the urgency of revenge. (Thus Lewis Carroll again; "I'll be judge, I'll be jury.") Love is not just the admiration of the other's virtues but a system of judgments about shared identities and interests, personal looks, charms, status and mutual concerns as well as a multitude of mostly absurd myths and metaphors that have infiltrated that system of judgments that we call "love." And the difference between envy and jealousy is not a single pair of judgments (e.g. a sense of entitlement to the coveted object); it too is a systematic difference, a difference in ways of seeing the world which might be illuminated but by no means wholly described by a single pair of differing judgments.

In *The Passions*, I distinguish a dozen or so judgment types that enter into emotions and form a multi-dimensional matrix within which our many emotions are differentiated and—just as important—interrelated. To focus on a single judgmental difference between two emotions may be useful and adequate for certain purposes, but it gives a false impression of the complexities of emotion. Just as it may serve the purposes of illustration and illumination to say that anger is a judgment of offense, to distinguish anger from mere irritation or frustration, for example, or to underscore the claim that an emotion is not merely a feeling or a physiological reaction, it is often instructive to pick out the dominant—or some overlooked but essential—judgmental component of an emotion. It is striking to learn, for instance, that one crucial ingredient in envy may be a judgment of one's own lack of self-worth. It seems to be edifying to hear (whether or not it is true) that love is an emotion with cosmic pretensions. But such abbreviated judgments do not capture the totality of emotion, and it is only to be expected that one might make just those abbreviated judgments, without the rest of the system of judgments, and not have the emotion in question, just as an undergraduate can learn the right formulation of the special theory of relativity without knowing the theory.

The system of judgments that make up an emotion does not consist exclusively of peculiarly emotional judgments. Just as the judgments that are typical of most emotions can be embedded in a context which is (relatively) unemotional, judgments that would seem to have nothing to do with emotion may be thoroughly embedded in an emotional context and so themselves be emotional. Consider the angry microbiologist's judgments, which might seem to be wholly concerned with microbiology and methodology ("your criticism of my experiment is invalid!"). It is not clear that such judgments should be treated only as the causal background of the anger rather than as part of it. Such judgments alone are not an emotion, but what makes them of particular significance to emotion is the context of other judgments, which we might summarize as the judgment that this is a matter of urgent personal importance. But judging that a matter is of urgent importance alone is not enough to constitute an emotion either; an emotion also needs its specific content (often summed up as the idea that emotions are 'intentional') such as that provided by the judgment that Jones is offensive, or by the judgment that the criticism of the experiment is invalid. We should not assume that the judgments constituting an emotion must all have some characteristic content or in themselves be particularly emotional. An emotion is the entire system of judgments, and the judgments that constitute the emotion are emotional by virtue of their place in that system.

The standard objection is more of a strategic maneuver than an argument. It is typically short and to the point. It shifts the burden to the strong cognitivist and then says, in effect, "whatever analysis of whatever emotion you give me in terms of judgments I will respond that one could make those judgments and not have that emotion." It is not surprising that a one-line analysis of an emotion in terms of a single judgment is always subject to such an objection, but it does not follow that the whole system of judgments is vulnerable to the same objection. Of course, it is incumbent upon the cognitive theorist to spell out in detail an adequate portrait of the various emotions, for it is this elaborate project—rather than the summary declaration of the cognitive position—that will make the case for cognitivism and render implausible the objection, "but couldn't you have all of that and still not have the emotion?" Unfortunately, there is also a very general problem of philosophical analysis here: the possibility of any adequate analysis of any concept in terms of necessary and sufficient conditions. Despite many decades of effort, there may be no such airtight analyses in philosophy; counter-examples may be inevitable—by way of showing the limitations of an analysis rather than deflating or refuting it altogether, and the business of the philosopher might be no more than to map out in detail a chart of the terrain. Furthermore, given the holism that lies behind much of my argument, it may be that all of the conditions and preconditions of even the simplest emotion would be as bewildering as the multitude of conditions Stephen Schiffer has catalogued concerning speech acts—leaving the impression that it is impossible for any ordinary human being to produce even the most ordinary, colloquial utterance (*Meaning*, Cambridge University Press, 1973). This is not the place to discuss these problematic metaphilosophical theses, but if an adequate analysis—that is, one that does not admit of any counter-examples, no matter how ingenious—may not be possible in any case, then the a prioristic strategy of the standard objection is hardly a boon to our understanding of emotions. The effort needs to be made to spell out the system of judgments that constitute a single emotion, Chisholming down the analysis to meet counter-examples. But this is very different from greeting the unsympathetic and non-specific rebuttle, "Ah, but I can make those judgments too without having the emotion." There will come a point in a thorough analysis where the rebuttle makes no sense; to make that holistic set of judgments *is* to have the emotion.

III. JUDGMENTS IN EMOTION AS ESSENTIALLY TIED
TO EXPRESSION IN ACTION

One way of explaining the difference between a system of judgments that make up an emotion and other judgments is to insist on their joint role in setting the circumstances for action. One recent theorist, Jennifer Church, has even argued that emotions should be construed as "internalized actions," a thesis not incompatible with the cognitivist thesis as I want to develop here. Emotions are intimately tied to their expression, and the expression of an emotion is not just an effect of the emotion. (See, e.g. Jerome Neu, "A Tear is an Intellectual Thing," 1985.) The system of judgments that make up an emotion do not just constitute a point of view, an observational framework or *Weltanschauung*; they also constitute a *scenario*, a behavioral stage setting in which the judgments dictate a set of behaviors, including, of course, verbal behavior. Ron de Sousa has offered the suggestive notion of a "paradigm scenario" to explain the nature of emotion; a paradigm scenario is that original situation in which emotional responses are learned. So too, situational scenarios, not abstract propositions, form the content of most emotions. The judgments that makeup an emotion are not just the components of a syllogism (as in Davidson's reconstruction of Hume's analysis of pride in the *Journal of Philosophy*, vol. 73 [1976]) but—to use a consciously Sartrian expression—an *engagement*. William James had it right when he insisted on "the urge to vigorous action," not as effect but as essence of emotion. (Like Hume, James overplayed the sensational element, at the detriment of the more insightful aspects of his analysis.) The judgments that make up emotion are not made in the merely observational mode. They are as a rule expressed in actions, even if those actions are usually truncated or displaced forms of full-blown, direct expressions (e.g., Wittgenstein's example of the angry man who smacks his cane against a tree). Some emotions (grief and embarrassment, for example) manifest themselves in seemingly pointless action, but they are still action—related in an important sense. Emotions sometimes constitute dramatic breakdowns in organized behavior, but (1) we hesitate to call the resulting awkwardness an "expression" of the emotion though we recognize this as an effect of the emotion, and (2) such breakdowns occur most often when the circumstances are unforeseen, when there is no practiced repertoire of expression. A man who is jilted by his lover for the first time will very likely find himself virtually paralyzed, or at best, able to produce a few childish expletives. A man who has had experience in such matters may, despite his despair, be able to bring off a quite polished performance.

The expressions of emotion are not independent of emotion but built into the system of judgments that constitute the emotion. Aristotle caught this in his insistence (in the *Rhetoric*) that anger includes—rather than causes—the desire for revenge. Now this might seem to support the anti-cognitivist argument, but only if one maintains—unreasonable, I think—that the intentions embodied in action are not cognitive because they are not 'purely' cognitive, or that the desires embedded in emotion can be sharply distinguished and separated from judgment. This is emphatically not to say that desire too is a species of judgment, or to deny that one can have the same desires in another context. It is to say that the context of an emotion is not just a cognitive context, but an active context in which we are engaged in a world that we care about. To insist on a concept of cognition (or judgment) that is essentially divorced from all such care and concerns is not only to adopt a wholly demeaning conception of emotion; it is also to accept a wholly useless concept of cognition and judgment.

IV. DISSOCIATED JUDGMENTS
(THE STANDARD OBJECTION AS PATHOLOGY)

The standard objection takes for granted the notion of dispassionate judgment and then challenges the cognitivist thesis to explain how a judgment—which is essentially dispassionate— can constitute an emotion. But this challenge can be turned around. Perhaps the meanest counter-argument against the judgments-without-emotion objection is one that I can honestly attribute to (blame on) Michael Stocker. The argument begins by noticing how odd it would be if a person were to make the system of judgments which compose an emotion without having the emotion— for example, the set of judgments appropriate (for most of us non-Davey Crockett types) as a large brown bear comes charging at us in the woods. Of course, we can all imagine a peculiar phenomenological circumstance in which one might dispassionately judge that "the fellow wearing the red shirt—namely me—is about to be mauled and caused considerable pain." But outside of philosophy seminars, such dispassion is better recognized as dissociation, a pathological condition. It is worth noting that the phenomenon of dissociation is what led Freud to distinguish "idea and affect," in order to explain how, for example, a patient could describe the most gruesome scene of murder and incest with the calm befitting a discussion about the weather. Which is to say that the content of a judgment is not wholly separable from the act and its context (which Husserl often emphasized) and, moreover, that the judgments that make up the emotion cannot be separated from the emotion except in the most unusual pathological cases. But then it is the pathology, and not the normal case, that needs to be explained.

One might object that though the circumstances of terror can rarely be conceived without terror, the circumstances of long term love or quiet pride can certainly be conceived of without passion. But what this shows—and can be shown on other grounds besides—is that many emotions do not depend on a specific, momentary context but involve complex sequences of judgments that may evolve over a period of days, weeks, or years. Not all passion is like explosive anger; indeed, the still popular distinction between occurent and standing emotions depends upon this false paradigm, and makes little sense without it. Hume had it right when he distinguished the violent versus the calm passions, by which he surely did not mean to eliminate the calm passions as passions. It is true that, over a long period of time, one finds oneself making more or less dispassionately a judgment that one remembers making rhapsodically, hysterically, only a few years before. But it is cynical, at least to say that such relatively dispassionate judgments—in long-term love, notably—indicate that there is no longer any emotion, now just opinion ("yes, you are indeed beautiful"). Again, it is the total context that counts, and the excitement that accompanies or fails to accompany a momentary judgment is not all there is to say about our emotional involvements in the world.

V. JUDGMENTS IN EMOTION DEFINED BY DESIRES

The judgments that make up an emotion have specifiable links with desires. It is not enough to say that emotions are composed of judgments that are *caused* by desires (as argued recently in *The Journal of Philosophy* by Jenefer Robinson, [vol. 80 (1983)]). The desire to be with Joe is not the cause of one's love for Joe (to use one of her examples); it is rather part of the emotion's essence, the motive definitive of—not just behind—the peculiar scenario which we call "love." It "fits" the scenario in a quasi-conceptually necessary way. Given Aristotle's description of anger as a perceived offense demanding punishment, for example, one can see that the urge to vengeance is something more than a cause or an effect (and something less than entailment—the awkward analysis suggested by the logical behaviorists). Judgments in emotion are judgments which have a quasi-conceptual connection with desires. (David Lewis calls such connections "loosely analytic.") This is suggested, for example, in our insistence that every emotion constitutes a scenario for action. It is explicit in our rejection of pathological dissociation as a paradigm for philosophy, and it is at least allowed for in our insistence that an emotional judgment is not just a proposition but also the way that a proposition is asserted, an entire mental act and not just a logical affirmation. Accordingly, the analysis of an emotion yields a more or less precisely circumscribed set of desires. Desire by itself is not an emotion, although it readily functions as a cause and a stimulus to emotion (is it easier to fall in love when hungry?). The desire to punish could not be a component desire of grief, though of course one could have the urge for revenge along with grief. In general, one might analyze the various emotions as judgmental structures enclosing a core desire which is both their motivation and their "conatus." But judgments and desires are not separate "components" of emotion (as, for example, John Searle argues throughout his book *Intentionality*). Many judgments have desires built right into them, for example, the judgment that something is desirable. (A reinterpretation of Mill's infamous argument lurks here.) The judgments that typically constitute the emotions—for example, judgments that something is offensive, desirable, tragic, lucky, degrading or an admirable achievement—have desires as their logical presuppositions. It is in this sense that the judgments that make up an emotion are to be characterized in part by desires, as part of, not in addition to, the strong cognitivist thesis.

One (but not "the") difference between anger and merely knowing that one has been offended is the fact that anger includes the desire for revenge—as Aristotle states so boldly. The statement seems bold and the ethics of anger behind it seems shocking because Aristotle, unlike a modern middle-class gentleman, did not see anger itself as offensive or irrational. Indeed, he even says (in the *Nicomachean Ethics*, Bk. IV, Ch. 5) that a man who does not get angry when anger is appropriate is a "dolt." Nevertheless, the connection between anger and the desire for revenge is (necessarily) very much intact in us, and while we might fudge elaborately and imaginatively in its expression, the logic of anger and what James called "the urge to vigorous action" are very much of a piece. Indeed, one of the problems with James's non-cognitivist theory is precisely that it does not and cannot explain the all-important connection between emotion and action, no matter how vigorously James insists on it.

VI. JUDGMENTS AS SUSTAINING, NOT INTRUSIVE, STRUCTURAL, NOT DISRUPTIVE

The aim of a cognitive theory of emotions is not to reduce the drama of emotion to cool, calm belief but to break down the insidious distinctions that render emotions stupid and degrading and eviscerate cognition. Part of the problem is the kind of limited examples philosophers often choose as instances of emotion; Shaffer, for instance, takes suddenly running across a log in the middle of the highway as a paradigm case. I would say that the resulting startle reaction is not an emotion at all, but the more general point is that, so long as examples of emotion tend to be cases of sudden shock or disclosure, the unintelligent, unprepared, dysfunctional and merely physiological aspect of emotion will always loom large, and the cognitive aspects of emotion will be comparatively inconspicuous. When, on the other hand, one starts with the grander passions as examples—Hume's sense of justice, the revolutionary's passion, the lover's life-long devotion—one gets a very different picture of emotions. And these, not being startled at the inopportune log in the road or the unwelcome sight of the bear, is where a more positive view of emotions, and a more cognitive view, is most plausible. We readily dismiss the three day flush of an adolescent as "not really love" and we recognize that a similar flush lasting several decades would be both an odd symptom of love and extremely unhealthy. A lover of many years has many *reasons* for love, and it surely makes no sense to suggest that such love is devoid of such judgments as respect and regard and a wide variety of judgments that are aesthetic and ethical as well as personal. The virtues (and vices) of emotion have to do with their endurance—even their intractibility—not sudden excitement and fleeting irrelevance.

This emphasis on the durability of emotion raises a problem, however, for the analysis of emotion in terms of judgment. I have not said anything in this essay to indicate why judgments should be favored among the variety of 'cognitive elements,' instead of beliefs or thoughts, for example. Beliefs (unlike judgments and thoughts) lack the requisite experiential component, although it still may be true to say that emotions presuppose certain beliefs. Thoughts (unlike beliefs) seem too episodic to account for emotions, even if, to be sure, every emotion is exemplified by characteristic thoughts, appropriate to the circumstances. Judgments seem to have the requisite place in experience (leaving aside the question of unconscious judgments), though we should certainly not say that what we experience in emotion is a system of judgments; it is rather the world as it is constituted through those judgments. The problem is that judgments, like thoughts and unlike beliefs, seem to be too momentary to account for long-term emotion, and although a judgment might initiate an emotion, it would seem strange to say that the emotion involves making that judgment continuously. One solution would be to say that an emotion is initiated by a judgment (or a system of judgments) but then carried on by (system of) beliefs, but this then fails to explain the experiential content of the on-going emotion. A very different solution is to suggest that emotions—like God's universe according to some theologians—require not just creation but an on-going effort. Thus one should think of judgment not as a momentary phenomenon at all, but as a continuous activity. Making an ethical judgment, for instance, does not consist just of the moment of deliberation and decision, and it is not just the event of pronouncement. It is a vision of wrong- (or right-) doing that is constantly (or inconstantly) renewed—which need not involve renewed deliberation or decision. So too, the judgment(s) one makes in emotion—that Jones is offensive or that one's lover is wonderful—are continually renewed, and one might speculate that the frequency and difficulty of renewal has much to do with the intensity and violence of the emotion. But in any case, the primary point is that emotions should not be construed as merely momentary intrusions into an otherwise orderly life but rather as dynamic structures of our experience that must be continually reanimated. Understanding emotions as judgments allows us to understand why this should be so and, a not undesirable benefit, helps us appreciate our active participation—as opposed to passivity—in our emotional lives.

Emotions are judgments, but not judgments in the sense that they are detached and disinterested momentary reflections about a world that does not deeply concern us. Rather, they are judgments which cannot be understood apart from the systematic connections with action and desire and a holistic view of our experience over time. Arguing that emotions are strongly cognitive does not make them philosophically less exciting. They can be just as subject to illuminating conceptual analysis as other more established topics in ethics and the philosophy of mind.

❧ RELATED APPROACHES ❧

The Thesis of Constructionism

Claire Armon-Jones

In the last ten years a new set of emotion theories has emerged. These theories (as represented, for example, in philosophy by Coulter, 1979; in social theory by Sabini and Silva, 1982; in psychology by Averill, 1980; and in anthropology by Lutz, 1982) retain the standard use of 'emotion' as a term to cover phenomena such as fear, anger, sorrow, joy, compassion, grief, remorse, envy, jealousy, guilt, pity, gratitude and other affective states. However, they are united by the principle that emotions are 'socioculturally constituted.' The principle of the 'sociocultural constitution of emotion' is one aspect of a general theory concerning the sociocultural constitution of individual experience, a theory which originated in the critical positivist tradition of post-enlightenment social philosophy. Mead regarded individual experience and behaviour as not prior to, but constituted by, the social group of which the individual is part: 'the behaviour of an individual can be understood only in terms of the behaviour of the whole social group of which he is a member, since his individual acts are involved in larger, social acts which go beyond himself and which implicate the other members of that group' (Mead, 1934).

Mead's theory was influential in promoting studies of the interdependence between social frameworks and the shaping of individual behaviour and experience. Similarly, Montesquieu's (1750) analysis of the sociological basis of political constitutions and civil law provided an inspiration for cross-cultural studies of the relation between individual experience and the religious beliefs, norms, political and social ideologies of particular cultural systems.

One outcome of these analyses is a model of general experience as constituted by what it is conceptualized as, and of conceptualizations as essentially deriving from the language, beliefs and social rules—the 'world view'—of the agent's cultural community. It is this model which provides the background to the constructionists' principle of emotion as 'socioculturally constituted.' The arguments which claim to justify this background model require more clarification than I will be able to provide in this outline. However some crucial aspects of what the constructionist means by 'socioculturally constituted emotions' can be outlined as follow:

1. According to constructionism, emotions are characterized by attitudes such as beliefs, judgements and desires, the contents of which are not natural, but are determined by the systems of cultural belief, value and moral value of particular communities: 'the capacity to experience either shame or guilt ... involves cultural knowledge and reasoning conventions' (Coulter, 1979). '... our capacity to experience certain emotions is contingent upon our learning to interpret and appraise matters in terms of norms, standards, principles and ends ... judged desirable ... or appropriate' (Pritchard, 1976).

2. Constructionists defend the view that emotion attitudes are culturally determined by the claim that the attitudes involved in emotions are learnt as part of the agent's introduction to the beliefs, values, norms and expectations of his/her culture. The acquisition of culturally appropriate emotion attitudes requires that emotions should be understood as elicited as a result of the agent's having acquired a culturally appropriate construal of the situation in which the situation is presented, and understood in terms of those values, etc., of his/her community: 'types of situation are paradigmatically linked to the emotions they afford by convention. The link is neither deterministic nor biological but sociocultural' (Coulter, 1979).

3. Thus far constructionism differs from naturalism in regarding emotions not as natural responses elicited by natural features which a situation may possess, but as socioculturally determined patterns of experience and expression which are acquired, and subsequently feature in, specifically social situations. However, constructionism adds to the claims above the following 'prescriptive' thesis: 'emotions are a socially prescribed set of responses to be followed by a person in a given situation. The response is a function of shared expectations regarding appropriate behaviour' (Averill, 1980). According to constructionism, there is a prescriptive implication embedded in the cultural situations in which emotions feature in that an emotion is not merely warranted by the situation as culturally construed but is deemed by members of a community to be a response which ought to feature in that situation because its presence would demonstrate the agent's commitment to the cultural values exemplified in that situation. This prescriptive relation between the emotion and the values it reflects is alleged by constructionists to have a crucial role in contributing to the acquisition of culturally appropriate emotions and to the subsequent regulation of the agent's responses to emotion-warranting situations.

4. The rationale for (3), according to constructionism, is that emotions are constituted in order to serve sociocultural functions: 'the meaning of an emotion—its functional significance is to be found primarily within the sociocultural system' (Averill, 1980). Emotions are regarded by constructionists as functional in that the possession of culturally appropriate emotions serves to restrain undesirable attitudes and behaviour, and to sustain and endorse cultural values: 'emotions are statements about, and motivations for the enact-

ment of cultural values' (Lutz, 1982). This functional account of emotion again differs from naturalism in that it requires that emotions are related in some way to agent responsibility. For example, according to constructionism, once emotion attitudes are acquired then agents can be held responsible for the adoption and expression of such attitudes in the contexts for which they are prescribed. Thus, unlike the alleged 'natural, passive state,' the adopted emotion is able to demonstratively reinforce the social value which commands the response and the agent's commitment to the value.

THE IMPLICATIONS OF CONSTRUCTIONISM

Constructionist theories of emotion, are I think, important and worth examining not only because they go beyond traditional theories of emotion as natural phenomena but because they have radical implications for both philosophical and practical ethics.

What implications does constructionism have for philosophical ethics? The ethical theories of, for example Kant (1949) and the Emotivists (e.g., Stevenson, 1937) are opposed in their views of the relation between emotions and moral discourse. According to Kant, moral discourse should be expressive of objectivity and consistency in rational judgement concerning moral matters. The emotions, being capricious and unevenly distributed natural dispositions, should not be motivations for, or involved in, such judgements. According to Emotivism, moral discourse is essentially functional, its function being to express the emotions of the speaker and incite emotions in others. Kant's theory is compatible with the view that moral training can educate and exert a controlling influence on natural emotional dispositions. However, both theories regard emotions as phenomena which are ontologically prior to moral judgement and action. Whereas for Kant emotions, as natural dispositions, should be ignored in moral judgement, for the Emotivists these natural dispositions are necessary conditions of moral judgement. Also, it was certain assumptions concerning the nature of emotion, which prompted the criticisms of Emotivism. According to Urmson (1963), Emotivism is false because emotions are not within our power to choose or reject and therefore could not be objects of moral incitement or influence.

However, constructionism disputes not only the grounds for this criticism but also the theories it addresses. According to constructionism, moral sentiments such as 'guilt' and 'pity' are not ontologically prior to moral judgement because a grasp of certain moral rules is a precondition of the capacity to feel the moral sentiments. Thus far, constructionism reverses the Emotivists' account in regarding such sentiments not as causal conditions, but as dependent upon the prior understanding of moral rules and discourse. In particular, according to constructionism, it is because the moral sentiments involve moral attitudes such as the evaluation of an act as morally wrong that, *contra* Urmson, such sentiments can involve agent responsibility and be subjected to rational appraisal and criticism. Moreover, as Williams (1972) suggests, in criticism of Kant's ethical theory, moral worth and emotion are not separable, since emotion has a crucial role in conveying the sincerity of moral worth. Here constructionism develops this role of emotion by explaining it as a social function of emotion, and the constitution of the 'moral sentiments' as part of moral training.

What implications would constructionism have for practical ethics? If, as the constructionist claims, emotions are functionally constituted for the maintenance of particular value systems, then a moral issue arises in that such organizations of human experience not only are socially based, but also can be evaluated as desirable and just. For example, during the early stages of the First World War recruitment of British soldiers was increased by propaganda aimed at the creation of an attitude which would enhance the motivation of young men to fight. The attitude in question, 'courageous patriotism,' qualifies as an emotion because it was clearly something felt, i.e., 'the fervour, shining eyes and heart swelling with pride,' etc. Moreover, the emotion itself was not clearly separable from its intended purpose, in that to feel 'courageous patriotism' was at the time, by social definition, to wish to be in the battlefields saving one's country and to believe that in performing such actions one's integrity as a citizen and as a man was preserved. Hence it was from such specific ends that the emotion derived its particular quality and content. The ethical issue which would arise here is whether it is morally acceptable to create an emotion which obscures the realities of war, diverts the person from other desires (e.g., immediate self-preservation) and responsibilities (e.g., family) and suppresses other emotions (e.g., compassion for the construed opposition).

THE ASSUMPTIONS OF CONSTRUCTIONISM

My aim in this chapter is to examine certain aspects of constructionism chosen with respect to both their foundational role in constructionist theory and their amenability to philosophical analysis. Given the varieties of emotions and of emotion theories, I will not be able to test the arguments proposed for every emotion, nor will I consider all the philosophical issues which constructionism might inspire. Descriptive work has been done by theorists, including those mentioned here, on the question of how emotions are socioculturally constituted. However, little philosophical attention has been paid to the question of how it is possible that emotions could be socioculturally constituted. So we need to specify the theory of mind that is presupposed in the constructionist account, and to consider various versions of constructionism.

First, constructionism would appear to require a theory of mind in which emotions, as instances of psychological states, are defined as cognition-based.

On the constructionist account culturally appropriate emotion attitudes are acquired by reference to those contexts for which the emotion is deemed to be desirable. This implies that, once the emotion has been acquired, then the agent's further ability to respond appropriately will depend crucially upon his/her ability to appraise a situation as warranting the emotion. The view that emotions depend upon appraisals is compatible with those contemporary philosophical theories which characterize emotions as cognitive in virtue of their dependence upon judgement and belief.

Second, and following from this, constructionism also appears to require a theory of mind in which emotions can be defined as in some sense world-dependent. The constructionist's account of emotions as responses appropriate to cultural contexts implies some kind of link between the emotion and external states of affairs. Post-Wittgensteinian philosophers have argued that psychological states such as emotion could not be identified via introspection alone because inner states lack the requisite identifying features. Emotions, they argue, are identified in part by behaviour, and in part by those external situations to which the emotion is directed. Constructionism is, it seems, committed to some version of this philosophical thesis in that, if it were possible to identify emotions via introspection alone, then the notion of 'appropriate context' would be redundant and could not have the explanatory role which the constructionist ascribes to it.

However, constructionism contains assumptions which go beyond the philosophical positions stated above. The philosophical theses make the minimal and general claim that emotions are world-dependent in so far as they are individuated by reference to behaviour and to appropriate object or situation types. But this thesis as it stands is still compatible with the naturalist views which constructionism disputes, since it is consistent with the claim that the external referents of emotions have a natural and universal status and give rise to responses constituted by natural beliefs and desires, etc. Constructionism maintains that emotions are constituted by non-natural attitudes, these being acquired in, and explicable by reference to, specifically sociocultural contexts.

This last claim requires that emotions are constituted by attitudes which are in principle learnable, and that such attitudes and their external referents are either irreducibly or significantly sociocultural in nature. The constructionist theses also require that emotions can be understood as prescribable for a social system, and that the sociocultural determination of emotion is revealed not only in semantics via its influence on our understanding of emotion terms but also in phenomenology via its penetration to the quality of emotion experience itself. So, while constructionism requires the minimal philosophical thesis above, in order to oppose the naturalist view constructionism also requires a validation of these further assumptions.

Third, constructionism opposes the traditional view expressed in philosophy in psychology that emotions are non-purposive forces which serve to disrupt rationality. Descartes and Darwin did allow that emotions are purposive in so far as they assist the survival of the individual. However, constructionism goes beyond this individualistic teleology in regarding the function of the emotions as essentially sociocultural and as serving individuals only as members of their community. This sociofunctional account of emotion exposes constructionism to the objection that it is not clear what kind of social function could be ascribed to phenomena such as ill-founded and negative emotions. Consequently, constructionism also needs to provide a plausible explanation of the way in which, and the extent to which, emotions can be understood as having a sociofunctional role.

CONSTRUCTIONISM VERSUS NATURALISM

The points made so far raise the question of how radical an alternative to the naturalist view of emotions constructionism intends to be. Here I will briefly outline two possible versions of constructionism which take the form of a strong and a weaker thesis. I will suggest that the weaker thesis is more plausible and is also sufficient to dispute some of the important premises of naturalism.

The strong thesis can be defined as one which claims that for any emotion, including the primary emotions, that emotion is an irreducibly sociocultural product. From this it would follow that no emotion can be a natural state, and therefore that the complex or sophisticated emotions cannot be regarded as cultural modifications of natural states. On this view the term 'emotion' derives from, and is central to, the sociocultural domain. The similarities between natural responses and 'emotions' are incidental. So to predicate the term 'emotion' of natural responses is to extend the term beyond its scope of legitimate application. This radical view gains support from two equally radical philosophical theses. First, the similarity between human and non-human behaviour cannot be used as evidence for the claim that emotions are natural states because emotions involve cognitions such as belief and judgement which cannot legitimately be ascribed to members of non-human species. Second, agents cannot be said to feel an emotion (E) unless they have a grasp of the concept E and can apply this concept to their own experience on appropriate occasions.

The weaker thesis can be defined as one which concedes to the naturalist the existence of a limited range of natural emotion responses. This view is implied by Averill, who states that 'the view that there is an invariant core to emotional behaviour which remains untouched by sociocultural influences is essentially a reification of emotion into a biological given' (1980). Averill's reference to emotions as 'untouched by sociocultural influences' appears to allow for the possibility of emotion responses as featuring prior to, and extra to, sociocultural influences.

One advantage of the weaker thesis is that, in conceding the existence of natural emotions, it escapes some of the difficulties of the strong view. For example, on the strong view it remains unexplained why, if emotions such as 'fear' are never natural responses, the humans who undergo these emotions exhibit much the same types of behaviour as some non-human species. Here it seems implausible to argue that responses which produce the same, or similar, effects are nevertheless entirely different. Also, given that it is such effects which provide evidence for the ascription of beliefs and judgements, etc., then it is not clear why these inferences from behaviour to mental state should be confined to humans. If such cognitive features can be ascribed to non-human species, then they need not serve as evidence for the non-naturalness of human emotions. In particular, the fact that we often regard non-verbal behaviour as sufficient for the ascription of emotions such as 'fear' to other persons suggests that mastery by them of the concept 'fear' is not a necessary condition of their experiencing this emotion. These points support our intuition that some objects or situations are natural referents of emotions such as 'fear' in virtue of their possessing features relevant to extra-social needs such as survival. For instance, no cultural significance need be attached by persons to a charging bull in order for it to be construed by them as dangerous and as warranting fear.

The strong view, in denying the existence of any natural emotions, is committed to refuting the points above and is in this respect problematic. However, the weaker version raises the question of exactly what is being asserted. Is it that some emotions, such as non-primary emotion types, are entirely socioculturally constituted? Or is it that all emotion types are socioculturally constituted to some extent? The first option is vulnerable to the naturalist objection that, for any emotion type, we can provide an instance of that type which is not specifically sociocultural—for example, instances of 'compassion' as generated by natural, empathic distress at the suffering of another being. So the second option seems preferable. It enables the constructionist to demonstrate the extent to which both primary and non-primary emotion types are socioculturally constituted, a position which is compatible with there being instances of both types in which they are natural responses to natural situations.

For the constructionist who adopts this version of the weaker thesis, the interest lies, I think, in the question of how much significance can be attached to the natural emotions relative to the socioculturally constituted emotions. For example, proponents of naturalism endorse the view that emotions, primitive and socialized, share the same biological bases and, where applicable, the same natural cognitions. Sociocultural variables, in so far as they feature in naturalist theory, have a peripheral influence, e.g., in reducing the intensity of the natural response and in determining the manner in which it is outwardly displayed. A proponent of this approach is Ekman

(1980), who introduces the term 'display rule' to explain the cultural prohibition and control of natural emotion states. For example, he claims that the exhibition of 'grief' at funerals in certain societies is a natural response constrained by norms which permit its expression only if the griever is close to the deceased.

The crucial point here is that the naturalist's predication of the term 'emotion' to both primitive and socialized emotions is justified by the view that both phenomena are sufficiently similar to fall under the same term. The weaker constructionist's objection to this account would be that, in so far as emotions involve specifically sociocultural attitudes, feature in specifically sociocultural contexts and bear a prescriptive, functional relation to such contexts, the naturalist cannot extrapolate his account of natural emotions in order to explain them. Furthermore, the naturalist's account is of limited scope since the salient aspects of an agent's emotional responses form part of a mental life, the interests, goals and general attitudes of which largely reflect the agent's membership of his/her cultural community. So the issue presented by the weaker constructionist is perhaps a more subtle one, inviting us to consider whether our application of the term 'emotion' both to natural and cultural instances of a response leads us to ignore their discontinuities.

The sense in which emotions can be understood as constituted by specifically sociocultural attitudes, and the prescriptive relation which emotions bear to sociocultural beliefs and values, is an issue which I have examined elsewhere (Armon-Jones, 1985). In this chapter I will describe some contemporary philosophical critiques of traditional theories of emotion, focusing in particular upon those features of the contemporary views which are compatible with, and might therefore provide a framework for, constructionism. I will suggest that the contemporary philosophical characterization of emotions as cognition-based and as involving attitudinal components should be understood as providing a basis for the constructionist principle of emotions as socioculturally acquired responses. I will also, having examined some theories of the role of sensation, and the subjective element in 'emotion feeling,' suggest that emotion feeling can be analysed as essentially constituted by the relevant attitudinal components. This claim is relevant to constructionism since, if sociocultural factors can determine emotion attitudes, then such factors should also be understood as determining emotion feeling via their determination of the attitudes by which emotion feeling is constituted.

THE REFUTATION OF THE TRADITIONAL THEORIES OF EMOTION

Philosophers traditionally defined the emotions as 'passions.' Passions were regarded as involuntary, non-cognitive phenomena which, like sensation and perception, are incorrigibly known simple impressions named by simple concepts: '[the passions] are received into the soul in exactly the same fashion as the objects of the exterior senses' (Descartes, 1952); '... a passion is an original existent' (Hume, 1978); '... [they] are so interior to our soul that it is impossible that they should be felt without their being in reality just as they are felt' (Descartes, 1952).

The traditional view is, first, subject to Wittgenstein's general critique of introspectionist semantics. According to this view, the inner feelings of both passions and sensations are contingently related to, and hence logically independent of, their expressions in verbal and physical behaviour. This view, Wittgenstein points out, renders the inner feelings themselves radically private. Against this, he argues that the inner feelings are not radically private but accessible since the terms via which we describe them depend upon objective criteria for their meaning and justification, and hence form a part of a shared public language: an "inner process" stands in need of outward criteria' (Wittgenstein, 1980).

Second, Wittgenstein points out that emotions and sensations are fundamentally dissimilar in that emotions, unlike sensations, are characteristically about an external object or situation, a reference which is apparent in the inclusion of a grammatical object in emotion sentences; for example, M is 'annoyed with x/afraid of x/grateful of x/angry that x,' x being some situation, person, action or attribute in the world which provides the extension of the emotion. Thus far, the general characterization of emotions as involving 'a reference to something beyond the person himself or beyond his present state' (Pitcher, 1965) already moves away from the traditional view of the passions as inner processes, logically distinct from the external world.

The analysis of the meaning of emotion terms also suggests that there are logical restrictions upon the type of object to which an emotion can refer. 'Envy' and 'jealousy,' for example, do not, within their grammatical rules, permit me to feel 'envious' or 'jealous' of myself, because these emotions share the feature that they are conceptually related to objects, the range of which excludes the subject of the emotion. By contrast, the subject can be included among the objects of emotions such as 'pride' and 'shame.' While M can also be proud or 'ashamed' of someone else, there must be some relation of responsibility or personal relevance here in order for M's emotion to qualify as 'pride' or 'shame.' For example, M's feeling 'proud' of his son's achievements requires that M regards himself as in some way responsible for, and able to take credit for, the events in his son's life. Similarly, although an agent can ascribe to himself the term 'annoyed' or 'angry,' he cannot ascribe to himself the term 'indignant' if the act of negligence which gives rise to his feelings is his own fault: only if the act of negligence is the fault of someone else could he describe himself as 'indignant.' So there are generally restrictions upon the sort of object to which an emotion type can be directed (see Bedford, chapter 2 above).

THE COGNITIVE ASPECT OF EMOTIONS

The examples considered so far enable us to illustrate the contemporary philosophical view (e.g., Kenny, 1963; Lyons, 1980; Gordon, 1969) that emotions are dependent upon cognitions. In order to be 'envious' I must believe that the object of my 'envy,' e.g., an attribute, belongs to another, and I must also believe that it is an attribute which I do not possess. Similarly, my being 'guilty' or 'ashamed' about an action requires that I believe that I am responsible for the action. However, while beliefs may be essential to the generation of emotions, they are not sufficient to constitute particular emotions because different emotions can be generated by the same belief. For example, the 'belief that x is dangerous' could provoke 'fear' in M and 'excitement' in S. The crucial differentiating factors are commonly the evaluative and appetitive attitudes which are also involved; for example, the difference between the two emotions above may be explained by the fact that S's 'excitement' about x is warranted by his desire to live dangerously, whereas M's 'fear' about the same x is warranted by his evaluation of x as menacing or threatening to him and his desire to avoid x.

Similarly, my feeling 'envious' requires that I hold the beliefs stated above in conjunction with other attitudes to which 'envy' is conceptually related, such as 'my evaluating the attribute as good' and 'my desiring the attribute for myself.' It is not a necessary condition of my being envious that I regard the attribute as desirable in all respects, only that, despite other opinions I may have about the attribute, I regard it as desirable in some respect. For example, while I may regard M's ruthlessness as undesirable in so far as it causes him to be selfish and inconsiderate towards others, I may also regard M's ruthlessness as desirable in so far as it gives him determination and assists his career. It would be correct to say that if I decide that, all things considered, M's ruthlessness is undesirable then I cannot be, or continue to be, envious. But I am not impelled to resolve my appraisals of the attribute in this way, in particular because they focus on different aspects and consequences of the attribute and are not therefore self-contradictory.

Exactly how the various attitudinal components which individuate the particular emotions are interrelated is a question debated by philosophical theorists of emotion. However, as a general theory the attitudinal account disputes the traditional theories of emotion in the following respects. As opposed to traditional views, the beliefs, evaluations and appetitive attitudes involved in an emotion are cognitive in that they depend upon the agent's knowledge and his capacity to judge and compare. Also, if emotions are constituted by particular conjunctions of attitudes, then they are not, as the traditional views claim, simple but complex phenomena; i.e., M can explain his 'anger' avowal by stating the object of his 'anger,' say, S's action; his belief, say, that the action was directed towards himself; his evaluation, say, of the action as an insult; and his desires, say, to seek revenge on S.

The attitudinal account also imposes restrictions upon the status of the object to which an emotion can be directed. If M's 'anger' is 'about x,' then x is the extension of M's emotion. However, given that it is M's attitudes towards x which generate his emotion, then x, in its role of explaining M's emotion, has to be characterized intensionally. This distinction can be elucidated by using Aristotle's account of 'anger' (in his *Rhetoric*) as 'a desire for what appears to be a revenge for what appears to be an insult.'

Let us suppose that the referent of M's 'anger' in Aristotle's example is A's doing x: 'letting his tongue protrude from his mouth.' Here it is not x as extensionally characterized, but x as construed as, or believed by the agent to be, 'an insult' which is conceptually related to 'anger' and which explains his 'anger' as warranted by the action. Similarly, as we saw in the case of 'envy,' the descriptions applicable to x such as 'ruthless' are not interchangeable *salva veritate* in their role of explaining M's 'envy,' because it is the attribute only as construed in terms of its advantages (promoting A's career) which warrants M's 'envy.' So while it is towards an object x that the agent's emotion E is directed, and it is x which provides the extension of E, it is x under the agent's descriptions that explains x as an object of E in particular.

If an emotion depends upon the construal of an object under those intensional descriptions which warrant the emotion, then this provides considerable latitude, both in the range of token extensional objects to which a particular emotion can be directed and in the range of third-person evaluations concerning the warrantedness of the emotion. For example, token objects of M's 'depression' can run the gamut from 'the weather' to 'work' to 'personal relationships.' These objects have few extensional properties in common; however, they warrant M's 'depression' in so far as they share the intensional feature of 'looking bleak to M,' etc. *A fortiori*, the third-person evaluation of an agent's emotion as warranted depends not only upon judgements concerning the extension of the object (e.g., that there really is an x of which M is afraid) but also upon agreement over the agent's construal as being a plausible construal of the object (e.g., that x can be construed as menacing or dangerous).

What relevance do the accounts outlined above have for constructionism? The characterization of emotion as attitudinal and cognition-dependent is crucial to constructionism in the following respects. According to constructionism, a socioculturally constituted emotion is an acquired response. This requires that the elements constitutive of the emotion are ones which are capable of being acquired by the agent. Consequently, it is essential to constructionism that an account of emotion be given in which emotions are neither identifiable with, nor have the same ontological status as, phenomena such as sensation and perception. This is so because, although perceptual skills, for instance, can be acquired, we also have reason to believe that perception and sensation are not essentially skills acquired by training but are natural phenomena which exist prior to the acquisition of any sociocultural frame of reference within which we might want to explain them. Hence, if an emotion was, as Aquinas believed (in 'The emotions'), a matter of a perception followed by a sensation, then this would cast doubt on the possibility of the emotion's being a socioculturally acquired phenomenon.

However, the contemporary accounts of emotion are consistent with constructionism in that the attitudes regarded by contemporary theorists as constituting emotions share the feature that they can in principle be acquired by training. While we regard some attitudes as natural (e.g., the desire to eat; the evaluation of wild beasts as dangerous), we regard other attitudes as dependent upon training and the introduction to a social custom (e.g., the desire to be polite; the evaluation of a Matisse as delicate; the belief that theft is a crime). Thus far, the contemporary accounts of emotion appear to provide an apposite framework upon which constructionists might build their explanation of how the attitudes which constitute the various emotions are socioculturally constituted.

Furthermore, the explanation of emotions as involving reference to an object or situation type enables the constructionist to demonstrate the extent to which such situations reflect the beliefs, values and expectations of particular cultures and the way in which such situations are used as contexts for the acquisition of the culturally appropriate emotion attitudes. Also, the constructionist can explain the agent's subsequent construals of situations as warranting certain emotions in virtue of the construal's involving attitudes which reflect the beliefs and values of the agent's community.

Finally, the attitudinal account opposes the Cartesian and Kantian view of emotions as opposed to the faculty of reason. If emotions are cognition-based, then this allows that they can be subjected to rational persuasion and criticism. For example, agents can be reasoned out of their 'anger' just because the emotion is based on attitudes which can themselves be critically appraised in respect of whether they form an accurate or reasonable construal of the situation. If the agent misinterprets the situation as an insult, then we expect and consider him able to relinquish his 'anger.' This point is relevant to constructionism because it allows that emotions can be endorsed or condemned with respect to the social appropriateness of the attitudes by which the emotion is generated, and that agents can be held responsible for the possession or absence of those emotion attitudes which are socially required for a situation.

The analysis given so far has characterized emotion in terms of the attitude complexes to which the various emotion types are conceptually related. According to some attitudinal theorists emotion feeling is not reducible to attitudes, in which case the analysis is, as it stands, incomplete in failing to incorporate emotion 'feeling' itself. This alleged incompleteness of a purely attitudinal account has led to various compromise views in which emotion 'feeling' is reintroduced by supplementing attitudinal components either with the notion of emotion qualia or with physiological features.

The motive for the introduction of emotion qualia is the belief that emotion feeling has a subjective element which is not reducible to the belief, desire and judgement components of the emotion. This subjective element is regarded as a phenomenally distinct feeling which, though evident in the experience of 'being moved' by an emotion, can only be 'vaguely approximated' via evocation and metaphor and so cannot be entirely captured via attitudinal analyses. For example, Arnold qualifies her cognitive account of emotion by adding to it an 'emotion quale [which] consists precisely in that unreasoning involuntary attraction or compulsion' (Arnold, 1960). Similarly, with reference to emotion conceptualizations, Leventhal maintains that 'the verbal, conceptual system ... is a way of representing and communication about feelings but not a representation of the feelings themselves' (Leventhal, 1980). The implication of these remarks is that there is a gap between emotion feelings themselves and the means by which they are conceptually represented.

The introduction of emotion qualia to the characterization of emotion poses a difficulty for constructionism in the following respects. The constructionist wants to argue that emotions are socioculturally constituted in that sociocultural factors determine not only emotion attitudes and their expression in language and behaviour, but also the experiential aspect of emotion via their determination of emotion feeling. The 'qualia' thesis outlined above requires that it is a necessary condition of a state's being a felt emotion that the attitudes involved are accompanied by an irreducible subjective feeling. The qualia thesis poses a difficulty for constructionism in virtue of its individualistic implications. It postulates a domain of individual emotion experience which is not reducible to emotion attitudes and expression and therefore can remain exempt from the sociocultural factors which are alleged by the constructionist to explain these latter components. Hence if the experiential aspect of emotion amounts to irreducible qualia, then this casts doubt on the possibility that emotion feeling could be socioculturally constituted.

The 'physiological' thesis (e.g. Perkins, 1966) poses a difficulty for constructionism in virtue of its naturalistic implications. Physiological factors such as chemically induced arousal and increased motor activity are biological events understood to be basic, natural and involuntary. Hence if these events are necessary components of a felt emotion, then this limits the scope of the constructionist's argument in that it reduces those components of the emotion which could be explained as socioculturally constituted. For instance, such physiological events could not be prescribed nor subjected to social endorsement and condemnation. The constructionist could argue here that, even if emotion feeling amounts to physiological events, this is not inconsistent with constructionism since it is the agent's attitudes, themselves socioculturally constituted, which cause the physiological events in question. Hence the 'physiological' thesis does not provide a strong opposition since it does not necessarily support naturalism. However this approach is unsatisfactory in so far as it requires constructionists to relinquish their view of emotion feeling as culturally constituted in favour of its being a natural response caused indirectly by cultural factors. While constructionists could take this approach, they do not need to do so since emotion feeling can, I believe, be adequately characterized without appealing to qualia or to physiological factors as necessary constituents of the total emotion event.

THE CONSTITUTION OF EMOTION FEELING BY ATTITUDES

Here I want to examine a distinction which Wittgenstein draws between emotion and sensation because it is relevant to the problem posed for constructionism by the qualia thesis. Despite contemporary philosophical agreement that psychological predicates require outward, critical justification, the qualia thesis above implies an adherence to the belief that criteria are expressive of an inner quale or irreducible raw feel not only in the case of sensation but also in the case of emotion. But this raises the question of what the 'feeling' term in an avowal such as 'I feel x' (where x stands for an emotion predicate) could refer to. The difficulty here is that, although the account above may apply to sensation, the notion of a residual qualia is not plausible in the case of emotion. Why not?

Wittgenstein, as already noted, argues that the terms for both emotion and sensation feelings are conceptually related to those verbal and physical expressions to which they give rise. However while in the case of sensation Wittgenstein does 'not deny the existence of the inner process' (*Philosophical Investigations*, 304), in the case of the emotion 'joy,' for example, he states: 'and of course joy is not joyful behaviour nor yet a feeling around the corner of the mouth and eyes. "But joy surely designates an inward thing?" No. Joy designates nothing at all. Neither any inward nor any outward thing' (Wittgenstein, 1981, p. 487).

From Wittgenstein's remarks on the failure of emotions such as 'joy' to 'designate anything' can be derived the following claims. First, the remark above is not meant to imply that 'joy' lacks any kind of referent, but is, as Green (1979) suggests, meant to criticize theoretical reductions of emotion to either inner feeling or outer behaviour, and to emphasize that no single item of verbal or physical behaviour can provide sufficient conditions for the ascription of an emotion.

Second, I would suggest that the reason why Wittgenstein confines 'reference to an inner process' to sensation terms is that sensation terms do refer to inner qualia in virtue of the fact that such qualia are not embraced by, and remain ontologically distinct from, the expressions to which they give rise and to which they are conceptually related. For example, the raw feeling of a pain cannot be constituted by 'my clutching my leg, believing that I am in pain, and making verbal avowals' because pain can be felt independently of such attitudes and their behavioural expressions. Hence Wittgenstein's claim that sensation feels are conceptually related to outward criteria in the form of the appropriate verbal and behavioural expressions is a purely semantic claim concerning conditions of meaningfulness for sensation terms, not an ontological claim about the existence of sensation feelings. The point here is that sensation terms refer to 'inner processes' just because, though conceptually related to, they are nevertheless ontologically distinct from the attitudes and behaviour to which they give rise. Thus far it is not to emotion feelings but to sensation feelings that Leventhal's distinction between representation and feeling really seems to apply.

However, with reference to the emotion 'joy,' Wittgenstein remarks:

> the gasp of joy, laughter, jubilation, the thoughts of happiness—is not the experience of all this: joy? Do I know then that he is joyful because he tells me he feels his laughter, feels and hears his jubilation—or because he laughs and is jubilant? Do I say 'I am happy' because I feel all that? ... the words 'I am happy' are a bit of the behaviour of joy. (Wittgenstein, 1980, p. 151)

Wittgenstein is, I think, making two points in this remark. The first point is that we do not recognize our 'joy' as a result of observing our thoughts and behaviour. I do not infer that I am joyful via induction from 'hearing my jubilation.' Rather, I simply think and behave in a joyful manner such that my recognition of my emotion, as expressed in the avowal 'I am happy,' is part of the expression of the emotion. The second point which emerges from the above remark is that 'the gasp of joy, laughter, jubilation, the thoughts of happiness' amount to—are identifiable with—the 'experience of joy.' Hence, unlike the case of sensation, in which attitudes and behaviour refer to an inner quale of which such factors are ontologically independent, in the case of emotions these factors are ontologically constitutive of emotion feeling.

A complication arises here because although, when considering the constitution of emotion feeling, Wittgenstein refers to 'the thoughts of happiness,' he nevertheless appears to focus on the expression of such thoughts in the form of outward verbal and physical behaviour. But 'feeling joyful' need not be overtly expressed. I can 'feel joyful' without allowing it to show in my verbal and physical behaviour. This is compatible with the possibility that, on occasions, 'feeling joyful' can be fully manifested in its outward expression, and also with the claim that such outward signs provide the criterial justification from which the term 'joy' derives its meaning. However, if 'feeling joyful' need not be made manifest, then Wittgenstein's reference to the constitution of emotion 'feeling' by 'expression' needs qualifying.

Here we can define 'expression' as criterial for 'feeling joyful' in so far as it manifests in verbal and physical behaviour those attitudes which are themselves constitutive of emotion feeling. First, this qualification remains compatible with the general point of Wittgenstein's remark that the 'feeling of joy' is not an inner quale. The avowal 'I am happy' is an expression of 'joy,' one which does not however refer to an inner quale but is expressive of the 'thoughts of happiness.' Second, I would suggest that the 'thoughts' in question can be analysed as the agent's complex realizations of the attitudes to which 'joy' is conceptually related. Let us suppose that M is 'feeling joyful about' x—'the news that his wife is not terminally ill after all.' Here M's dwelling on the occasion of his hearing the news, his visions of his wife returning home, his plans for their future, etc., can be defined as realizations of those attitudes towards x which constitute his 'feeling joyful,' such as his belief that his wife is not terminally ill, his evaluation of the news is good, his strong desire for her to live and remain his companion, and so on.

The points made so far suggest that the feeling of 'joy' is not an ontologically distinct inner quale but is constituted by those thoughts which provide the particular content of the attitudes to which 'joy' is conceptually related; moreover, that the 'feeling' term does not in this case refer to an inner quale but to those attitudes which are constitutive of 'feeling joyful.' This account of 'joy feeling' as constituted by the relevant emotion attitudes can, I think, be generalized to other emotions, as I will try to show. First, we need to clarify the relation between emotion attitudes and their expression in verbal and physical behaviour.

This relation can be clarified by distinguishing between the overt expression and the covert entertaining of emotion attitudes. For example, in overtly expressing his 'anger,' the angry person tends to convey his feelings towards the offender via spoken appraisals such as (P) 'wretched bastard ... get out!' and he may also behave in a violent manner; whereas in covertly entertaining an emotion such attitudes and behaviour remain undisplayed. Here the antagonist's claim that linguistic and behavioural expression does not represent inner feeling is correct in so far as overt expression can be a refined version of the inner feeling. For example, my 'feeling angry' can, and often does, amount to more than 'my shaking my fist' and stating P. But it does not follow that what is actually omitted from overt emotion expression must be omitted because of its alleged irreducibility to the attitudes constitutive of 'feeling angry.' In particular, the covertly entertained emotion is a mode of experiencing the emotion which share the same features as the overt expression to which it is conceptually related; for example, in feeling inwardly angry the agent responds to the occasion of his being wronged by experiencing angry thoughts such as P above. However, P shares the same descriptive features as the overt communication. Here P, whether conveyed or merely thought, represents the agent's attitudes to the offender, e.g., the judgement that S has wronged him and his desire to 'seek revenge.' While in the case of a covert entertaining of 'anger' we may also experience violent urges, the urge again has the same descriptive features as the overt act of violence in that the urge takes form not of a sensation but of a bodily rehearsal of the display of 'anger.'

However, the distinction between overt and covert emotion feeling is not sharp. The angry person may convey his attitudes but restrain his behaviour. Alternatively, he may prevent a full statement of his attitudes by letting his 'anger' be known in a stilted or ambiguous way, e.g., 'it is remarkable how mean some people can be isn't it S?' etc. The two modes of emotion expression differ in the following respects. An overt expression of emotion feeling is frequently a communicative act and hence leads to particular consequences. One effect of overt 'sadness' is consolation or commiseration from others. Also, in communicating an emotion we do, I think, commit ourselves to being a possessor of that emotion. By contrast, undisplayed feeling can remain ambiguous and hence is more amenable to self-deception. If M suppresses the outward signs of his 'sorrow' then it is easier for him to pretend, or to persuade himself, that he does not in fact 'feel sad.' Nevertheless, both modes can be equally constitutive of emotion feeling. Just as the consequences of overt emotion expression may enhance feeling (e.g., M's display of anger may instigate a fight which in turns intensifies his angry feelings), so covert emotion feeling can be as intense, if not more so, than the display. (For example, 'anger' can build up for being suppressed; similarly 'grief, sorrow and fear' can feed upon themselves unless conveyed and discussed.) but if to feel these emotions is either to express overtly or entertain inwardly the relevant attitudes, then how, it may be objected, can this account allow us to measure the intensity of emotion feeling? How can the possession of such attitudes provide an account of the agent's being moved by an emotion?

So here we want to ask: what has to be added to these emotions for them to qualify as emotions by which the agent is moved? In the case of 'regret,' for example, I would suggest that the recollections and wishes of the agent must first be vivid, in that agents could not reasonably be said to feel intensely regretful about an event which they barely remember. Second, such attitudes must be serious, in that to feel intensely regretful requires more than a passing acknowledgement of something that the agent wishes had not happened. In particular, a usual feature of intense regret is that the emotion is at least tinged with sorrow about the event. Third, such attitudes must be consuming, since to be moved by 'regret' the agent's recollections and wishes must not only be occurrent, but must also greatly or totally preoccupy the agent's attention. Similarly, in order to feel intense 'fear' the agent must not merely surmise, but must have a firm conviction, that the object x of his 'fear' is dangerous; he must construe x not as faintly threatening, but as vividly menacing; his attention must be totally absorbed by x and he must also have a strong or urgent desire to avoid x.

Here it seems reasonable to suggest that the inner array of events described above constitutes a typical state of feeling 'regretful' or 'afraid' and hence explains sufficiently what it is to be moved by these emotions in a particular case. Consequently, in the case of 'regret,' for example, a report such as 'I wish that x had not happened,' although a refined expression of the agent's attitudes, is not an 'approximation of the subjective element' but is at most a summary of, and at least a selection from, these attitudes. Hence the antagonist's reference to 'vagueness' as a descriptive feature of the subjective element seems misdirected. If I can only vaguely describe my 'regret' or 'anger,' whether mild or moving, then I cannot properly be said to feel these emotions. Hence if 'feeling' is not easily conveyable via language and behaviour, this is because it is barely a feeling, not because it is a 'bare feeling.'

THE ROLE OF BODILY FEELING

So far I have suggested that emotion feeling is constituted by the appropriate attitudes, whether such attitudes are covert or overtly displayed. Against this account the antagonist might object that it fails to explain why we have the term 'feel' in our emotion repertoire. Perkins, a proponent of the compromise view, argues that one role of the term 'feel' in the case of emotion is to designate bodily feeling: 'bodily feeling is indispensable to ... our practice of ... conceiving emotions as felt' (Perkins, 1966). This view requires some consideration as an alternative to the attitudinal account of emotion feeling advanced so far.

Perkins wants to argue that an emotion is a double aspect phenomenon such that attitudinal and behavioural components can qualify as a 'felt emotion' only if they give rise to some kind of bodily sensation. Sensation is understood by Perkins as a non-specific aspect of the total emotional event and hence differs from the traditional James-Langian account of emotions as individuated by, and reducible to, specific or unique disjunctions of sensation. On Perkins's view it is a necessary condition of an event x's being a felt emotion that a non-specific bodily feeling (S) features in the total emotional event. Perkins, in using the necessary condition S, seeks to provide a criterion for placing psychological phenomena in the class of 'emotion.' So far the criterion remains uninformative about the nature of particular emotions. He can avoid this objection by maintaining that it is in the realm of sufficient conditions that the nature of particular emotions is revealed. Nevertheless, we have to consider particular emotions in order to establish whether the criterion works for emotion generally. While it would be wrong to claim that S never features in an emotional event, the claim that S is a necessary condition for an event's being a felt emotion, is, I think, dubious.

If S does feature in an emotional event, then this occurrence of S is surely related to the intensity of the emotion feeling. And 'being intensely felt' is not a defining feature of emotion feeling. Extreme 'anger' or 'sorrow' might, on occasions, be accompanied by S. But S is not necessarily present in less extreme versions of the same emotion types. I can for instance be 'mildly angry' or 'faintly melancholy' without the presence of S; whereas Perkins's argument commits him to the view that anything less than an extreme case cannot qualify as a felt emotion. The antagonist might argue here that extreme emotion occurrences do necessarily involve S; moreover, that such occurrences provide the paradigms upon which mild occurrences are conceptually dependent. But first, even if this claim were true, it would not establish that S is a necessary feature of any instance of a felt emotion. Second, it is not clear that S is a necessary feature even of extreme, or intensely felt, emotions. As already argued, the crucial measure of the intensity of, say 'envy' is the extent to which the attitudes involved are vivid, serious and occupy the agent's attention. Whether or not I feel any twinges or palpitations, if my thoughts are totally consumed by a 'strong desire for an object which I do not possess and which belongs to another,' then I can be said to feel 'extremely envious.' This point applies equally to the emotions 'sorrow' and 'anger' discussed above. 'Anger,' for example, may give rise to S, but the criterion of its being intensely felt is the quality and force of the attitudes and behaviour it generates. Hence if S is neither essential to emotions as moderately felt nor essential to emotions as intensely felt, then it would seem that it is not an intrinsic defining feature but a contingent fact about emotions that they can give rise to S.

THE ROLE OF THE TERM 'FEEL'

While the arguments of the compromise view are problematic, the re-emphasis on 'feeling' in the explanation of emotion is, I think important in that it serves to remind us that emotions can be qualitative, experiential states. This aspect of emotions is not, as I will go on to argue, incompatible with constructionism. However, it does provide an explanation of the use of the term 'feel' in our emotion repertoire. Here it is useful to examine some actual contexts in which we would tend, or prefer to use the locution 'feel x.' I do not wish to imply that the following examples are exhaustive; however, they do illustrate some ways in which emotion 'feeling' terms can have legitimate applications without referring to emotion qualia or physiological changes.

We tend to use 'feel' for occurrent emotions, e.g., 'I feel afraid of x (now),' and 'am/is' for standing emotions, e.g., 'M is (tends to be) afraid of loud noises'; 'I am still in love with J.' However, constructionism can trade on the fact that, in general, sentences such as 'I feel x' (where x is an emotion predicate) are synonymous with 'I am x' and therefore that the feeling term does not designate anything over and above those attitudes constitutive of 'being x.' For example, 'I am/feel afraid (now)' are intersubstitutable without loss or change of meaning.

Another use of 'feel' can be derived from the fact that in the case of emotions the expression of which has a performatory role (e.g., to praise, blame, criticize or congratulate), it is possible to isolate the phenomenological aspect of the agent's emotion reaction from the performatory aspect of the emotion. By this I mean that agents reserve the locution 'feel' for reporting their introspective emotion experience, reports which are confined to 'how' the agent feels and do not include a reference to the agent's possible intention in expressing E. Let us suppose that person J was wronged or failed the expectations of person M in some way. The communicative intention of a statement made by M such as (P) 'I am angry with you/ashamed of you, J' is to criticize J. Here it is surely the case that the force of M's negative appraisal would not be successfully conveyed to S via a statement such as 'I feel angry/ashamed with you,' in that there is no reason to suppose that J would regard himself as admonished by a mere introspective report of how M happens to feel. The point here is that the performatory use of statements such as P (e.g., as a criticism of J) is not effectively conveyed by the 'feel' locution. However in those contexts in which M's critical intention is absent or no longer necessary, then M may revert to the 'feel' locution in describing his 'anger' or 'shame.' If M is musing to himself or a neutral party about the situation concerning J, he may describe himself as 'feeling' or as 'having felt angry/ashamed' because he is attending to the qualitative, experiential aspect of his emotion and not to its performatory aspect, being his criticism of J.

The above account also suggests another use of 'feel,' which is to express uncertainty as to whether we ought to 'be in' a particular emotion state. For example, 'I am angry about it' implies more strongly than does 'I feel angry about it' that the emotion in question is justified and reasonable. In particular, the overlap between the use of the term 'feel' to refer both to sensation and to emotion suggests that agents can use the term 'feel' to interpret their emotion as, like sensation, not self-initiated. In the 'anger' example above the use of 'feel' may have an excusatory function in that the strategic redescription of 'being angry' as 'feeling angry' enables the agent to entertain this emotion without assuming the responsibility which would subject the emotion to moral censure or rational criticism. For example, in a sentence such as 'I just feel angry about it, although I know I shouldn't be' the use of 'feel' can be understood as mitigating the acknowledged irrationality of the 'anger' by excusing its presence as involuntary.

The points above would appear to remain compatible with constructionism in the following respects. While, as I suggested, the locution 'feel' may be reserved for describing the phenomenological aspect of an emotion, this aspect shares the same form as the covert emotion feeling which itself essentially consists not of irreducible qualia, nor of physiological changes, but of those attitudes which are constitutive of the emotion. In the example above, M's retrospective report of having 'felt angry' would consist of the same desires, beliefs and evaluations concerning J as the overt performance, the difference being only that M is not, or is no longer, actually conveying his critical judgement of J's behaviour. Similarly M's report that he 'feels ashamed about J's failure of his (M's) expectations' would consist of the same attitudes (i.e., the desire and the belief that J could have met M's expectations, and the evaluation of J as at fault for having failed to do so) which are conveyed as criticisms in the overt performance. In this case the identity between the phenomenological report and the overt performance obtains in that M's report of 'feeling angry/ashamed' shares the same attitudinal structure as M's 'being overtly angry/ashamed.'

I would also argue that, although the locution 'feel' may have a role in expressing only the experiential aspect of the emotion, this focus of attention is a contingent and context-dependent feature, not a logical feature of emotions, since the ability of agents to confine their attention to the phenomenological aspect of their emotion – to 'how E feels to me' – logically presupposes their having a conception of the situation as appropriate to E and, in cases where it applies, of the performatory use of E. Here the constructionist can assert that in these cases not only is M's 'feeling' report a result of his original critical appraisal of J, but this performatory role of the emotion depends crucially on social expectations concerning those situations which are deemed to warrant 'anger' or 'shame.'

So far I have suggested some ways in which emotion 'feeling' terms are used to convey the phenomenological, as distinct from the performatory, aspect of an emotion. But this is not to deny that agents feel something while conveying their critical evaluation. This point is important because it allows the constructionist to explain how emotions can be qualitative states while simultaneously fulfilling some cultural expectation. In particular, on this point constructionism has a certain strength in being able to unify various disparate philosophical emotion theories.

To illustrate this, consider Bedford's claim that emotions 'form part of the vocabulary of appraisal and criticism' (Bedford, 1967). This claim expresses Bedford's view that emotion sentences have a performatory role in that they can be used to praise or condemn agents for their behaviour. Sentences, such as 'I am ashamed of you,' he suggests, serve a 'judicial function' rather than reporting the feelings of the speaker. Unfortunately, Bedford makes two unwarranted assumptions here: that performatory functions such as these are primary, and, following from this, that emotion predicates need not be treated as denoting psychological states 'at all.'

Bedford's denial that emotion terms primarily denote psychological states is extreme and provokes a dichotomy in philosophical emotion theories between the performatory aspect of emotions, i.e., the use of emotions to convey appraisals relating to some standard or value, and the phenomenological aspect of emotions, i.e., as denoted by emotion 'feeling' terms. Also any theory which denies emotion terms a central role in reporting our mental life is neither plausible nor appealing. My analysis of emotion 'feeling' in the previous section was intended to show, among other things, the way in which emotion feeling terms are about experiential states.

However, Bedford's unwarranted conclusions need not be fatal to his general argument concerning the performatory aspect of emotions. If his account of the performatory aspect of emotion could be made compatible with an account of emotions as experiential states, then this would make his arguments both more plausible and more interesting. And here constructionism does offer an account which unites these two aspects in that it can explain emotions as culturally constituted responses which are simultaneously experiential and performatory. For example, self-ascriptions such as 'I feel ashamed' frequently serve the function of expressing the agent's feelings; but this expressive function is surely not incompatible with the ascription's being a self-criticism and an acknowledgement of the agent's act as wrong by reference to some social standard of desirable behaviour. In particular, this compatibility enables the constructionist to assert that the 'feeling of shame' in the above case is socioculturally constituted just because the attitudes which constitute the 'feeling' are explainable as internalizations of the beliefs and values of the agent's cultural community.

RECAPITULATION

In this chapter I have suggested that contemporary philosophical theories of emotion are consistent with constructionism in that the characterization of emotions in attitudinal terms not only rejects the traditional view of the emotions as simple, non-cognitive phenomena, but also provides a basis from which emotions can in principle be explained as acquired responses which are determined by sociocultural prescription and training. I have further suggested that the phenomenological aspect of emotion which has been emphasized by the recent theoretical interest in emotion feeling does not present a difficulty for constructionism because, unlike the case of sensation, emotion feeling terms do not refer to irreducible emotion qualia or to sensations; rather, the ontology of emotion feeling should be analysed in terms of the emotion attitudes by which the emotion feeling is constituted. I explained this account by distinguishing between the covert entertaining and the overt display of emotion attitudes, and by introducing the notions of 'vividness, seriousness and inclusivity' of emotion attitudes as sufficient conditions of an emotion's being 'felt.' The advantage of this account is that it allows the phenomenological aspect of emotions to be accommodated within the constructionist's framework of explanation. Having considered some uses of the locution 'feel' which are compatible with the 'attitudinal' theory of emotion, I concluded by suggesting some ways in which constructionism can offer an account of emotion which unifies their social, performatory aspect with their experiential aspect.

THE RATIONALITY OF EMOTION

Ronald de Sousa

Le coeur a ses raisons, que la raison ne connaît pas. —Blaise Pascal

[In] rare moments of experience ... we feel the truth of a commonplace, which is as different from what we call knowing it as the vision of waters upon the earth is different from the delirious vision of the water which cannot be had to cool the burning tongue. —George Eliot

RATIONAL DESIRE

Some people think assessments of emotional rationality can only be strategic. Like Protagoras, the partisans of that view hold that the measure of an emotion lies in whether it makes you feel good, promotes your goals, and perhaps disposes you to behave in commendable ways.

On this view, one might concede that our emotions provide information, but only about the likelihood of future behavior, satisfaction, or practical success: they would not be subject to cognitive rationality. They would be only *natural signs*. A natural sign can be interpreted as providing information in the light of natural regularities; but that it is so interpreted is not its function in the sense explicated in chapter 4 (see Millikan 1984, 120). If emotions are natural signs, they can provide information without being truly representing states on the model of perceptual or cognitive ones.

Among the partisans of such a pragmatic or strategic view of the role of emotions were many philosophers in the eighteenth-century tradition. They saw some emotions, the "moral sentiments," as forming the basis of social and moral life (see Rorty 1982). But however important that role might be, it ascribes only instrumental value to emotions. And that raises a dilemma: if you make the value of an emotion depend on its consequences, you need criteria of assessment for those consequences themselves. Some of them are likely to be further emotional states, if only of felt happiness or misery. If you know how to evaluate emotional states, you didn't need to inquire into these remote ones. But if you don't, they are of no help anyway. It seems therefore that we still need a criterion of *intrinsic* rationality for emotions and desires. Could such a criterion still be of the strategic kind?

AUTONOMY

One proposal that might help here is due to John Elster. Elster endorses the idea (consonant with our principle (R4) about origins)[1] that a belief or desire is irrational if it has been "shaped by irrelevant causal factors." In the case of beliefs the capacity for appropriate shaping amounts to *judgment*, "defined as the capacity to synthesize vast and diffuse information that more or less clearly bears on the problem at hand" (Elster 1983, 16). In the case of desire the analogous notion is *autonomy*: any inappropriate external influence on my desires will make them irrational, just as an epistemically irrelevant cause of belief would make my belief irrational. (Note that Elster's concept differs from the more usual notion of autonomy, which precludes any external cause. See Morgan, unpub.) Obviously, these characterizations beg for a more substantive criterion of appropriateness and relevance. Like the concept of judgment, that of autonomy has little content. Both should be taken as something like regulative concepts. But for our purposes that is not important. At this stage I will be content with the general shape of the right view.

The conception of rational desire implied by this proposal seems to be that of individual, self-generated will. This agrees in flavor with Parfit's suggestion that a rational desire provides reasons to act, without making the objectionable claim that this fact is criterial. If my desire is not really my own (if, like Titania's love, it has been induced by some chemical means, for example), then it is not autonomous and hence not rational. Elster's concept of autonomy also stresses the contrast between a criterion for "mind-world" matching, which suits judgment, and one aimed at some kind of coherence within the agent. It may seem, for this reason, more akin to the strategic than the cognitive model. But let us see how this squares with some examples of desires assessed for rationality.

Parfit (1984, chap. 8) describes three types of cases, illustrating respectively (1) clear cases of desires that are intrinsically irrational, (2) clear cases of desires that cannot be irrational, and (3) interesting controversial cases.

Clearly irrational desires include wanting to suffer great pain at some time in the present or future, without any other goal to which this might be a means; a desire to jump off a high place (without either a parachute or a death wish); and desires involving certain second-order preferences based on completely arbitrary lines, such as *future-Tuesday indifference*, which means not caring about anything that happens on a future Tuesday however painful or pleasant it might be (Parfit 1984, 124).

Desires that cannot be irrational, as Parfit describes them,

> are the desires that are involved in purely physical pains or pleasures. I love cold showers. Others hate them. Neither desire is irrational. If I want to eat something because I like the way it tastes, this desire cannot

be irrational ... even if what I like disgusts everyone else (Parfit 1984, 123).

Controversial cases include various kinds of *temporal bias*: caring more about the present than about the future, or on the contrary discounting the future, or transferring from the past or from the future the motivating force of desires that are not presently felt. Those particular controversial cases will be dealt with in chapter 8. Now let us see what lessons may be gathered from the (supposedly) clear cases.

Clearly Irrational Desires. The three cases under this heading are quite heterogeneous.

What is irrational about merely desiring pain? It violates no *logical* constraints. Parfit does not speculate about how the desire originated. But it is hard to imagine any normal origins, compatible with autonomy, for the desire for gratuitous pain. Pain is the paradigm of what is intrinsically undesirable. This has nothing to do with either its causes or its consequences: rather, it seems to be just a fact. So far, if either model fits, it is the cognitive. But rather than saying it is irrational gratuitously to desire pain, perhaps we should say that it is just a misdescription. The case is *impossible*: a violation of minimal rationality.

The impulse to jump, by contrast, is clearly possible. And its intuitive irrationality seems to have everything to do with strategic considerations. The impulse to jump is irrational, because it might incline you to jump, and jumping would be bad for you. This does not preclude an explanation in terms of autonomy, but to give such an explanation we would again need to rely on some substantive notions of what is or is not normal.

Whatever is wrong with future-Tuesday indifference is not based on any standard specific to desire. It violates one of the constraints mentioned in (R5): the requirement that cases not be differently treated arbitrarily. But this requirement of reason is not one that necessarily sits well with the ideal of autonomy. Existentialists might claim that it is of the essence of autonomous desire that it eludes any requirement of nonarbitrariness. If my desires are arbitrary, that makes them all the more my own. So the evident irrationality of future-Tuesday indifference again seems to demand an explanation in terms of the cognitive rather than the strategic model.

Can we categorize, in terms of Parfit's intuitions, the case of the person who says she *just* wants a saucer of mud? Remember that as the case was described, she wants it not under the false impression that it is nutritious, nor, like Nagel's case of parsley on the moon, as an aesthetic whim, nor because it is pleasant to look at or muck about in. She just wants it.

What should we say of this case? It is not painful, like the first clear case. Is it irrational because it is like drawing an arbitrary line (she doesn't want other things that are like mud *even a tiny little bit*)? Is it irrational because it is a case of desiring "something that is in no respect worth desiring" (Parfit 1984, 123)? Or is it of the sort that cannot be irrational because, like a bodily sensation, it is irreducible and undiscussable? My intuition is that none of these explanations is very plausible. We need instead a *history* that will connect the desire both with particular events in which it had its origins and with the general facts about human instincts that made it possible for those particular events to result in just this desire.

Desires That Cannot Be Irrational. The need for a history supplemented by biology can be further illustrated in terms of the cases that Parfit says cannot be judged either rational or irrational. The claim that his examples are of this sort is unconvincing. Recall that a desire induced by direct chemical intervention would typically be non-autonomous: clearly it is not *my* desire, even though I am the one to experience and perhaps act on it. "Purely physical" desires, therefore, can also be alienated. And if by direct intervention, why not by psychological means? An orthodox psychoanalyst might claim that the causal story that it is necessary to tell in order to explain certain desires (coprophilia, for example, or certain other forms of masochism) is altogether incompatible with the development of a fully autonomous self. Now this might be hard to establish, but it seems to me that the conceptual apparatus that it presupposes makes sense. What is lurking here, once again, is the difficult concept of *normality*: a desire is not autonomous if it did not originate in some normal way. Since origins are relevant to both strategic and cognitive models, however, this will not help us to decide between them.

The cases I have looked at have alternately seemed to favor the strategic and cognitive model, without fitting either very neatly. In cases of the second type, where the criterion of autonomy held sway, the strategic model seemed plausible; but some desires of the first type— where intelligible at all—drew us to the cognitive model. One possible explanation is that we are dealing with two different sorts of desires or emotions. Let us explore this possibility.

SUBJECTIVE AND OBJECTIVE DESIRES

The Devil's Bargain: A Moral Tale

Once upon a time there was a man who aspired to emulate Faustus, though he was not as clever. In the usual manner he summoned the Devil, and slyly he offered his soul in exchange for the granting of a single wish. The Devil smiled, but the man didn't worry. "My soul," he offered, "for the promise that I shall have what I desire forever." The Devil's smile grew wider. But what could go wrong?

Had the man been a little smarter, he would have remembered Bertrand Russell and specified the scope of the quantifiers. What he meant was this:

At any future time t, let me have at t what I desire to have at t.

But what the Devil agreed to was this:

At any future time t, let me have at t what I now desire to have.

So the man lived forever, in what soon turned out to be Hell, and never even got to meet Faustus.

At first the moral of this story seems trivial. Of course we change, and to have always what I desire just now would indeed be hell. (Sometimes Dante's damned are punished in the surfeit of what they sinfully desired.) So the simple moral is, When you are making plans, allow for changes of heart.

But things are not so simple. When we desire food, drink, sex, or sleep, it is usually obvious to us that the desire will last only as long as it is not gratified. We expect our moods and our whims to be similarly transient. But other desires and emotions—admiration, love, the sense of beauty, and perhaps, sometimes, even regret or revenge—seem to come with a secondary desire for their own continuation: it is painful, while one is in their grip, to think of them as ephemeral. The latter kind feel this way because they seem to correspond to some *objective value*. Grief typifies a third category in which one is pulled both ways at once: in grief one wants the pain to go away, but if the grief is caused by the loss of a loved one, the very thought that grief will subside can itself be a source of renewed grief. People who divorce sometimes long to be released from the pain of missing a presence they no longer enjoyed, while saying they will regret forever (and never want to cease regretting) a certain kind of failure—the breakup of a family, the failure of understanding—that the divorce entails.

Perhaps our pseudo-Faustus would have foiled the Devil, if only he had desired, at the time of his wish, only objectively valuable things. For what could go wrong then?

The idea of objectively valuable objects of desire brings us back to one of my central motivating problems, the question asked of Euthyphro. Do we desire something because it is desirable, or is it desirable because we desire it?

One modern answer is that it depends on the desire. One kind, *subjective* desires, comprise roughly what Parfit calls "mere preferences," providing *agent-relative* reasons. The other class are *objective* desires, which in the *Euthyphro*'s terms are desired because they are desirable. They are roughly Parfit's *agent-neutral* desires, corresponding also to what Stephen Schiffer has called *reason-providing* desires, as opposed to *reason-following* desires.[2] I stick with "subjective" and "objective," because I will shortly introduce a third category of "self-related" desires, and because although subjective desires are not subjective in all of the four (or five) senses distinguished in chapter 6, they are both relative and potentially projective.

This distinction between the two kinds of desire naturally evokes the cognitive model with its core metaphor of matching. Nevertheless, one might seek to account for it entirely from the strategic point of view. Here is how a proposal on these lines might go.

Think of subjective desires as those that we do not mind thinking of as changing. By contrast, it will be painful to envisage the loss of those desires that appear to be for something objectively good:

Nay, if I wax but cold in my desire,
Think heaven hath motion lost, and the world, fire.
(John Donne, Elegy XII: "His Parting from Her")

The presumption of objectivity in the latter desires does not commit us to a Platonic view: it does not imply that nothing is objectively valuable except what is eternal. It implies only that the *value* of what is valuable is timeless, not that what is valuable must exist forever. (Compare: the truth of what is true is timeless, though the things and events of which it is true need not be.) To take an extreme case, one of the things we might prize as having objective and timeless value may be *fleeting pleasure.* "Death is the mother of beauty," said Wallace Stevens in "Sunday Morning." By definition, fleeting pleasures would lose their identity, and therefore their value, if they were to persist forever.

Armed with these distinctions, let us return to our pseudo-Faustus: from the strategic point of view, it seems he might have foiled the Devil even without any knowledge of true value. Perhaps he need only have included among his present desires a second-order desire that his desires remain constant. Would this idea have saved him?

Some desires come with positive second-order desires. Others come with a negative second-order desire: a desire that they not continue. Second-order desires are easy to confound with judgments of objective value, because in most cases they are the foundations for such judgments (see Frankfurt 1971). But this is not a necessary feature of such desires. One can imagine wanting a certain desire never to stop (thus having the positive second-order desire) but knowing, at the same time, that this second-order desire is merely incontinently caused by the first-order desire. Perhaps this was the case with Augustine when he uttered his prayer: "Give me chastity, but not yet."

Now the fact that second-order desires can be either positive or negative, regardless of whether they are thought to represent objective value, might seem to undermine the project of distinguishing subjective from objective desires in terms of attitudes to their future alteration. But we might save it by appealing to a third-order level of desire. Even when my first-order desire D1 (a simply physical desire, let us say) generates a second-order desire D2 that D1 continue, the test of a sincerely negative evaluation of D1 is that there be a desire D3 for D1 (and perhaps also D2) to disappear. In this way, then, we might still make the distinction between objective and subjective desires in terms of attitudes to the future.

Nevertheless, this attempt to deal with the difference between subjective and objective desires solely in terms of the strategic point of view will not work. The reason is that there is a third category of desires, which are clearly not objective and yet meet the strategic criterion for being so.

SELF-RELATED DESIRES

People change, and so do their emotions and desires. Our pseudo-Faustus might have tried to protest that changes in his own desires were not part of the bargain, but the Devil would not have been impressed. We all have emotions and desires the loss of which we would deplore, because we would feel our own self-concept undermined. They do not have to be virtues: I love my stamp collection; I am a woman who needs to feel glamorous; I live only for the moment's passion; I am a man given to indignant rages. Yet we are not so mad as to think that any of these idiosyncrasies reflects objective value. If I projected the formal object of my emotion, taking it for a real feature of the world, I would be clearly self-deceived. But I need not do so. And yet emotions in this category can be vital to my individual well-being. The emotional quality of intense passions and simple appetites of youth are an example. One might quite intelligibly celebrate their loss in old age, as Cephalos does in the opening pages of Plato's *Republic*, but it is more usual to mourn them, as does Yeats:

> I have not lost desire
> But the heart that I had;
> I thought 'twould burn my body
> Laid on the death-bed,
> *For who could have foretold*
> *That the heart grows old?*
> (W.B. Yeats, "A Song")

Such desires seem to be a proper domain of Elster's category of autonomy. They are the ones that spring from our own being, and their value is undiminished by the fact that they are liable to change in ways we can neither predict nor control. Sometimes, indeed, one might claim that a certain degree of mutability in such desires is itself valuable. We would then have a second-order desire—the desire for mutability—that could be considered an objective desire defining a timeless value.

The deceptively simple parable of the Devil's Bargain has led me to distinguish three kinds of desires: those that we regard as intrinsically subjective, those in which we cherish constancy because they have moral or aesthetically objective import, and finally those that are morally significant not simply because of the value of their object but because of what our *having* such desires means for our self-concept, our energy, or our integrity. The existence of the self-related desires in this third class, however, is incompatible with the purely strategic perspective on the contrast between subjective and objective desires.

It is time, therefore, to return from the perspective of strategic rationality, rooted in the idea of practical success, to the alternative perspective rooted in the idea of matching. Taking the hint from the cases considered a few pages back, in which the rationality of emotional desires seemed to hang on their history, I shall now explore the conditions of rationality of emotions in terms of their origins. What follows can be viewed as first steps in search of a *semantics* of emotions.

PARADIGM SCENARIOS

We have already seen how classical writers on the emotions, from Descartes on, are fond of making lists of primitive emotions, then going on to show how the more complex are built out of those. The diversity in the resulting lists is warning enough that this is an unpromising method. And yet it cannot be denied that there are, in other animals as in human babies, modes of behavior that we take to express something like human emotions. I think we can understand, in principle, how our repertoire of emotions gets built up, without positing a set of "primary emotions" that get combined like basic blocks or even mixed like primary colors. We do need a repertoire of primitive instinctual responses, but emotions are not mere responses.

My hypothesis is this: We are made familiar with the vocabulary of emotion by association with *paradigm scenarios*. These are drawn first from our daily life as small children and later reinforced by the stories, art, and culture to which we are exposed. Later still, in literate cultures, they are supplemented and refined by literature. Paradigm scenarios involve two aspects: first, a situation type providing the characteristic *objects* of the specific emotion-type (where objects can be of the various sorts identified in chapter 5), and second, a set of characteristic or "normal" *responses* to the situation, where normality is first a biological matter and then very quickly becomes a cultural one. It is in large part in virtue of the response component of the scenarios that emotions are commonly held to *motivate*. But this is, in a way, back-to-front: for the emotion often takes its name from the response disposition and is only afterward assumed to cause it.

Recent work on the development and function of smiling in infants provides a striking illustration of this last point. According to Daniel Stern, babies are born with an innate capacity to smile. At the very earliest stage, smiling seems to be a purely biological function, which elicits adult responses without involving any intentional communication. Between six weeks and three months, the baby begins to use the smile "instrumentally," that is, "in order to get a response from someone" (Stern 1977, 45). This does not affect the way the smile looks: in some way it is the same response. But what has changed is how it originates (p. 44).

From this stage on, the behavior needs to be reinforced visually if it is to persist: blind children seem to lose expressiveness in their smiles. The necessary reinforcement comes, of course, from feedback provided in interaction with caretakers. But we should not assume, as both psychoanalysis and behaviorist psychology might incline us to do, that the child is merely a passive recipient of shaping by parental and other external influences. For there is evidence that the feedback received in turn depends on the innate character of the infant's smile. How an infant is treated determines the paradigm scenarios that define its emotional repertoire; but its treatment, in turn, partly depends on its own innate facial characteristics and behaviors. To that extent, physiognomy is destiny.

Those original facial characteristics and behaviors of the infant are spontaneous and purely physiological: at that stage they *mean* nothing at all (Stern 1977, 43-44). Yet we might read these facts as telling us that, in a way, the ultimate initiative in determining the infant's emotional constitution belongs largely to the infant itself. This may be, in the end, what the notion of emotional temperament amounts to. If so, believing in temperament does not require us to believe in primitive emotions: the primitives out of which emotions emerge are not emotions.

A child is genetically programmed to respond in specific ways to the situational components of some paradigm scenarios. But what situational components can be identified depends on the child's stage of development. An essential part of education consists in identifying these responses, giving the child a name for them in the context of the scenario, and thus teaching it that it is experiencing a particular emotion. That is, in part, what is involved in learning to feel the right emotions, which, as Aristotle knew, is a central part of moral education (*Nicomachean Ethics*, II.2).

The process whereby emotions are constructed out of dispositions to respond can be observed from the first few months of life.[3] Mere feedback loops give way to complex interaction that it is plausible to think of as scenarios. First, between six and nine months one can generally make a baby smile by smiling, and cry or frown by frowning. There is "vicarious resonance," but no intentionality. At the next stage the caretaker's expressions have become signs to the infant of what it can expect her to do and feel. After nine months this includes looking to her for guidance as to what to look at and how to feel about it. The infant will follow the caretaker's gaze and, more important, look to her to learn how to react. Late in the second year of life toddlers seem already to have the sense of the existence of other subjects. They become aware that different participants in the same scene will, by virtue of their different roles, feel differently from each other. As we should expect if paradigm scenarios indeed define the very character of our emotions, we acquire the capacity to talk about emotions in terms of the stories that give rise to them sooner than we can talk about the origins of other mental states such as perception. Before the age of three, toddlers can understand that one person's action may lead to another's distress and that certain types of events typically cause certain emotions. They also know that by taking a sequence from an emotional scenario out of context, one can play-act or "pretend" emotions that are not actually being felt. And by the time toddlers are four or five years old, they have a very good sense of what kinds of stories lead to what simple emotions. Learning these scenarios continues indefinitely, however, as the emotional repertoire becomes more complicated. (Sentiments of guilt and responsibility are not generally understood by six-year-olds well enough for them to infer who is feeling what in stories where such sentiments would be appropriate.)[4] Indeed, perhaps we enlarge our repertoire, much as we increase our mastery of language, well into adult life, though with increasing resistance.

This fits in with the fact that some emotions are more thought-dependent than others. It depends on the paradigm scenarios to which they are related. If the paradigm scenario cannot be apprehended without complex linguistic skills, for example, we shall not expect to find in someone who lacks those skills an emotion specifically tuned to that scenario. That is why, as Iris Murdoch has put it, "the most essential and fundamental aspect of culture is the study of literature, since this is an education in how to picture and understand human situations."[5]

On the other hand, prelinguistic responses such as flight or attack can subsist to define so-called primitive emotions of fear and rage. Thanks, perhaps, to their dependence on relatively separate parts of the brain, they retain their power even over individuals whose repertoire includes the most "refined" emotions. We observe this most easily in other people.

THE PRINCIPLES OF RATIONALITY APPLIED

In sum, the role of paradigm scenarios in relation to emotions is analogous to the ostensive definition of a common noun.[6] Their role can be sharpened by relating it to the principles of rationality elaborated in chapter 6.

According to (R1), formal objects define a state's criterion of success. Where the state is an emotion, its formal object is fixed by a paradigm scenario, which defines an axiological quality. The emotion is objective, self-related, or subjective, depending on whether the qualities in question are legitimately attributed to the real world or are merely projected onto it. The essentially dramatic structure of the formal object helps to set the axiological level apart from the cognitive and strategic levels of appraisal on which it is partly modeled. But it does not stop axiological properties from having a phenomenological aspect: every scenario has its own feel.

The dramatic structure of the formal objects of emotions has another important consequence. In a sense, we might characterize an emotion's formal object as its *mode of appropriateness*. But that carries a misleading suggestion that emotions as a class have a single specific formal object, which is to all emotions as truth is to beliefs and desirability to wants. In view of the diversity in logical structure of different emotions as it emerged in chapter 5, it would be better, though messier, to concede a sense in which emotions do not form a kind in the same way as do wants or beliefs (see Rorty 1980). There is no general criterion for a set of things to constitute a "natural kind" (see de Sousa 1984). But the view of formal objects I have been expounding suggests a strict criterion for the limited category of representational states: A group of such states form a natural class, if and only if they have the same formal object.

Appropriateness is the genus of the formal object in question. But that genus includes truth and goodness too. It tells us nothing about the differentiae of success conditions for emotions. I have argued that axiology has some features in common with the cognitive, and some with the strategic forms of rationality. But in the end even axiological success is only a genus. Even emotion must find, in the peculiar character of its paradigm scenario (enraging, engaging, sinister, shameful, and so on), its own specific formal object. This explains, as I shall argue more fully in chapter 12, why there are, in the words of Bernard Williams, "few, if any *highly general* connections between emotions and moral language" (Williams 1973a, 208).

In relation to paradigm scenarios the principle of minimal rationality (R2) works like this. Since emotions are learned in terms of paradigm scenarios, they cannot, at least within a given social context, be criticized for inappropriateness if they occur in response to a relevantly similar situation. Here we must carefully distinguish the emotion itself from the behavioral response that the scenario might involve: it does not follow from the rationality of the emotion evoked that the stock response will continue to be seen as rational. Where the response is an action or strategy, it needs to be assessed in its own terms. It may be that a further narrowing of the context is needed before the minimal rationality of the behavior is guaranteed. Surprising one's lover in bed with someone else, one may react with jealousy and rage. In our culture this situation maps onto some primal sense, first rehearsed in infancy, of being robbed by another of vital physical attention. It has become the paradigm scenario for jealousy and so the emotion aroused by it must be counted appropriate. (In other cultures where polygamy is the rule, infantile jealousy may come to be represented by rather different situations.) but even if the original scenario, as learned, involves the response of murderous aggression, this will not necessarily make murder rational. That act will have its own minimal rationality as an extreme act of revenge, but the mere existence of the scenario will not determine whether extreme revenge is ever rational.

The intentionality principle (R3) stipulated that (categorial) rationality applies only to intentional states. Accordingly, as I stressed in my brief discussion of the role of development in the setting up of paradigm scenarios, there are responses before there are intentional states, but there are no scenarios, and therefore no emotions, until those responses can be integrated into an intentional structure, enabling the child to understand the meaning of different possible roles.

The bearing of the fourth and fifth principles is best understood by considering them together. Constraints, in the sense of principle (R4), are most easily understood as applying to *transitions* between states and to the *coexistence* of states. We do not usually judge a belief in isolation, for example, except on those rare occasions when we can directly assess its truth. Hence the emphasis on origins prescribed by principle (R5). For two reasons, the importance of origins in the assessment of rationality carries over with especial force to the axiological sphere. The first reason is that judgments of transition and coherence tend to be uncertain in the domain of emotions. (One example, which I shall consider at length in chapter 11, is the question of whether the same thing can be both comic and tragic at the same time.) The second is that for beliefs, origins are merely a clue to the likely attainment of the formal object; but here—in the form of paradigm scenarios—they constitute the formal object's very definition.

SOME OBJECTIONS

One problem raised by the present account is this. It appears to suggest that the rationality of an emotion is fixed irretrievably by its origins in socialization and that nothing can affect the appropriateness of an emotion provided the evoking situation fits the paradigm. What then of the changes in emotional dispositions that we call "maturing emotionally"? and what of the possibility of striving for greater emotional rationality? Can we not, for example, repudiate certain scenarios altogether in an effort to be rid of sexist or racist emotions?

This objection parallels the charge, justly laid against a certain kind of "Oxford philosophy" a couple of decades ago, of misusing the notion of paradigm. The smiling bride, according to a once popular argument, is the paradigm of a free agent: "If you want to know whether we ever act freely, look at the smiling bride. That's what it is, by (ostensive) definition, to act freely.

So, as you can see, there are free acts." But that a concept is learned in a given context does not mean that the concept cannot be revised and refined, that our understanding of it cannot be deepened to the point where we are able to ask without contradiction whether it is appropriate to the paradigm itself. A smiling bride, we say, is *a picture of happiness*. But what a picture *shows*, it does not typically *instantiate*.

A paradigm can always be challenged in the light of a wider range of considerations than are available when the case is viewed in isolation. It can be revised in the light of competing paradigms that are also applicable to the situation at hand. However, the emotion will retain its basic intelligibility (its minimal rationality) provided it can be seen in the light of its own, narrowest, proper scenario. Further, a scenario can become completely inert, obsolete: this will take place if every situation that fitted the original scenario comes to be seen, from a more comprehensive perspective, as fitting another (set of) scenario(s). In some North American subcultures, for example, the sentiments and scenarios once associated with such notions as "chastity" or "satisfaction in affairs of honor" have altogether lost their power to move either to feeling or to action. Situations that would once have evoked those sentiments are now simply felt in terms of quite different scenarios.

This suggests the following principle:[7]

> (PEC) *Principle of emotional continence.* Let your emotions be appropriate to the widest possible range of available scenarios.

Here is a somewhat politically charged example. How do you feel about prostitution? The answer will depend on the model to which—emotionally— you assimilate it: Is it wage labor? (Or is wage labor just prostitution?) (See Jaggar 1980.) Is it free-enterprise independent business? Oppression of women? Oppression of men? Therapy? Or theatre? A mature emotional reaction to prostitution, according to (PEC), is one that is tested against all these potentially applicable scenarios.

The complications of working out what (PEC) would mean in practice are enormous, because—as I shall explain—the emotional level of rationality is the deepest and most inclusive. But the attempt to restructure one's emotions by "consciousness raising" is based on something like the principle of emotional continence. Beyond a certain point, moral progress is often a matter of rising above principle—by getting a more adequate feel for a certain situation in all its ramifications, by viewing it as a complex scenario. Almost by definition, a moral principle is bound to construe any situation to which it is applied simplistically.[8]

Mark Twain's Huckleberry Finn provides a savory example of emotion successfully rising above principle. Although tortured by his moral conscience, Huck gives in to what he assumes must be emotional and moral weakness.

When he refrains from turning in Jim, the fugitive slave, he does what he "knows" is wrong according to every principle of honesty and gratitude known to him (see Bennett 1974).

Nevertheless, an objector might ask, in what sense can we maintain that the process of one paradigm being supplanted by another is rational? And to what extent can it be maintained that there is any objectivity involved here? Am I not saying that attitudes, dispositions, and habits may change unaccountably, since what leads to change—what one might barbarously call "emotional regestalting"—is simply beyond the pale of rationality? Do emotions not remain as subjective after as before such changes?

My brief answer is no: not all changes of mind are equally subjective or irrational. The tendency to think otherwise springs from an unrealistic picture of the rationality of belief changes and from unwarranted standards for "objectivity." I said that an emotion is appropriate (or minimally so) in a given situation if and only if that situation is relevantly similar to (can accurately be "gestalted" as) a suitable paradigm scenario. To be sure, what can be seen as similar to a given scenario admits of a certain amount of leeway. Can the complicated friendships of sophisticated Bloomsburyites adequately be seen as instantiating "the Eternal Triangle," for example, or would that scenario be truly stifled, in those circles, by a metascenario in which it appears as vulgar? We can hardly expect mathematically precise answers to such questions. But not just anything goes, either, as some have learned to their cost, like Pentheus in Euripides' *Bacchae*, who have attempted to "rationalize" their lives in terms of invented scenarios insufficiently rooted in human nature and the facts of life. True irrationality of emotion involves the perception of a situation in terms of a scenario that it does not objectively resemble. I shall discuss an important class of such cases in chapter 8. Change of mind rests on unconscious links and transformation rules that have turned one situation into another. Emotional irrationality is a matter of muddled scenarios: a loss of reality, intensified in neurosis and extreme in psychosis. The minimal rationality of those emotions must be sought in terms of the scenario unconsciously evoked. Psychotherapy typically looks for clues to the transformation in free association, and it is a sound principle of therapy not to rest in the search for the original scenario until the emotion inappropriately evoked is accounted for as minimally rational.

Two further complications block any easy answers to questions about rationality in practice. (This is lucky for my theory, since if easy answers to complex problems could be deduced from it, they would constitute a quick reductio.) The first complication stems from the fact just noted, that a given situation and response may evoke several clashing scenarios. Emotions are not necessarily compatible, even when they are all equally adequate. (The perception analogy will help again to see how this is possible: when you are looking at a Necker cube ⬡ or a duck-rabbit picture ⇒ you cannot see both cubes or both animals at once; yet what you are interpreting as one or other is in some sense just one thing.) In some cases emotions mix, in varying proportions; in other cases one emotion, like a perceptual gestalt, crowds out another. The rules governing these phenomena are among the "constraints" of axiological rationality demanded by (R5). Unfortunately, I don't know what they are.[9]

The second obstacle to finding clear-cut examples of those constraints at work is the variety of formal objects. Rational coexistence is a matter of consistency, not compatibility. The latter concerns simultaneous satisfaction, whereas the former concerns simultaneous success. The two are easily confused, since they coincide for the case of beliefs. But they do not coincide for goodness, or for the different species of axiological appropriateness. Wants are consistent, not if their objects can all be *true* together, but if they can all be *good* together. Similarly, the condition of consistency for emotions is not whether their targets, motivating aspects, or propositional objects are compatible but whether their formal objects are logically consistent. And if each emotion has its own formal object, then the constraints of consistency will only relatively rarely have occasion to apply.

Let me repeat an important consequence of this last point: the objectivity of axiology does not imply that there must be uniqueness of axiological "correctness." This fact, amounting to the *multidimensionality of value,* will prove crucial when we come (in chapter 12) to looked at the contributions of emotions to ethical life.

In effect, I have been arguing that paradigm scenarios, in setting up our emotional repertoire, quite literally provide the meaning of our emotions. There will be more to say in later chapters about the axiological level of reality that they pick out. For the rest of this chapter I want to switch back to the strategic model, guided by the metaphor of success, and return, though at a more abstract level, to the question of the biological function of emotions considered in chapters 3 and 4. In the next sections I offer a new speculation about what that biological point might be. This will fulfil my promise to say something about the role of emotion in rationality as a whole, and it will also tell us something more about the nature of emotional appropriateness.

WHAT ARE EMOTIONS FOR?
A NEW BIOLOGICAL HYPOTHESIS

As we saw in chapter 3, there are many speculative theories in the field about the biological usefulness of emotions. Most of them relate to the survival value of such basic behavior patterns as the traditional "four F's." But the relevance of those speculations to my present purposes is limited. The reason is that I am specifically interested in emotions as such. (Even where for simplicity I speak of desire, I am interested chiefly in what I have called 'emotional desire.') And those basic survival functions have no need for emotions at all. It is logically possible that evolution might have set us up simply to want the right things and to have true beliefs or perceive the relevant aspects of our environment. This fact is reflected in traditional theories of rational decision-making, in which emotions have acquired their bad reputation. For in those theories there is neither need nor room for emotions, except as disrupters of the orderly course of rational deliberation.[10] Since I have insisted all along that emotions are not reducible to desires and beliefs, it is time to say more positively what, in relation to rational behavior and belief, the role of emotions might be.

The suggestion I want to make is best approached by elaborating on a thought experiment broached in chapter 1. Let us try to imagine what it would be like for us to be without emotions. This must not be confused with the speculation that we might be without "functional wants," or even without a certain class of wants, of the sort attributed to "emotional" people. The confusion is common in science fiction attempts to describe emotionless beings, who generally turn out merely to lack concern for other people, or else are inhumanly single-minded and constant over time. In fact, the problem is deeper and more abstract than is imagined in such stories.

I see two forms that such beings could take. A truly emotionless being would be either some kind of Kantian monster with a computer brain and a pure rational will, or else a Cartesian animal-machine, an ant perhaps, in which every "want" is preprogrammed and every "belief" simply a releasing cue for a specific response. My hunch here is that it is because we are neither one nor the other, "neither beast nor angel," that we have emotions as well as beliefs and desires. But let me try to do a little better than a hunch.

What is it that animal-machine and Kantian angel have in common? I submit that it is *complete determinacy*: in the first by mechanism, in the second by reason. In fact, of course, the two monsters are equally mythical. The fact of biological variability precludes any animal-machine of the sort just described. Two individual ants, even two individual viruses, will not do exactly the same thing under every condition. But they come close enough: close enough in particular so that individual ants have no need of a special clue to tell them how, from a repertoire of equally probable alternatives, other ants are likely to react. Ants, unlike primates, have no need for communicativeness of emotional expression. But among animals like us, to read the emotional configuration of another's body or face is to have a guide to what she is likely to believe, attend to, and therefore want and do. Such dispositions tend to be given different names depending in part on their duration: a short one is an emotion, a longer one a sentiment, and a permanent one a character trait. Ants need no character, and if they emoted, they would not need to know it of one another.

What about angels? There, I suggest, full predictability would also elude us:

not because of angelic variability, but because there is no such thing as fully determinate rationality. This is true of both the cognitive and the strategic varieties.

Consider the cognitive level. On many issues, logic gives no unique prescription. Logic suggests that in consistency we should avoid false beliefs and pursue true ones: "Don't believe an inconsistent set," but "Believe the consequences of your beliefs." Plausible as they are, these principles are not always compatible in their application, nor do they prescribe their own ordering. Even at the lowest level we require informal policies to supplement hard logic. More important areas of indeterminacy have to do with what subjects to investigate and what inductive rules to adopt. No logic determines *salience*: what to notice, what to attend to, what to inquire about. And no inductive logic can make strictly rational choices between the extremes of "soft-headedness" and "hard-headedness." (The terms are borrowed from the *Theaetetus* (191c), where Plato describes two sorts of "tablets" in the mind. Soft ones easily take impressions but just as easily lose them; hard ones are difficult to scratch but once imprinted are less easily erased.) Plato's problem was what statisticians now call the problem of the choice of *significance level*: how probable must it be that your hypothesis is true on the evidence, and how improbable must it be that it should be false on the evidence, before it is rational to accept it? Inductive logic does not tell us, and statistics offers only sophisticated rules of thumb.

But there is an even worse problem, not reducible to those of either logic or induction. It is not just that we know too little and are not powerful enough logicians to make the best even of that. We also know too much.

KNOWLEDGE ACCESS
AND THE PHILOSOPHERS' FRAME PROBLEM

The recognition of a class of problems generated by the fact that we know too much is a major contribution of artificial intelligence to philosophy.

Because a machine starts out knowing nothing, the task of getting it to act intelligently reveals how much we know—but didn't know we knew. One class of such knowledge is constituted by what we might call "Piaget-processes"—pieces of knowledge that we acquire very early, by some mixture of maturation and learning, and that have to do in some way with "the way the world works." (I am not speaking here of procedural knowledge, or "knowing how." We need to learn to do things too, of course; but here I am concerned only with factual knowledge.) I know, for example, that when I've poured the beer into the glass, it's not in the bottle any more. This kind of knowledge is constantly required to interpret the simplest of instructions, as well as to disambiguate simple sentences.[11] The extent of such knowledge is vast: it is not merely semantic but encyclopaedic: one does not acquire it by simply having a good grammar and knowing the meanings of the words involved.[12] Think, for example, of the general knowledge required to know that snow-shoes, alligator-shoes, and horse-shoes are not respectively made of snow, worn by alligators, or used to walk on horses.

Even an encyclopaedia may not be enough. John Haugeland has called this the "No Topic" problem:

> "I left my raincoat in the bathtub, because it was still wet." Does 'it' refer to the bathtub or the raincoat? To the raincoat, obviously, because 1. a raincoat's being wet is an intelligible (if mildly eccentric) reason to leave it in a bathtub, whereas 2. a bathtub's being wet would be no sensible reason at all for leaving a raincoat in it. But where are these reasons to be "filed"? They hardly seem constitutive of the general, commonsense concepts of either raincoats or bathtubs (let alone wetness); nor are they part of some other concept, for which there just doesn't happen to be a word in the given sentence. (Haugeland 1985, 202)

Assume encyclopaedic knowledge, supplemented by an appendix entitled "No Filable Topics." The worst problem still remains: how will the system have access to this knowledge, and how will it ignore what is not relevant?

Both aspects concern, not the acquisition of knowledge, but the use we make of the stupendous quantity of knowledge we already have. When we plan some action, we can assume that the vast majority of the world's facts will remain unaffected by it (see Hayes 1987). Yet some will not: we can never do just one thing at a time, and some of the side effects of what we do may turn out to be important. When we act, we need to track relevant change and "bear in mind" what does not change for possible future reference. But the number of facts that change, and the number of facts that stay the same, are both unmanageably large. Assume all the powers already listed—logic, induction, and more-than-encyclopaedic knowledge: the *philosophers' frame problem*, roughly, is how to make use of just what we need from this vast store, and how not to retrieve what we don't need.[13] Daniel Dennett has given the problem a vivid illustration. He imagines a robot being informed that a bomb is about to go off in its hangar. The robot duly decides to leave the hangar, but, alas, the bomb is on the robot's own wagon: though it knew this and many other things about the environment, it had not "thought" to draw the inference. So its designers instruct it, in future, to draw the consequences of what it knows. Unfortunately, when the experiment is repeated, the robot sits, lost in computation, long past the time for action; at the time the explosion occurs it has "just finished deducing that pulling the wagon out of the room would not change the price of tea in China." In the newest version the designers try again, instructing it, this time, to ignore irrelevant implications:

[T]heir next model [was] the robot-relevant-deducer ... R2D1. When they subjected R2D1 to the test ... , they were surprised to see it sitting, Hamlet-like, outside the room containing the ticking bomb.... "Do something!" they yelled at it. "I am," it retorted, "I'm busy ignoring some thousands of implications I have determined to be irrelevant...." but the bomb went off. (Dennet 1987, 42)

The philosophers' frame problem is not reducible to the problem of induction. The problem of induction is about what inferences are warranted. What gives rise to the philosophers' frame problem is that we need to know whether a consequence will turn out to be relevant *before drawing it*. If it is relevant and we have not retrieved it, we may act irrationally. But if it is irrelevant and we have already drawn it, we have already wasted time. This is the problem at its most virulent: How do we know without finding out what not to find out if we know?

THE STRATEGIC INSUFFICIENCY OF REASON

The deficiencies of pure reason apply not only to cognitive problems but also to choices of strategies in the light of existing desires. Where action is concerned, all our uncontroversial principles of rationality are captured by Bayesian decision theory, which is based on the idea that life consists in gambles. Its maxim is "Maximize expected gain." Expected gain is the sum of gains and losses afforded by each possible outcome, weighted by its probability. (Pascal's bet, described in chapter 6, is an application of Bayesian theory.) But Bayeasian theory is not enough to yield unequivocal outcomes to practical problems. For suppose you are considering whether to take a fair bet. By definition, from the Bayesian point of view, a fair bet is equivalent to no bet at all: its expected desirability is zero. Whether we make a bet, therefore, requires additional principles. Yet there is clearly a significant option between the choice to minimize the greatest possible losses ("maximin") and the choice to maximize the greatest possible gains ("maximax"). One can make up a principle here, of course, as one can for consistency or for induction. But no principle can claim to be dictated by rationality alone.

A little paranoia would help in these various cases, both with knowing too little and with knowing too much, as well as with the insufficiency of strategic reason. The point of the bathtub scene, for example, will be more immediately obvious to anyone who has a fetish about getting things wet. An entire scenario will flash before such a person, and the question of "how to file" the information will be answered in terms of the importance of that kind of scenario and its typical features. And the choice between maximin and maximax strategies is obviously associated with such emotional and character traits as boldness or timidity. In all these cases we may surmise that emotions are one source of the necessary supplemental principles.

To see how this might work, think of some conditions in which the philosophers' frame problem will not arise. I argued that it must arise for angels, which are logically perfect but finite in knowledge and in power. (God, as I pointed out, needs no principles of rationality of any kind.) But it will not arise for ants: a completely mechanistic system will need no devices for solving the frame problem. The motor system of ants, I surmise, is controlled by information confined to a limited range to which their sensors are attuned.[14] Similarly, as Jerry Fodor and Zenon Pylyshyn have argued, we ourselves get around in the world with the help of sensors, or perceptual modules, which in themselves do not work significantly differently from those of the ants: they are informationally encapsulated. The frame problem arises only when we consider what to do with information interpreted and stored in an intentional system. The role of emotion is to supply the insufficiency of reason by imitating the encapsulation of perceptual modes. For a variable but always limited time, an emotion limits the range of information that the organism will take into account, the inferences actually drawn from a potential infinity, and the set of live options among which it will choose. This, then, is my biological hypothesis:

> (BH1) *New Biological Hypothesis* 1. The function of emotions is to fill gaps by (mere wanting plus) "pure reason" in the determination of action and belief, by mimicking the encapsulation of perception: it is one of Nature's ways of dealing with the philosophers' frame problem.

Consider how Iago proceeds to make Othello jealous. His task is essentially to direct Othello's attention, to suggest questions to ask: "Did Michael Cassio, when you woo'd my lady / Know of your love?" and then to insinuate that there are inferences to be drawn without specifying them himself, so that Othello exclaims (III, iii, 106-108):

> By heaven, he echoes me
> As if there were some monster in his thought
> Too hideous to be shown.

Then more directly Iago advises, "Look to your wife." Once attention is thus directed, inferences which on the same evidence would before not even have been thought of are experienced as compelling: "farewell, the tranquil mind..."

In this example the emotion is changed via the manipulation of what Othello thinks about, notices, and infers. But such manipulation is not always possible. It can be blocked by the grip of pre-existing emotion. Even where an emotion is already regnant, the order of causal accessibility of emotion and attention is not fixed. As commonsense "psychologists" we learn to "play on" people's emotions—sometimes the more abusively for being more shrewd. Iago is a master psychologist in that sense: a con man, which is to say, a sophist of the emotions. The con artist and the sophist differ in the emphasis they place on different methods, but in each there is some of the other. A sophist needs to divert attention from her most slippery arguments, and one way to do it is by manipulating emotion or else overtly inducing it by the use of rhetoric. This is the art of the political orator, as well as the wooing lover. But a con artist must also be, like Iago, adept at "passing" bad arguments by making them look plausible. In the light of this example, the present hypothesis can be restated as follows:

(BH2) *New Biological Hypothesis* 2. Emotions are species of determinate patterns of salience among objects of attention, lines of inquiry, and inferential strategies.

SOME CONSEQUENCES

To get a better feel for this hypothesis, let us see how it bears on some of the questions addressed in this book.

Emotions Set the Problems

First, we can now see why, though emotions are neither judgments nor desires, it has been tempting to assimilate them to one or to the other. On my view, emotions set the agenda for beliefs and desires: we might say they ask the questions that judgment answers with beliefs and evaluate the prospects to which desire may or may not respond. As every committee chairman knows, questions have much to do with the determination of answers: the rest can be done with innocuous facts. In this way emotions can be said to be judgments, in the sense that they are what we see the world "in terms of." But they need not consist in articulated propositions. Much the same reasons motivate their assimilation to desire, of which one kind or component, as I have argued, can itself be classed as an emotion. Logic leaves gaps. So as long as we presuppose some basic or preexisting desires, the directive power of "motivation" belongs to what controls attention, salience, and inference strategies preferred.

For this reason emotions are often described as guiding the processes of reasoning—or distorting them, depending on the describer's assessment of their appropriateness. Indeed, this is in great part what all good novels are about. In extreme cases we think of reasoning as being distorted into self-deception: but there is seldom a sharp mistake in logic of which the self-deceiver can be accused. As I shall argue in chapter 9, self-deception is not different in kind or mechanism from normal cases of reasoning about matters of concern. The difference may largely rest in the relation of a piece of reasoning to what is expected in the circumstances.

Consider for example the way that we are wont to discount experience for distance in space, time, or affection: we care less about pain if it is far enough in the past or the future, and we are relatively indifferent to distant disasters. This seems reasonable, within vague bounds: but are there no rules of rationality that prescribe the rate of discount? The thought of our own death is subject to this discount. We are usually curiously indifferent to it, but as Tolstoy vividly shows in *The Death of Ivan Ilyich*, the prospect of death might provoke such a shift in a man's patterns of salience that an entire life is seen aright for the first time: Ivan Ilyich's emotions are axiologically adequate only when he faces death.

The Irrationality of Emotions

Although emotions are manipulators of reasoning, the experience of emotion tends to be an "intuitive" one: it is not easy to formulate reasons for one's shifts of attention. To be sure, there are great differences between types of emotion on this point: it does not clearly apply to indignation, surprise, or embarrassment. But many emotions do not come fully equipped with reasons on which they are based. This applies not just to the most diffuse or least "thought-dependent," such as joy or depression, but also to those, like love or mistrust, that are specific in their targets and sometimes even loquacious about their propositional objects. Even these are often not given to much pretense of having been brought about by reasons: "I can't explain: he just gives me the creeps." An explanation sometimes offered for this is that emotions are somatic phenomena; that they consist largely in autonomic reactions, of which the phenomenological component consists in dim awareness. We found some support for this view in the modularity of some of our mental mechanisms. But from the point of view of the theory of rationality a preferable explanation can be given in terms of the model I have sketched: paying attention to certain things is a *source* of reasons, but it comes *before* reasons. Like scientific paradigms, in the sense of Thomas Kuhn (1969), emotions are better at stimulating research in certain directions than at finding compelling and fair reasons for their own adoption. They are too "deep" for that, too unlike specific beliefs.

Not only are emotions not assimilable to beliefs: often they are experienced as "gut feelings" in direct opposition to overt belief. Consider for example the fear of flying.[15] Those who suffer from fear of flying are likely to remain unaffected by sound statistical knowledge about the relative safety of air travel. They can be distracted from it, but mere argument is unlikely to dispel the fear. This need not be, as so often thought, because the emotions are not cognitive at all but merely bodily phenomena. Instead, it can be due to the fact that the body contributes to the phenomena at hand a different pattern of emphasis that merely cognitive considerations cannot overcome. The beliefs themselves may be common to both the state of calm and the state of fear. (In chapter 9 I shall go further into the question of the peculiarly unconvincing character of what, by synecdoche, I shall call *lovers' arguments*.)

Emotional Transitions

I have argued that there is bound to be a good deal of biological atavism, and considerable variation in the levels of antiquity, in the determinants of our emotions. And this means that they will be variously well adapted to the circumstances in which they are now likely to arise. On the present account, this is to be expected. For to be inclined to look to certain things may have a very different utility in different circumstances. Here, as elsewhere, the overall usefulness of some device of nature is quite compatible with its noxiousness in particular cases, as Descartes noticed when he explicitly linked the variable utility of emotions with what one might call their inertia (see chapter 3; also Rorty 1978). But inertia is not, as on Descartes's view it should be, the general case. What we find instead are variable patterns of continuity and transformation between emotions. Here are some examples:

In some cases the discovery that an emotion was premised on a false belief, instead of simply canceling the emotion, will transmute it into another. Indignation can turn into remorse upon finding that it was unjust; and we have all seen a parent punish a lost child when, on finding it, anxiety turned to anger. In such cases the focus of attention is not changed by the mere change of belief: so there is a kind of inertia of attention. But since the facts are now different, new features of the situation naturally become salient to the same attentive set, in turn provoking shifts in the dominant patterns of concern.

In other cases the emotion's habit of looking for certain sorts of facts and facilitating certain sorts of inference will simply look for more. There is a good example in George Eliot's *Middlemarch*. When Mrs. Farebrother learns that Lydgate is not the natural son of Bulstrode, she does not take this to be sufficient grounds for ceasing to think ill of Bulstrode: "the report may be true of some other son." Here the emotion can be clearly seen as a disposition to persist in asking certain questions.

Conversely, there are cases where something comes to change that disposition without any change in the object or in any directly relevant belief. A friend of mine felt intimidated by a man she met, apparently because of his character. Later she discovered that the man had been her student. "I'm not afraid of him any more," she said, although not claiming to perceive any difference in his character, "because I have this maxim that you can't be afraid of students." From the point of view of a teacher, signs of intellectual threat are not salient, nor are they easily inferred. The story is a good illustration of the fact that although we usually think of emotions as grounded in beliefs, they operate by evoking whole scenarios, at a metalevel in relation to beliefs.

Arbitrators of Weakness of Will

These facts about emotional change are related to a more general point about the voluntariness of emotions. In spite of the "irrationality of emotions" tradition, we commonly hold people responsible for their emotions. This seems to presuppose that emotions are at least to some extent in our power. The hypothesis I have offered suggests an explanation for the limited extent to which this is true: namely, the limited extent to which attention is itself in our power. This sometime leads to paradox, as we shall see in chapter 9. It is also related to the fact that emotions are widely reputed to play an important part in the genesis of *akrasia*, or weakness of the will, defined as *doing something intentionally that one has overriding reasons not to do*. The problem of akrasia has been one of philosophy's most notorious conundrums ever since Socrates tried to prove the concept self-contradictory. The best modern account of the phenomenon is that of Donald Davidson (1970a).[16] His solution is inspired by a familiar fact about statistical inference. Statistical premises support their conclusions only if they take account of the whole of the relevant available evidence. Otherwise, it could be true both that there is a high probability of rain tomorrow (say, on the basis of the cloud pattern) and that there is a very low probability of rain (say, on the basis of wind or temperature). Similarly, reasons for action provide only undetached conclusions of the form 'On the basis of R_1, I should do A,' which is compatible with 'On the basis of R_2, I should refrain from doing A.' In order to detach a categorical practical conclusion, there must be an additional factor. Davidson argues that whatever the causal status of that additional factor, it must satisfy a certain rationality condition, which he calls the *principle of continence*. This principle, on which (PEC) was modeled, enjoins that one should act on the most comprehensive set of available reasons.

Akratic actions fail this condition. This means that there must have been some causal condition, other than whatever it is that results in the implementation of the principle of continence, that somehow plugs the output of some partial argument into the motor system.

The best candidate for the agency that plugs one argument over another into the motor system is emotion. The reason is this. It cannot be a merely physiological factor that is in itself arational, that is, beyond the reach of assessment for evaluative rationality. Otherwise, Elster's principle of autonomy is violated, and it becomes unclear whether the action is an intentional act of the subject's at all. On the other hand, the causal factor in question can be neither a desire nor a belief. The reason for this was expressed with characteristic pith (and uncharacteristic wit) by Aristotle himself: "when water chokes, what will you wash it down with?" (*Nicomachean Ethics*, VII.3). By hypothesis all the reasons, both cognitive and desiderative, are already in. So whatever tips the balance cannot be another reason. It must be something that, in some sense, acts on reasons.

So the additional factor required to turn the argument into an action (to "detach" the practical conclusion) can be neither a purely nonrational factor, nor a belief, nor a desire. Only emotions are left. Since they can, as I have argued, be assessed for rationality, they are not excluded by the first constraint. And if, as claimed in my central hypothesis, their essential role lies in establishing specific patterns of salience relevant to inferences, then they are perfectly tailored for the role of arbitrators among reasons.[17]

This is interesting not only for what it tells us about akrasia and for the neatness with which it fits the central hypothesis. It also adds a powerful argument to those I have already offered against the reductive view of emotions as just complexes of beliefs plus desires. For since emotions play a role in akrasia that is available neither to belief nor to desire, they cannot consist in either.

Salience and Paradigm Scenarios: The Euthyphro *Once More*

I have been expanding and illustrating the idea that our emotions underlie our rational processes. This claim—this model of emotions and what at the most general level they are for—was introduced to make it plausible that there is some objectivity, related to biological significance, to the proper objects of emotions. But it is time to address a problem.

In the last chapter and the first part of this one I offered a defense of a cognitive-perceptual analogy to axiological properties. On this view, paradigm scenarios determine characteristic feelings, and an emotion can be assessed for its intrinsic rationality—a kind of correctness or incorrectness—in terms of the resemblance between a presenting situation and a paradigm scenario. This suggests an objectivist answer to the *Euthyphro* question: emotions—at least objective ones—are not mere projections but apprehensions of real properties in the world.

In the second part of this chapter my thesis has been that emotion deals with the insufficiencies of reason by controlling salience. And the answer to the *Euthyphro* question suggested by that, it might seem, is a subjectivist one. For salience would seem to be a matter of rearranging things that are already there, rather than discovering new ones.

How can these theses harmonize, if they amount to opposite answers to the *Euthyphro* question?

The answer lies in attending to the distinctions made in chapter 6 between different kinds of subjectivity: phenomenology, relativity, projection, and perspective. *Phenomenology* does not preclude correspondence to a real property. Indeed, it usually indicates such correspondence. I argued that a measure of *relativity* is just what we would expect from taking seriously the analogy of perception. If the world is real, it will look different as we move around. When a paradigm scenario suggests itself as an interpretation of a current situation, it arranges or rearranges our perceptual, cognitive, and inferential dispositions in terms of some real configuration of human experience. *Perspective* is just the mysterious fact that whatever we are aware of must be apprehended from some point of awareness: it is irrelevant to whether what we are taking in is really there or not.

That leaves *projection*, which is the only sense of subjectivity in question in the *Euthyphro*. We need to ask, therefore, whether the control of salience effected by emotions amounts to projection.

The answer in outline is simple: projection interferes with objectivity when it is illegitimate and does not when it is appropriate. But that sounds too easy to be helpful. The point will acquire substance if we think back to the psychoanalytic context for the notion of projection.

A psychoanalyst typically works by making inferences about the patient's condition. But such inferences can be made in two ways. One consists in fitting the situation of the patient into a plausible scenario ("an Oedipal problem," for instance) and making inferences "by the book" about how the patient feels in the real predicaments of life. The other involves the therapist's own feelings as an additional source of inferences. The latter method, called "working with the countertransference," is a valuable tool to a good analyst. But obviously it involves the risk that, if the therapist has not been "successfully analyzed," her feelings will be mere projection in precisely the sense that precludes objectivity. In one case the feelings evoked in the analyst will enable her to lock into a patient's actual scenario, in terms of which she can then "read off" other features that might have taken a long time to uncover by a more analytic route. Here we have legitimate "projection." In the contrary case the scenario is not really the patient's but one springing from the analyst alone. It can therefore tell her nothing useful about the patient.

Outside the therapeutic environment the situation is much the same. By controlling salience, the paradigm scenario mimics the encapsulation of perception. This inhibits certain perceptions and inferences and fosters others. But if the resulting pattern is appropriate to the situation, it does not constitute illegitimate projection.

But how are we to interpret the notion of appropriateness involved here? There are two possible routes. One is to look for some insight into what the normal scenarios dictated by human nature may be. On this view, emotions will be objectively correct if and only if they correspond to scenarios stemming normally from human nature. This is more or less Aristotle's route. But it is not one that is appealing in practice, simply because of the difficulty of giving substance to the idea of a human nature. But there is no reason to feel thus confined. The standards of normality involved may be social as well as biological. Further, there is also room, I believe, for a notion of *individual normality*.

To those who assume that normality must ultimately always point to some statistical facts, this may sound self-contradictory. But two sorts of considerations support it. One goes back to some of the facts of biology surveyed in chapter 4. We saw there that individual variation is a basic fact of biology. Earlier in this chapter I also cited some facts about emotional development suggesting that the very social genesis of the paradigm scenarios that will define an infant's emotional repertoire may be at least partly controlled by individual temperament. For these reasons, if it makes sense to speak of normality for a social group, it also makes sense to speak of the normality of a single individual, as something only partly shaped by the former. In chapter 9 I shall develop some of the consequences of this idea.

The argument begun in chapter 6 offered what I take to be plausible theses about the conditions for ascription of rationality. In this chapter I have tried to show how these can be applied to emotions. The main conclusion for which I have argued is that axiological rationality is distinct from both the cognitive and the strategic kinds, though it bears instructive analogies to both. Despite familiar claims about the subjectivity of emotions, I have argued that an objectivist answer to the *Euthyphro* question can sometimes be supported: emotions tell us things about the real world. To be sure, their mode of objectivity is relative to the characteristic inclinations and responses of human and individual nature. The biological function that makes them indispensable to complex intentional organisms—ones unlike either ants or angels in that they are not subject to simple determinisms—is to deal with the philosophers' frame problem: to take up the slack in the rational determination of judgment and desire, by adjusting salience among objects of attention, lines of inquiry, and preferred inference patterns. In this way emotions remain sui generis: the canons of rationality that govern them are not to be identified with those that govern judgment, or perception, or functional desire. Instead, their existence grounds the very possibility of rationality at those more conventional levels.

This role, with its possibilities for self-justification or bootstrapping, carries risks. In the next two chapters I shall look at some of the pathological excesses to which such bootstrapping is prone.

Notes

1   [References (R1) through (R6) speak to six principles of rationality that de Sousa discusses in a previous chapter. It may help the reader if I quote them here. Ed.]

(R1) *Success.* The formal object of a representational state defines that state's criterion of success, in terms of which the rationality of that state is assessed.

(R2) *Minimal rationality.* It is a necessary condition of an intentional state or event's being describable as *categorially* rational, that under some true description it can properly (though perhaps vacuously) be said to be *evaluatively* rational.

(R3) *Intentionality.* The teleology implicit in rationality applies only to intentional acts or states.

(R4) *Origins.* The assessment of rationality of any act or belief looks both forward to consequences, logical and causal, and backward to origins.

(R5) *Constraints.* Rationality never prescribes, but only constrains, by proscribing inconsistency and distinctions without a difference.

(R6) *Cognitive and strategic rationality.* A representational state can be assessed in terms of the value of its probable *effects* (in the causal sense): this evaluates its *strategic* rationality, or utility. By contrast, a state is *cognitively* rational if it is arrived at in such a way as to be probably adequate to some actual state of the world that it purports to represent.

2   See Parfit 1984, 143ff., and Schiffer 1976. Thomas Nagel speaks in a similar vein of "subjective" and "objective" *reasons* in Nagel 1970 but adopts Parfit's terminology in Nagel 1986.

3   The description in this paragraph draws liberally from Bretherton et al. 1986, 534ff.

4   Inge Bretherton also gives a telling example of a six-year-old's fully developed sense of the difference it makes which role one is playing in a scene:

Mother. "It's hard to hear the baby crying like that."
Child: "Yes it is. But it's not as hard for me as it is for you."
Mother. "Why not?"
Child: "Well, you like Johnny better than I do! I like him a little, and you like him a lot, so I think it's harder for you to hear him cry." (Bretherton et al. 1986, 541)

5   Murdoch 1970, 34. For an eloquent defense of the idea that a novel can itself be a moral achievement, see also Nussbaum 1985. There are difficult and fascinating questions about the extent to which literature can *invent* scenarios that when applied to one's own life result in "authentic" emotions.

6   In term of Saul Kripke's theory of naming, the experience of paradigm scenarios is something like the original baptism that gives its sense to a natural kind term (Kripke 1980). In terms of Ruth Millikan's theory, where "real value" is the kind of thing an "intentional icon" "Normally" (that is, in accordance with normally established functions) maps onto, paradigm scenarios determine the class of real values to which emotions, as meaningful states are supposed to correspond (see Millikan 1984, 112). Some important qualifications to this picture will emerge in chapter 9.

7   (PEC) is modeled on the "Principle of Continence" introduced by Donald David-

son (1970a) as the rule of rationality that is specifically broken in cases of weakness of will. It was itself modeled on a principle of statistical rationality introduced by Carl Hempel (1965).

8   Nel Noddings (1984) has begun to explore an alternative to an ethics of principle, based on adequate emotional response.

9   Patricia Greenspan has argued that it is in the nature of emotions to allow "ambivalence in persons not so irrational as to hold genuinely contrary judgments" (Greenspan 1980, 223).

10 See Jeffrey 1965. The view of emotions as disruptive of normal capacities and activities has not been confined to philosophers. For an attack on this conception in psychology, by a psychologist, see Leeper 1948.

11 I once heard Paul Ziff offer a charming example: "I saw her duck ... when they were throwing rotten eggs ... and then I saw it swim out to the middle of the lake." Note, here, how our cognitive system somehow automatically retrieves the information needed for our flip-flops of interpretation.

12 According to John Haugeland (1985, 174), Yehoshua Bar-Hillel was the first (in Bar-Hillel 1960) to draw this moral from early failures to produce machine translation.

13 I call the problem I am concerned with the *philosophers' frame problem*, mostly to avoid being accused of misunderstanding the *real* frame problem. According to members of the AI community, this is their problem and all philosophers misunderstand it. See, for example, McDermott 1987 and Hayes 1987; but see also Dennett 1987 and Fodor 1987 in the same volume.

14 Compare the fascinating thought experiments of Valentino Braitenberg (1984). Because his vehicles are *constructed*, with the aid of gradual complications in the application of simple principles of afferent-efferent connections, it is easy to see the kind of behavior of which such constructions would be capable. But if we look at their behavior itself, its sheer phenomenological complexity is baffling, and we can hardly resist the temptation to honor them with the intentional labels—fear, aggression, love, anxiety, and so forth—with which Braitenberg graces, with tongue somewhat in cheek, the various stages of his vehicles' increasingly sophisticated meanderings. But his vehicles do not yet suffer from the philosophers' frame problem.

15 The example of fear of flying is discussed in unpublished work by both Michael Stocker and Patricia Greenspan.

16 For further discussion, see de Sousa 1974a.

17 Note that since emotions also sometimes conflict, other tools of rationality may be brought in to determine the issue in those sorts of conflict. There is no inconsistency here, if the person is, as I suggested in chapter 3, a heterarchic system.

❧ RECONSIDERING THE OPTIONS ❧

STARTLE[1]

Jenefer Robinson

Philosophers tend to take very sophisticated and culture-bound emotions as their paradigms for emotion in general. So Gilbert Ryle discusses an interest in symbolic logic; William Lyons discusses being awestruck by the beauty of a golden eagle; Patricia Greenspan talks about being warily suspicious of an insurance salesman; and Robert Gordon talks about being embarrassed about the publicity of one's wedding.[2] Psychologists, on the other hand, tend to stick to very different examples; several of them have studied the startle reaction as an example of an emotion, a suggestion most philosophers would consider laughable. I shall argue that startle does belong to the spectrum of emotional response, and that indeed, if we abstract from the startle response, we can come up with a useful model of emotional response in general.[3]

I shall be implicitly criticizing throughout the "judgmentalist" theories of emotion currently fashionable among philosophers for neglecting the "primitive" end of the emotional scale and for focusing on the cognitive complexity of sophisticated examples of emotion instead of analyzing the noncognitive aspects of emotion, in particular the role of emotional *response*. Thus, Gordon and Gabriele Taylor[4] both provide illuminating analyses of the cognitive structure underlying various emotional states, but pay no attention to the physiological or noncognitive elements in emotion. Greenspan spells out in great detail the peculiar nature of the cognitions central to emotion, but again has little or nothing to say about their physiological concomitants.

Many different phenomena go by the name 'emotion,' including complex patterns of attitude and behavior (love of Mary, awe of Mozart, contempt for one's boss), moods (gloomy, joyful, nervous), traits (choleric, chronically pessimistic), and disorders (depression, anxiety disorder). I shall focus on a class of phenomena that I believe are central to our ordinary concept of emotion, namely, episodes of emotional *response*. I shall develop a model of emotional response based on the startle reaction and argue that this model helps us to understand the structure and function of emotional response in general. Moreover, I shall claim that my analysis of emotional response can explain phenomena that are recalcitrant to "judgmentalist" theories of emotion, such as the biological adaptiveness of emotion, the "inertia" of some emotional states, and the irrationality of some emotion responses.

Although I have a theory of emotional response, I do not make any explicit connections between emotional responses and such "long-term" emotional
states as being in love with Mary or in awe of Mozart. I believe, however, that
when such long-term states are properly describable as "emotions," they must
at the very least include episodes of emotional response such as I shall
discuss.[5]

I

Before developing a theory of emotional response based on the startle mechanism, I have to try to justify my contention that startle deserves to be treated
as an emotional or proto-emotional occurrence, on the same spectrum of
phenomena as episodes of fear, anger, or joy.

I shall begin by describing what is known about the startle response. The
startle response is an invariant response in humans to a sudden, intense stimulus, such as a loud noise like a revolver shot. In their pioneering study of
startle, C. Landis and W.A. Hunt[6] describe the response as including:

> blinking of the eyes, head movement forward, a characteristic facial
> expression, raising and drawing forward of the shoulders, abduction of
> the upper arms, bending of the elbows, pronation of the lower arms,
> flexion of the fingers, forward movement of the trunk, contraction of
> the abdomen, and bending of the knees (*ibid.*, p. 21).

The characteristic facial expression involves the immediate closing of the
eyes, followed by a widening of the mouth "as though in a grin, although this
only occasionally leads to a real baring of the teeth" (*ibid.*).

The startle response is a universal response, found in humans from infancy
to old age, and in primates as well as many other mammals. Not all people
exhibit all the elements in the response, but the eyeblink is always present and
most people show some head movements and some bodily movement. The
startle response happens very fast, ranging from a mild response taking 0.3 seconds to an intense response lasting 1.5 seconds. Normally, the whole process
takes less than half a second. It is involuntary and cannot be deliberately controlled or successfully imitated. Simulations of the startle response are always
much too slow. People are often unaware of their response. Thus, trained
marksmen who had spent their lives on pistol ranges were surprised to learn,
when presented with photographs of their startle reactions, that they blinked
and "made faces" when a pistol was fired (*ibid.*, p.37). In addition to changes in
facial expression, there is an immediate galvanic skin response ("A sudden
loud sound is the best and most reliable stimulus for a drop in the electrical
resistance of the skin") and cardiac changes: there is an increase in blood pressure; breathing is momentarily checked, then accelerated (*ibid.*, p. 129).

II

Philosophers who tend to focus on emotions that require a complex cognitive structure, such as pride or shame, or a complex cultural context, such as Western romantic love or Japanese *amae*, are likely to repudiate the suggestion that startle even belongs to the emotional spectrum.[7] Since it is involuntary and universal it does not require any cultural context, and since it is evident in "lower" mammals from the Cape ground squirrel to the two-toed sloth as well as in species of fish, it does not seem to require any complex cognitive structure either.

There are at least two good reasons to think that startle *does* belong on the spectrum of emotions, however, even if it is on the very end of that spectrum. The first reason is that startle has many of the important features of more standard cases of emotion, such as fear, anger, or joy. In particular, startle is characterized by a particular pattern of neural firing, by characteristic autonomic nervous system changes and by a characteristic facial expression.

Not surprisingly, the psychologists who are most comfortable with the idea that startle is an emotion or proto-emotion are those who emphasize somatic factors and motor output. "Facial feedback" theorists, such as Silvan Tomkins and Carroll Izard,[8] think of emotions or "affects" as responses in the autonomic visceral system and, in particular, the somatic system, including the finely differentiated somatic muscles of the face. According to this theory, awareness of some external or internal stimulus causes a change in the gradient of neural stimulation which in turn produces a preprogrammed facial expression.

Paul Ekman's[9] studies strongly suggest that for certain emotions, at least, there is an inborn relation between the emotion and a particular facial expression. He has shown that there is remarkable agreement among different researchers using different methods about the facial expressions of at least seven "basic" emotions (happiness, surprise, fear, anger, sadness, disgust/contempt, and interest). Ekman hypothesizes that emotional expressions are biologically important for communicating to others (and perhaps oneself) the emotional state of the organism (*ibid.*, esp. ch. 3). He accounts for the apparent variation in our expression of emotions by showing that we can mask the spontaneous expression of emotion and assume a "learned" facial expression that obeys what he calls the "display rules" for emotion in force in our particular culture. Thus, for example, the Japanese have a display rule that forbids the exhibition of negative emotion in the presence of an authority figure. When Japanese and American subjects were shown an unpleasant, gory film, their expressions were identical when they thought they were unobserved but when they knew they were being watched by a scientist, the expressions of the two groups diverged.[10] Ekman's findings suggest that *some* spontaneous change in facial expression is part of any emotional response and that, where it is absent, it has to be deliberately suppressed.

Ekman has also shown that several emotions can be distinguished by their somewhat different patterns of autonomic nervous system activity. He directed subjects to move their facial muscles in certain ways (without specifying the emotional expression aimed at) and found that once the expression was posed, he could discriminate differences in autonomic nervous-system activity.[11] Again, the available empirical evidence suggests, therefore, that an emotional response includes a particular pattern of autonomic nervous-system activity and that these patterns may differentiate (some of) the various emotions.

Now, as we have seen, startle, like happiness and anger, also has a universal facial expression and a characteristic pattern of autonomic nervous-system changes. There is also a characteristic pattern of neural firing: startle is activated by a sudden sharp increase in the rate of neural firing. In short, startle shares important features with what are clearly bona fide kinds of emotional response.

The second reason for thinking that startle belongs on the spectrum of emotions is that it is a developmentally early form of two emotions in particular, namely, fear and surprise. There is some dispute about the exact biological function of the startle mechanism. Tomkins suggests that the role of startle is as a "circuit-breaker," an interrupter of ongoing brain activity: it is "a common way of clearing the central assembly" in order to ready it for the access of new information (*op. cit.*, pp. 499-501). Both he and Izard therefore link startle with surprise. For Izard, the primary function of "startle/surprise" is "to help prepare the individual to deal effectively with the new or sudden event and with the consequences of this event" (*op. cit.*, p. 281). This is not a completely satisfactory analysis, however. For one thing, unlike surprise, the startle reaction does not depend upon the unexpectedness of the stimulus; even if I fire the gun myself and know exactly when the sound will come, I still exhibit the startle response. Secondly, what we know about startle is also consistent with the view that it is closely related to *fear*.

Landis and Hunt point out that no matter where the gun is fired (above the head, below the knee, etc.) the startle pattern remains the same. They therefore link startle with surprise rather than fear, since one would expect fear to produce a directional response away from the cause of fear (*op. cit.*, p. 31). There is evidence, however, that startle does function as an immediate nondirectional fear response in some organisms, designed to get the organism out of danger as fast as possible, before giving way to more directed escape behavior.[12] The psychologist Nico Frijda[13] supports the fear hypothesis on slightly different grounds: he argues that the startle response in humans should be considered as a protective response, in particular "as protection of the vulnerable vital organs, including the eyes" (*ibid.*, p. 16). He links the startle response to "the flinch and shrink movements found in both humans and chimpanzees" (*ibid.*). It would seem that startle is a primitive form of both surprise (the readying of the organism to deal with a new situation) and fear (an escape or protection reaction). Since both surprise[14] and fear count as bona fide emotional responses, it is reasonable to propose that startle, too, deserves to be called an emotion or proto-emotion.

III

There are also reasons, however, for thinking that startle is *not* an emotional or even proto-emotional response. Indeed, even those theorists who think of emotions as being partly defined in terms of facial expression (such as Izard and Ekman) have expressed doubts as to whether startle is a "real" emotion. Izard comments that compared with fear, anger, or joy, startle is "so fleeting and motivates very little thought and action" (*op. cit.*, p. 281). Ekman interestingly seems to think of startle as the same sort of phenomenon as emotional response, but he nevertheless distinguishes it from "real" emotions on the grounds that, unlike fear, anger, and joy, it cannot be successfully inhibited or simulated. Furthermore, it is reliably produced by a sudden loud noise, whereas there is no single stimulus that universally produces fear, anger, or joy.[15]

These reasons for thinking that startle is not an emotion are connected with what philosophers are likely to think of as a more important reason, namely, that startle does not seem to involve any evaluation of, or judgment about, the environment. Startle is a reflex, an involuntary response that requires no prior learning and occurs too rapidly for there to be any cognitive activity at all. Now, it seems to me that the importance of cognition to emotion has been overemphasized, chiefly because philosophers have tended to study only the most complex of emotional phenomena. If we turn our attention to the primitive end of the emotion scale, we find there is both phylogenetic and ontogenetic evidence that emotional or proto-emotional responses can involve "evaluative judgments" of only the most primitive kind, and that many sophisticated human emotions develop out of primitive reflex responses. Furthermore, there is some evidence that emotions employ different neurological pathways from ordinary, nonemotional evaluative judgments.

In his compendious treatment of emotion, Frijda cites evidence that a number of primitive emotional responses, such as the orienting response to the novel or unexpected, are responses to "unlearned stimuli." As examples of strangeness evoking fear, he cites fear in dogs and apes for people dressed or behaving in unfamiliar ways, fear in horses for flapping plastic bags, and terror in Rhesus monkeys for mechanical moving monsters. Other responses, though requiring learning, are very readily acquired, for example, fear of spiders and snakes in humans (*op. cit.*, pp. 272-73).

The psychologist Robert Zajonc[16] has argued that affect (emotion) can precede cognition and hence does not require it. He cites a wide variety of evidence from the primitive end of the emotion spectrum. Among many examples (including the startle reaction), he cites the "mere exposure effect," that is, the fact that "preferences for stimuli (tones, polygons) can be established by repeated exposures," R.S. Lazarus's and R.A. McCleary's subception experiments, and the establishment of taste aversion even when any possible association between the food and the nauseous substance administered has been "obliterated by anaesthesia."[17] Zajonc's examples suggest that many primitive or proto-emotional responses are immediate and automatic, and do not require "conceptual processing" of information stored propositionally. He himself has argued that the *motor* system may provide one way in which information is processed emotionally.[18]

The second set of evidence that emotions need not involve full-fledged evaluative judgments of the environment and can begin life as reflexes comes from the study of infantile human development. In some early and notorious studies with neonates, the behaviorist psychologist John Watson[19] found that restraining the infant's ability to move its head was a universal stimulus for rage, that sudden loss of support (dropping the neonate!) was a universal stimulus for fear, and that gentle caresses universally elicited pleasure (Watson says "love"). Studies in the emotional development of infants and small children have shown how more sophisticated emotional responses grow out of primitive, apparently prewired responses. For example, the earliest examples of rage occur when some ongoing activity is interrupted; later, the infant gets angry when some specific object is made unavailable; a little later still, anger may occur when the cause of anger is not present, as when the infant gets mad at the absent mother only when she returns.[20] True, the early rage response seems to be a kind of "reflex," but it is distinguishable from other reflexes, such as the knee-jerk reflex or the constriction of the pupil of the eye in bright light, by the fact that it is a developmentally early form of emotion "proper"; it seems to have the same biological function or motivation as the later emotion. Both the neonate cry of rage and the later expression of full-fledged anger communicate frustration of desire. Similarly, the startle response registers a novel and/or intense stimulus, readies the organism for the new information, and initiates a movement of flight and/or self-protection, just like the later surprise and fear responses.[21]

Finally, there is some recent evidence from neurophysiology that suggests that emotional processing may sometimes be independent of cognitive processing. According to some recent work by Joseph Ledoux,[22] emotion may be mediated by subcortical centers, especially a structure called the amygdala. In particular, Ledoux has tried to show that fear in rats can be acquired without cognitive mediation. The inference is that the fear conditioning is mediated by subcortical centers, probably by thalamo-amygdala pathways.[23] Such as it is, then, the evidence from neurophysiology suggests that emotions are not necessarily dependent upon cognitions, and that the "appraisals" they involve may be as rudimentary as that involved in the startle mechanism.

IV

Even though startle does not involve any "cognitive evaluation" of the environment, it is nevertheless a way in which the organism focuses on some event in the (internal or external) environment and registers it as significant to its goals, wants, or motives. The startle response is the way in which the organism focuses on a sudden loud sound and registers it as a significant piece of information: the response "tells" the organism that the event is a significant event, something potentially dangerous which needs investigating further.

If we now generalize from this account of startle, we come up with a conception of emotional response which downplays the role of cognition and instead emphasizes that an emotional response is a bodily response that serves to call attention to (make salient) those features of our environment which most urgently affect our well-being, our interests, our goals, and our desires.[24] I would like to urge that startle provides a rather useful model of emotional response, and one that captures the whole spectrum of such responses, from the primitive to the sophisticated. I suggest that an emotional response should be thought of, on the model of the startle response, as a response that focuses our attention on (makes salient) and registers as significant to the goals (wants, motives) of the organism something in the perceived (remembered, imagined) environment; this response characteristically consists in motor and autonomic nervous system changes, including changes in the facial musculature, which may be part of a motivated action sequence (such as fight or flight) or function chiefly as communication to oneself and others of the state of the organism. In humans (and perhaps other species) the response is sometimes subjectively experienced as a recognizable "feeling."

On this model, an emotional response is distinguished as having three main features. It is (1) a bodily response that (2) makes something salient to the organism (focuses the organism on something), and (3) what it makes salient or focuses on is something registered as significant to its well-being. Moreover, the fact that the emotional response is a bodily response with observable characteristics, notably a change in facial expression, means that it also communicates to others the state of the organism, in particular the fact that something significant has affected it. On this view, the function of an emotional response is to pick out from the mass of information available to the organism in its environment those things which the body registers as significant to the organism's well-being. What is thus picked out can just be something perceived, such as a gunshot, or it can be something remembered or imagined or just thought about. If what is picked out by the emotional response is a complex conception of an event or situation, then obviously the emotional response presupposes some complex cognitive activity, such as the formation of this conception. The formation of complex conceptions is *not*, however, an essential constituent of an emotional response. In particular, an emotional response need not make salient a conception of a situation in propositional form.

On my view, there is a range of cases of emotional response from the primitive, such as startle or the newborn baby's rage response, which seem to require no prior cognitive activity, to the sophisticated, such as an indignant response to U.S. policy toward Haitian refugees or a compassionate response to Anna Karenina, which pre-suppose complex cognitive activity. At the primitive end of the spectrum are responses that alert the organism to some situation (of danger or frustration, for example) which the organism perceived in its immediate environment and which it registers in an automatic, pre-programmed way. As we move further along the spectrum, cognitive activity becomes more important, so that, in the most sophisticated cases, what is responded to is a complex conception of the situation, expressible in propositional terms. Even fish and frogs can have primitive emotional responses to things perceived in the immediate environment, but only beings with complex cognitive abilities can have emotional responses to a conception of U.S. foreign policy or the fate of Anna Karenina.[25]

Suppose that I respond emotionally to a news story about the plight of Haitian refugees and the fact that the U.S. Coast Guard has been rounding them up and sending them back to Haiti. Suppose I respond with indignation to the thought of the refugees travelling across the sea in dangerously frail boats and then being picked up by the Coast Guard and sent back to the wretched and threatening conditions that prevail in Haiti. I may begin reading the story in a dispassionate or even uninterested way, but after a while I begin to get "worked up": I fidget, clench my fists, my facial expression changes, my heart rate picks up, etc. In an extreme case perhaps my stomach churns and I start to sweat and tremble a little. This response is how my body registers that the situation is significant to me personally, to my values, interests, wishes, and goals, and how it focuses my attention on the situation conceived of in this way.

Now, of course, my conception of the situation depends on thoughts, opinions, and beliefs of various sorts. If I respond indignantly to the situation as I see it, then I must have a conception of the situation according to which the U.S. government is acting immorally, the Haitians' suffering is unjustifiable, and so on. I *think of* the government as acting immorally and the Haitians as being mistreated.[26] In short, what is made salient and registered as significant to my personal well-being is a complex conception that only a creature with sophisticated cognitive and moral competence could achieve. Nevertheless, even in this case, what makes the response an *emotional* response is that (1) it is a bodily response of a certain characteristic sort, (2) it directs attention to the conception that causes it, and (3) it picks out that particular conception for me to focus on from the myriad other thoughts and imaginings jostling for my attention, because the body "tells" me that *this* conception is significant to me and my well-being. As we have seen, developmentally sophisticated emotional responses requiring cognitive activity grow out of primitive responses that do not. Moreover, in every case from the primitive to the more sophisticated, the response itself serves the same purpose: to make salient some situation or conception of a situation, and register it as significant to the organism.

If I am right, then the formulation of beliefs, judgments, and conceptions about a situation is not necessary to an emotional response. It is also true, moreover, that cognitive activity of this sort is not *sufficient* for a emotional response.[27] Even in those cases where I am emotionally responding to a cognitively complex conception of a situation, merely having such a conception is not sufficient for the emotional response. After weighing up the political and moral implications of a situation, I can formulate a complex system of judgments or thoughts about Haitian refugees, all of which are characteristic of moral indignation, for example, and yet remain "unemotional" about the situation. It is only if my conception of the situation affects my own desires and my sense of my own well-being that it will provoke a bodily reaction, and by the same token it is only in these circumstances that I can be said to respond *emotionally* to the situation. Perhaps I can even dislike the situation without getting emotional about it, if the situation does not affect me so personally that it causes bodily changes that focus my attention on its significance to me. By contrast, if I am an African-American who identifies with the Haitians as victims of a colonial past and I am indignant that the U.S. fails to succor them, I may feel *myself* threatened by U.S. policy, and consequently respond emotionally to my conception of the situation.

We should, then, distinguish between merely viewing some situation in an indignant way—having an indignant conception of it—and an emotional response of indignation. If I respond emotionally with indignation, then my body alerts me to my conception of the situation and registers it as personally significant to me. *What* is registered as significant may be a complicated set of thoughts and beliefs, but *how* it is registered by the body may be relatively crude, as in the startle response: the body registers even the most complex conception merely as something I like or do not like, something threatening or frustrating, something that gives me pleasure or displeasure, something that is unexpected or novel, and so on.[28]

Interestingly, I may only begin to realize what conception I have of a situation if my body forces me to pay attention to it. I often respond emotionally to some event without realizing why; my body registers the event as significant to me, but I have only inchoate thoughts about it and have not made any conscious judgments about it. In such cases, I can and often do try to articulate what my thoughts about the situation are in order to explain and understand my emotional reaction. Thus, I may realize that I am angry about something without being able to articulate my "angry conception" of the situation. I may well have to engage in a great deal of thought before I can figure out what exactly my conception of the situation is and why my body is behaving in this peculiar way.[29]

My concept of an emotional response is broad enough to include both the startle response and the emotional response of moral indignation. It does not include everything that anyone has ever claimed to be an emotion, however. Ryle's example of an interest in symbolic logic would seem to be one case that fails to fit. It is only if I have a *passionate* interest in symbolic logic that a response to a particular logical dilemma may count as an emotional response. If a problem in symbolic logic causes me to get "worked up" in a bodily way, and if my bodily disturbance focuses my attention on the personal significance of the problem for me, then we can say that my response is emotional.[30]

At the other end of the spectrum, my concept of emotional response rules out certain reflexes as emotional. The knee-jerk reflex does not serve to alert me to an important condition of my body—or anything else. Some other responses, however, may turn out to be closer to emotional responses than has often been thought. Hunger, pain, and sexual desire are names of conditions that may satisfy the requirements on emotional response. If it turned out that there were identifiable bodily responses characteristic of these conditions which in turn served to alert the organism to the presence of these conditions—which are certainly of significance to the organism—then it may well be that these responses belong on the emotional spectrum, too.

V

I shall now briefly defend my model of emotional response by showing how it explains three things that the judgmentalist theories cannot. First, it explains the biological purpose of emotion; if emotional responses were just unreliable judgments, it is unclear what survival value they would have. The registration of significance by physiological means is nature's way of enabling us to pick out from the mass of information that bombards our senses that particular information which is significant to our goals and desires. Sometimes we need to respond very quickly to this information, so again nature has provided us with a means for quick responses where necessary: the information is registered automatically and the response is immediate. In other cases, a great deal of information has to be processed before the response is possible, as when I need to have a great deal of information about politics and morality before I can respond with moral indignation to the plight of the Haitian deportees. Even in this case, however, my response may be automatic and immediate if the relevant underlying beliefs and conceptions are deeply entrenched, perhaps in motor memory.

Emotional responses of all sorts can become entrenched, so that they are elicited in an automatic way rather like the startle mechanism. If I repeatedly hear about the Haitian situation and my conception of the situation is reinforced, eventually the mere mention of Haiti may provoke my emotional response of indignation.[31] If Zajonc is right, our emotional responses can get ensconced in motor memory, so that a particular stimulus will immediately produce a particular emotional response. Just as I am always startled by a gunshot, so, given the right reinforcement, I automatically respond angrily to talk about Haitian refugees.[32]

In any event, when my response is emotional rather than dispassionate, it is a characteristic bodily response which draws my attention insistently to the situation and its significance to me and may also prepare me for appropriate action.[33] Moreover, the force of the emotional (bodily) response is correlated with the perceived significance of the information to my goals and desires. Even a mild emotional response therefore differs from a "mere judgment": a mild emotional (bodily) response reflects the mildness of my concern for what I perceive; it is significant to my goals and desires, but not very. Unlike a "mere judgment," however, it is still a means of alerting me to the way the environment is affecting those goals and desires.

The bodily nature of emotional response also explains how our emotional responses may be connected with our physical states, how fatigue makes us more susceptible to anger or depression, for example, and how caffeine makes us prone to nervousness and irritability. Furthermore, it suggests a solution to the problem of the so-called "passivity" of emotion or "passion." If making cognitive evaluations were essential to emotion, then it would be odd to think of the emotions as passive phenomena. I suggest that emotions are passive in the sense that emotional responses alert us to particular features of our internal or external environments in a bodily way that, as it were, bypasses our willing or rational consent. Given our desires and goals, our thoughts and beliefs, the body responds willy-nilly to situations it registers as significant. We can try to control our desires and our goals; we can try to change our beliefs and conceptions; but it is very difficult, perhaps impossible, to control the emotional response itself. In this respect, too, all emotional responses are somewhat like the startle response.[34]

Secondly, the startle model of emotional response can explain emotional inertia, that is, the way that change of belief does not always bring change in the (apparently) corresponding emotion. I can continue to respond fearfully to spiders even though I firmly believe that spiders are not dangerous.

Despite my dispassionate judgment that spiders are harmless, my body responds automatically when I see (or imagine) a spider and "tells" me that the spider is indeed threatening to me. Again, it is probable that such responses are programmed into motor memory and use different neurological pathways from dispassionate judgments. Greenspan discusses a more interesting example of a similar phenomenon. Suppose, she says, I am in a car accident in a blizzard from which results a fear of skidding.

> On a later occasion, for instance, with someone else driving at a slow speed on an isolated road, a very slight skid and the momentary sensation of uncontrolled movement had me gasping audibly for a second out of fear.[35]

Greenspan uses this example to argue that since I do not on this occasion judge that I am in danger, my emotion of fear cannot be identified with such a judgment. So far so good. She goes on to claim, however, that in this situation I must be entertaining a *thought* of danger, since on her account emotions always have propositional content. But in this particular example where there is no evidence that there is such a thought present it is much more plausible to suppose that a representation of the earlier skid has been stored in perceptual/motor memory and that the present skid evokes the response in a rapid, automatic way, independently of any higher cognitive activity. On my model, such phenomena are easily explained.

The third point in favor of this account is connected to the second. The startle model of emotional response helps us to understand certain kinds of emotional irrationality which arise when my emotional responses seem to be inconsistent in some way with my dispassionate judgment of a situation. One kind of irrationality occurs when my emotional response seems to be caused by a particular *judgment,* but in fact I know the judgment to be false. For example, I respond fearfully to spiders but sincerely claim that I believe them to be harmless. Such irrationality can occur because, while my emotional response draws attention to and registers as significant a conception of spiders as threatening (nasty hairy crawly things that suddenly drop down on you from above), on my dispassionate view of spiders they are nonthreatening. Moreover, my response to spiders may be automatic and immediate, and not even caused by a conception of the situation.[36]

There is a second way in which an emotional response seems to be inconsistent with one's epistemic state, as when I respond angrily to Mary because she has "deliberately flouted my wishes" but I am uncertain as to whether she did or not. Unlike the spider case I do not believe that Mary did not flout my wishes; I do not know whether she did or not. I respond, however, as if I did believe she had flouted my wishes. I just cannot help thinking of Mary as someone who always flouts my wishes given half a chance. My emotional response is a bodily response to a conception of the situation which is inconsistent with my dispassionate "evaluative judgment." Moreover, this conception of Mary may have become entrenched so that my emotional responses to Mary are automatically elicited: I dislike her so much that my body immediately responds to her behavior (whatever it is) in a negative way. My conception of Mary is so deeply embedded that it evokes an emotional response independently of my rational assessment of the situation.[37]

Finally, a third type of emotional irrationality occurs when my emotional response is inappropriate in its intensity. Perhaps on another occasion Mary does flout my wishes on an issue I acknowledged (dispassionately) to be insignificant and I know that she has so flouted my wishes. My response, however, may be one of violent rage, inappropriate to my dispassionate assessment of the situation. Again, my bodily response may register the situation as *very* significant to my wants and interests, while dispassionately I know it is not. The startle model explains such cases, by suggesting that an emotional response is a bodily response which registers significance physiologically and which can—although it need not—be independent of one's dispassionate evaluation of the situation.

In all three cases I have examined, it is appropriate to call my emotional response "irrational" because it focuses on a conception of the situation which is inconsistent with the relevant beliefs or judgments. Thus, I register the spider as fearsome but acknowledge dispassionately that it is harmless. I respond to Mary as if she deliberately provoked me but am not sure whether or not she deliberately provoked me, or I respond to Mary as if she had delivered a terrible insult though I judge dispassionately that the insult is insignificant. In each case, irrationality arises because the emotional (physiological) focus of attention is on a situation conceived of and hence registered as significant in a particular way, and this particular way is inconsistent with my dispassionate evaluation of the situation. Moreover, the irrational conception I have of a situation may be entrenched so that my responses are elicited in a quasi-automatic way, not unlike the startle mechanism.

VI

I would now like to contrast my "startle" theory with some of the more prominent "judgmentalist" theories that I have been implicitly criticizing in this essay.

The judgment theory that might seem at first glance to have the most in common with my theory is that of Lyons, since he, too, emphasizes the importance of physiological response to emotion. On Lyons's view, an emotional state is "a physiologically abnormal state caused by the subject of that state's evaluation of his or her situation" (*op. cit.*, p. 58). Now, I am not sure that everything classifiable as an "emotional state" requires physiological arousal, but, as I have argued, an emotional *response* is indeed always a physiological response. On my view, however, this response does not need to have been caused by any "cognitive evaluation" of a situation.[38] More importantly, perhaps, Lyons ignores the *role* of physiological change, which I have tried to stress in this paper. On Lyons's view, it is entirely mysterious why certain "cognitive evaluations" produce abnormal physiological states and what function these physiological states might have. I have tried to show that whether or not produced by an "evaluation" of a situation, an emotional response always serves the function of drawing our attention to something that is registered as significant to us.

According to Robert Solomon,[39] emotions *are* judgments of a certain sort, namely, "self-involved and relatively *intense* evaluative judgments" which are "especially important to us, meaningful to us, concerning matters in which we have invested our Selves" (*ibid.*, p. 188). Elsewhere,[40] he says that emotions are "urgent" judgments, and emotional responses "emergency behavior." On my view we cannot *identify* emotions with the kinds of complex judgments discussed by Solomon. If I am in an emotional state of embarrassment, for example, my emotion cannot be identical to "my judgment to the effect that I am in an exceedingly awkward situation,"[41] since it is perfectly possible to make this judgment without being in the corresponding emotional state. I might even have an "embarrassed conception" of my situation but without being emotional about it. Moreover, I have argued that it is possible to respond emotionally to something without having any conception of the situation at all: an emotional response can be an automatic response, much like the startle reaction.

If we view Solomon's remarks not as remarks about emotion as such but as about emotional response, however, then what he says is much closer to the truth. As I have argued, emotional responses are indeed self-involved and have degrees of intensity corresponding to the intensity of our desires; they register the personal significance of something: they "tell" us what is especially important to us, meaningful to us, and what concerns "matters in which we have invested our Selves." Moreover, our emotional responses may indeed be urgent responses and "emergency behavior." In general, an emotional response registers the significance to us of some situation or conception of a situation, just as the startle reaction registers the significance to us of a sudden loud sound. Speaking very broadly—indeed, metaphorically—we can say that when we are startled, our bodies "judge" that we are in a potentially threatening situation that needs immediate attention, but we must remember that this "judgment" does not require cognitive activity or the formulation of any beliefs or conceptions of the situation in propositional form.[42]

Unlike Solomon, Gordon does not *identify* emotions with judgments; rather, he argues that certain emotional states are *caused by* particular cognitive states. According to Gordon, it is the *cognitive aetiology* of an emotional state that makes it the state that it is. On my view, Gordon gives subtle analyses of the *conceptions* that underlie some emotional states, such as fearing or hoping that *p*, and being angry or delighted that *p*, but he does not shed any light on what it is to have an emotional response of fear, hopefulness, anger, or delight.[43] Significantly, Gordon has virtually nothing to say about the physiological components of emotional states.[44]

The trouble with his "judgmentalist" assumption that cognitive aetiology is crucial to emotion is that, as we have seen in our discussion of Zajonc's results, although emotional responses *can* be caused by cognitive evaluations of complicated sorts, they do not *have* to be. Fear that my boss will rebuke me in public for erasing a vital computer program can only be caused by a complex evaluation of a situation, but fear of spiders apparently does not have to be similarly caused. Moreover, Gordon's overemphasis on the cognitive elements in emotional states leads him to the counterintuitive conclusion that there is a radical difference between emotion in humans and emotion in nonhuman animals.

Gordon distinguishes between fearing that *p* and being in a state of fear. Fearing that *p* (for example, fearing that it will rain) is an epistemic state confined to human beings which entails being uncertain whether or not that *p* and wishing that not-*p*. In contrast to *fears* of this sort is the state of *fear* that according to Gordon is a "complex evolutionary experiment, perhaps universal among mammals, involving physiological (especially autonomic) arousal, the riveting of attention, readiness for flight, and a disposition to flee."[45] Since on Gordon's view only states with a certain cognitive aetiology qualify as fears and since the state of fear need not have this cognitive aetiology, Gordon claims that it is a quite different phenomenon. Thus, while lower animals can be in the state of fear, they cannot have fears.[46]

I have defined an emotional response throughout in terms of its effects rather than its causes: an emotional response is one that alerts the organism to something important in the environment. If the function of emotional response is to alert the organism to something significant to it in the environment, and if the startle model is an informative model of emotional response, then all mammals and, indeed, many other species have emotional responses and these responses are crucially important to the survival and the flourishing of the organism. It is true that thoughts can cause emotional responses in humans, but it does not follow that animals who do not think cannot have emotions. Thus, both animal fear and human fears, when truly emotional phenomena, have the same structure and function, to draw attention to something significantly threatening in the environment.

Finally, much that I have said is consistent with Greenspan's view that emotions are "states of comfort or discomfort directed toward evaluative thoughts that they serve to hold in mind" (*op. cit.*, p. 63). In my terms, Greenspan holds that an emotional response registers as liked or disliked, pleasurable or painful, some conception of a situation which is not a "judgment" but an "evaluative thought." On her view, though emotions do not involve judgments, they nevertheless have propositional content since they are always directed toward "thoughts," whether these are believed or merely entertained or even imagined. Thus, like Gordon, she wants to make a sharp distinction between human emotion and emotion in lower animals. She claims, for example, that a cat cannot be said to be genuinely *angry* unless we can "attribute to it at least some evaluation of the situation." Without a propositional object, the cat's state cannot properly be termed "emotional"; it is rather a "pure feeling of arousal" which humans, thinking anthropomorphically, and finding in the cat's behavior the same kind of perceptual causes and behavioral effects as we find in human anger, mistakenly term 'anger' (*op. cit.*, p. 48). As I have argued, however, while emotional responses are always responses *to* something, this "something" might just be a gunshot; it need not be a *thought* and it need not have intentional content. Consequently, there is no big gap between human anger and animal anger. Anger is not a "pure feeling of arousal," since it is physiologically distinct from other states of arousal (such as joy or fear). Furthermore, anger does not always require "thoughts": humans and cats can both respond angrily in an automatic immediate way to some perceived stimulus.

VII

I have drawn attention to the "primitive" end of the emotion spectrum, with particular emphasis on the startle response. I have urged that the startle response gives us a more useful model of emotional response in general than the cognitively sophisticated emotions emphasized by most philosophers. Our mature emotional life has its roots in the "primitive" emotional responses of infancy and shares its most characteristic features with them. And however cognitively sophisticated we become, our moral indignation, awe, and embarrassment crucially resemble the humble startle response.

Notes

1   I am deeply indebted to William Dember, who introduced me to the psychological literature on the emotions. I should also like to thank Dember, Christopher Gauker, Robert M. Gordon, and Robert C. Solomon for their critical comments on this paper, as well as the Charles Phelps Taft fund and the University Research Council of the University of Cincinnati for financial support while I was writing it.

2   Ryle, *The Concept of Mind* (New York: Barnes and Noble, 1949); Lyons, *Emotion* (New York: Cambridge, 1980); Greenspan, *Emotions and Reasons* (New York: Routledge, 1988); Gordon, *The Structure of Emotions* (New York: Cambridge, 1987).

3 I am not discussing 'being startled' in the sense of "being astonished by," as in 'I was startled by her sudden change of opinion.' As will become clear, I am talking about the "reflex" reaction of startle which typically occurs when one is subjected to a sudden loud sound.

4 *Pride, Shame, and Guilt: Emotions of Self-assessment* (New York: Oxford, 1985).

5 I leave open the possibility that love and awe are not always emotions. In general, I think the concept of emotion in ordinary use does not name a "natural kind." I think, however, that the core of the ordinary concept will be captured by my analysis of emotional responses. Lyons distinguishes between "occurrent" episodes of emotion and "standing" emotional states. In his terms, my analysis is of *occurrent* emotions, which I believe are always responses to some thought or perception.

6 *The Startle Pattern* (New York: Farrar and Rinehart, 1939; repr. New York: Johnson Reprint, 1968). This book is the only full-length study of the startle mechanism of which I am aware. The contemporary psychologists Paul Ekman and Carroll Izard have devoted some attention to the issue, however, as I shall mention later.

7 In particular, this suggestion is likely to be repudiated by social construction theorists of emotion. See, for example, James Averill, "A Constructionist View of Emotion," in R. Plutchik and H. Kellerman, eds., *Theories of Emotion* (New York: Academic, 1979); Robert Levy, "Emotion, Knowing, and Culture," in R. Schweder and R. LeVine, eds., *Culture Theory* (New York: Cambridge, 1984); and Catherine Lutz, *Unnatural Emotions* (Chicago: University Press, 1988).

8 Tomkins, *Affect-Imagery-Consciousness, Volume I: The Positive Affects* (New York: Springer, 1962); Izard, *Human Emotions* (New York: Plenum, 1977).

9 Ed., *Emotion in the Human Face* (New York: Cambridge, 1982; 2nd ed.).

10 See Ekman, "Expression and the Nature of Emotion," in K. Scherer and Ekman, eds., *Approaches to Emotion* (Hillsdale, NJ: Erlbaum, 1984), pp. 320-21.

11 "Expression and the Nature of Emotion," pp. 324-28. It may be that some people can suppress or mask ANS activity as well as facial expression. See Ekman's studies of the polygraph, the so-called "lie-detector," in *Telling Lies* (New York: Berkley, 1985), esp. ch.7.

12 See, for example, the studies of F.B. Krasne and J.J. Wine on crayfish tailflip manoeuvres and Robert Eaton and John Hackett on fast-starts involving escape in teleost fishes, in Eaton, ed., *Neural Mechanisms of Startle Behavior* (New York: Plenum, 1984).

13 *The Emotions* (New York: Cambridge, 1986), p. 16.

14 Surprise, like startle, is not commonly discussed by philosophers of emotion, but it is one of the basic emotions, according to both Izard and Ekman, chiefly because of its distinctive facial expression.

15 Cf. Ekman, "Expression and the Nature of Emotion," p. 329.

16 "On the Primacy of Affect," *American Psychologist*, XXXIX (1984): 117-23; see also his "Feeling and Thinking: Preferences Need No Inferences," *American Psychologist*, XXXV (1980): 151-75.

17 "On the Primacy of Affect," p. 120. In the mere exposure experiments, subjects are differentially exposed to a variety of stimuli, such as nonsense syllables, and then asked to give a liking rating. It was discovered that subjects gave a higher liking rating to those syllables they were exposed to more often. In some experiments, the stimuli are presented too fast for recognition, and the mere exposure effect still obtains. In the subception experiments, subjects are presented with ten nonsense syllables, five of which are associated with electric shocks. Eventually, the subject gets a galvanic skin response before the shock occurs. Then the stimuli are presented very fast and the subject asked to guess what they are. Even when the subjects guess wrong, the level of galvanic skin response is higher for the stimuli that were associated with the electric shocks: the subjects' skin "knew" which ones were associated with shock, although the subjects did not!

18 Zajonc and Hazel Markus, "Affect and Cognition: The Hard Interface," in Izard, J. Kagan, and Zajonc, eds. *Emotions, Cognition and Behavior* (New York: Cambridge, 1984), pp. 73-102.

19 *Psychology from the Standpoint of a Behaviorist* (Philadelphia: Lippincott, 1929: 3rd ed.). More recent research has shown that even in the first weeks of infancy the neonate "smile" can be regularly elicited by the mother's smiling face. See T.M. Field, et alia, "Discrimination and Imitation of Facial Expressions by Neonates," *Science*, CCXVIII (1982): 179-81. See also Alan Sroufe, "The Organization of Emotional Development," in Scherer and Ekman, esp. pp. 114-15.

20 Sroufe, pp. 112-114.

21 Klaus Scherer has observed that the development of emotions in the very young child corresponds to the increasing sophistication of what he calls "stimulus evaluation checks." Thus, on his view, startle and displeasure are present at birth; surprise appears between one and three months; joy between three and five months; fear between five and nine months; shame between twelve and fifteen months, etc. Corresponding stimulus evaluation checks are: novelty (for startle), intrinsic pleasantness (for displeasure), "goal/need conduciveness" (for surprise), "goal/need conduciveness and coping potential" (for fear), "norm/self concept compatibility" (for shame), etc. Until the child is capable of the appropriate stimulus evaluation check, it is incapable of being in the corresponding emotional state. See Scherer, "On the Nature and Function of Emotion: A Component Process Approach," in Scherer and Ekman, pp. 293-317, esp. p. 314.

22 "Cognitive-emotional Interactions in the Brain," *Cognition and Emotion*, III (1989): 267-89. Ledoux also points out that there are interactions between amygdala and neocortex and hippocampus which mediate cognition.

23 It also seems to be the case, however, that elimination of the conditioned fear response needs to be cognitively mediated. Ledoux, L. Romanski, and A. Xagoraris, "Indelibility of Subcortical Emotional Memories," *Journal of Cognitive Neuroscience*, I (1989): 238-43.

24 Amelie Rorty urges the importance to emotion of "patterns of intentional salience"—"Explaining Emotions," in Rorty, ed., *Explaining Emotions* (Berkeley:

California UP, 1980), p. 112. Ronald de Sousa suggests that emotions be identified with "species of determinate patterns of salience among objects of attention, lines of inquiry, and inferential strategies"—*The Rationality of Emotion* (Cambridge: MIT, 1987), p. 196.

25 The idea that there is a spectrum of emotional responses corresponding to the kind of processing that mediates the response has been suggested by Howard Leventhal in "A Perceptual Motor Theory of Emotion," in Scherer and Ekman, pp. 271-91, esp. pp. 274-78. Scherer more plausibly ties the development of emotional sophistication to cognitive development—"On the Nature and Function of Emotion: A Component Process Approach."

26 See my "Emotion, Judgment, and Desire," *The Journal of Philosophy*, LXXX, 11 (November 1983): 731-41, where I explain why I think we have to specify that the relevant cognitions are "conceptions" or "thoughts" about a situation rather than "judgments" about it.

27 I defend this view in "Emotion, Judgment, and Desire." In particular, I argue there that I can experience the occurrent emotion of nostalgia simply by thinking certain thoughts. I would now want to say that, although this may be true, if I have an emotional *response* of nostalgia to something, then my desires and my sense of my own well-being must be so centrally involved that my body is affected and focuses me on those thoughts.

28 Perhaps this helps us to understand the perennial search for so-called "basic emotions." As Ekman, Izard, and others have shown, the repertoire of bodily responses that distinguish particular emotional states seems to be relatively small. Complex conceptions serve to demarcate more complex emotional states, but the bodily registration of significance can only demarcate emotional states in a rudimentary way. Those emotions which *can* be so distinguished perhaps deserve the name 'basic emotions.'

29 R.G. Collingwood makes a distinction between the "betrayal" of emotion by physiological symptoms that are typically beyond our control, and what he calls the "expression" of emotion by which he means the articulation and elucidation of emotion in language or art: we become *conscious* of our emotional states, he says, when we attempt to "express" them. Collingwood can perhaps be interpreted as adumbrating a distinction between the bodily registering of some conception as something significant to me and the articulation of that conception in propositional form—*The Principles of Art* (New York: Oxford, 1938), esp. ch. VI, "Art Proper: (1) As Expression."

30 Whether it still counts as mere "interest" rather than something stronger, may be questionable. Of course, this is not to say that only violent responses can be emotional. Emotional responses can be more or less calm or violent, but they must involve a focus of attention on a situation as it is significant to my goals and wishes.

31 Significantly, such a response is sometimes referred to as a "knee-jerk" response. Of course, some cognitive activity must have preceded the development of such a response; however, it seems that cognitive activity is not necessary to elicit the

response once it becomes entrenched. LeDoux's results may be relevant to this point. Incidentally, I am not claiming that repeated exposure to a situation *always* reinforces the initial emotional response: my emotional response may change or it may fade into indifference.

32   Interestingly, one of the main therapies for treating depression is behavior therapy. The therapy aims to change motor habits in order to change emotional state. See, for example, Peter M. Lewinsohn, et alia, *Control Your Depression* (New York: Prentice-Hall, 1986).

33   Greenspan emphasizes the role of emotional "discomfort" as motivating action. She would want to say that it is my uncomfortable feeling of indignation that is in part responsible for the action I take (so that I can get rid of the discomfort). See, for example, Greenspan, pp. 52-53.

34   As Ekman has noted, subtle changes in facial expression may be crucial to identifying an emotion but difficult to simulate. For example, deliberate smiles are more often asymmetric than spontaneous ones, and among asymmetric smiles the deliberate are more often than the spontaneous stronger on the left side of the face. On the other hand, some people are able to prevent any "leakage" of their emotions through facial expression. Even where an emotion is completely inhibited, however, "nonvisible expression may still be detectable electromyographically. No one yet knows whether inhibition can take place *centrally*, preventing the efferent impulses from reaching the peripheral expressive equipment"—*Expression and the Nature of Emotion*, esp. p. 322 and pp. 335-36.

35   Greenspan, pp. 18-19.

36   Frijda cites Ohman's results showing that "fear for some kinds of stimuli is much more readily learned than for others. The organism is apparently 'prepared' for them. Human beings very readily learn to be afraid of spiders and snakes" (*op. cit.*, p. 272).

37   Compare Rorty's example of Jonah's deeply embedded hostility to women in authority which is incompatible with his actual *beliefs* about such women— "Explaining Emotions," esp. pp. 106-11.

38   In "Emotion, Judgment, and Desire," I also criticize Lyons's explanation of a "cognitive evaluation."

39   *The Passions* (New York: Doubleday, 1976).

40   "Emotions and Choice," in *Explaining Emotions* p. 264.

41   *The Passions*, p. 187.

42   In conversation, Solomon has remarked that he has a very broad notion of the concept of "judgment." I would still want to deny that an emotional response is *identical* to a judgment, however, even in a broad sense of "judgment."

43   Gordon admits that his analyses may not be true of emotions per se: "I shall not pretend to be talking about every state we are wont to call an emotion, nor indeed that my generalizations do not apply to some states that one might balk at calling emotions. The term 'emotion' will serve only as a rough guide to the initial scope

of this investigation. The final scope may be defined as those states of which my generalizations hold true"—*The Structure of Emotions* p. 22.

44   Taylor, like Gordon, gives illuminating accounts of emotional states such as pride, shame, and guilt in terms of the "judgments" that on her view constitute these emotions; see her *Pride, Shame and Guilt.* Many of the older accounts of emotion in the history of philosophy (e.g., Aristotle, Descartes, Spinoza) also give us analyses of this sort.

45   Gordon, *The Structure of Emotions,* p. 71. Significantly, the argument could be adapted to other emotions, too, such as being angry or pleased. I can be angry or pleased that p without being in an emotional state of anger or pleasure.

46   In his comments on an earlier version of the present paper (American Philosophical Association Central Division Meeting, Chicago, April 1993), Gordon comes closer to acknowledging that cognitive aetiology is not always definitive of an emotional state. He notes that we often use the same term (such as 'fear') to cover both "cognitive and noncognitive aetiologies." As he says, I can be disturbed (noncognitively) by your typing or disturbed (cognitively) by the fact that you were typing. Gordon grants that there are "important similarities in the effect the cognitive and noncognitive cause has on us," but he still wants to insist that the differences are more important than the similarities, because he is wedded to the idea that cognitive causal structure is what defines some classes of emotions. He says that "the various emotions, those with a cognitive causal structure and those with a noncognitive aetiology, those which incline us toward characteristic intentional action and those which do not, those which involve much agitation or emotion and those which do not, appear to be linked together only by a number of overlapping family resemblances," and rejects my idea that there is a spectrum of emotional response, from the cognitively sophisticated to the noncognitive, based on the structure and function of the response.

MODULARITY AND THE
PSYCHOEVOLUTIONARY THEORY OF EMOTION

P.E. Griffiths

I INTRODUCTION

Everyday discourse classes emotions into kinds like fear, anger, love, disgust and sadness. It would be a mistake to assume that this is the best classification for all scientific purposes. First, even the most superficial conversation about emotion soon leads to a wish to distinguish more kinds of emotion than we have names for. It is not difficult to find counterexamples to even the most mundane assertions about love or anger. The next conversational step is to insist that what we say is true of one kind of love, or anger or whatever, but not of others. So even in casual conversation, we do not take the standard emotion vocabulary to be definitive.

Secondly, members of other cultures seem to experience emotions that are unknown to us. The Japanese experience called 'amae' is not one which westerners can readily imagine, and certainly not one most westerners would claim to have experienced.[1] It follows that the emotion vocabulary of English is at least incomplete. Other facts about the cultural diversity of emotional experience suggest that even for the domain of emotions it describes, our vocabulary may not capture the definitive distinctions between one emotion and another. Heelas (1986) introduces the notions of 'hyper-' and 'hypo-cognition.' A particular emotion category may be central to a culture. In consequence, a larger segment of the emotional experience of individuals in that culture may be conceptualized in that category. Alternatively, a category may be squeezed into insignificance, or even non-existence, by the expansion of other categories, or by the direct hostility of the culture to that category. In current western culture, 'love' may be hyper-cognized in comparison with other cultures, and 'piety' hypo-cognized in comparison with previous stages of our own culture. States that were classified under one head in one time or place are now classified under another.

These facts about emotion make it unwise to assume that our current vocabulary draws all and only those distinctions which will be required for the scientific study of emotion.[2]

There are two main strands to our everyday discourse about emotion. The first strand contrasts emotion with rational thought and action. Emotions are conceived as 'passive,' or involuntary. They are intrusive elements in our motivation, interfering with rational action based upon justified beliefs and stable desires. This element of everyday discourse also links emotions to various physiological events. Emotions take over systems whose operation is usually voluntary, causing behaviours such as flinching and orienting. They also divert from their usual paths systems whose operation is characteristically involuntary, such as the beating of the heart, or sweat glands. It is this strand of our thought that motivates philosophers like William Lyons (1980), who believe that a mental state cannot count as an emotion unless it causes physiological disturbance.

The second, contrasting strand of everyday discourse treats emotions as intentional states, embodying judgements of various kinds. Fear is an attitude we have to certain kinds of objects. It somehow embodies the judgement that those objects are threats to us. This strand of our thought lies behind the major philosophical approach to emotion of the last 25 years—the cognitive theory. Philosophical cognitivism centers around two claims. First, that the occurrence of propositional attitudes is essential to the occurrence of emotions. Second, that the identity of particular emotions depends upon the kinds of propositional attitudes they involve. The philosophical cognitivist claims that it is a necessary condition of fearing something that you believe it to be dangerous, and desire to avoid the danger. An extensive philosophical literature defends this position against various counterexamples, and relates the cognitivist orthodoxy to questions concerning the rationality and moral status of emotions.[3]

There are a number of problems with the idea that having an emotion involves having appropriate beliefs and desires. The content of some emotions blatantly contradicts the contents of our beliefs, as when a person is afraid of what they are sure is a harmless earthworm. The cognitive contents associated with some emotions are also liable to occur without the emotion occurring. For example, people face terrible dangers, and with no apparent death wish, remain unafraid, and take sensible decisions.

A number of authors have suggested more or less ad hoc additions to the theory in the hope of making it extensionally adequate. Among the more notable suggestions, William Lyons (1980) suggests that the cognitive state must cause physiological disturbances of some kind if it is to count as an emotion. Michael Stocker (1987) has suggested that the cognitive contents must be held "emotionally," as well "evidentially." The contents must be "entered into," or "lived." As Stocker admits, these notions are "difficult to characterize."

I have argued elsewhere (Griffiths 1989b) that none of the sophisticated versions of cognitivism succeed in overcoming the original array of difficulties. In the same article I show that even if cognitivism were able to provide an extensionally adequate taxonomy of emotions, this would fail to fulfill many of the desiderata for a theory of emotions.

One of the continuing attractions of the cognitive approach is that it promises a theory of emotion that preserves the categories used in our every-day discourse. I have suggested, however, that there is good reason to doubt whether these categories are definitive. The alternative approach which I describe in this paper—the psychoevolutionary theory—will not preserve the traditional categories. First, it does not pretend to be a theory of all the things which can properly be called 'emotions' in English. Secondly, it revises those emotion categories which it does attempt to explain. I shall defend this revisionary approach in two ways. First, I show that the new categories of emotion are far more theoretically fruitful than the old in ethology, evolutionary theory and in the neurosciences. Thus, even if we were to retain the old vocabulary, we would need the new vocabulary in order to state a body of important generalizations about emotional phenomena. Secondly, I shall show that using the new vocabulary we can give a partial account of the origins of the old vocabulary, and explain why theories which use that old vocabulary encounter characteristic difficulties.

II   THE PSYCHOEVOLUTIONARY THEORY OF EMOTION

The psychoevolutionary approach to emotions was pioneered by Darwin (1872). Darwin used the French anatomist Duchenne's data on facial musculature, obtained by electrical stimulation of the facial muscle groups, to put forward *component analyses* of particular emotional expressions. He also pioneered the *judgement test*, in which a subject's ability to recognize emotion on the basis of photographed faces is assessed.

These two techniques have remained the most important tools in the investigation of facial expressions. In this section I outline some of the most telling of those modern experiments. I describe a judgement test with isolated New Guinean subjects, a comparative component analysis carried out on American and Japanese subjects, and some work on facial expression in deaf and blind born infants. The tendency of all this work is to show that there are some patterns of emotive response, which occur in all cultures. These results contradict the orthodoxy which prevailed before the 1960's. Previously, authors like La Barre (1947) and R.L. Birdwhistell (1963) had popularized the view that emotions are expressed in a culture-specific, learnt code, akin to a language. This view was made tenable by a reliance upon anecdotal evidence, a conflation of facial expression with other behaviours, such as gestures, and the phenomenon of display rules, which we discuss below. This position still seems to be favoured by authors such as Rom Harré (1986).

Ekman and Friesen (1971) conducted an experiment with subjects from the Fore language group in New Guinea. These subjects had seen no movies or magazines, they neither spoke nor understood English or pidgin, they had not lived in any western settlement or government town, and they had never worked for a white man. Forty photographs were used in experiments with 189 adults and 130 children from the Fore.

Ekman and Friesen utilized a judgement task originally designed for work with children. The subject was given three photographs at once, each showing a face. The faces were selected, on the basis of a previously devised component theory, to be clear expressions of one basic emotion. The subject was then told a story which was designed to involve one of these emotions. Finally, they were asked to say which photograph showed the person described in the story. The stories described situations with emotional significance in the life of the Fore speakers, such as the death of a child, or an unarmed encounter with a wild pig. This method has the advantage of avoiding the necessity of translating emotion terms from one language to another.

High degrees of agreement were observed between the categories which the pictures were intended to represent and the categories which they were chosen as representing by the Fore. For example, photographs intended to represent sadness, anger and surprise were shown to the New Guineans, who were asked to select which picture represented the face of a man whose child had just died. Seventy-nine percent of adults and 81 percent of children selected the face intended to represent sadness. These results confirm the view that similar facial behaviour is selected for the same emotion in visually isolated preliterate cultures. Ekman and Friesen also conducted a reverse test using their New Guinean subjects. They asked members of this culture to show how their face would appear if they were the person described in one of the emotion stories that had been used in the judgement test. Video tapes of nine New Guineans were shown to thirty-four U.S. college students. Except for the poses of fear and surprise (which the New Guineans had difficulty in discriminating), the students, who had never seen anyone from New Guinea, accurately judged the emotion intended by their poses. This reverse test further confirms the results of the study.

Ekman and Friesen (1980) also conducted a component analysis of spontaneous facial expression. Twenty-five subjects from the University of Berkeley and twenty-five subjects from the Waseda University, Tokyo, watched a neutral and stress-inducing film whilst alone in a room.[4] They were aware that skin conductance and heart-rate measures were being taken but unaware that a video tape of their facial behaviour was being made. The facial behaviour of both groups during the stress film was radically different from that during the neutral film. When the repertoire of facial behaviours shown during the stress phase by the two sets of subjects were compared it was very similar.[5] Correlations between the facial behaviour shown by Japanese and American subjects in relation to the stress film ranged from 0.72 to 0.96, depending upon whether a particular facial area was compared or the movement of the entire face.

Perhaps the most interesting result from this experiment was that when an authority figure was introduced into the room and asked questions about the subject's emotions as the stress film was shown again the facial behaviour of the Japanese differed radically from that of the Americans. The characteristic difference was that the Japanese showed more positive emotion than the Americans and less negative emotion. The Japanese appeared to have masked their negative feelings by politely smiling. Slow-motion videotape analysis showed the micro-momentary occurrence of characteristic negative emotional expressions, and then showed them being replaced with a polite smile. This behaviour appears to have been unconscious and relatively automatic on the part of the Japanese. This is a classic example of so-called 'display rules' in operation. A display rule is a means whereby an individual, or more often a whole society, habitually mask or suppress a natural emotional response in order to conform more closely to some norm or ideal. The existence of display rules may have played a role in making plausible the view of La Barre and others that even basic emotional expressions are culture specific.

Finally, we can turn to component analyses on the deaf and blind born. Eibl-Eibesfeldt (1973) analyzed the facial movements of infants born deaf and blind and of normal infants when exposed to the same stimuli. He discovered that the same patterns of muscular activity were used to display the same kinds of emotions in both groups. This finding confirms the results of Thompson (1941) and Fulcher (1942), both of whom discovered the same patterns of muscular activity in the blind and seeing for each type of emotional behaviour. This result seems to have been fairly well confirmed and has extremely important implications for our theory of emotion.

III   ARE EMOTIONAL RESPONSES INNATE?

The evidence just reviewed will be used below to support the idea that certain emotional displays are controlled by "affect-programs." An affect-program is a neural circuit, probably in the hypothalamus and associated regions. When triggered, it initiates the complex series of reactions which make up an emotional response. These are generally thought to include facial expression, vocalization and expressive vocal changes, skeletal muscular reactions, such as orienting or flinching, and changes in autonomic nervous system activity, leading to alterations in heart rate, skin temperature and so on.

However, the issue of whether affect-programs exist must not be confused with the issue of whether they are innate. In principle, an affect-program may be entirely innate, entirely learnt, or a mixture of the two. These are questions about how the circuitry gets built, not about whether it exists. It is not possible to argue from the fact that emotions are controlled by affect-programs to the fact that they are innate.

There is, however, an argument in the other direction. If emotional responses are innate, this would provide support for the view that there are affect-programs. The argument is something like this. If there are complex, co-ordinated responses, involving many different physiological systems, and these depend upon an innate factor, our present scientific understanding makes a circuit in the central nervous system just about the only mechanism that could be built by the genes and then lead to the production of these complex sequences of behaviour. In this section I assess the evidence for the innateness of the various elements of the affect-program response.

The results on facial expressions gathered by Ekman and Friesen are evidence for the innateness of those expressions. They are particularly good evidence because facial expressions are mostly arbitrary behaviours. In humans, the fact that the fear expression expresses fear and the joy expression expresses joy, cannot be explained by any intrinsic appropriateness of those expressions. Only surprise retains its utilitarian purpose (it serves to increase uptake of visual information). If these arbitrary expressions were the results of learning or social training, the use of the same expression for the same purpose in different cultures would be inexplicable.[6]

The data gathered by Eibl-Eibesfeldt is also good evidence for innateness. It is implausible to suppose that deaf and blind born infants have learnt the correct facial expression for joy or disgust from those around them.

Unfortunately, the research on the innateness or otherwise of other postulated affect-program elements is not as decisive. We know that orienting to the stimulus is part of the surprise response, other than that I am not aware of any studies of muscular/skeletal response in humans. Panksepp (1982) has worked on affect-program controlled muscular/skeletal responses in animals, and claims to have isolated a number of behaviour sequences. I doubt, however, whether these results can be carried over to humans. I discuss my reservations on this point in section 6. I also know of no solid data on vocal responses.

Turning to ANS responses, there is a massive body of research, dating back to W.B. Cannon in the inter-war years. Unfortunately, most of it is addressed to the question of the specificity of ANS arousal to particular emotions, not to the innateness of that arousal (the two issues are connected, but in a way too complex to go into here). Anecdotally, it seems plausible that adrenalin release and the accompanying heart rate and other changes accompany fear in the New Guineans, as well as in westerners, but there are no studies that I know of. A further problem is raised for such research by the direct utility of some such ANS responses. Studies would have to rule out the possibility that adrenalin release is a learnt response which occurs in all cultures because it is always useful. Studies on infants, as well as cross-cultural studies, would be necessary to ascertain this.[7]

As a consequence of the lack of research on these topics, it must be concluded that if there are affect-programs their contents are at least partly innate, but that the boundary between the innate and the learnt is unclear.

IV   THE AFFECT-PROGRAM THEORY

The idea that there are affect-programs controlling the various pancultural emotional responses received some support from the fact that those responses are at least partly innate. But the main argument for the existence of affect-programs is the following argument to the best explanation. There are a number of important characteristics of emotional responses that seem to stand in need of explanation. They are often brief, quick, complex, organized and to a greater or lesser extent involuntary. Let us consider these characteristics in a little more detail. If emotions are distinguished from moods (Griffiths 1989a) they are typically *brief*, they may last as little as a few seconds. The onset of an emotion may be so *quick* as to be regarded as near instantaneous. An emotional response is both *complex* and *organized*. It typically involves at least four kinds of coordinated changes. Firstly, there are skeletal/muscular changes such as flinching, orienting or relaxing. Secondly, there are changes in the facial musculature, leading to emotional expressions. Thirdly, there are vocalizations and more general changes in the vocal muscles leading to expressive tones of voice. Fourthly, there are autonomic nervous system responses, such as sweating, secretion of adrenalin and changes in heart rate. The characteristic sensations of the various emotions might also be mentioned. Perhaps the most important feature of emotional responses is that they are typically *involuntary*. They occur without the conscious instigation of the subject. In this they are rather like reflexes, but they are unlike reflexes in being more complex and organized. The argument for the existence of affect-programs is simply that the features of emotion just described, and particularly the last feature, can best be explained on the hypothesis that a neural program stores a predetermined set of responses which are activated in a co-ordinated fashion in rapid response to some external stimuli. This argument has been advanced forcibly in a number of works by Paul Ekman (1972, 1973, 1980).

The existence of neural circuits that are partially innately specified, and which control the rapid responses uncovered by the psychoevolutionary theory is the best evidenced part of the affect-program theory. In addition to the data and arguments already given, there is a body of neuroscientific work which has attempted to map such circuits in the limbic system. This is reviewed in section 6. These neural circuits, and their surface manifestations, may be regarded as the 'output side' of the psychoevolutionary/affect-program theory, dealing with what happens when an emotional response is triggered. The 'input side,' dealing with the events that trigger the emotional response, is in a somewhat less developed state.

The fact that the elements of the affect-program responses are at least partially innate tells us nothing about whether there are any stimuli to which the affect-programs are innately sensitive. But there is a considerable amount of research which throws light on this question. J.B. Watson (1925) found that new-born babies are afraid of loud sounds and loss of balance, but almost nothing else. More recent research has suggested that the new-born are sensitive to one further class of stimuli, namely the facial expressions of caregivers (Trevarthen 1984). It might, therefore, be concluded that the system which triggers the affect-programs has very few innate elements. But this makes no allowance for responses which emerge during maturation, or for the possibility of learning preparedness (Seligman 1970). Experience may be needed to produce a response, but if less experience is needed to produce a response to one object than to another, the explanation of this 'preparedness' to learn may involve genetic factors.

There is experimental evidence for learning preparedness in the cases of fear and disgust. Seligman (1971) has argued that phobias are best understood as cases of highly prepared (often one-trial) learning of fear responses. He suggests that the stimuli for which humans are predisposed to acquire fear are those which would have been prevalent sources of danger during human evolution. Ohman et al. (1976) conducted conditioning experiments on human beings in an attempt to test a similar proposal. They found that associations between classic phobic stimuli, such as snakes, and aversive stimuli, in this case electric shock, were more resistant to extinction than associations established with a similar number of trials between shock and neutral stimuli, such as flowers, or arbitrary stimuli, such as shapes. They were also more resistant than associations between phobic stimuli and non-aversive stimuli, in this case, sounds. They concluded that the association of certain classic phobic stimuli with danger is a prepared association in humans.

Disgust responses have been widely studied in animals under the heading of 'taste aversion.' Many species exhibit a marked inability to associate anything but ingested substances with nausea, and have remarkable capacities to identify and avoid noxious substances in their diet. Various authors have suggested the existence of specialized mechanisms for associating illness with tastes (Rozin and Kalat 1971, Garcia et al. 1974). Logue et al. (1981) attempted to show that the same phenomenon is found in humans. It appears that in humans, as in other animals, there is a strong tendency to acquire disgust for a taste which has been followed by illness, even where higher-level cognitive systems are aware that no causal connection exists between the food and the illness.

The data suggests that affect-program responses are innately sensitive to very few stimuli. Most of the contents of the triggering system are learnt. There is, however, considerable evidence that this learning mechanism is biased. It is not a general-purpose mechanism, equally capable of learning any facts that the world may embody. Some kinds of fact are easier to learn, and some harder. Although the organism does not arrive in the world with a preconceived map of what is emotionally significant, it does bring with it some preconceived ideas about what is *likely* to be emotionally significant.

This picture of the triggering of affect-programs makes considerable evolutionary sense. Affect-programs are adaptive responses to events that have a particular ecological significance for the organism. The fear response is adapted to dangers, the disgust response to noxious stimuli, the anger response to challenges, the surprise response to novel stimuli. The local events which possess the properties of being dangerous, noxious or novel may be very different from one environment to the other. If affect-programs are to be of significant adaptive advantage to an organism over an evolutionarily significant time period, it would be advantageous for them to be linked to some mechanism which can interpret the broad ecological categories of danger, novelty and so forth, in the light of local conditions, and equate them with detectable features of the local environment. So it comes as no surprise that organisms have to learn which events in their particular environment should trigger the affect-programs.

There are, however, certain constancies in the environment which a learning system can be pre-programmed to take account of. The disgust response is designed to prevent the ingestion of noxious substances. It would be extremely inefficient if the disgust response were to be elicited by non-gustatory stimuli, however well those stimuli might correlate with illness. Such responses would be useless, and probably counterproductive. A constraint on the learning mechanism which helps to restrict disgust to gustatory stimuli would be advantageous.

The other sort of constraint on learning discussed above, a preparedness to associate particular stimuli with danger, has obvious adaptive advantages. A prepared learning mechanism of this sort makes it possible to compromise between the advantages of flexibility in the face of environmental variation, and of inheriting the experience of past generations.

There may be another adaptive advantage to the neonate's apparently innate sensitivity to the facial expressions of caregivers. Learning the significance of the facial expressions of conspecifics would be a complex and probably lengthy task, and it would be highly advantageous to have this data available as early as possible. Responding appropriately to the emotional state of caregivers may well be directly advantageous to the infant. Furthermore, the significance of events in the current environment can be very rapidly assessed by noting the assessment of those who have already lived in that environment. Very few children have been hurt by snakes, or spiders, or the dark, but it seems that only a slight demonstration of revulsion or anxiety by adults is needed to produce a powerful aversion to these things in the young. An innate capacity to interpret the emotional responses of conspecifics would facilitate learning of this kind.

Finally, it may be possible to give an evolutionary explanation of the irrational persistence of judgements about the emotional significance of the environment. A single display of fear by a caregiver may result in a fear of the dark that will be retained despite any amount of information about the harmlessness of darkness. Emotional responses do not seem to adjust themselves as readily as beliefs when new information is acquired about the environment. Sustained counter-conditioning seems to be needed to delete an assessment once it has become linked to an affect-program response. This could be due to the evolutionary advantages of 'false-positive' responses. The costs of failing to respond to dangers, challenges, noxious stimuli, and so on may well outweigh the costs of responding unnecessarily. Failing to respond to danger may lead to death, while responding unnecessarily merely wastes a little energy. In evolutionary terms, phobias and irrational distastes may have much to recommend them.

V   AFFECT-PROGRAMS AND MODULARITY

I have argued that the systems which trigger affect-programs must learn the emotional significance of features of the local environment. This learning is constrained in various ways which may have evolutionary explanations. In this section, I want to argue that these, at least some of the systems which trigger affect-programs, are distinct from the systems that create the model of the world which guides rational action, that is, from the system of beliefs and desires.

The main reason for supposing that there is such a separate system is the need to explain the ways in which emotional responses can conflict with other cognitive activity. There is some sense in which fear embodies the judgement that something is dangerous. But it is common for a person to display the symptoms of fear when confronted by a stimuli they know to be harmless. The same is true of the other affect-program responses. They frequently occur when their occurrence is irrational in the light of our beliefs and desires. This suggests that there is a process which is capable of evaluating stimuli and triggering the appropriate affect-program, but which is separate from the process which leads to the fixation of belief.

This process would be 'modular,' in something like the sense popularized by Fodor (1983). Fodor was primarily concerned to argue that there are modules responsible for processing sensory data to the point where it becomes a conscious perception. Perception, he argues, is informationally encapsulated. We know that a complex process of interpretation is required in order to construct, say, a visual image. The process has access to information which allows it to establish prior probabilities for various possible interpretations of the data, but it does not have access to everything known to the subject. The fact that the mask in the concave mask illusion feels concave does not affect the visual perception of a convex mask. This process's operation is also mandatory. We cannot decide whether to process visual data in this way. Finally, the process is opaque to introspection. There is no conscious awareness of the complex act of interpretation that gives rise to the perception.

The way in which certain kinds of emotional response, notably those dealt with by affect-program theory, can conflict with other cognitive processes would be neatly explained if there are processes that trigger affect-programs which are 'informationally encapsulated.' In that case, there would not be a free flow of information between them and the rest of the mind. It is possible for a modular system to respond as if a certain state of affairs obtains although the organism as a whole believes that that state of affairs does not obtain. Informational encapsulation is perhaps the most important feature of modular systems. It captures what we mean when we say that modular processes are 'separate' from the rest of the mind. The system(s) which triggers affect-programs has other features which Fodor thinks characteristic of modular systems. Its operation is mandatory. We do not choose to respond with fear or anger to a given stimulus. The system is largely opaque to our central cognitive processes. We are aware of its outputs, which are the affect-program responses themselves, but not aware of the processes that lead to them.

The suggestion that the affect-program triggering system is a module fits neatly into the evolutionary perspective on emotion that gave rise to the affect-program view. Fodor, drawing on Rozin (1976) and others, gives a psychoevolutionary account of the existence of modules in minds such as ours which are capable of more general intelligence. Modules, argues Fodor, originated in phylogenetic predecessors who did not have this general-purpose intelligence. They provide relatively unintelligent but effective ways of performing certain low-level cognitive processes such as perception, and, I am suggesting, immediate response to certain important kinds of stimuli. We have retained these modules, Fodor argues, because the very unintelligence of modular systems gives them a number of advantages. Among these are the very short response times that can be obtained by having a mandatory system and a limited data base. If a system is mandatory there is no decision time incorporated in the response time. If the system operates on a limited data base, which is chosen for its relevance to the question in hand, the procedures through which it must go in order to make its decision may be more rapid. Finally, and most interestingly, Fodor suggests that there are penalties to allowing our general cognitive processes to interfere too freely with certain areas of mental activity. He points out that, in the case of perception, it is vital for an organism to be able to accept data which contradicts even its most firmly held beliefs. If perception were an entirely top-down process then the perception of novelty would be impossible. The modularity of our perceptual processes means that we are compelled to consider data hostile to our present beliefs even if eventually we decide not to change them on the basis of that data.

Similarly, the modularity of affect-program responses can be seen as a mechanism for saving us from our own intelligence. Consider the startle response experienced when confronted with novel stimuli. No matter how much we may want to appear blasé, we are forced to gather as much information as possible from the novel stimulus. The affect-program causes us to orient towards the stimulus, to open our eyes widely and to direct our attention largely towards the stimulus. It also triggers preliminary elements of a flight or fight response in case this should be necessary when the stimulus has been evaluated. Similar observations can be made about the fear response. No matter what our higher cognitive processes tell us about the situation, if we have experienced an object as harmful in some past segment of our learning history, the appraisal mechanism will trigger our fear affect-program and this will initiate expressive facial changes and the necessary autonomic nervous system changes for a flight or fight response. When it comes to dangers, false positives are usually preferable to false negatives!

It is, of course, not necessary to the argument that any particular modular process, or even modular processes generally, are useful to us today. It is only necessary that in some previous state, preserving our modular responses may have been more useful than incorporating those areas of our activity into general intelligence.

The modularity of the systems which trigger affect-programs differs in one important respect from that of perceptual input systems. The output of perceptual systems is a mental event, a perception, whereas that of the emotion system is behavioural. But this does not conflict with the Fodorean approach of modularity. Fodor establishes the notion of a modular system by analogy with reflexes, which, of course, have a behavioural output. Fodor draws the analogy in the following, typically Fodorean, words:

> ... reflexes are informationally encapsulated with bells on ... you have come to know perfectly well that under no conceivable circumstances would I stick my finger in your eye.... Still, if I jab my finger near enough to your eye, you'll blink. To say, as we did above, that the blink reflex is mandatory is to say, inter alia, that it has no access to what you know about my character, or, for that matter, to any other of your beliefs, utilities and expectations. For this reason the blink reflex is often produced when sober reflection would show it to be uncalled for ... it is prepared to trade false positives for speed.
>
> That is what it is like for a system to be informationally encapsulated. If you now imagine a system that is encapsulated in the way that reflexes are, but also computational in the way that reflexes are not, you will have some idea of what I'm proposing that input systems are like. (1983, pp. 71-72)

Given the data that I have reviewed about the triggering of affect-programs, a great deal would be explained by considering the proprietary appraisal mechanism for the affect-programs as a module of this sort—a system akin to a reflex in its encapsulation and mandatory operation, but with relatively sophisticated information-processing arrangements of the interpretation for the stimulus.

It may be the case that affect-programs can be triggered by other routes, in addition to this modular one. The existence of a relatively unintelligent, dedicated mechanism does not imply that higher-level cognitive processes cannot initiate the same events. Perhaps affect-programs can be triggered voluntarily as well as involuntarily, in something like the way that heart rate can be brought under voluntary control by the use of bio-feedback devices. Even if this is not possible, there may be certain higher-level processes, such as the imaginative representation of emotion-inducing stimuli, that can trigger the affect-programs.

VI   THE NEURAL BASIS OF THE AFFECT-PROGRAMS

Research on the neural substrate of the affect-programs suggests that they are subserved by neural circuits in the limbic system, the phylogenetically old portion of the cortex which surrounds the brainstem, or in associated brainstem structures. The hypothalamus in particular is a plausible locus for many of these responses. The central role of the hypothalamus in emotion was first stressed in the classic work of W.D. Cannon in the 1920's, and has been reiterated by many later authors.

The role of these sub-cortical structures in emotion has led P.D. MacLean, in a long series of papers (MacLean 1952, 1969, 1970, 1980), to argue that emotions represent a phylogenetically more primitive way of processing important information and directing our responses to that information, than that localized in the neo-cortex. This idea is supported by Fodor's explanation of the retention of modular systems in animals equipped with higher cognition. Modules evolved in our forebears for want of a powerful general-purpose cognitive mechanism to bring to bear. They were retained because of their efficiency as dedicated systems for those tasks. If such an account is accepted, the natural place to look for the localization of such brain functions is in the parts of our own brains equivalent to the brains of our evolutionary forebears. It is by no means safe to assume that inheritance of structure carries with it inheritance of function, but it does provide a rational basis for a research strategy, and evidence such as MacLean's which supports this approach should be taken seriously.

A recent attempt to locate the neural circuits subserving emotional responses is to be found in Panksepp (1982). Panksepp suggests that four circuits can be found in the hypothalamus in certain animals. He calls these the "expectancy," "fear," "rage" and "panic" pathways. His main technique for locating such pathways is direct stimulation of cells in the hypothalamus, evoking various sorts of behaviour. The aim is to find areas which trigger a substantial series of connected behaviours in order to demonstrate the existence of a hard wired basis for complex behaviour sequences which could be triggered relatively automatically by major life-challenges, such as danger or the presence of a potential fulfiller of a basic need. Panksepp's approach has met with some success, enough to lead him to propose his four pathways. He is also admirably conservative in refusing to posit any hypothalamic emotions for which he is unable to locate a pathway and specify a set of resultant behaviours. But I do have certain reservations about his methodology. I suspect that Panksepp's concentration on longer-term responses, such as sequences of movements, will make his results less applicable to humans than might otherwise have been the case. It seems plausible that in humans, only short-term responses are controlled by the affect-program, longer-term responses, such as attack or flight, being predominantly under the control of higher cognitive processes. The predominant features in the human response seems to be the expressive and ANS elements. The expressive responses are present in animals, as Darwin showed, and attempts to evoke expressive responses in other primates might reveal pathways that would be directly relevant to the realization of the affect-programs in humans.

VII   THE SIGNIFICANCE OF THE PSYCHOEVOLUTIONARY THEORY

The psychoevolutionary theory describes a set of well-defined physiological responses that can be used to create a new classification of emotional responses. Ekman and his co-workers call the responses they have isolated fear, anger, joy, surprise, disgust and sadness. They use these traditional labels because the new categories coincide more or less well with the occurrent, phenomenologically salient instances of these traditional categories. I shall refer to these six categories as the affect-program responses.

This new way of classifying emotions abstracts away from causes. The identity of an emotion depends upon the character of the response, not on the nature of the stimuli. This puts it on one side of a dichotomy which has been nicely characterized by Paul Rozin:

If one focuses on traditional definitions of emotion, which emphasize visceral and expressive responses, disgust can be viewed as an extension of the set of stimuli or contexts that elicit a fundamental rejection (distaste-disgust) emotion. In the same manner, we typically describe both the negative response to a looming object in infants and the response to the threat of nuclear war in adults as fear, presuming that the same underlying internal response is generated by different situations at dif-

ferent levels of cognitive sophistication. We [*Rozin and his co-worker*] prefer a conception in which the interaction of the subject with the object
or context is a critical part of the definition of emotion. (Rozin 1987, p.
35)

I advocate abstracting away from the objects or contexts that cause emotion,
because they vary enormously in response to local culture and individual
learning. Concentrating on the response makes it possible to discern what is
common to emotions in all humans, and even in related species. Once we
have these response-based categories, it becomes possible to provide an evolutionary explanation of them. Furthermore, the new classifications appear to
link up with some promising work in the neurosciences. This is surely ample
theoretical justification for introducing an 'output side' classification.

Although the new categories are defined in terms of the emotional
response itself, the new theory does provide insights into the causes of emotion. The psychoevolutionary perspective, as I have tried to show, gives us the
rationale of the way in which affect-program responses are triggered and the
way in which the contents of the triggering mechanism are sensitized to certain stimuli.

I have no desire to ban the kind of 'input side' taxonomy Rozin suggests.
Viewed as a total account of emotional phenomena the psychoevolutionary
perspective is seriously incomplete. Clearly, in addition to the affect-program
responses, the traditionally defined realm of emotion involves higher-level
cognitive phenomena. It also, and very importantly, involves learnt, culture-
specific elements. In understanding an emotion like romantic love, it is vital
to understand that it is culturally prescribed for certain classes of objects. The
nature of the response, in such a case, may not be the most important characteristic of the emotion, and may alter so as to reflect societies changing attitude to the prescribed object.

Accepting the affect-program taxonomy does not exclude the delineation
of more complex states, involving cognitive and cultural factors, and perhaps
building in one or more of the affect-program responses. Attention to the
input-side may well be important in deriving such a taxonomy. But the introduction of these states must have some theoretical utility. It is not enough that
the new category achieve a rough extensional equivalence with one of the
pre-scientific categories. The temptation to reconstruct the traditional categories of pre-scientific English without any other theoretical payoff should be
resisted. An analogy may help to show why such a salvage job would not be
useful. Consider the pre-scientific concept of heat. What was called 'heat'
turned out to be a complex phenomena, derived from our sensory experience of several genuine physical properties. Prominent amongst these are
temperature (mean molecular kinetic energy), quantity of heat (total molecular kinetic energy), and conductivity (a matter of the relative ease with

which electrons are detached from atoms of different elements). An understanding of the folk concept of heat involves all these factors. What is more, the folk concept is less a useful amalgam of these factors than a misleading conflation of them! Using the folk concept we have no means of explaining how a person can touch a very hot piece of aluminum foil and remain unharmed. Similarly, it must have seemed to Wenceslaus's peasant, as he gathered winter fuel, that the handle of his axe was warmer than the blade, simply because wood is less conductive than metal. The folk concept is a liability when it comes to physical theory. It is of (limited) utility only in certain practical applications.

To continue the analogy, it may be possible to describe a complex property which answers to the pre-scientific concept of heat. But this property does not have much theoretical utility. Quite simply, you can't do physics with it, whereas you can do physics with the concepts of atom, molecule, electron and kinetic energy. The only thing the complex property might be needed for is to explain how the pre-scientific notion of heat arises, and why it is useful in a limited range of everyday applications.

I suggest that emotion is a complex phenomena like heat. Emotional phenomena involve psychoevolved adaptive responses, cognitive factors and cultural factors. All of these are needed to give an adequate account of what underlies folk discourse about emotion. It is also possible, as we shall see below, to give an account of the origin, and limited utility, of the folk taxonomy, much as we can give an account of the origin, and limited utility, of the folk conception of heat. I also suggest that emotion and the folk categories of emotion, are not kinds that will be of interest to a developed science. For the purposes of psychology and the philosophy of mind, a new taxonomy is required, and the affect-program states are a contribution to that.

In the final section of the paper I want to show how the psychoevolutionary theory can be used to illuminate the pre-scientific conception of emotion, and explain its characteristic strengths and weaknesses.

VIII   EXPLORING THE FOLK CONCEPTION

I said in my introduction that there were two strands of the pre-scientific conception of emotion. The first emphasizes the involuntary and disruptive effects of emotion, both physiological and motivational. The second stresses their intentionality. In everyday discourse, emotional responses are assigned intentional objects, with assertions such as 'They are afraid of that spider.' The cognitivist claims that this emotion embodies the judgement that spiders are dangerous. This claim is firmly grounded in the everyday conception of emotion. It is intuitively paradoxical to say 'I don't think it's dangerous, but I'm afraid of it.' However, if the theory I have outlined is correct, the relationship between emotions and cognitive states is more complicated than in the pre-scientific conception. People often experience so-called 'irrational' emotions.

The affect-program theory can account for the occurrence of irrational emotional responses, and also for their appearance of paradox. The judgement that the current stimulus is dangerous can occur in two ways. First, it can arise through the normal processes of belief fixation. Secondly, the modular triggering system may class a stimulus as falling into one of the emotion evoking categories, and trigger the affect-program response. If these processes run in tandem, as they often do, the subject will both exhibit the symptoms of fear, and assert that the cause of his fear is dangerous. In this situation, both elements of the folk-conception of emotion are satisfied. A cognitive state is present, and an involuntary response is evoked. If, however, only the affect-program system classes the stimulus as a danger, the subject will exhibit the symptoms of fear, but will deny making the judgements which folk theory supposes to be implicit in the emotion. Conversely, if only the belief system classes the object as a danger, the subject may take steps to avoid it, but will not have any of the symptoms of fear, and may hotly deny being afraid.

The ability to draw this distinction is a considerable advance, as it avoids the paradoxes which have dogged the cognitive theory of emotions. Emotions radically at odds with our beliefs and desires are in fact commonplace. Other traditional problems for cognitivism also become more tractable. It has traditionally been thought paradoxical that fictional presentations can evoke emotional responses, or that imagined events can evoke real emotions. In both cases, the cognitive factors required by standard theories are, *ex hypothesi*, absent. Michael Stocker (1987) has argued that this paradox can only be resolved by allowing the cognitive content of emotions to be different in kind from the cognitive content of beliefs. The present proposal allows us to flesh out this suggestion, not by positing a new and mysterious class of mental states, but by utilising notions like modularity and informational encapsulation that are already deployed elsewhere in psychology. The occurrence of emotions in the absence of suitable beliefs is converted from a philosophers' paradox into a practical subject for psychological investigation.

As well as explaining some of the paradoxes generated by the pre-scientific conception of emotion, the psychoevolutionary and affect-program accounts allow us to explain the origins of that conception. Affect-program responses can be seen as paradigmatic mental events around which other relevantly similar events are gathered. Jerome Schaffer (1983) has pointed out that, if emotions were merely collections of beliefs and desires, it would be hard to account for the distinctions we draw between emotional and rational action, and for the deep-seated belief that emotions are disruptive events that are often at odds with other sources of motivation. The nature of the affect-program responses makes these elements of our concept of emotion easier to understand.

The affect-program system is precisely a source of disruptive motivations not integrated into the system of rational action on the basis of belief and desires. It is the characteristic properties of the affect-program states, their informational encapsulation, and their involuntariness, which necessitate the introduction of something other than belief and desire into our conception of ourselves.

If we take the affect-program responses as the paradigm emotional events, there are two ways in which higher cognitive elements might be introduced into our conception of an emotion. First, there is the fact that in many cases, central belief formation and affect-program triggering run side by side. It would be understandable if these cognitive elements were to be regarded as part of the emotional response. The emotion term might then be applied to the cognitive elements even when they occur in isolation, as it is to the affect-program element occurring in isolation. Furthermore, it seems plausible that the use of an intentional content based classification of mental states is a basic element of our pre-scientific understanding of ourselves. If this is correct, our everyday discourse lacks the resources to make the distinctions between fear as it occurs in "John was afraid of the spider" and as it occurs in "John is afraid we will be a little late for the meeting."

If some of our traditional emotion categories are derived from affect-program responses in this way, this will make it possible to explain the way in which folk psychology selectively parcels up cognitive states, and labels some of these parcels, but not others, "emotions."

Emotion types which don't correspond to known types of affect-programs cannot be explained in this way. Jealousy, hope and envy, all of which may be such types, seem to be based on more or less common arrangements of desires. The idea that an emotion is an isolated source of motivation may help here. Perhaps it is the common occurrence and relative isolation of these sets of desires that leads us to class them as emotions. The irruption of such strong desires for particular outcomes is relatively involuntary, and disruptive of our pursuit of more general, long-term projects, in much the same way as the occurrence of affect-program responses.

It might seem that states of this kind are just what the cognitivist originally promised us. A purely cognitive specification picks out an emotion type. Even in this case, however, the cognitivist is unable to provide us with much of a *theory* of these states. We want, above all, to know why it is these sets of desires occur so commonly, and not some of the myriad others that the cognitive taxonomy makes room for (Griffiths 1989b). Perhaps psychoevolutionary factors are at work in creating common patterns of human motivation such as these. This idea, however, is highly speculative. If these largely cognitive emotion types turn out to be culture-specific, there will be a very different etiological story to be told.

The nature of the affect-programs may also be of the first importance in understanding the social construction of emotion categories, and emotional responses. The role of the affect-programs would be akin to that of the real physiological or mental disorders upon which certain societies' model mythical diseases (Newman 1960). Similarly, the construction of social models of emotional response proceeds in accordance with the societies understanding of emotion. It is often the special status which emotions have in virtue of being thought involuntary that constructed-emotions seek to share. It may be that socially constructed emotions, such as romantic love, mimic the general features of affect-program phenomena, and perhaps of those cognitive states that resemble affect-program states in their motivational isolation and involuntariness. Such constructed emotions purport to be urgent, involuntary aberrations from the usual patterns of action rationalized by beliefs and stable desires, whereas they are, in fact, subconsciously directed intentional actions, reflecting roles available in a culture, and assisting the individual to achieve various social ends. Some authors have provocatively compared such emotions to hysterical illnesses (Averill 1980a, 1980b).

Notes

1   It is sometimes described as taking moral satisfaction in one's childlike dependency on someone. The Japanese are said to experience this as a basic emotion.
2   This argument will have less force for social constructionist theorists, such as Claire Armon-Jones (1985, 1986a, 1986b), who believe that emotions can be exhaustively understood as learnt behaviours reflecting surrounding social norms. On such a picture, our emotion vocabulary is a critical part of the apparatus by which people are taught to have the emotions of the local culture. This makes it more likely that the local vocabulary will reflect the psychological reality of emotion in that culture.

   I have argued elsewhere (Griffiths 1988) that social constructionist ideas can shed light upon some emotional phenomena, and upon some ways that emotions are classified. However, the view that all emotions are learnt behaviours reflecting local social norms is not credible. One of the largest problems for this view is the body of data on the evolution of emotion that is summarized in this paper.
3   A seminal cognitivist work is Kenny (1963), classic presentations include Solomon (1977) and Lyons (1980).
4   Previous research in Japan had established that having subjects watch certain stress-inducing films led to self reports of similar emotions in both Japanese and United States subjects.
5   Judgements as to similarity in facial expression are made using FAST (facial affect scoring technique). FAST is an atlas of pictures of three areas of the total face. Judges are asked to class a picture of one area of a subject's face, by comparing a photograph of that area to the standard samples in the atlas. Their judgements

collectively determine a classification of the expression as one, or none, of the known responses.

6   In Darwin's own words: "Whenever the same movements ... express the same emotions in the several distinct races of man, we may infer with much probability that such expressions are true ones—that is, are innate or instinctive. Conventional expressions ... would probably have differed in different races, in the same manner as do their languages ..." (Darwin 1872, p. 15). Darwin also pioneered the explanatory scheme which is now used to account for the form of the various emotional expressions. He tried to show that these responses are relics of functional responses, tooth-baring in human anger, for example, being a relic of tooth-baring in preparation for attack. Darwin stressed the similarities between the emotional responses of man and of allied, primate species, suggesting an origin for the response in a common ancestor. In humans, these responses are retained because they have acquired a role in intra-specific communication.

7   The idea that ANS response differs from one emotion to another is the subject of considerable controversy. It would be congenial to the psychoevolutionary perspective if they did differ, as this would allow them to be adaptations to particular kinds of emotion-inducing situations. The debate is widely thought to have been settled by S. Schachter and J.E. Singer (1962). Schachter and Singer showed that subjects could be induced to label the same drug-induced physiological disturbance as one emotion or another depending on the available cognitive cues. They concluded that the feelings caused by physiological disturbance were the same for the various emotions, and that cognitive factors identified the emotions. But this result is less conclusive than has been claimed. First, it is well established that subjects who are unable to account for their current introspective state will invent an explanation that allows them to make sense of their condition, and claim that the explanation is the result of direct knowledge of their own mental processes (the phenomenon of 'confabulation'; Gazzaniga and Smylie 1984, Nisbett and Wilson 1977). Schachter and Singer's subjects may have been doing this, rather than experiencing emotion in any normal sense. Secondly, contradictory results have been obtained elsewhere by using what are arguably more sensitive experimental techniques (Ekman 1983).

On Feeling Angry and Elated

Stephen Leighton

However it is to be described, feeling angry is not much like feeling elated. Whether these feelings are constituents of emotions or sometimes accompaniments, certain feelings seem relevant to particular emotions, whereas certain other feelings seem irrelevant to the same emotions and, sometimes, irrelevant to any emotion whatsoever.

The appropriate description of these features is one issue. A prior issue, the one to be discussed here, concerns the basis or bases of specification for such noticed differences in the identity of feelings. In the following, I consider possible bases, defend one, and fend off objections to the solution proposed. I shall begin with some assumptions.

A relatively safe assumption is that specifiable cognitive states, including evaluations, are constituents of each and every emotion.[1] For example, whereas anger involves judgments that the object of anger has frustrated one's aims or insulted one in some fashion, elation does not, but rather involves judgments about the exceptional way things have gone, are going, or are expected to go. Since neither the above mentioned judgments nor more intricate complexes of them are thought sufficient for emotions, an assumption only somewhat riskier is that there must be components of emotion additional to these cognitive ones.[2] Whether the additional components are feelings, desires, physiological changes, or some combination thereof remains sufficiently controversial to bar further assumption if we are to consider our question in the least question-begging fashion possible.

Some general observations about feelings are also in order. Feelings, though always attractive as a constituent of emotion, run into a host of problems which has deterred consideration of them as more than a sometime or frequent accompaniment of emotion.[3] Serious discussion of feelings is made difficult because feelings, whatever their precise nature and role, occupy a particularly private part of our psychic life: comparison and contrast is not easy; the lack of subtlety found in the language of feelings is not surprising. Since these difficulties are inherent in the subject matter, we can never enjoy the sort of sophistication in discrimination or comparison concerning feelings which we enjoy with, say, the cognitive components of emotion.

These difficulties, then, bear on the precision attainable concerning the basis for, and specification of, the feelings relevant to emotion, suggesting that it must remain general and in outline. Such generality, however, should not be misconstrued, taken to show that consideration of feelings is misguided, inappropriate, or to be avoided. Rather, it indicates the sort of precision the subject matter admits of, and thereby sets the bounds of reasonable expectations.

Now to our question. Our ability to identify certain feelings, to cite them as relevant or irrelevant to an emotion or emotions, requires that said feelings are specifiable and appropriate.[4] But in what sense and upon what basis?

One possible specification of feelings is in terms of the emotion itself. The feelings relevant to particular emotions are those of that emotion: the feelings relevant to elation are those of elation; the feelings relevant to anger are those of anger, etc.[5] Feelings that are not of elation are not relevant to that emotion; feelings that are not of any emotion are feelings which are not relevant to emotion. The basis of specification and relevancy of certain feelings is the emotion the feelings are feelings of. One is able to determine feelings to be of a certain sort on the basis of knowledge of the emotion, and knowledge that said emotion has certain feelings associated with it.

Although as a characterization this may contain some truth, it does not provide an adequate basis to specify the feelings involved in particular emotions, or to exclude feelings as relevant to particular emotions or any emotions whatever. Quite aside from the vagaries of identification by emotion, specifying feelings by emotion is helpful only if feelings are something incidental to and not strictly a part of emotion. Now, this role for feelings may prove true. But, since identification by emotion simply begs the question against certain theories of emotion and feeling (i.e., theories of emotion and feelings in which feelings stand as an independent component), we must look to see whether a more neutral basis for specification is possible. If one is, then a prominent role for feelings in and out of emotion becomes plausible; if one is not, then doubts about any prominent role for feelings must surely be strengthened.

A promising line of inquiry involves sifting through the various senses of 'feeling' distinguishing perceptual, exploratory, propensitory, localized sensation, mock, propositional, etc., senses of the term and isolating a sense or senses relevant to the emotion.[6] William Alston finds a sense, the general condition, which covers four further senses, one of which seems helpful in picking out the sorts of feelings most plausibly involved in the emotions.[7] Such delimitation by elimination, though unattractive inasmuch as it does not so much characterize as distinguish the relevant feelings, does help narrow down the feelings relevant to emotion.[8]

One way to augment the account would be to allow that any feeling from this narrowed grouping is relevant to any emotion, so long as it is conjoined with, associated with, etc., the appropriate cognitions.[9] Emotions are, at least, cognitive complexes, ones which may have feelings involved or associated with them; particular emotions are distinct from one another in terms of differences in cognition; particular kinds of emotion have no distinct feelings associated with them other than that they are among the group of feelings deemed relevant to emotion. Any further differences of feeling among emotions would be wholly accidental.

Certainly some will feel that this is as far as one can push the matter. But it has not solved our problem about feelings. For even if we are relatively happy that the feelings relevant to emotion had been or could be separated off in the sifting fashion, still one must specify the feelings that are relevant to particular emotions, say, feeling angry versus feeling elated. Eliminating sorts of feeling as relevant to emotion does not itself provide a basis for differentiating among those feelings which are relevant to emotion. Nor does conjunct identification further the matter. Quite the contrary: conjunct identification has not taken seriously the thought that different feelings associated with certain emotions are recognizably different and appropriate to certain emotions, much less does it provide a basis for this. As we have seen, however, some basis is needed.[10]

A better way to augment the sifting method would be to suggest that of the group of feelings deemed relevant to emotion (as determined by the sifting method), the feelings relevant to particular emotions are the ones standardly caused by or typically conjoined with the independently specifiable cognitions constitutive of particular emotions.[11] As a basis this would allow us to say that, since being elated standardly feels in one way and being angry in a quite different way, then, should a feeling like that of elation arise, we can identify it as such—even if it should arise in a context normally associated with a different or no emotion. The feeling remains one of elation. For it is the sort of feeling that is standardly caused by elation.

This explanation is a significant improvement because it does provide a basis for discrimination among the feelings relevant to emotion, including some and excluding others as relevant to particular emotions. It thereby provides a basis for the opening observation that feeling angry is not much like feeling elated.

As it stands, however, there is something of a problem. For speaking of feelings "standardly" caused or "typically" conjoined seems to have some statistical, empirical content.[12] What, then, if people should "standardly" come to feel as they do when elated, but in the context of evaluations relevant to anger, and vice versa? Should we allow that, due to possible changes in the regularities of the universe, angry feelings would come to be those previously known as feelings of elation, and vice versa?

Followers of Hume would be prepared to accept this consequence. According to Hume, pride is a pleasant passion, whereas hatred is a painful one. There is no reason for this; it is how we find the world. Presumably, if we were to find the world otherwise, painful feelings could be feelings of pride, while pleasant feelings could be feelings of hatred.

A position with such extreme consequences is not desirable. For it seems simply absurd that the feelings we ascribe to grief are so contingently connected with grief that grief feelings could conceivably come to be those which we presently ascribe to joy. Instead, let us seek an analysis in which there is not this contingency associated with the nature and role of feelings.

I believe that the standard cause solution can be modified so as to allow us to say that feeling and being angry feel in a certain way whatever the empirical regularities. One, then, is not forced to the contingent view about the nature of feelings, suggested by the Humean. To meet this challenge, however, it is necessary to distinguish an identifying and defining project.

Standard cause seems to provide a noncircular way to identify or pick out the feelings relevant to emotion and particular emotions, allowing that certain feelings are recognizable and relevant to emotions and to particular emotions. The identifying project proposals of standard cause do rely on the world being as it is. Should the world turn Heraclitean in the relevant way, yet should we wish to deny the contingency of feelings as just suggested, we may well have to develop different identifying strategies. But in order to deny that contingency of feelings, a related (though distinct) project of defining or delimiting the feelings relevant to particular emotions must be accomplished, and accomplished in a way which does not rely on the contingencies of this world, or at least not in the way the identifying method does. This type of specification, then, is central to an account of feelings which would allow them to be independently specifiable and nonreliant upon the regularities of experience. How, then, is the defining project to be accomplished?

The proposal, mentioned near the outset, that the feelings relevant to emotions are defined by the emotion can be revived here, but, once again, not for those not wishing to foreclose the question of the relative independence of feeling. A different strategy remains necessary.

An assumption at the outset was that judgments constitutive of emotions are specifiable. One can describe, compare, and contrast the judgments involved in, say, anger, versus elation. One thing notable about many of the constitutive judgments is that they value the world in certain ways, e.g., anger involves judgments of insult, whereas elation involves judgments concerning the exceptional way things are going. Furthermore, feelings seem to be valued in and of themselves.[13] For example, painful feelings, aches, etc.—quite apart from their functional utility, etc.—are valued in a certain way, whereas various sorts of pleasant feelings are valued in quite another way. Whether or not the pain of remorse leads to amends, the pain is negatively valued.

Now, if one grants that the feelings relevant to particular emotions should cohere with the evaluations constitutive of emotions if one is to have a coherent emotion complex, then upon that basis one can justify saying things such as "this feeling is not appropriate to this sort of emotion, whereas this one is." The reason for the lack of appropriateness is that the evaluation constitutive of the emotion and the evaluation of the feeling are out of harmony; and the evaluation constitutive of the emotion is emphasized in setting out the emotion, its feelings, and so forth. The reason for appropriateness is a harmony of feeling and the evaluation constitutive of the emotion.[14]

Thus when one judges in a fashion appropriate to depression but exquisite feelings of pleasure are had, one does not feel depressed, nor is one depressed—whatever people standardly feel in such situations. The valuation of depression involves a grim world, whereas the feeling of pleasure mentioned has a very positive evaluation. So here there is a lack of harmony in combining a positive valuation with something that has a negative one. For depression, both ought to be negative. Similarly, an amused feeling had upon seeing someone's undeserved pain or distress is not part of pity nor appropriate to the emotion. For the evaluation we give of the amused feeling and the evaluation of an undeserved pain are at odds.[15]

The contrariness of evaluation need not be this extreme in order to exclude certain feelings as relevant to particular emotions or to certain sorts. For example, it might be that a feeling is too intense in comparison with the valuation of the judgment. If one supposes that the evaluational difference between fear and terror has to do with the extremities of danger, then to judge something somewhat dangerous, yet to feel incredibly distraught and overwhelmed by it, betrays a certain inappropriateness or lack of harmony such that one is puzzled about just what to make of the person's emotional state. It is not clearly a case of terror or fear; it has affinities with each, but the state remains confused. More relevantly, the feelings are not those of a normal, ordinary fear, but those of terror. Feeling that distraught is to feel terror, not to feel fear.[16]

Notice that evaluational specification does not require the presence of the emotions, say, anger, to determine the presence of the feelings, angry feelings. Nor does it require the presence of the evaluations necessary to the emotion. Rather, to be able to determine that a present feeling is or is not an angry feeling presupposes familiarity with anger and its valuation at some level, but not thereby the presence of the anger or the relevant evaluation.

The way evaluational specification provides a basis for the specification of the felt component can be more complex than indicated so far. Consider the pain of love, or delight had in anger when taking vengeance. How are these to be explained? On the surface of it, love seems to involve a rather positive evaluation and thereby should involve corresponding feelings, whereas anger involves a negative evaluation and thereby should require painful feelings. Indeed, these explanations are appropriate as far as they go.

One way to deal with this apparent incongruity of feeling would be to maintain, say, that the pain sometimes associated with love is had at love's frustration or loss, not as part of the love itself. Similarly, the pleasure associated with anger is a pleasure of taking vengeance as a result of anger, not as part of anger itself. Thus, love remains a certain sort of pleasure; anger, a certain sort of pain. The apparent incongruity of feeling is explained away as a feeling which, strictly speaking, is not a part of the emotion—though related to the emotion in specifiable ways.

One difficulty with this response is that, unless one is prepared to maintain that the person having incongruous feelings necessarily is in a mixed feeling state, it suggests that those enjoying vengeance are no longer angry and those pained in love are no longer in love. A claim of a mixed state or the postulation of discontinuance of emotion, however, do not suffice as interpretations of all the relevant experiences. Love, at times, is sheer pain.

A better solution would be to admit that love involves specifiable sorts of evaluations that would require certain pleasant feelings, but add that, when the aims of the evaluation are frustrated or lost, that frustration or loss is itself valued, which, in turn, explains the appropriate place of being pained while in love.[17] Thus, we say that, other things being equal, love is a pleasure, but that, when it is frustrated or lost, because of the meaning of that frustration or loss, frustrated love (and unrequited love) is painful or involves pain. Thus, if someone tries to say that feelings of love are feelings of pain and misery, even sweet misery—even if it is true that this is the plight of most of us most of the time—we can explain why such claims are misleading. Similarly, we say that, other things being equal, anger is distressing and feels so, but that, when the desire for revenge is entertained, set upon, accomplished, it can be most pleasant. Thus, the experience of anger while taking revenge or even contemplating it can end up being rather different from the experience of anger when that revenge is not occurring, anticipated, or possible. Angry feelings, according to this view, can differ. Even so, we can see why it would be highly misleading to say, without further ado, that said feelings are rather pleasant.

In such states, the complicating factors may take over and, say, the love becomes sheer pain, or it may not take over and leave one with mixed feelings. Exactly what sort of feeling state obtains will have to do with one's situation and one's focus of attention.

Evaluational specification eliminates a good many feelings as relevant to particular emotions, while supporting others as feelings of various emotions, and does so in a way that does not depend on empirical regularities.

To be sure, evaluational specification offers only very general determinations of the feelings relevant to particular emotions. If my earlier thoughts about precision were correct, this is to be expected and is not itself damaging to the proposals. Still, the generality of the account may be worrisome. Let me anticipate and consider some specific objections.

One objection is that the generality of evaluational specification is evidence for the original alternatives of identification by emotion or standard cause. These, after all, were put to the side as less desirable, not proven wrong. If this objection is correct, feelings cannot be an independent constituent of emotion, but must be parasitic upon the emotion and do rely upon empirical regularities. If correct, the only means to determine that feeling angry is not much like feeling elated is to determine the presence of the emotions or the cognitions and judge what the feelings are upon that basis, or to see whether the feeling is the one that is standardly caused by the emotion or cognition.

Yet I do not think this objection works. For the alternatives for identifying feelings (identification by emotion or standard cause) are no more specific. Setting out the feelings relevant to emotion in terms of the emotion itself (identification by emotion) might have the advantage of trivial truth, but it is not very informative about which among a group of feelings is relevant. For either it simply denies the opening observation that feeling angry and feeling elated were not much alike, or it is an appeal to empirical regularities (standard cause), or it is a shorthand for the evaluational method I recommend. If it is the first, it runs contrary to experience. If it is the second, then, when the issue of changes in regularities is considered, it proves much less specific than evaluational specification. If it is a shorthand for the method suggested here, then the disagreement is verbal, not substantive. Hence, the objection to evaluational specification by virtue of a comparative generality in identification of said feelings is lost. The alternatives are in no better, indeed worse, position.

A second objection from generality is not comparative in nature. The thought behind this objection is that, whatever the attractions of the described method, any procedure that is so general in result must be of little value. For the evaluational method seems unable to exclude feelings that typify anger as feelings of, say, fear. For the disvaluing involved in the cognitive content of each is, on the surface of it, not able to distinguish feelings of anger from feelings of fear. Yet this is absurd: some differentiation is desirable.

The conclusion that the evaluational method, as given, is not able to differentiate feelings of anger versus those of fear seems correct. Moreover, this consequence does seem somewhat absurd.

One can, of course, respond by pinning some hope to future discriminations. After all, no claim has been made that the discriminations discussed are all the relevant evaluational discriminations. Presumably more will be forthcoming; perhaps some which will make the difference concerning feelings of fear and anger. Again, one can re-affirm that the generality with which feelings relevant to emotion can be delimited might not be the disadvantage the objection implies. For exactly which feelings are and are not relevant to which emotions is rather ill-determined; whether to allow certain feelings as relevant to particular emotions is hard to say with precision. Perhaps, then, a means which allows for certain general determinations, but yet which is not terribly specific and precise, reflects not an absurdity for the method of determination, but an appreciation of the rather wide ranging possibilities open to the feelings relevant to emotions.

Although I take it that there is something to these responses, a hope for future discriminations and the recollection of the ill-determinateness of the territory still does not really dispel all our unease about feelings of fear and anger. Fortunately, a further response is available.

We have distinguished the empirical identifying project of standard cause from a nonempirical, evaluational defining project. So far the two have been kept quite separate. Yet the two projects can be combined. That is, we should be able to say, regarding feelings found in anger versus feelings found in fear, that the feelings relevant to each do differ on the basis of certain empirical regularities. Thus, should a feeling like that found in fear arise, even in the context of anger, one is justifiably able to say that it is not a feeling of anger. The basis for saying so is an appeal to standard cause. Pressed on the conceptual point, whether it could be otherwise, we would have to agree with the Humean that, given some conceivable regularities in the universe, the feelings we speak of in fear could be considered feelings of anger—though at the moment they are not. What would not be possible, due to evaluational specification, is that the feelings which we presently find in anger or fear could be considered feelings of elation, or vice versa—no matter the regularities in the universe.

Thus, we use the evaluational method to provide a basis for certain discriminations in the identity of feelings, and add standard cause to base further discriminations. The refinements based on standard cause are apt to our world of experience, but do not go beyond this; the distinctions based on evaluations go beyond our experience of the world.

The bifurcating here—the notion that a basis for certain discriminations is limited to our world of experience, whereas the basis for other discriminations transcends this—may seem terribly odd. Perhaps we have avoided one absurdity by embracing another. The following thought experiment may help to dispel that suggestion.

Imagine that we were to be structured in a way which means that all painful feelings were like those we now associate with fear. Then, should we have such feelings in the context of judgments of anger, it seems rather plausible to say that we still have anger and feelings of anger. In such circumstances, feelings of fear versus feelings of anger do not differ, much like, say, joy and elation. In contrast, were we to be restructured in a way that meant that all our feelings were like those we now associate with joy, then should we have the feelings of which we are capable in the context of judgments of anger, it seems that we have a different sort of emotion, rather than anger. Certainly we do not have feelings of anger.

Using the evaluational method for certain discriminations, then augmenting it with standard cause for certain additional discriminations in given contexts seems advantageous. Our bases for specifying the feelings relevant to certain emotions becomes flexible enough to allow for certain alignments to be otherwise than we presently find them, but firm enough to prevent any conceivable alignment calling for a change in the identity of feelings.

Hence, the second objection fails to show any disadvantage in the method recommended. What it has brought out, however, is that there is room to be made for the method of standard cause when it augments evaluational discriminations in restricted contexts. Earlier I suggested that standard cause, because of its empirical content, cannot be the whole story. We see now, what was suspected then, that it is a part of the story. It makes discriminations additional to those made by evaluational specification, but discriminations which depend upon the empirical regularities of the world, the constitution of the subjects, etc. To an extent, then, we should agree with the followers of Hume.

An objection with a similar upshot but different in approach notes that the evaluational method rests on the sifting method. Since the sifting method is a contingent methodology, it is possible that the feelings of anger—though still having to satisfy the determinations of evaluational specification— nonetheless could, in different contingencies, turn out rather differently than they presently do. As the above response suggests, however, properly understood this does not seem an unacceptable consequence.

A different objection from contingencies notes that, in the method espoused, one uses evaluations constitutive of the emotion to provide a basis for the specification of the feeling relevant to the emotion. Assumed is a necessary connection between emotion and evaluation. But perhaps this is not so. If the evaluations relevant to certain emotions are only contingently connected with particular emotions, ultimately the connections between feelings of grief and grief must be wholly contingent.

The suggestion here of a contingent connection between emotion and evaluation is peculiar, and contrary to most recent work in emotion. Thus, the objection seems to create little pressure. But even should it be the case that the connection between emotion and evaluation is contingent, that does not show that the feelings are contingent given the evaluations. Thus, even if it is a contingent matter that grief values the world in a particular way and joy in a very different way, it will not follow that the feelings relevant to grief or joy are contingent given these evaluations.

It would seem that we have bases for specifying the feelings relevant to emotion such that we can make sense of the independence of feeling suggested in my opening remarks about feeling angry and elated. In so doing, we make room for the possibility that feelings, at least some of the time, stand as nondependent constituents of emotion.

Notes

1   This seems to me to be one result—though not an uncontested one—of recent work in the analysis of emotion. See, for example, Errol Bedford, "Emotions," *Proceedings of the Aristotelian Society* (1956/7): 281-304; William Lyons, *Emotion* (New York: Cambridge, 1980); Joel Marks, "A Theory of Emotion," *Philosophical Studies*, XLI (1982): 227-242; Stanley Schachter and Jerome E. Singer, "Cognitive, Social and Physiological Determinants of Emotional States," *Psychological Review*, LXIX, 5 (1962): 377-399; Robert Solomon, *The Passions* (Garden City, NJ: Anchor, 1977); but compare William P. Alston, "Emotions and Feelings," *Encyclopedia of Philosophy*, Paul Edwards, ed. (New York: MacMillan, 1967), pp. 479-486; and Patricia Greenspan, "Emotions as Evaluations," *Pacific Philosophical Quarterly*, LXII (1984): 158-169.

2   See, for example, the criticisms of wholly cognitive analyses by Greenspan, "A Case of Mixed Feelings: Ambivalence and the Logic of Emotion," in *Explaining Emotions*, Amelie Rorty, ed. (Berkeley: California UP, 1980), pp. 223-250; my "The New View of Emotions," *American Philosophical Quarterly*, XXII, 5 (1984): 133-141; Lyons, *op. cit.*; Marks, *op. cit.*; Jenefer Robinson, "Emotion, Judgment and Desire." *The Journal of Philosophy*, LXXX, 11 (Nov. 1983): 731-741; and Jerome Shaffer, "An Assessment of Emotion," *American Philosophical Quarterly*, XX, 2 (1983): 161-173.

3   That feelings are attractive as a constituent of emotion is born out by their frequent role in analyses of emotion prior to this century. Our present century has found such serious problems with that placement that talk of feelings has become something of an embarrassment. But for certain notable exceptions, discussions tend to be dismissive of a place and significance for feelings.

4   I shall use the 'relevant to' and 'associated with' language in a way which is uncommitted as to whether the identity of the feelings "relevant to" an emotion presupposes or requires that emotion in an important way.

5   Hereafter, identification by emotion.

6   Alston [*op. cit.*; and "Feelings," *Philosophical Review*, LXXVIII (1979): 3-34] and Gilbert Ryle ["Feelings," *Philosophical Quarterly*, 1, 3 (1951): 193-205] have developed this line of thought most usefully. Hereafter, I shall refer to this as the sifting method.

7   According to Alston, under general conditions we have (a) emotional, (b) mood, (c) general bodily conditions, and (d) behavioral tendencies. I suggest that one difference between the feelings associated with behavioral tendencies and those of emotion is the former's prima facie link with behavior and the latter's absence of such a link. A difference between feelings of general bodily conditions and the feelings relevant to emotions is that the former are not intentional, whereas distinctively emotional feelings are intentional. Perhaps one can draw the same contrast between mood feelings and emotional feelings. The nonintentionality of mood feelings, however, is more controversial. One may

have to make room for both emotional and mood feelings as feelings relevant to emotion.

8   I do not mean to suggest that the last word on this project has been written, only that the project does seem to be identifying a sense of 'feeling' which allows us to distinguish the feelings particularly relevant to the emotions.

9   Hereafter, conjunct identification.

10   In "Feelings and Emotion" [*Review of Metaphysics*, XXXVII (1984): 303-320], I argue, in effect, both that many hold that the solution of conjunct identification is about as much as one can say about the role of feelings, and that that thesis is too modest. Here I suggest how a stronger relationship might be justified.

11   This seems to be Anthony Kenny's [*Action, Emotion and Will* (Boston: Routledge & Kegan Paul, 1963)] position on feeling and emotion. Hereafter, standard cause identification.

12   Henry Laycock brought to my attention this consequence of standard cause.

13   Stronger positions about certain feelings and evaluation are taken. For example, the pleasure taken in something is essentially the same as the evaluation of that thing. Such a position would tend to support, but is not necessary to, the project undertaken here. See Jan Narveson, *Morality and Utility* (Baltimore: Johns Hopkins, 1967), p. 65.

14   Hereafter, evaluational specification. This attempt has a certain kinship with attempts, such as Franz Brentano's [*Psychology from the Empirical Standpoint*, D.B. Terrell, trans. (Boston: Routledge & Kegan Paul, 1971)], to find basic positive and negative emotions from which all others are to be explained. Both projects help us see that more Humean views about feelings, such as the following by Bedford and Solomon, are just too strong: "It may be said that an emotion is unjustified when a feeling is inappropriate or unfitting to a situation. But I find this unintelligible. Feelings do not have a character that makes this realistically possible" (Bedford, *op. cit.*, p. 21); "But I do know that it does not even make sense to say that one feels angry if one is not angry" [Solomon, "Emotions and Choice," *Review of Metaphysics*, XXVI, 1 (1973): 24).

15   The example is C.D. Broad's ["Emotion and Sentiment," in *Broad's Critical Essays in Moral Philosophy* (London: Allen & Unwin, 1971), pp. 283-301]. Broad speaks of fitting and appropriate emotions, but leaves the notions unanalyzed. Here I offer a part of that analysis.

16   An example which frequently causes us much trouble and which parallels the fear/terror contrast in a rather interesting way is the contrast between being fond of or liking someone and the associated feelings, versus being deeply in love with a person and the associated feelings—though here the difference may not be so much that of intensity, but of the depth and durability of the feelings.

17   The solution suggested here seems implicit in Aristotle's remarks about anger in his *Rhetoric*, 1378bl-10.

FROM *THE THERAPY OF DESIRE*

Martha C. Nussbaum

II

Among the most notorious and paradoxical theses in the history of philosophy is Chrysippus' theses that the passions are forms of false judgment or false belief.[1] On its face this claim seems bizarre indeed. For emotions such as fear, grief, anger, pity, and erotic love seem to us (and seem to the Stoics too, when they write about them concretely) to be (as their name implies) violent motions or upheavals in the soul, quite unlike the calm graspings and placings of reason. To equate passion with belief or judgment seems, furthermore, to ignore the element of passivity that installed the term "passion" as another generic name. For judgments seem to be things that we actively make or do, not things that we suffer. In short: to feel love or fear or grief or anger is to be in a condition of tumult, violent movement, and vulnerability. Nikidion will ask: how can this condition possibly be equivalent to judging that such and such is the case?

We can readily see why the Stoics might have wished to defend this strange claim. For it helps them in no small measure to establish the necessity and efficacy of philosophy as the art of life. If passions are not subrational stirrings coming from our animal nature, but modifications of the rational faculty, then, to be moderated and eventually cured they must be approached by a therapeutic technique that uses the arts of reason. And if judgments are all that the passions are, if there is no part of them that lies outside the rational faculty, then a rational art that sufficiently modifies judgments, seeking out the correct ones and installing them in place of the false, will actually be sufficient for curing Nikidion of the ills that are caused by the passions.[2] False beliefs can be altogether removed, leaving no troublesome trace behind them. If, in addition, the curing of the passions (which, as we shall see, means their total extirpation) is the central task for which Nikidion requires an art of life, then philosophy, in showing that it can cure them, will establish its own practical sovereignty. So the analysis of the passions and the description of a philosophical therapy go hand in hand. Chrysippus wrote, we are told, four books on the passions. In the first three he argued for his analysis of passion and gave his accounts and definitions of the particular passions. The fourth book turned from this theoretical basis to the practice of curing. It was called the *therapeutikon*, the therapeutic book, and also the *ēthikon*, the one concerned with ethical practice. Clearly this book required and rested on the analysis for which the first three books had argued.[3]

But it is one thing to see why a certain thesis is important to a philosopher, quite another to assess its truth. A closer analysis shows, however, that the apparently strange thesis is not merely a handy theoretical tool imposed by force upon the experience of life. It is one of the most powerful candidates for truth in this area; and it is also far less counterintuitive than we might at first think.

These two issues—intuitive acceptability and truth—are closely linked in most contemporary ethical thought. They were also closely linked in the thought of Chrysippus. It would be surprising indeed if he had completely missed the mark where ordinary belief and experience are concerned. For more than any other ancient philosopher, with the possible exception of Aristotle, he is constantly, deeply, and almost obsessively concerned with the close investigation of ordinary thought and language. It is clear that his book on the emotions is no exception to this general policy. Aristotle characteristically begins an inquiry with a brief dialectical summary of ordinary beliefs and sayings on a topic. Chrysippus goes further,[4] filling much of his four-book work with scores of observations on ordinary usage, on common expressions, on literary passages used as evidence for ordinary belief, and even on our gestures as evidence of our common conceptions. He clearly thinks that our language and our daily practices reveal truth, and that philosophical theory ignores these data at its peril. Some of the examples recorded by Galen seem tendentious or naïve; many more seem, to me at least, to reveal a subtle and careful attention to the nuance of what we say and the conceptual structure revealed in what we say. And it is very clear indeed that Chrysippus thought that his theory of the passions was the one to which everyday intuitions gave strongest support. Galen sometimes objects to his arguments on the grounds that experience refutes them. But more often, and revealingly, he mocks Chrysippus for spending too much time on what non-experts and poets say, too little on the theories of the philosophical experts.[5] This all indicates that we cannot claim to have understood Chrysippus' theory unless we have seen not only how it coheres with his other theories, but also how it might be defended, and commended to a non-Stoic Nikidion, on intuitive and experiential grounds.

As we have seen, there is in Greek thought about the emotions, from Plato and Aristotle straight on through Epicurus, an agreement that the emotions are not simply blind surges of affect, stirrings or sensations that are identified, and distinguished from one another, by their felt quality alone. Unlike appetites such as thirst and hunger, they have an important cognitive element: they embody ways of interpreting the world. The feelings that go with the experience of emotion are hooked up with and rest upon beliefs or judgments that are their basis or ground, in such a way that the emotion as a whole can appropriately be evaluated as true and false, and also as rational or irrational, according to our evaluation of the grounding belief. Since the belief is the ground of the feeling, the feeling, and therefore the emotion as a whole, can be modified as a modification of belief. We have seen how these ideas provided Aristotle with accounts of emotions like anger and pity; we have seen how they were put to work in Epicurean therapy.

Two further elements of continuity in the tradition prepare the way for Chrysippus' move. First, the beliefs on which emotions are based prominently include our evaluative beliefs, our beliefs about what is good and bad, worthwhile and worthless, helpful and noxious. To cherish something, to ascribe to it a high value, is to give oneself a basis for the response of profound joy when it is present; of fear when it is threatened; of grief when it is lost; of anger when someone else damages it; of envy when someone else has it and you don't; of pity when someone else loses such a thing through no fault of his or her own. Second, as chapter 3 argued, the evaluative beliefs on which the major emotions rest all have something in common. They all involve the ascription of a high value to vulnerable "external goods"—to items that are to some extent not in the full control of the agent, items that can be affected by happenings in the world. They presuppose, then, the non-self-sufficiency of the most valuable things (or some of them). They embody a conception of the agent's good according to which the good is not simply "at home" inside of him, but consists, instead, in a complex web of connections between the agent and unstable worldly items such as loved friends, city, possessions, the conditions of action. They presuppose that we have hostages to fortune. In this sense, we notice that there is a remarkable unity among the emotions. They share a common basis, and appear to be distinguished from one another more by circumstantial and perspectival considerations than by their grounding beliefs. What we fear for ourselves we pity when it happens to another; what we love and rejoice in today engenders fear lest fortune should remove it tomorrow; we grieve when what we fear has come to pass. When others promote the vulnerable elements of our good, we feel gratitude; the same relation to an external good gives rise to anger, should the action of others prove maleficent.

In all these cases the emotion will not, Aristotle stresses, get off the ground unless an evaluative belief ascribes not only worth, but also serious or high worth, to the uncontrolled external item. Fear requires the thought that important damages can happen to us through no fault of our own; anger, again, requires the thought that the item slighted by another is of serious value. I do not go around fearing that my coffee cup will break; I am not angry if someone takes a paper clip. I do not pity someone who has lost a toothbrush. My breakfast cereal does not fill me with joy and delight; even my morning coffee is not an object of love.

These examples suggest a further thought, one that will be exploited by

Stoic therapy. The damages of fortune, when they are seen as trivial or light, and thus prove insufficient to ground an emotion, are frequently seen this way because the object damaged or promoted is itself seen, with respect to its value, as replaceable. Coffee cups and paper clips are rarely reasons for grief, because we don't care which one we use. There is a readily renewable supply, and all alike serve the function for which we value that item. If we try to imagine a case where the loss of a coffee cup would be an occasion for grief, we find ourselves imagining a case in which the particular item is endowed by the owner with a historical or sentimental value that makes it a unique particular. This suggests that the removal of the sense of particularity and specialness, in big things as well as small, might contribute to the eradication of fear, anger, and even love, should we wish to effect their eradication.[6]

This tradition of Greek thought about the emotions seems, so far, to be not bizarre, but intuitively quite plausible. If Chrysippus does indeed end up in a counterintuitive position, he starts from a basis that seems to articulate our intuitions about the emotions as well as any philosophical reflection on this topic ever has. Chrysippus places himself within this tradition; but he also makes a radical departure from it. To see what he has done, we need to distinguish four theses that are defended within this tradition about the relationship between belief or judgment and passion.

1. *Necessity.* The relevant belief[7] is necessary for the passion.
2. *Constituent Element.* The belief is a (necessary) constituent element in the passion.
3. *Sufficiency.* The belief is sufficient for the passion.
4. *Identity.* The belief is identical to the passion.

To be precise enough, this classification would need several refinements. First, we would need to distinguish occurrent passions from entrenched dispositional states. Stoic theory does this well, as we shall later see. Second, we would need to get clear in each case about exactly what level of belief we are working with, and about how the different levels interact. Generic beliefs that at least some external uncontrolled items have high value; more concrete beliefs that there are serious damages that I may suffer by another's agency, through no fault of my own; the very concrete belief that X has wronged me in such and such a way just now—all of these are at work in the passion of anger; they need to be distinguished and their role in the passion assessed. Again, the Stoics thought carefully about this. For now, however, I shall be thinking of a specific occurrent evaluative belief (for example, "X has seriously damaged an important element of my good life just now") that is the basis for a concrete episode of passion; this specific belief of course presupposes the more general ones, and would be removed with their removal.

To put things roughly and somewhat crudely: Plato and Epicurus hold (1) and possibly none of the other theses—though their position on (2) is unclear, and Epicurus might be prepared to grant (3).[8] Aristotle, I have argued, holds (1) and (2). His position on (3) is unclear, but his rhetorical strategies rely on the *usual* sufficiency of belief for passion. Zeno, Chrysippus' predecessor, seems to have held (1), in a causal form that is incompatible with (2), and also (3). He says that the belief reliably causes a fluttering feeling, and that this feeling, not the belief, is what the passion itself is. He appears to deny (2); and yet there is need for caution here. For it appears that he individuates and defines passions at least partially via their causes, the beliefs; and it seems to be his view that the very same feeling not only could not be caused in another manner, but would not, if it were otherwise caused, count as that pathos.[9] All of these people, then, defend a close and intimate connection between passion and belief; but this connection stops short of identity.

III

Now we want to know: what leads Chrysippus to take the final step?[10] We might have thought that the Zenonian and/or the Aristotelian position would have been sufficient to defend whatever picture of philosophical therapy the Stoics wish to defend. Now clearly Chrysippus does not ignore or deny the affective and kinetic aspects of passion—for he says that the judgment that is identical with the passion is itself a *pleonazousa hormē*, an excessive inclination.[11] But he wants to say that the sort of tumultuous movement it is, is a judgment; and that its seat is the rational soul. Why does he want to say this?

Here we frequently get a superficial answer. The Stoics, we are reminded, recognize only a single part to the soul, namely the rational part. They reject Plato's division of the soul into three distinct elements. Hence they have to make all psychological conditions conditions of this one element, no matter how odd or implausible this might seem.[12] This seems to me quite inadequate, as an answer. It was not an item of unargued dogma for the Stoics that the soul has just one part; it was a conclusion, and a conclusion of arguments in moral psychology, prominently including arguments about the passions. Galen tells us that Chrysippus argued first for the existence of some *alogos dunamis*, some irrational capability, in the soul, and then went on to consider the relative merits of a view that separates passion from judgment and the view he finally adopted, arguing against a pluralist psychology and in favor of his own one-part account of passion, as the view that best explained human irrationality.[13] Posidonius, a perfectly good Stoic, takes the opposite course, restoring the three parts of the soul and placing emotion in an irrational part, because he felt that this gave Stoicism its best account of human irrationality.[14] So what needs explaining is precisely the fact that is being invoked as an explanation—namely, why Chrysippus decides to make all passional states the conditions of a single part or faculty, and the same faculty that does our practical reasoning. Why does he think this the best and most plausible account?

We must begin by noting that a judgment, for the Stoics, is defined as an assent to an appearance.[15] In other words, it is a process that has two stages. First, it occurs to Nikidion, or strikes her, that such and such is the case. (Stoic appearances are usually propositional.) It looks to her that way, she sees things that way—but so far she hasn't really accepted it. She can now go on to accept or embrace the appearance, commit herself to it; in that case, it has become her judgment. She can also deny or repudiate it: in that case, she is judging the contradictory. Or, like the Skeptic she was in chapter 8, she can live with it without committing herself one way or the other. Recall Aristotle's similar analysis. The sun strikes Nikidion as being about a foot across.[16] (That's the way it looks to her, that's what she sees it as.) But if she has acquired a belief, to which she is committed, that the sun is larger than the inhabited world, she will reject the appearance. She distances herself from it, she does not accept or embrace it—though of course it may go on looking that way to her. She says to herself, "That's the way it looks to me, but of course that's not the way things really are." In this simple perceptual case there seems to be nothing odd about saying both that the appearance presents itself to her cognitive faculties and that its acceptance or rejection is the work of those very faculties. Embracing or acknowledging an appearance, committing oneself to it as true, seems to be a task that requires the discriminating power of cognition. And unless we have an anachronistic Humean picture of cognition, according to which it is motionless, performing calculations without commitment, it seems in no way strange to say that it is reason itself that reaches out and takes that appearance to itself, saying, so to speak, "Yes, that's the one I'll have. That's the way things are." The classic way of distinguishing humans from other animals, from Aristotle on, is, in fact, to point to the fact that animals just move in the way appearances cause them, without making judgments.[17] They move the way things strike them, without commitment. The extra element of selection, recognition, and commitment that sets us apart from the beasts is taken to be the contribution of reason. In fact, we might say that this is paradigmatically what reason is: that faculty is virtue of which we commit ourselves to a view of the way things are.

Let us now examine a different case.[18] A person Nikidion loves very much has died. It strikes her, it appears to her, that something of enormous and irreplaceable value that was there a short time ago is there in her life no longer. If we want to display the appearance pictorially—a conception of appearing that some Stoic texts occasionally suggest—we might think of a stretch of daily life with a big empty space in it, the space that the loved person used to fill by his presence. In fact, the representation of this evaluative proposition, properly done, might require a whole series of picturings, as she would notice the person's absence in every corner of her existence,[19] notice the breaking of a thousand delicate and barely perceptible threads. Another sort of picturing would also be possible: she could see that wonderful beloved face, and see it both as enormously beloved and as irretrievably cut off from her. What we must insist on, however, is that the appearance is propositional: its content is that such and such is the case; and it is evaluative. Whether pictorially displayed or not, it represents the dead person as of enormous importance, as unlike anything or anyone else in the world.[20]

So far, we are still at the stage of appearing. Now several things might happen. She might reject or repudiate the appearance, push it away from her—if, for example, she decides that it is a nightmare or a morbid imagining. She might, if she is still a Skeptic, get herself into an attitude of complete neutrality about it, so that she neither commits herself to it nor rejects it. But suppose that she embraces it, really accepts or assents to it, commits herself to it as the way things are. Is a full assent to the idea that someone tremendously beloved is forever lost to her compatible with emotional equanimity? Chrysippus' claim is that it is not. She cannot really perform that act of recognition without profound upheaval. Not if what she is recognizing is that proposition with all its evaluative elements. Suppose she says, quite calmly, "Yes, I know that the person I love most is dead and I'll never see him again. But I feel nothing; it does not disturb me at all." (Remember Cicero's story about the father who says, on learning of his son's death, "I was already aware that I had begotten a mortal.") Chrysippus will say, "This person is in a state of denial." She is not really assenting to that proposition. She may be saying the words, but there is something in her that is resisting it.[21] Or if she is assenting to something, it is not to that same proposition. She may be assenting to the proposition that a mortal human being has died: even (just possibly) to the proposition that X (the man she loves) has died; what she has not assented to is the proposition, that the person whom she loves and values above all others,[22] has died. For to recognize this is to be violently disturbed.

Notice the crucial importance of getting clear about which proposition we have in mind here. Some of the literature about Chrysippus' view makes the salient proposition one without any evaluative element, say "Socrates is dead." We have already seen that the beliefs or judgments that are hooked up with emotion in the pre-Stoic tradition are judgments about value: cherishings and disvaluings of external uncontrolled items. We should now insist that the appearances that the Stoic agent either acknowledges or does not are, similarly, appearances with a marked evaluative element. To be more precise, in order to be equivalent to a passion they must have three features. First, they must make a claim about what, from the point of view of that agent, is valuable and fine, or the contrary. The texts speak always of the "opinion of good and bad," the "supposition of good and bad"—both in giving the general theory and in defining particular passions (e.g., *SVF* III.385, 386, 387, 391, 393, 394).[23] And we should insist here that the propositions express not simply the agent's desires and preferences, but his or her values: the scheme of ends believed choiceworthy, by which she chooses to live. Thus several texts insist that the agent not only believes that something bad is at hand, but believes that it is the sort of bad thing about which it would be right to be upset.[24] This added element of affirmation shows us that we are not talking about mere desiderative whim and caprice.

Second, the propositions ascribe to the item in question not only some value, but a serious or very high value (or disvalue).[25] Chrysippus tells us explicitly that the mistake, and the passion, come not in thinking the things in question to be good, but in thinking them to be much better than they are—in fact, to be the most important things (cf. *PHP* 5.5.20-22, 262D= *SVF* III.480; compare Galen's paraphrase, which adds the word *megista*, "greatest"—264D). Similarly, accounts of the dispositional conditions that underlie particular episodes of passion make them equivalent to a belief that something is very worth pursuing (*valde expetenda*, Cic. *TD* 4.26 = *SVF* III.427, Sen. *Ep.* 75.11 = *SVF* III.428; the Greek has *sphodra*, cf. *SVF* III.421), although that thing is in fact either only slightly choiceworthy or not choiceworthy at all. Again, a passage of Posidonius, reporting Chrysippus, speaks of a conviction that a thing contains a "great benefit" (fr. 164 E-K). The belief that money is a good thing is said to turn into a chronic infirmity only "when one holds that money is the greatest good and even supposes that life is not worth living for the man who has lost it" (*PHP* 4.5.25, 264D).[26]

Finally, the belief must have a certain content: it must be concerned with vulnerable external things, things that can fail to be present, that can arrive by surprise, that are not fully under our control. This is common ground between Chrysippus and the pre-Stoic tradition. The Stoics do not explicitly include this in their definitions, though they repeatedly underline the connection between passion and a concern with external goods, and emphasize that a person who ceases to be concerned with externals will be free of passion. For this failure to be explicit they are reproached by Posidonius, who points out that the wise man ascribes the highest possible value to his wisdom, and yet does not feel fear for its loss, longing for its presence, and so forth (fr. 164 E-K, 266D).[27] Again, sometimes the texts speak as if the relevant group of judgments was identified by its falsity, relative to Stoic moral theory. This seems to be a strategic error too, since the Stoics claim to be able to persuade pupils like Nikidion, who start out with another conception of good. The passion-beliefs all share, as the more concrete definitions make clear, a subject matter; and they can and should be identified and defined with reference to that subject matter. This would answer Posidonius' worry and make more perspicuous the motivations behind the theory and the call for extirpation.

So far we have gotten only to thesis 3 on our list. We have argued that a judgment is an embracing of an appearing proposition; and that the real embracing of or assent to a certain sort of evaluative proposition is sufficient for being moved emotionally. It entails the emotion; if emotion is not there then we are entitled to say that real acknowledgment of the proposition is not (or not yet) there. But all of this—though it goes against Aristotle's claim that the belief-component of the emotion is independent of the feeling—could, apparently, be satisfied by a causal picture like Zeno's, in which the belief of necessity produces the passion, which is still seen as a distinct item. We still need to know, then, what leads Chrysippus to make the emotion itself a function of reason, and to make it identical with the assent that is the judgment.

First, then, why should the upheaval be seen as a state of reason? Well, what is it that gets the terrible shock of grief? Nikidion thinks of the person she loves—she embraces in her mind the fact that that extraordinary person will never be with her again—and she is shaken. Where, she asks herself? Is the grief a fluttering off in her ear, or a trembling in her stomach? Is it a movement in some animal appetitive nature that she shares with rabbits and birds?[28] No, these answers seem wrong. It seems clear that we don't want to relegate the grief itself to such trivial and undignified seats as these. We want to give it a seat that is specifically human, and discerning enough, complex enough, to house such a complex and evaluatively discriminating response. What part of me, she asks, is worthy of grieving for the person I love? Perhaps we could invent a special emotional part of the soul to house it. But in order to be capable of housing it, this part would have to be capable of conceiving of the beloved person in all his beauty and specialness; of comprehending and responding to the evaluative proposition on which the grief is based, even of accepting it. It would have to be able to know and properly estimate the richness of their love for each other; to insist on the tremendous importance of that love, even in the face of Stoic arguments belittling it; and so forth.[29] But then it will need to be very much like reason: capable of the same acts of selection, evaluation, and vision that are usually taken to be the works of reason. It then begins to seem peculiar to redouble faculties. If we have a faculty on hand that can perform this job, we surely would do best to make the grief a state of that same faculty. The point is, once we make the emotions as cognitive and selective as Chrysippus, building on his tradition, argued that they must be, Reason looks like just the place to house them.

But, one might object, this is not yet clear. For if it is true that emotion's seat must be capable of many cognitive operations, there also seems to be an affective side to emotion that we have difficulty housing in the soul's rational part. We have already begun to respond to this point by stressing the fact that Stoic reason is dynamic, not static. It moves, embraces, refuses. It can move rapidly or slowly; it can move directly or with hesitation. We have imagined it entertaining the appearance of the loved person's death and then, so to speak, rushing toward it, opening itself to take it in. So why would a faculty this dynamic, this versatile, be unable to house, as well, the disorderly motions of the ensuing grief? Sophocles' Creon, confronted by the death of his only son, says, "I accept this knowledge and am shaken in my reason" (*Antigone* 1095). What Chrysippus wants us to see is that this can happen; reason is capable of that. But if this is so, why push off the affect into some corner of the soul more brutish, less discriminating, less closely connected with the cognitive and receptive processes that we have seen to be involved in grieving? "I recognize this and (incidentally) I am shaken in my gut." Here we lose the close connection between the recognition and the being shaken that Chrysippus' analysis, and Creon's speech, give us. No, we want to say, the recognizing and the upheaval belong to one and the same part of her, the part with which she makes sense of the world.

I have spoken of the recognition and the "ensuing" upheaval. The final stage in Chrysippus' argument is to tell us that this distinction is wrong and misleading. When Nikidion grieves, she does not first of all coolly embrace the proposition, "My wonderful lover is dead," and then set about grieving. No, the real, full recognition of that dreadful event is the upheaval. It is like putting your hand straight down on the sharp point of a nail. The baneful appearance sits there, asking her what she is going to do about it. If she goes up to embrace it, if she takes it into herself, opens herself to receive it, she is at that very moment putting the world's knife into her own insides.[30] That's not preparation for upheaval, that's upheaval itself. That very act of assent is itself a wrenching, tearing violation of her self-sufficiency and her undisturbed condition. The passion is a "very violent motion" that carries us along, "pushing us violently" toward action (*SVF* III.390). But this does not imply that it is not a form of recognition. For, as Chrysippus insists, "It is belief itself that contains the disorderly kinetic element" (*SVF* III.394). Knowing can itself be violent.

Seneca adds a useful distinction. Sometimes, he says, the presence of an appearance might evoke a reaction even when the appearance itself is not accepted or taken in, but, so to speak, just strikes against your surface. Sudden pallor, a leap of the heart, sexual excitation—all of these bodily movements may be caused by the appearance alone, without assent or judgment.[31] But these are not passions: these are mere bodily movement.[32] It is only when the appearance has been allowed in, that we get—in the very act of recognition—the tumult of the mind that is the passion (*Ir.* 2.3).

In short: we have here a dynamic conception of practical knowing or judging, in which a judgment is not a cool inert act of intellect set over against a proposition, but an acknowledgment, with the core of my being, that such and such is the case. To acknowledge a proposition is to realize in one's being its full significance, to take it in and be changed by it. On this conception—which seems to me to be a powerful one—there is every reason to insist that passion and judgment do not come apart: rather, the passion is itself a certain sort of assent or acknowledgment: an acknowledgment of the tremendously high importance of something beyond my control, an acknowledgment appropriately called "excessive" because it transgresses the limits prescribed by right reason for our relation to things external.[33]

Chrysippus adds one further significant element to his account. The judgment, to be equivalent to a passion,[34] must be *prosphaton*: not yet spoiled or digested, "fresh." This word, used frequently of food, and also of corpses newly dead,[35] implies that no decomposition has yet set in—the item in questions still has its pristine character. The point of this seems to be to allow for certain sorts of affective distancing, especially over time, compatibly with the retention of the same belief or judgment. When the person Nikidion is mourning has been dead for a long time, she will no longer have the violent recognition of his death that is identical with grief. Without the supplement, Chrysippus would then have been required to say that she no longer judges or believes that he is dead; or, equally implausible, that this cool and distant recognition is itself identical with grief. He does not wish to say either of these things. For there are many ways to acknowledge an irreplaceable loss, and over time those ways naturally transform themselves. When, like food, the loss has been assimilated or digested, she will still have the same judgment and the same recognition, but it seems wrong to say that she still has the passion. Loss of "freshness" is usually portrayed in the texts as a temporal matter; though we might be able to imagine other factors that might distance her from passion without entailing a refusal to recognize or admit the proposition.

It may seem that here Chrysippus gives the game away. For isn't he admitting after all that there is something more to grieving than believing that ...? And isn't this something, this "freshness," an irrational element that has nothing to do itself with grieving? Yes, and no. Yes, having a certain belief is not, we now see, sufficient for grieving (though we should remember that Chrysippus advances this point with uncharacteristic tentativeness, saying that the phenomenon is "hard to understand" [*asullogiston*]). No, because the difference is itself a cognitive difference—a difference in the way that proposition is active in, received by, the self; above all, a difference in its relation to other propositions. The "fresh" acceptance is something tearing and wrenching. Since it concerns her deepest values and projects, it upsets everything in me, all the cognitive structures of hope, cherishing, and expectation that she has built up around those values.[36] But when the proposition has been there for a long time, when the element of surprise and tearing is gone, it has lost its extreme sharpness, its intrusive cutting edge, since she has by that time adjusted her life and the rest of her beliefs to fit with it. It does not assault the other beliefs, it sits alongside of them. For example, she doesn't any longer look forward to happy times that she will share with her lover. She doesn't have the belief that he will be with her tonight, or expect to see his face when she opens the door. These, however, are cognitive changes. It was the discrepancy of the death-proposition with so many others that gave grief its bite, and time removes this discrepancy—not because the grief-proposition changes, but because other related propositions change. As Chrysippus says in this very passage, "Things don't present the same appearances."[37]

Chrysippus' picture has interesting implications for the analysis of ethical conflict. On the parts-of-the-soul view, conflict is viewed as a struggle between two forces, different in character and simultaneously active within the soul. Reason leads this way, desire pushes that way. The outcome may or may not be a matter of sheer strength; what is crucial is that both forces are active together, until one wins. Suppose that Nikidion is mourning for the person she loves; suppose she is also, at the same time, striving to be a good Stoic, distancing herself from grief with the thought that virtue is sufficient for happiness. The parts view will say that her irrational element is doing the grieving, while the rational part is thinking philosophical thoughts and endeavoring to restrain her from grief. Chrysippus would urge us, instead, to regard the conflict as an oscillation of the whole soul between recognition and denial. He speaks of the soul "turning and shifting as a whole," "not the conflict and civil war of two parts, but the turning of a single reason in two different directions, which escapes our notice on account of the sharpness and swiftness of the change" (*SVF* III.459 = Plut. *Virt. Mor.* 441C, 441F).[38] At one moment, she assents (her whole being assents) to the idea that an irreplaceable wonderful person has departed from her life. At another moment, she distances herself from that knowledge, saying, "No, you will find someone else." Or, "that is just one person like many others." Or, in the words of Seneca: "You have buried the one you love; go look for someone to love. It is better to replace your love than to weep for him" (*Ep.* 63.11). Then the thought of her lover, with his particular eyes, his ways of moving and talking, overwhelms her, and she assents, once again, to the thought that something has gone from her life that she can never replace. Chrysippus claims that this story of oscillation and shifting perspective is a more accurate account of the inner life of mourning than the story of battle and struggle. The oscillation may of course be extremely rapid; his point is that in this rhythm of embracing and denial, this uneven intermittance of vision, we have a more accurate analysis of the struggle of mourning than the parts model can provide. When she denies the evaluative proposition about her lover's specialness, at that moment she really is not grieving. When she is fully acknowledging that irreplaceability, she is not at the same time committing herself to a Stoic view of the good. We cannot fully comprehend the complex agony of these conflicts if we downplay their cognitive content, thinking in terms of contending forces. They must be seen as urgent struggles of reason with itself concerning what is valuable and fine in the universe, concerning nothing less than how to imagine the world. To struggle against grief is to strive toward a different view of the universe, in which that face does not appear, luminous and wonderful, on every path; in which places, no longer seen as habitations for that particular form, flatten out and lose their agonizing sharpness.

The picture of oscillation can explain one further feature of the experience of mourning that the parts model fails to notice. In my example, the thought of the Stoic attitude toward loss and the relapse into grief were not accidentally connected; one can be seen to have been, in a strange way, the cause of the other. It was the fact that Nikidion noticed herself looking for someone else to love—she caught herself saying Seneca's cold words about replacing—that threw her back, so to speak, into the arms of her grief. It was the cognitive content of one picture that reminded her violently of the opposing picture: the very suggestion of other replacements that prompted the return of that one face—as the ebbing tide is followed inexorably by the flood. The parts model cannot explain this rhythm, except to say that sometimes one force, sometimes the other, wins the upper hand. Chrysippus' view strikingly anticipates the account of mourning in Proust, when it suggests that the explanatory connections are tighter, and work through the very cognitive content of the opposing pictures. Just as it is the thought of making love with other women that awakens Marcel's grief and love for Albertine, until that love, like a raging lion, takes over the heart with its own violent view of the world, so here it is the vision of undifferentiated flatness that summons the vision of the single point, which returns with triumphant force as, in pain, she embraces it.

Notice that we have here, subtly delineated, two conceptions of mourning: the mourning of time, which is compatible with the retention of recognition and acknowledgment, and the mourning of denial, which cuts short the natural process of grief's digestion by veering over to a different view of the world. If Nikidion mourns in the first way, the way most people mourn, she will find her grief diminishing gradually, as her judgment loses its "freshness." She will eventually stop grieving altogether, but she will continue to retain the very same judgment.[39] She never tells herself that the person who died was not uniquely beloved. She never alters her fundamental commitment to that love. She may in time find another love; but she will not for that reason give up her thought that the first person was unique and irreplaceable; she will not go over to Seneca's flattened view, and she will probably continue to find it a shocking view. This means that she will be likely to see her new love, too, as a unique and irreplaceable individual, qualitatively distinct from the other, and indeed from all other people in the universe. So she will still be loving in a way that leaves her vulnerable to loss in the future. Because she has not altered her judgments, she remains the sort of person for whom grief is possible and natural. If she mourns in the second way, the way described in my example, the extinction of grief is the result of a more fundamental restructuring of her cognitive commitments. The grief is extinguished by the refusal of the evaluative proposition and the acceptance of a contradictory proposition. By the time that grief is gone, she will have denied the value of something she once valued supremely; and her attitude to a new love can hardly fail to be different in consequence. (Proust, mourning in the second way, comes to understand that each beloved woman is simply an instantiation of the "general form" of his needs and desires, and that love has, really, nothing to do with the individuating qualities of the loved one.) She will be removed in a global way, from the possibility of future grief. As Chrysippus would say (recommending the second way),[40] she will be that much closer to being really cured. We shall shortly see how he argues for the second way.

IV

As we by now expect, the Stoic passions will be very close to one another, resting, as they all do, on some kind of high evaluation of externals. And they are classified accordingly in the formal definitional accounts that become canonical in the school, with reference to two distinctions: the distinction between good and bad, and the distinction between present and future, as these opposites figure in the propositions to whose content passion is a response.[41] Thus, there are four basic emotions: (1) judgment that what is presently at hand is good: called delight (*hēdonē*); (2) judgment that something still in the future is good or valuable: called longing or appetition (*epithumia*); (3) judgment that what is presently at hand is bad: called distress (*lupē*); and (4) judgment that what is still in the future is bad: called fear (*phobos*).[42] (Note that to recognize that a possible or future item is good or valuable is ipso facto to reach out for it; that's what it is really to have that recognition.) There are in each case numerous subspecies, depending upon the specific subject matter of the content of the proposition. Pity is distress at the undeserved sufferings of another; envy is distress at the good fortunes of another, viewed as a bad thing for me; mourning is defined as distress at the untimely death of a beloved person; and so forth.[43]

In some cases as well, we find the definition mentioning the specific kinetic character of the recognition or judgment: depression (*achthos*) is a distress "that weighs us down"; exasperation (*enochlēsis*) is "a distress that coops us up and makes us feel that we haven't got enough room"; confusion (*sunchusis*) is "an irrational distraction that scrapes away at us and prevents us from seeing what is at hand" (DL 7.112 = *SVF* III.412; cf. Andron, in *SVF* III.414). These wonderful phenomenological descriptions show us that the Stoics are not neglecting the way passions feel. What they insist is that, in each case, the thing that feels like this is an act of assent or acknowledgment. Some recognitions feel like embracing a nail; others like rubbing yourself across a rough, grating surface; other propositions "cut" differently, so other acceptances have a different phenomenological content.

These emotions, we have said, are concrete episodes of passion, to be identified with highly specific evaluative beliefs about one's situation. But we have also said that the Stoics recognize the importance of more general beliefs in generating the passions: the entrenched beliefs about the value of certain sorts of externals that, internalized in a person's ongoing conception of value, are the stable basis for concrete outbursts of passion. This level of belief figures, as well, in their formal theory, which here relies explicitly on the medical analogy. The soul of an ordinary person says Chrysippus, is like a body that is prone to various diseases, some large, some small, which may arise from chance causes (*PHP* 5.23, 294D). These diseases are diseased conditions of belief. A *nosēma* or chronic illness of the soul is a stable condition of the personality that consists in accepting a value-judgment that leaves its holder susceptible to passions. It is defined as "a belief in the desirability of something that gets strengthened into a disposition [*hexis*] and hardens, according to which they take things that are not choiceworthy to be strongly choiceworthy" (Stob. *Ecl.* 2.93.1 = *SVF* III.421; cf. DL 7.122). The belief that money is extremely important, the belief that passionate love is extremely important, these would be *nosēmata*.[44] So too, presumably, would be the more concrete belief that X is extremely important—an entrenched belief that could become the basis for a concrete episode of love, fear, or grief. Chrysippus added that when such an illness is deeply enough entrenched and generates psychological weakness, we should call the condition of *nosēma* plus weakness an *arrhostēma*, or infirmity.[45]

What this schema implies, among other things, is that (if we confine ourselves to the big generic categories and some especially prominent subspecies) Nikidion cannot have one emotion without letting herself in for many others: perhaps even, given the fullness of time, for all the others. Once she has hostages to fortune, the very course of life will bring her now to grief, now into fear, now into intense joy. "Those same things in whose presence we experience distress are objects of fear when they are impending and approaching" (Cic. *TD* 3.14; cf. 4.8). "If the wise man should be open to distress, he would also be open to anger ... and also to pity and envy" (3.19-20). "Where you take greatest joy you will also have the greatest fear." Just as there is a unity among the virtues, all being forms of correct apprehension of the self-sufficient good, just so there is a unity to the passions—and also to their underlying dispositional states. But this means, too, that there is a unity to the cure of the passions. "You will cease to fear, if you cease to hope. ... Both belong to a soul that is hanging in suspense, to a soul that is made anxious by concern with the future" (Sen. *Ep.* 5.7-8). The world's vulnerable gifts, cherished, give rise to the passionate life; despised, to a life of calm. "What fortune does not give, she does not take away" (Sen. *Ep.* 59.18).

Notes

1   Chrysippus seems to have used both the word *doxa*, usually translated "belief" or "opinion," and the word *krisis*, usually translated "judgment": the latter more often in general assertions (the *pathē* are *kriseis*), the former more often in concrete definitions ("grief is a fresh *doxa* that something bad is present"). *Hupolēpsis*, "supposition," is sometimes used as well. (See, e.g., DL 7.111, where in reporting Chrysippus' view Diogenes shifts from *krisis* in the statement of the general view to *hupolēpsis* in particular examples.) Most of the canonical definitions use *doxa*. The Latin sources show the same pluralism of use: *iudicium* occurs alongside both *opinio* and *opinatio*. (Cic. *TD* 3.61 uses *opinio et iudicium* in defining grief.) Since the Stoics are unusually careful to say exactly what sort of cognitive activity they have in mind, this does not cause a problem for their argument.

2   Later Stoics who reject Chrysippus' view and posit a natural irrational part of the soul are led to the view that philosophy must be supplemented by music (understood in a rather non-cognitive way) which alone can tame this animal part. See especially the fragments of Diogenes of Babylon *On Music* in *SVF* III, pp. 221-35. Early Stoics value poetry, but on cognitive grounds. Seneca follows the approach of Chrysippan Stoicism: see chapter 12. On all of this see Nussbaum (1993a).

3   On the four-book structure of Chryssipus' *Peri Pathōn*, see *PHP* 5.6.45-46, 336D = *SVF* III. 458, and 5.7.52, 348D = *SVF* III. 460. In citing from the fourth book, Galen sometimes calls it the *therapeutikon*, sometimes the *ēthikon* (once *therapeutikon kai ēthikon*, 5.7.52). Here Galen says that the fourth book was written "apart" from the other three, "added on" (*epigraphomenon*) "on its own" (*idia*). But he consistently speaks of the work as a single four-book whole, or *pragmateia* (e.g., 272D); and his citations from the therapeutic book make clear its closeness to the others in argument and purpose. Indeed, from the surviving fragments it is difficult to see any clear difference—though presumably the final book would have included detailed material on the treatment of the passions that does not survive because Galen is not interested in it. Galen describes the purpose of the fourth book as "to know all the causes" of irrational action (272D); later he says that the fourth book sets out to describe the proportion or harmony according to which the soul is said to be healthy or diseased (304D). One further remark of Galen's is probably misleading. In a different work (*De Loc. Affect.* 3.1 = *SVF* III.457) he uses Chrysippus' books to illustrate his own distinction between the *logikōtera*, i.e., "those that going beyond us examine the nature of things as they are in their own being," and writings intended for use. But a Chrysippan Stoic would be unlikely to make this distinction in this sphere (cf. chapter 9.) In any case, the surviving quotations show us that the fourth book contains a lot of theory, and that the earlier books discuss the emotions in a way that is highly relevant to practice. Judging from Galen's remarks about the relative length of Chrysippus' books and his own, the *On Passions* must have been fairly long: about 250 printed pages in a standard typeface.

4   Chrysippus and Aristotle seem to be close here. But I think that their reasons for interest in ordinary use are subtly different. For Chrysippus, language reveals a rational structure that exists in the universe; it is important as a sign of that independently existing reality. For Aristotle, use is itself more intimately connected with truth, since (or so I think) the reality use reveals does not exist as a set of distinct items in nature, independently of the demarcating activities of mind. However, when we remember that the Stoic universe is itself a rational animal, and that the structure revealed by *logos* is itself, in this way, a homoiomorphic conceptual structure or *logos* (and not only similar in structure, but the larger whole of which this *logos* is a part), the difference becomes far subtler. Neither thinker believes that the universe has a structure apart from *logos* and reason's conceptualizing activity; and this is one reason why, for both, the study of the conceptual structures of discourse is of the highest importance.

5   See, e.g., *PHP* 3.5.23, 204D: Galen has so far criticized only "all the arguments that have some plausibility and do not invoke the testimony of women, non-experts, etymologies, motions of the hands, upward or downward movements of the head, or poets."

6   For a typical example of a Stoic therapeutic exercise focusing on this idea, see Epict. *Ench.* 3. And see also Sen. *Ep.* 63.11, cited later. There may be antecedents of this therapy in Plato's *Symposium*: see Nussbaum (1986a) chapter 6.

7   Of course it may also be a complex family of beliefs.

8   See also Galen *PHP,* 240D, who identifies Epicurus' position as (3) and links it with Zeno's.

9   For Zeno's position, see *SVF,* 1.205-15; the relevant passages of Galen are 1.209, 210. See also Galen *PHP* 4.3.1-2, 246D; 5.1.4, 292D; 4.2.6-7, 240D. Galen consistently insists on the difference between Zeno and Chrysippus. There is some evidence, on the other hand, that Zeno on occasion did identify passion and judgment—see, e.g., Cic. *TD* 3.74-75 = *SVF* 1.212, where Zeno is said to have added "fresh" (cf. subsequent discussion) to the definition of distress as *opinio praesentis mali.* The general classification of the *pathē*, along, perhaps, with the canonical definitions, is ascribed to Zeno (and Hecato) by DL 7.110-11. Just after this, Diogenes Laertius writes, "They believe that the *pathē* are judgments as Chrysippus says in his *Peri Pathōn.*" "They" presumably means "Stoics": but it is significant that Diogenes Laertius saw no significant shift of ground here. At any rate, it is clear that both Zeno and Chrysippus had "one-part" views of passion; neither recognized an independent emotional part of the soul. I do not agree with Inwood (1985) that the difference makes no difference, for there are important intuitive differences, as we shall see; and we should emphasize that to preserve intuitions was one of Chrysippus' goals and achievements.

The substantial literature on the possible differences between Zeno and Chrysippus is summarized in Inwood (1985). Some major contributions are Pohlenz (1938, 1970), Voelke (1965), Gilbert-Thirry (1977), Rist (1969), Lloyd (1978).

10 Major discussions of Chrysippus' theory include Frede (1986), Lloyd (1978),

Inwood (1985); see also Pigeaud (1981), and the works cited in the previous note. On Posidonius' criticisms of Chrysippus, see Kidd (1971b).

11 Cf. Plut. *Virt. Mor.* 449C = *SVF* III.384, and especially Galen *PHP* 4.8.2-18, 240-42D =*SVF* III.462. Chrysippus writes as if he is explicating the traditional Zenonian definition.

12 This answer is first given by Galen (drawing perhaps on Posidonius), who thinks that all intuitive evidence about the *pathē* points in the direction of the tripartite view. It recurs in many accounts. Lloyd (1978) concludes that Chrysippus could not have really had the view that emotions are simply judgments: he must have meant "judgments that lead to irrational feelings." But this seems to go against the evidence of Galen, which says that Chrysippus argued against the view that passions are things supervening on judgments and in favor of the view that they are the judgments.

13 Galen, *PHP* 4.1.14ff., 4.3.1ff. Galen reproves Chrysippus for not considering Plato's view, but arguing instead only against the view that passions are irrational items that supervene on or follow on judgment. But it is not clear that we should believe this. Chrysippus may not have spent time quoting Plato; but he clearly produced, by Galen's own account, a great deal of intuitive and literary evidence in favor of his view and against the view that the passions inhabit a separate irrational part. For a fine discussion of Chrysippus' use of literary examples, see Gill (1983).

14 See Kidd (1971b), who, however, insists that Galen is not to be altogether trusted in his assimilation of Posidonius to Plato, and who shows that Posidonius retains many essential points of Chrysippus' view.

15 See also Frede (1986).

16 *Insomn.* 460b19. On *phantasia* and belief, and Aristotle on the emotions of animals, see chapters 3 and 8, and also Sorabji (1993).

17 Cf. Aristotle *EN* 1147b3-5, *Metaph.* 980b25-28. On this view of reason and belief, see also Burnyeat (1980a).

18 Grief and mourning were central examples for Chrysippus—cf. *PHP* 4.7.

19 I have depicted the grief as self-referential: strictly speaking, there seem to be two aspects here. I mourn the dead person both as a part of my existence and experience, and also for his own sake, mourning the loss of life and activity to him. It is not clear that the Stoics make this distinction.

20 Strictly speaking, the recognition of qualitative uniqueness does not seem to be necessary—for I might believe that each and every human life is of enormous importance and value, no matter how like or unlike humans are to one another in both intrinsic and historical/relational characteristics. But the ascription of an extremely high value to a particular object is frequently connected with, and also nourished by, the thought that the object is irreplaceable.

21 Cf. Aristotle on the akratic: he mouths the words of the correct proposition, but doesn't really activate it in his life. He is like an actor, or like a drunk reciting the words of Empedocles. Aristotle adds that it is like this with a pupil who recites a

lesson, but can't be really said to have, as yet, the relevant knowledge: it must "grow to be a part of him, and this requires time" (*EN* 1147a10-24).

22   I do not intend to suggest that loving implies high *moral* evaluation; I mean only to say that it implies thinking of the object as of tremendous importance, however that importance is to be understood.

23   There are several roughly equivalent ways in which we could express the proposition, and its evaluative element. The definition of *lupē* (grief or distress) is "a fresh belief that a bad thing is present." This suggests that in my example the proposition about the lover's death should be, "A very horrible event is here at hand." The evaluative element would be the strong disvalue of that event. I have instead placed the evaluative element on the other side, so to speak, by attributing high positive value to the lover who is said in the proposition to be irretrievably lost. The texts insist (cf. section IV) that it should not matter which conception we adopt. For if something has a very high positive value for us we view its destruction or loss as a correspondingly bad thing. One might dispute the connection in a number of ways. For example, Epicurus would say that to value highly the life of a friend will not, in rational people, lead to the judgment that the friend's death is bad—not for him at any rate, and possibly not for you. But the Stoic equivalence view does seem to capture well the structure of most people's desires.

24   Cf. *SVF* III.391.

25   Frede (1986) seems to take this element of seriousness or intensity to be not a part of the content of the proposition itself, but rather to be a way this proposition has of appearing to a certain agent. Although it is true that *phantasiai* contain more than their strictly propositional contents, the textual evidence strongly and without any exception I know of supports the view that the intensity of concern with the object is part of the propositional content.

26   This is actually Galen, imagining how Chrysippus would develop his view further in reply to objections. He is staying close to Posidonius' account of the orthodox Stoic view.

27   Posidonius also considers the attitude of the person who is making progress toward wisdom. Here it is less obvious that the attitude in question could not be a *pathos*—given the elusive character of wisdom and the absence of sufficient conditions for its acquisition. But it is clear that the Stoics are committed to saying that it is not.

28   Galen and Posidonius treat it as obvious that animals and young children have the same *pathē* that we do, and they use this as a point against Chrysippus. I believe that they are correct only insofar as it would also be correct to ascribe to children and to certain animals complex cognitive attitudes. Seneca and other Chrysippans regard it as obvious that animals do not have full-fledged passions: see, e.g., *Ir.* 1.3.6-8.

29   Chrysippus stressed this element of deliberate evaluation and even deliberate rejection of contrary arguments, in distinguishing between *pathē* and other errors

of reason. Passionate people have cognitive commitments; when they knowingly go against the correct Stoic course, it is not because some force just blows them away. They are led by a contrary view of things, they (often consciously) disobey reason—something that the tripartite people often say, but which their view cannot explain, since it makes the "disobeying" part too brutish even to understand the opposing argument. Cf. *PHP* 4.2 and 4.6, passim.

30   For related imagery in Seneca, see chapter 12.

31   See Chapter 3 on Aristotle's *MA* chapter II.

32   For a convincing defense of the view that Seneca is an orthodox Chrysippan on this point, see Inwood (1993).

33   For this interpretation of "excessive" as "transgressing the limits set by right reason," see also Inwood (1985), with a convincing discussion of Chrysippus' use of the phrase *logou summetria*, the balance of commensurateness of reason.

34   Strictly speaking, "freshness" is involved in the definitions only of passions relating to the present, not the future: *SVF* III.391.

35   Representative examples: of corpses, Hom. Il 24.757, Hdt. 2.89, 2.121-24; of food and drink, Ar. *HA* 520b31, *PA* 675b32; Ps-Ar *Probl.* 924b28; of actions and events, Aes. *Cho* 804, Soph, fr. 130, Ar. *HA* 509b31, *GA* 764a6, *Rhet.* 1375b27, 1376a7, Ps-Ar. *Probl.* 907b25; of emotions and thoughts, Lys. 18.19, Ar. *EE* 1237a24, *MM* 1203b4; and see LSJ s.v.

36   This shows us a further reason why a Stoic will not grieve: through the practice of *praemeditatio* she will have accepted bad things before they happen and will adjust her hopes and expectations to the knowledge of life's tremendous uncertainty. For just a few of the hundreds of references to the technique in Stoic texts, see Cic. *TD* 3.29-34, 4.57; Epict *Disc.* 1.4.20; *Ench.* 21; Sen. *Ep.* 4.6; 14.3; etc.

37   *SVF* III.466 = Galen *PHP* 4.7.12ff. Chrysippus says that the opinion that remains is that "a bad thing is present"—i.e., I still judge the death to be a bad thing, not just to have been at one time a bad thing. (See also Cicero's explanation of *recens* at *TD* 3.74ff.) Freshness figures only in the definitions of the present passions. Inwood connects loss of freshness with ceasing to accept the proposition that it is appropriate to be upset. There seems to be no evidence for this; and we have seen that that opinion is really a part of the evaluative content of the main proposition.

    Two further suggestions have now been made in Duncan (1991), a very subtle treatment of this entire topic. First, he notes that when a bad event such as a death is recent, many cues in my environment will call the relevant impression to mind; as time goes on, I have fewer occasions for thinking about it. This seems true, but not likely to be an explanation of Stoic "freshness," which has to concern some change in the way the proposition itself strikes me, not just the number of times it strikes me. Duncan's second suggestion is, however, a valuable alternative to my interpretation. He points out that over time, as memory fades, the particular value my lover (for example) had for me becomes vague, and the corresponding propositional appearances likewise. "Particular experiences, we claimed, gave rise to particular types of value. Without a continual supply of such experiences to nourish it, the true character of valuations perhaps fades for want of sustenance." He adds that, when memory brings back that full particularity, we are often thrown back into "the pronounced disorder of our initial grief."

Finally, in my 1993 Gifford Lectures (Nussbaum, *Upheavals of Thought*), developing a quasi-Stoic theory in my own way, I argue that over time the proposition alters with respect to its eudaimonistic content, as I reshape my life and goals. It was once true that "a person who is absolutely central to my life has died." Over time, the centrality shifts into the past tense, as I find myself able to go on living without that person, and adopt other attachments. Studies of disordered mourning—e.g., in Bowlby (1980)—show that the failure of grief to fade over time is usually connected to a failure to reformulate a conception of what is most important in one's life: the person remains fixed on the lost object as still of central, even paramount, importance for her entire life.

38 For an excellent treatment of this part of Chrysippus' view, with reference to his interpretation of Euripides' *Medea*, see Gill (1983); see also Campbell (1985). For this interpretation of Euripides' Medea's conflict, see also Epict. *Disc.* 1.28.7.

39 If we accept Duncan's proposal, however (see n. 59), the judgment will remain the same only in its general outlines, and will shift in its degree of concreteness. If we accept my Gifford Lecture proposal, the tenses in a part of the judgment will shift.

40 Chrysippus suggests, however, that the two sorts of mourning can be connected: for when grief has lost freshness one may also hope that "reason will make its way in and take up its place, so to speak, and expose the irrationality of the affection" *PHP* 4.7.26-28, 286D = *SVF* III.467.

41 There is some evidence that the Stoics (or some of them) regarded the two future emotions as prior in some way: they "lead-off" (*prohēgeisthai*); the present species are the "subsequent" responses to the results of our longings and fears, "pleasure occurring when we get what we desire or escape what we try to avoid and pain when we miss what we desire or run into what we fear" (see Arius Didymus in Stob. *Ecl.* 2.88-89, translated and discussed in Inwood [1985] 146). Epictetus makes a similar remark about the relationship among the four, though without any claim of priority. The claim seems to be (pace Inwood) no more than a straightforward remark about temporal sequence: for any imagined good or bad event (relative to my scheme of values) it will be in the future for me, and so an object of fear or longing, before it is (if it ever is) in the present for me.

42 I have used "delight" and "distress" to translate *hēdonē* and *lupē*, rather than the more obvious "pleasure" and "pain." I have done so because these are genera that have as their species only specifically human emotions, and not the bodily feelings and reactions that we share with animals. I believe that the Stoics were not giving a surprising analysis of bodily feeling, or denying that animals feel simple bodily pleasures and pains, such as thirst and hunger. They were using these words in a rather special sense, for want of any better generic words. Cicero remarks on this double use at *Fin.* 3.35: "what, giving a single name to both a bod-

ily and a psychological phenomenon, they call *hēdonē*." Cicero himself removes the ambiguity where *lupē* is concerned, using *aegritudo* rather than *dolor* for the emotion genus. In the case of *hēdonē*, he is again at pains to indicate that it is not the ordinary sense of *voluptas* that is meant here: he speaks of *voluptas gestiens, id es praeter modum elata laetitia (TD* 3.24). At other times he simply uses *laetitia* (4.14). On the double sense of *voluptas*, see also Sen. Ep. 59.1.

43   For the canonical definitions, see DL 7.110-14; Cic. *TD* 4.14-22; Andronicus *Peri Pathōn* 2-5 = *SVF* III.397, 401, 409, 414. The reader of these lists will be struck by the prevalence of terms designating angry and hostile feelings. Under *lupē* we find jealousy, envy, spite, annoyance; under longing, we find hatred, love of quarreling, anger (*orgē*), wrath (*mēnis*), resentment—and only two other species. Even under delight we find hostility: one of the four species mentioned is malevolent joy at another's sufferings, *epichairekakia*. If one were to inquire into the motivations behind the Stoic condemnation of the passions on the basis of these lists alone, one would have to conclude that worries about malice and anger are central. The rest of the evidence confirms this.

44   Examples in Diogenes Laertius are love of fame and love of pleasure. Stobaeus adds love of women, love of wine, love of money—and also the hatreds corresponding to each of these.

45   One further category is *euemptōsia*, or susceptibility to a particular passion. Examples given include irascibility, enviousness, fearfulness. It is not entirely clear how these tendencies are supposed to be related to the beliefs that are the *nosē mata*. I shall not discuss here the problems raised by Cicero's confused and careless account of these categories at *TD* 4.23ff. He expresses irritation with Chrysippus' extended probing of the medical analogy (*nimium operae consumitur*, 4.23), and concludes that we may neglect the fine points of the medical analogy and occupy ourselves with the main outlines of the argument. This leads him into confusion.

References and Further Readings

Alexander, S. (1911). "Foundation and Sketch-Plan of a Conational Psychology." *British Journal of Psychology.*

Alston, W. (1967). "Emotion and Feeling." *The Encyclopedia of Philosophy*. Vol. 2. Ed. Paul Edwards. New York: MacMillan and the Free Press.

—. (1969). "Feelings." *Philosophical Review.*

—. (1967). "Emotions and Feelings." *Encyclopaedia of Philosophy*. Ed. Paul Edwards. New York: MacMillan.

Angell, R. (1980). "The Sporting Scene—Distance." *The New Yorker*, September 22.

Aquinas, Thomas. (1939). "The Emotions." *Summa Theologia*. Vol. 19. Trans. Eric D'Arcy. London: Blackfriars and Eyre and Spottiswoode.

Aristotle. (1984). *The Complete Works of Aristotle*. Edited by J. Barnes. Princeton, NJ: Princeton University Press.

Armon-Jones, C. (1985a). "Towards a Constructionist Theory of the Emotions." Dissertation. Oxford University.

—. (1985b). "Prescription, Explication and the Social Construction of Emotion." *Journal for the Theory of Social Behaviour* 15.

—. (1986a). "The Thesis of Constructionism." *The Social Construction of Emotions*. Ed. R. Harré. Oxford: Blackwells.

—. (1986b). "The Social Functions of Emotion." *The Social Construction of Emotions*. Ed. R. Harré. Oxford: Blackwells.

Armstrong, D.M. (1968). *A Materialist Theory of Mind*. New York: Routledge and Kegan Paul.

Arnold, M. (1960). *Emotion and Personality*. New York: Columbia University Press.

—. (1969). "Human Emotion and Action." *Human Action: Conceptual and Empirical Issues.*" Ed. T. Mischel. New York: Academic Press.

—, ed. (1968). *The Nature of Emotion*. Harmondsworth: Penguin.

—, ed. (1970). *Feelings and Emotions: The Loyola Symposium*. New York: Academic Press.

Aune, B. (1963). "Feelings, Moods and Introspection." *Mind* 72.

—. (1977). *Reason and Action*. Dordrecht: Reidel Publishing Company.

Austin, J.L. (1962). *How To Do Things with Words*. Oxford: Clarendon Press.

Averill, J.R. (1980a). "Emotion and Anxiety: Sociocultural, Biological and Psychological Determinants." Rorty 1980.

—. (1980b). "A Constructionist View of Emotion." Plutchik and Kellerman 1980.

Bedford, E. (1967). "Emotions." *Proceedings of the Aristotelian Society* 57.

Bell, C., Sir. (1972). *The Anatomy and Philosophy of Expression.* London: H.G. Bonn.

Ben Z'ev, A. (2000). *The Subtlety of Emotions.* Cambridge, MA: MIT Press.

Birdwhistell, R.L. (1963). "The Kinesic Level in the Investigation of the Emotions." Knapp.

Blackburn, S. (1992). *Ruling Passions.* Oxford: Oxford University Press.

Block, N. (1979). "Troubles with Functionalism." *Minnesota Studies in the Philosophy of Science.* Vol. 9. Ed. W. Savage. Minneapolis: University of Minnesota Press.

Brady, J.V. (1970). "Emotion: Some Conceptual Problems and Psychophysiological Experiments." Arnold 1970.

Braitenberg, V. (1984). *Vehicles.* Cambridge, MA: MIT Press.

Brentano, F. (1971). *Psychology from the Empirical Standpoint.* Trans. D.B. Terrell. Boston, MA: Routledge and Kegan Paul.

—. (1977). *The Psychology of Aristotle.* Trans. R. George. Berkeley, CA: University of California Press.

Bretherton, I.J., et al. (1986). "Learning to Talk about Emotions: A Functionalist Perspective." *Child Development* 57.

Broad, C.D. (1971). "Emotion and Sentiment." *Broad's Critical Essays in Moral Philosophy.* London: Allen and Unwin.

Brunschwig, J., and Nussbaum, M., eds. (1993). *Passions and Perceptions: Proceedings of the 4th Symposium Hellenisticum.* Cambridge: Cambridge University Press.

Campbell, K. (1985). "Self-mastery and Stoic Ethics." *Philosophy* 60.

Cannon, W. (1927). "The James-Lange Theory of Emotions: A Critical Examination and an Alternative Theory." *American Journal of Psychology* 39.

Collingwood, R.G. (1938). *The Principles of Art.* New York: Oxford.

Coulter, J. (1979). *The Social Construction of Mind.* London: Macmillan.

Cranach M.V., and Vine I., eds. (1973). *Social Communication and Movement.* New York: Academic Press.

Damasio, A.R. (1994). *Descartes Error.* London: Macmillan.

—. (1999). *The Feeling of What Happens.* New York: Harcourt Brace and Company.

Darwin, C. (1872). *The Expression of Emotion in Man and Animals.* New York: Philosophical Library.

Davidson, D. (1970). "How is Weakness of the Will Possible?" Feinberg 1970.

—. (1974). "Belief and the Basis of Meaning." *Synthèse.*

—. (1976). "Hume's Cognitive Theory of Pride." *Journal of Philosophy.* LXXII,19.

de Sousa, R. (1979). "The Rationality of Emotion." *Dialogue.*

—. (1980). "Self-Deceptive Emotions." Rorty 1980.

—. (1991). *The Rationality of Emotion.* Cambridge MA: MIT Press.

Dennet, D. (1987). "Cognitive Wheels: The Frame Problem in AI." Pylyshyn 1987.

Dent N.J.H., and Benson J. (1976). "Varieties of Desire." *Proceedings of the Aristotelian Society.*

Descartes, R. (1952). "The Passions of the Soul." *Descartes' Philosophical Writings.* Trans. N. Kemp Smith. London: Macmillan.

Dewey, J. (1971). "The Theory of Emotions." *The Early Works (1882-98).* Vol. 4 Carbondale, IL: Southern Illinois University Press.

Dumas, G. (1948). "Leeper's ÔMotivational Theory of Emotion.'" *Psychological Review* 55.

—. (1968). "Emotional Shocks and Emotions." *La Vie Affective.* Trans. Begin and Arnold. Arnold 1970.

Duncan, C.M. (1991). "Diseases of Judgment: The Emotions in Stoic Psychology and Ethics." Undergraduate honors thesis, Department of Philosophy, Brown University.

Duncker K. (1940). "On Pleasure, Emotion, and Striving." *Philosophy and Phenomenological Research.*

Eibl-Eibesfeldt, I. (1973). "The Expressive Behaviour of the Deaf and Blind Born." Cranach and Vine 1973.

Ekman, P. (1972). *Emotions in the Human Face.* New York: Pergamon Press.

—. (1980) "Biological and Cultural Contributions to Body and Facial Movements in the Expression of Emotions." Rorty 1980.

—. (1983). "Autonomic Nervous System Activity Distinguishes Among Emotions." *Science* 221.

—. (1984). "Expression and the Nature of Emotion." Scherer and Ekman 1984.

—. (1985). *Telling Lies,* New York: Berkley.

—, ed. (1973). *Darwin and Facial Expression.* New York: Academic Press.

Ekman, P., and Davidson, R. (1994). *The Nature of Emotion, Fundamental Questions.* New York: Oxford University Press.

Ekman, P. and Friesen, W.V. (1971). "Constants Across Cultures in the Face and Emotion." *Journal of Personality and Social Psychology* 17, 2.

Erikson, E. (1964). *Insight and Responsibility.* New York: W.W. Norton and Co.

Feinberg, J. ed. (1970). *Moral Concepts.* London: Oxford University Press.

Field, T.M., et al. (1982). "Discrimination and Imitation of Facial Expressions by Neonates." *Science.* CCXVIII.

Fodor, J. (1983). *The Modularity of Mind.* Cambridge, MA: MIT Press.

—. (1987) "Modules, Frames, Fridgeons, Sleeping Dogs and the Music of the Spheres." Pylyshyn 1987..

Frankenhaeuser, M. (1975). "Experimental Approaches to the Study of Catecholamines and Emotion." Levi 1975.

Frede, M. (1986). "The Stoic Doctrine of the Affections of the Soul." Schofield and Striker 1986.

Frijda, N. (1986). *The Emotions.* New York: Cambridge University Press.

Fuicher, J.S. (1942). "Voluntary Facial Expression in Blind and Seeing Children." *Archives of Psychology* 38, 272.

Garcia, J., Walter, G.H., and Rusiniak, K.W. (1974). "Behavioural Regularities in the Milieu Interne in Man and Rat." *Science* 185.

Gardiner, H.J., et al. (1970). *Feeling and Emotion: A History of Theories*. Westport, CT: Greenwood.

Gazzaniga, M.S., and Smylie, C.S. (1984). "What Does Language do for a Right Hemisphere?" *Handbook of Cognitive Neuroscience*. Ed. M.S. Gazzaniga. New York: Plennum Press.

Gean W. (1979). "Emotion, Emotional Feeling, and Passive Bodily Change." *Journal for the Theory of Social Behaviour*.

Gill, C. (1983). "Did Chrysippus Understand Medea?" *Phronesis* 28.

Goldie, P. (2000). *The Emotions*. Oxford: Clarendon.

Goldstein, D., Fink, D. and Metee, D. (1972). "Cognition of Arousal and Actual Arousal as Determinants of Emotion." *Journal of Personality and Social Psychology* 21.

Gordon, R. (1969). "Emotions and knowledge." *Journal of Philosophy* 66.

—. (1974). "The Aboutness of Emotion." *American Philosophical Quarterly* 11.

—. (1987). *The Structure of Emotions*. New York: Cambridge University Press.

Goshen, C. (1967). "A Systematic Classification of the Phenomenology of Emotions." *Psychiatric Quarterly* 41.

Gosling, J.C. (1969). *Pleasure and Desire*. London: Oxford University Press.

Green, O. (1979). "Wittgenstein and the Possibility of a Theory of Emotion" *Metaphilosophy* 10, 3/4.

Greenspan, P. (1978). "Behavior Control and Freedom of Action." *Philosophical Review* LXXXVII, 2.

—. (1980). "A Case of Mixed Feelings: Ambivalence and the Logic of Emotion." Rorty 1980.

—. (1984). "Emotions as Evaluations." *Pacific Philosophical Quarterly* LXII.

—. (1988). *Emotions and Reasons*. New York: Routledge.

—. (1995). *Practical Guilt*. New York: Oxford University Press.

Griffiths, P.E. (1988). "Emotion and Evolution." Dissertation, Australian National University.

—. (1989a). "Folk, Functional and Neurochemical Aspects of Mood." *Philosophical Psychology* 2.

—. (1989b). "The Degeneration of the Cognitive Theory of Emotion." *Philosophical Psychology* 2.

—. (1997). *What Emotions Really Are*. Chicago and London: The University of Chicago Press.

Grimal, P. (1968). *Larousse world Mythology*. Paris: Larousse.

Hampshire, S., ed. (1966). *The Philosophy of Mind*. New York: Harper and Row.

Hare, R.M. (1979). "What Makes Choices Rational?" *The Review of Metaphysics*.

Harré, R., ed. (1986). *The Social Construction of Emotions*. Oxford: Blackwells.

Harris, P. (1989). *Children and Emotion*. Oxford: Blackwell.

Haugeland, J. (1979). "Understanding Natural Language." *The Journal of Philosophy.*

—. (1985). *Artificial Intelligence: The Very Idea.* Cambridge, MA: MIT Press.

Haymaker W. et al., eds. (1969). *The Hypothalamus.* Springfield, IL: Thomas.

Heelas, P. (1986). "Emotions Across Cultures." Harré 1986.

Hempel, C. (1965). *Aspects of Scientific Explanation.* New York: Free Press.

Hume, D. (1978). *A Treatise of Human Nature: Book II.* 2nd ed. Oxford: Oxford University Press.

Inwood, B. (1985). *Ethics and Human Action in Early Stoicism.* Oxford: Oxford University Press.

Izard, C.E. (1972). *Patterns of Emotions: A New Analysis of Anxiety and Depression.* New York: Academic Press.

—. (1977). *Human Emotions.* New York: Plenum Press.

Izard, C.E., et al., eds. (1984). *Emotions Cognition and Behavior.* New York: Cambridge University Press.

Jacobson, E. (1971). *Depression.* New York: International University Press.

James, W. (1890). *Principles of Psychology.* New York. Holt

—. (1880). "The Feeling of Effort." *Anniversary Memoirs of the Boston Natural History Society.*

—. (1884). "What is an emotion?" *Mind* 9.

Jeffery, R.C. (1965). *The Logic of Decision.* New York: McGraw-Hill.

Kant, I. (1949). *Critique of Practical Reason.* Trans. Beck. Chicago, IL: University of Chicago Press.

—. (1952). *Critique of Judgment.* Trans. Meredith. Oxford: Oxford University Press.

—. (1991). *The Metaphysics of Morals.* Trans. Gergor. Cambridge: Cambridge University Press.

Kenny, A. (1963). *Action, Emotion and Will.* London: Routledge and Kegan Paul.

Kernberg, O. (1975). *Borderline Conditions and Pathological Narcissism.* New York: Jason Aronson.

Kidd, I.G. (1971). "Posidonius on Emotions." Long 1971.

Knapp, P.H., ed. (1963). *Expression of the Emotions in Man.* New York: International Universities Press.

Kohut, H. (1971). *The Analysis of Self.* New York: International Universities Press.

Krasne, F.B., and Wine, J.J. (1984). *Neural Mechanisms of Startle Behavior.* New York: Plenum.

Kripke, S. (1980). *Naming and Necessity.* Cambridge, MA: Harvard University Press.

La Barre, W. (1947). "The Cultural Basis of Emotions and Gestures." *Journal of Personality* 16.

Landis, C., and Hunt, W.A. (1939). *The Startle Pattern.* New York, Farrar and Rinehart. Repr. (1968) New York: Johnson Reprint.

Lange, C.G. (1922). *The Emotions.* Baltimore: Williams and Wilkins.

Lawrie, R. (1980). "Passion." *Philosophy and Phenomenological Research.*

LeDoux, J. (1988). *The Emotional Brain.* London: Orion Books.

—. (1989). "Cognitive-emotional Interactions in the Brain." *Cognition and Emotion* III.

Ledoux, L., et al. (1989). "Indelibility of Subcortical Emotional Memories." *Journal of Cognitive Neuroscience* I.

Leighton, S.R. (1984). "Feelings and Emotion." *Review of Metaphysics* XXXVII.

—. (1985). "The New View of Emotions." *American Philosophical Quarterly* 22.

—. (1988). "On Feeling Angry and Elated." *The Journal of Philosophy.*

Leventhal, H. (1980) "Towards a Comprehensive Theory of the Emotions." *Advances in Experimental Social Psychology* 13.

—. (1984). "A Perceptual Motor Theory of Emotion." Scherer and Ekman 1984.

Levi, L., ed. (1975). *Emotions: Their Parameters and Measurement.* New York: Raven Press.

Lévi-Strauss, C. (1966). *Mythologique.* Vol. I. Paris: Plon.

—. (1963). *Pensée Sauvage.* Paris: Plon.

Levy, R. (1984). "Emotion, Knowing and Culture." Schweder and LeVine 1984.

Lewinsohn, et al. (1986). *Control Your Depression.* New York: Prentice-Hall.

Lloyd, A.C. (1978). "Emotion and Decision in Stoic Psychology." Rist 1978.

Logue, A.W., Ophir, I., and Strauss, K.E. (1981). "The Acquisition of Taste Aversions in Humans." *Behavior Research and Therapy* 19.

Long, A.A., ed. (1971). *Problems in Stoicism.* London: Athlone Press.

Lutz, C. (1982)."Parental Goals, Ethnopsychology and the Development of Emotional Meaning." *Ethos.*

—. (1988). *Unnatural Emotions.* Chicago: Chicago University Press.

Lycos, K. (1964). "Aristotle and Plato on 'Appearing.'" *Mind* 73.

Lyons, W. (1980). *Emotion.* New York: Cambridge University Press.

MacLean, P.D. (1952). "Some Psychiatric Implications of Physiological Studies on Fronto-temporal Portions of the Limbic System." *Electroencephalography and Clinical Neurophysiology* 4.

—. (1969). "The Hypothalamus and Emotional Behavior." Haymaker 1969.

—. (1970). "The Triune Brain, Emotion and Scientific Bias." Schmitt 1970.

—. (1980). "Sensory and Perceptive Factors in Emotional Functions of the Triune Brain." Rorty 1980.

Marañon, G. (1924). "Contribution a l'étude de l'action emotive de l'adrénaline." *Revue Française d'Endocrinologie* 2.

Marks, J. (1982). "A Theory of Emotion." *Philosophical Studies.*

Matthews, G. (1980). "Ritual and Religious Feelings." Rorty 1980.

McDowell, J. (1978). "Are Moral Requirements Hypothetical Imperatives?" *Proceedings of the Aristotelian Society* 52

—. (1979). "Virtue and Reason." *The Monist.*

McTaggert, J.M.E. (1927). *Nature of Existence.* Vol. 2. Ed. C.D. Broad. Cambridge: Cambridge University Press.

Mead, G. (1934). *Mind, Self and Society.* Chicago: University of Chicago Press.

Millikan, R.G. (1984). *Language, Thought and Other Biological Categories: New Foundations for Realism.* Cambridge, MA: MIT Press.

Mischel, T., ed. (1969). *Human Action: Conceptual and Empirical Issues.* New York: Academic Press.

Montesquieu, C. (1970). De l'espirit de lois. Paris: Gallimard.

Murdoch, I. (1970). *The Sovereignty of Good.* London: Routledge and Kegan Paul.

Nagel, T. (1970). *The Possibility of Altruism.* London and New York: Oxford University Press.

Neu, J. (1977). *Emotion, Thought, and Therapy.* Berkeley, CA: University of California Press.

—. (1987). "A Tear is an Intellectual Thing." *Representations.*

—. (2000). *A Tear is an Intellectual Thing.* Oxford: Oxford University Press.

Newman, P.L. (1960). "'Wild Man' Behaviour in a New Guinean Highland Community," *American Anthropologist* 66.

Nietzsche, F. (1954). *The Gay Science. The Portable Nietzsche.* Ed. and trans. W. Kaufmann. New York: Viking.

Nisbett, R.E., and Wilson, T. DeCamp. (1977). "Telling More Than We Can Know: Verbal Reports on Mental Processes." *Psychological Review* 84.

Noddings, N. (1984). *Caring: A Feminine Approach to Ethics and Moral Education.* Berkeley and Los Angeles: University Press of California.

Nussbaum, M.C. (1978). *Aristotle's De Motu Animalium.* Princeton, NJ: Princeton University Press.

—. (1990). *Love's Knowledge.* Oxford: Oxford University Press.

—. (1993). "Poetry and the Passions: Two Stoic Views.." Brunschwig and Nussbaum 1993.

—. (1994). *The Therapy of Desire: Theory and Practice in Hellenistic Ethics.* Princeton, NJ: Princeton University Press.

—. (2001). *Upheavals of Thought: The Intelligence of Emotions.* Cambridge: Cambridge University Press.

Oakley, J. (1992). *Morality and the Emotions.* London: Routledge.

O'Shaughnessy, B. (1980). *The Will.* Cambridge: Cambridge University Press.

Ohman, A., Fredrikson, M., Hugdahl, K., and Rimmo, P. (1976). "The Premise of Equipotentiality in Human Classical Conditioning." *Journal of Experimental Psychology.*

Olafson, F. (1975). "Consciousness and Intentionality in Heidegger's Thought." *American Philosophical Quarterly.*

Panksepp, J. (1982). "Towards a General Psychological Theory of Emotions." *Behaviour and Brain Sciences* 5.

Parfit, D. (1984). *Reasons and Persons.* Oxford: Oxford University Press

Perkins, M. (1965). "Seeing and Hearing Emotions." *Analysis* 26.

—. (1966) "Emotion and Feelings." *Philosophical Review* 75.

Peters, R.S. (1961). "Emotions and the Category of Passivity." *Proceedings of the Aristotelian Society* suppl. LXII.

Pigeaud, J. (1981) . La maladie de l' âme Étude sur la relation de l' âme et du corps dans la tradition medico-philosophique antique. Paris: Société d'édition Les Belles lettres.

Pitcher, G. (1965). "Emotion." *Mind* 74.

Plato. (1997). *Plato: Complete Works.* Ed. J.M. Cooper. Indianapolis: Hackett Publishing Company.

Platts, M. (1980). "Moral Reality and the End of Desire." *Reference, Truth, and Reality.* Ed. M. Platts. London: Routledge and Kegan Paul.

Plutchik, R., and H. Kellerman, eds. (1980). *Emotion: Theory, Research and Experience.* Vol. 1. New York: Academic Press.

Pritchard, M. (1976). "On Taking Emotions Seriously." *Journal for the Theory of Social Behaviour* 6, 2.

Pugmire, D. (1998). *Rediscovering Emotion.* Edinburgh: Edinburgh UP.

Putnam, H. (1975). "The Mental Life of Some Machines." *Mind, Language, and Reality.* Cambridge: Cambridge UP.

Pylyshyn, Z., ed. (1987). *The Robot's Dilemma: The Frame Problem and Other Problems of Holism in Artificial Intelligence.* Norwood, NJ: Ablex Publishing.

Rawls, J. (1971). *A Theory of Justice.* Cambridge, MA: Harvard University Press.

Rey, G. (1980). "Functionalism and the Emotions." Rorty 1980.

Rist, J., ed. (1978). *The Stoics.* Berkeley, CA: University of California Press.

Robinson, J. (1983). "Emotion, Judgment, and Desire." *Journal of Philosophy.* LXXX, 11.

—. (1995) "Startle." *Journal of Philosophy* XCII, 2.

Rorty, A. (1978). "Explaining Emotions." *Journal of Philosophy* LXXV, 3.

—, ed. (1980). *Explaining Emotions.* Berkeley. CA: University of California Press.

Ross, D.W. (1939). *Foundations of Ethics.* Oxford: Clarendon Press.

Rozin, P. (1976), "The Evolution of Intelligence and Access to the Cognitive Unconscious." *Progress in Psychobiology and Physiological Psychology.* Vol. 6. New York: Academic Press.

Rozin, P., and Fallon, A. (1987). "A Perspective on Disgust." *Psychological Review* 94.

Rozin, P., and Kalat, J.W. (1971). "Specific Hungers and Poison Avoidance as Adaptive Specializations of Learning." *Psychological Review* 78.

Russell, B. (1921). *The Analysis of Mind.* London: Allen and Unwin.

Ryle, G. (1949). *The Concept of Mind.* London: Hutchinson.

—. (1951). "Feelings." *Philosophical Quarterly.*

Sabini, J., and Silva, M. (1982). *Moralities of Everyday Life.* New York: Oxford University Press.

Sartre, J.P. (1956). *Being and Nothingness.* Trans. H.E. Barnes. New York: Philosophical Library.

—. (1971). *Sketch for a Theory of Emotions.* London: Methuen and Co.

Schachter S., and J.E. Singer. (1962). "Cognitive, Social and Physiological Determinants of Emotional States." *Psychological Review* LXIX, 5.

Schachter, S. (1970). "The Assumption of Identity and Peripheralist—Centralist Controversies in Motivation and Emotion." Arnold 1970..

Schaffer, J.A. (1983). "An Assessment of Emotion." *American Philosophical Quarterly* 20.

Scheffler, I. (1977). "In Praise of the Cognitive Emotions." *Teachers College Record.*

Scheler, M. (1973). *Formalism in Ethics and Non-Formal Ethics of Values.* Evanston, IL: Northwestern University Press.

Scherer, K. (1984). "On the Nature and Function of Emotion: A Component Process Approach." Scherer and Ekman 1984.

Scherer K., and Ekman P., eds. (1984). *Approaches to Emotion.* Hillsdale, NJ: Erlbaum Associates.

Schiffer, S. (1973). *Meaning.* Cambridge: Cambridge University Press.

—. (1976). "A Paradox of Desire." *American Philosophical Quarterly* 13.

Schmitt, F.O., et al., eds. (1970). *The Neurosciences.* New York: Rockefeller University Press.

Schneider, G.H. (1990). *Der Thierische Wille.* Leipzig: A. Abel.

Schofield M., and Striker G., eds. (1986). *The Norms of Nature.* Cambridge: Cambridge University Press.

Schweder R., and R. LeVine., eds. (1984). *Culture Theory.* New York: Cambridge.

Searle, J.R. (1983). *Intentionality, an Essay in the Philosophy of Mind.* Cambridge: Cambridge University Press.

Seligman, M.E.P. (1970). "On the Generality of the Laws of Learning." *Psychological Review* 77.

—. (1971). "Phobias and Preparedness." *Behaviour Therapy* 2.

Solomon, R. (1973). "Emotions and Choice." *Review of Metaphysics* XXVI, 1.

—. (1977). *The Passions.* New York: Anchor Books.

Solomon, R.C. (1977). "The Logic of Emotion." *Nous.* XI, 1.

Spinoza, B. (1955). *On the Improvement of the Understanding: The Ethics; Correspondence.* Trans. R.H.M. Elwes. New York: Dover.

Sprigge, T. (1979). "Physicalism, and Animal Rights." *Inquiry.*

Sroufe, L.A. (1984). "The Organization of Emotional Development." Scherer and Ekman 1984.

Stevenson, C. (1937). "The Emotive Meaning of Ethical Terms." *Mind* 46.

Stocker, M. (1976). "The Schizophrenia of Modern Ethical Theories." *The Journal of Philosophy*.

—. (1979). "Desiring the Bad—An Essay on Moral Psychology." *The Journal of Philosophy*.

—. (1980). "Intellectual Emotion, Desire, and Action." Rorty 1980.

—. (1987). "Emotional Thoughts." *American Philosophical Quarterly* 24 (1).

—. (1996). *Valuing Emotion*. Cambridge: Cambridge University Press.

Stout, G.F. (1910). *Manual of Psychology*. 2nd ed. London: Clive.

Strasser, S. (1977). *Phenomenology of Feeling*. Pittsburgh: Duquesne University Press.

Taylor, C. (1964). *The Explanation of Behavior*. London: Routledge and Kegan Paul.

—. (1975). "Justifying the Emotions." *Mind*.

—. (1985). *Pride, Shame, and Guilt: Emotions of Self-Assessment*. New York: Oxford.

Thompson, J. (1941). "Development of Facial Expression of Emotion in Blind and Seeing Children." *Archives of Psychology* 37, 264.

Tomkins, S. (1962). *Affect-Imagery-Consciousness, Volume I: The Positive Affects*. New York: Springer.

Trevarthen, C. (1984). "Emotions in Infancy: Regulators of Contact and Relationships with Persons." Ekman and Scherer 1984.

Urmson, J. (1963). *The Emotive Theory of Ethics*. London: Hutchinson.

Warner, R. (1980). "Enjoyment." *Philosophical Review*.

Watson, J. (1989). "Cognitive-emotional Interactions in the Brain." *Cognition and Emotion* III.

Watson, J.B. (1925). *Behaviourism*. London: Kegan Paul, Trench, Trubner and Co.

—. (1929). *Psychology from the Standpoint of a Behaviorist*. Philadelphia: Lippincott.

Weinrich, J.D. (1980). "Towards a Sociobiological Theory of the Emotions." Plutchik and Kellerman 1980.

White, A.R. (1964). "The Notion of Interest." *Philosophical Quarterly*.

Williams, B. (1972). *Problems of the Self*. Cambridge: Cambridge University Press.

—. (1973) "Ethical Consistency." *Problems of the Self*. Cambridge: Cambridge University Press.

Wittgenstein, L. (1980). *Remarks on the Philosophy of Psychology*. Vol. 1. Trans. G.E.M. Anscombe. Oxford: Blackwell.

—. (1981). *Zettel*. 2nd ed. Trans. G.E.M. Anscombe. Oxford: Blackwell.

Wolheim, R. (1999). *On The Emotions*. New Haven, CT: Yale University Press.

Zajonic R.B. (1980). "Feeling and Thinking." *American Psychologist* XXXV.

—. (1984). "On the Primacy of Affect." *American Psychologist* XXXIX.

319   References and Further Readings

Zajonic R.B., and Markus, H. (1984). "Affect and Cognition: The Hard Interface." Izard et al.